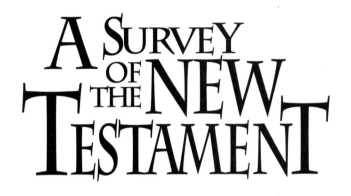

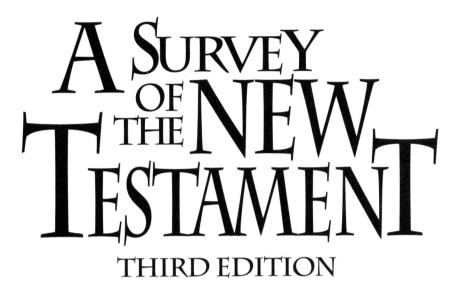

A SURVEY OF THE NEW TESTAMENT

THIRD EDITION

ROBERT H. GUNDRY

ZondervanPublishingHouse

Grand Rapids, Michigan

A Division of HarperCollins*Publishers*

A Survey of the New Testament, Third Edition

Copyright © 1994 by Robert H. Gundry

Address inquiries to:
Zondervan Publishing House
5300 Patterson Avenue S.E.
Grand Rapids, Michigan 49530

Library of Congress Cataloging in Publication Data

Gundry, Robert Horton.
    A survey of the New Testament / Robert H. Gundry. — 3rd ed.
        p.   cm.
    Includes bibliographical references and indexes.
    ISBN 0-310-59550-9 (hard)
    1. Bible. N.T. — Textbooks. I. Title.
BS2535.2G85   1994
225.6'1—dc20   94-17738
                                                   CIP

Cover design by Kirk DouPonce

Printed in the United States of America

99 00 /❖ DH/ 15 14 13

This edition is printed on acid-free paper and meets the American National Standards Institute Z39.48 standard.

CONTENTS

Preface 11

Introduction 15

Part One: Political, Cultural, and Religious Antecedents

1. Intertestamental and New Testament Political History 21

2. The Secular Settings of the New Testament 43

3. The Religious and Philosophical Settings of the New Testament 56

Part Two: Literary and Historical Materials

4. The Canon and Text of the New Testament 85

5. The Study of Jesus' Life 94

6. An Introductory Overview of Jesus' Public Life and Ministry 111

Part Three: The Four Canonical Gospels and Acts

7. Mark: An Apology for the Crucifixion of Jesus 125

8. Matthew: Handbook for a Mixed Church Under Persecution 159

9. Luke: A Promotion of Christianity in the Greco-Roman World at Large 205

10. John: Believing in Jesus for Eternal Life 252

11. Acts: A Promotion of Christianity in the Greco-Roman World at Large (Continued from the Gospel of Luke) 295

Part Four: The Epistles

12. The Early Epistles of Paul 341

13. The Major Epistles of Paul 359

14. The Prison Epistles of Paul 390

15. The Pastoral Epistles of Paul 409

16. Hebrews: Jesus as Priest 421

17. The Catholic, or General, Epistles 431

Part Five: The Apocalypse

18. Revelation. Jesus Is Coming! 457

In Retrospect 477

Indexes 482

Illustrations, Maps, and Charts

ILLUSTRATIONS

Bust of Alexander the Great, Original in Louvre
    Museum, J. Kuhn   22
Antiochus IV, Israel Museum, Jerusalem   24
Modein, Israel Government Press Office   26
Roman Forum, Dan Bahat   28
Arch of Titus, Israel Government Press Office   29
Augustus Caesar   30
Tiberius Caesar, The British Museum   31
Nero, Carta, Jerusalem   31
Herodian Masonry, Israel Exploration Society   32
Ruins at Caesarea, Israel Exploration Society   33
Masada, Israel Exploration Society   34
Roman Road, Dan Bahat   45
Roman Warship, Photo Sadeh, Haifa   45
Palestinian Housing, Israel Government Press Office   48
Palestinian Merchant, University Library, Istanbul   50
Chariot Race, The British Museum   52
Roman Theater, Ecole Biblique et Archéologique Française,
    Jerusalem   52
Tholos of Delphi, Dan Bahat   57
Assyrian Amulet, Reunion des Musées Nationaux   60
Books from Nag Hammadi Library, Institute for
    Antiquity and Christianity, Claremont, California   61
Scroll of Isaiah, Israel Museum, Jerusalem   63
Floorplan and Facade of Capernaum Synagogue,
    Carta, Jerusalem   64
Ruins of Capernaum Synagogue, Israel Government
    Press Office   65
Herod's Temple, Israel Government Press Office   66
Floorplan of the Temple, Carta, Jerusalem   67
Temple Mount, Carta, Jerusalem   67
Portion of Septuagint, Studium Biblicum Franciscanum   70
Qumran Caves, Israel Government Press Office   72
Qumran Ruins, Israel Exploration Society   76
Luke in Greek Text, Foundation Martin Bodmer   89
Coverdale's Bible, The British Library   91

ILLUSTRATIONS   *Gospel of Thomas*, Institute for Antiquity and Christianity,
Claremont, California   95
Jordan River, Duby Tal   132
Galilean Boat, Israel Government Press Office   138
Divorce Certificate, Israel Museum, Jerusalem   145
Wild Donkey, Israel Government Press Office   148
Fig Branch, Israel Government Press Office   148
Denarii, Israel Museum, Jerusalem   149
Coin of Elagabalus, Israel Museum, Jerusalem   154
Church of the Holy Sepulchre, Zev Radovan   155
Burial Cave, Zev Radovan   157
Nazareth, Israel Government Press Office   173
Judean Wilderness, Zev Radovan   175
Horns of Hattin, Israel Government Press Office   176
Mustard Plant, Cana, Jerusalem   183
Farmer Plowing Field, Israel Government Press Office   184
Double Drachma, Israel Museum, Jerusalem   190
Vineyards, Israel Government Press Office   192
Aerial View of Jerusalem, Zev Radovan   193
Lamps, University of Haifa   198
Shepherdesses and Flock, S. Zur Picture Library   199
Valley of Hinnom, Duby Tal   202
Bethlehem, Israel Government Press Office   216
Cliff Near Nazareth, S. Zur Picture Library   220
Ruins at Capernaum, Studium Biblicum Franciscanum   222
Gerasa, Garo Nalbandian   225
Frigidarium, Zev Radovan   232
Headdress, Zev Radovan   233
Beggar in Jerusalem, Zev Radovan   237
Pilate Inscription, Zev Radovan   246
Ruins of 'Imwas, Zev Radovan   249
Papyrus, John Rylands Library, Manchester, England   255
Temple Mount, Israel Government Press Office   266
Mount Gerizim, Israel Government Press Office   269
Pool of Bethzatha, Zev Radovan   270
Pool of Bethzatha, L. Ritmeyer   271
Stone Carving of Menorah, S. Zur Picture Library   276
Shepherds and Their Flock, Zev Radovan   278
Alabaster Flask, Israel Museum, Jerusalem   281
Mount of Olives, Israel Government Press Office   286
Garden of Gethsemane, Israel Government Press Office   287

Fisherman, A. Oppenheimer 290
Cilician Gates, Dan Bahat 294
View of Jerusalem, Zev Radovan 304
Gateway to Straight Street, Studium Biblicum
   Franciscanum 309
Antioch, Syria, Ecole Biblique et Archéologique
   Française, Jerusalem 314
Theater at Perga, Dan Bahat 316
Aqueduct at Antioch, Studium Biblicum Franciscanum 316
Prison in Philippi, Zev Radovan 320
Mars' Hill, G. Nowotny 322
Temple of Apollo, Studium Biblicum Franciscanum 323
Statue of Artemis, Duby Tal 327
Arcadian Way of Ephesus, Dan Bahat 328
Greek Tablet, Israel Antiquities Authority 330
Theater at Ephesus, Duby Tal 330
Aqueduct Near Caesarea, Israel Exploration Society 333
Roman Colosseum, G. Nowotny 336
Arch of Titus, Dan Bahat 342
Arch of Galerius, Zev Radovan 352
Ruins of Corinth, Studium Biblicum Franciscanum 371
Ruins at Ostia, Studium Biblicum Franciscanum 377
Gate of St. Paul, Dan Bahat 391
Ruins of Babylon, Staatliche Museen zu Berlin 438
Roman Head in Marble, Israel Museum, Jerusalem 439
Fragment of Dead Sea Scrolls, Israel Antiquities Authority 447
Pergamum, Dan Bahat 458
Temple of Artemis, Dan Bahat 467
Temple of Zeus, Ecole Biblique et Archéologique Française 467
Lime Deposits, Dan Bahat 469

Maps	Hellenistic Empires	23
	Hasmonean Kingdom	27
	Roman Empire	28
	Herodian Kingdoms	36
	Road System in Palestine	42
	Dead Sea Area	77
	Palestine in the Time of Jesus	84
	Egypt	90
	Jesus' Trial, Judgment, and Crucifixion	112
	Paul's Journeys	311
	Athens in the Time of Paul	324
	Roman Provinces in Asia Minor	345
	Patmos and the Seven Churches of Asia	456

Charts	List of Roman Governors over Judea	37
	Review of Late Old Testament, Intertestamental, and New Testament History	38
	Partial Genealogy of the Herodian Family	40
	Jewish Religious Calendar	69
	Solutions to the Synoptic Problem	100
	Comparison of the Four Gospels	292
	Paul's Missionary Journeys: A Synchronized Summary	312
	Books in the New Testament	480

PREFACE

A TEXTBOOK SURVEYING the New Testament should bring together the most salient items from New Testament background, technical introduction, and commentary. Nearly all surveys of the New Testament suffer, however, from a deficiency of comments on the biblical text. As a result, study of the survey textbook often nudges out a reading of the primary and most important text, the New Testament itself.

Since many beginning students have never read the New Testament systematically or thoroughly, the present survey prompts them to read it by carrying on a continual dialogue with it. This dialogue takes the form of comments on and references to the New Testament sections assigned for reading. By tracing the flow of thought from section to section, students will gain a sense of logical progression. By this means it has also proved possible to move at least some of the background material concerning intertestamental history, Judaism, and other matters, which seem tortuous to many students, from the first part of the book to later parts, where such items elucidate the biblical text directly. This procedure is superior in that it reduces the discouragingly long introduction to the typical college course in New Testament survey, better enables students to see how background material helps interpret the text, and, above all, keeps the textbook from supplanting the New Testament.

To be sure, the procedure demands brevity in the treatment of intertestamental and Roman history. But brevity is just as well for the beginning student, for at least we do not obscure the big picture by dwelling on the unessential details of Hasmonean family squabbles, political intrigues within the Herodian household, and similarly incidental matters.

After the necessary introductory material, then, the four gospels receive separate treatment suitable to their individual emphases. Even though they were not the first books of the New Testament to be written, they come under consideration first because their subject matter provides the basis for all that follows. To avoid discontinuity, the study of Acts proceeds without interruption. The epistles of Paul, Hebrews, the general epistles, and Revelation follow in roughly chronological order (so far as that can be determined) with indications of their relation to events in Acts. Throughout, comments on the biblical text (in addition to introductory discussions) do not merely summarize or rehearse what is self-evident, but concentrate on what is not readily apparent to uninitiated readers.

Leading questions introduce chapters and sections as a teaching device to invite expectancy, induce right questioning of the material by students, and launch their thinking into proper channels. Sectional headings and marginal headings for paragraphs and groups of related paragraphs keep students oriented. Outlines systematize the scriptural material. Questions for further discussion assist not only review of the material, but also its application to the contemporary scene. Suggestions for further investigation (collateral reading) include commentaries and other standard works, ancient primary sources, topical works, and related literature.

The theological and critical perspective of this textbook is evangelical and orthodox. In a survey, considerations of space and purpose rule out a full substantiation of presuppositions and method, as well as a complete consideration of opposing views. Nevertheless, frequent note is taken of other positions; and literature of different persuasions often appears among the suggestions for collateral reading. Instructors will be able to guide their students further in evaluating these supplementary sources. Grateful acknowledgment is made to the publishers Charles Scribner's Sons and Harper & Row for permission to quote from works duly noted in the following pages. Biblical quotations represent my own translation, which is fairly standard.

The third edition of this textbook includes updating of bibliographies, improvement of maps and pictures, and upgrading of English style. In addition, a number of substantive changes (the largest: shortening the harmonistic treatment of Jesus' life, advancing it into the section on historical background, and expanding individual treatments of the four gospels—a more biblical approach) have been made. The good reception of the first two editions has seemed to imply the inadvisability of radical changes. The editorial staff at Zondervan Publishing House deserve a great deal of credit for the improvements made in this third edition.

Robert H. Gundry
Westmont College
Santa Barbara, California

INTRODUCTION

Approaching the New Testament

AN ANTHOLOGY OF twenty-seven books of varying lengths, the New Testament forms Part Two of the Bible, but has only one-third the bulk of Part One, the Old Testament.[1] On the other hand, the Old Testament covers thousands of years of history, the New Testament only one century. This century, the first one A.D., formed the crucial era during which according to Christian belief the fulfillment of messianic prophecy began, the divine outworking of human salvation reached a climax in the coming of God's Son, Jesus Christ, and the new people of God, the church, came into existence—all on the basis of the new covenant, under which God forgives the sins of believers in Jesus Christ by virtue of his vicarious death and bodily resurrection.

New Testament, in fact, means "new covenant," in contrast with the Old Testament, or "old covenant," under which God forgave sins provisionally by virtue of animal sacrifices. But those sacrifices only anticipated the truly adequate self-sacrifice of Christ (Heb. 9:11–14; 10:1–18). His self-sacrificial death inaugurated the new covenant and made possible a full remission of sins (1 Cor. 11:25; Heb. 9:15–17).

Tradition ascribes the books of the New Testament, written in Greek about A.D. 45–95, to the apostles Matthew, John, Paul, and

---

1. *Old Testament and New Testament are Christian, not Jewish, designations, since Jews accept only the Old Testament as Scripture. Nowadays the Old Testament is often called "the Hebrew Bible" because, unlike the New Testament, it was originally written in the Hebrew language (with the exception of Ezra 4:8–6:18; Dan. 2:4b–7:28, written in the sister language, Aramaic).*

Peter and to their associates Mark, Luke, James, and Jude, the last two also being half brothers of Jesus. In our Bibles the New Testament books do not appear in the chronological order of their writing. With the possible exception of James, for example, Paul's early epistles, not the gospels, were the first to be written. Even in the grouping of Paul's epistles the order does not follow chronology, for he wrote Galatians or 1 and 2 Thessalonians well before Romans, which stands first because it is the longest; and among the gospels Mark, not Matthew, appears to have been written first.

The order of books, then, follows a certain logic and developed as a matter of Christian tradition. The gospels appear at the beginning because they describe the momentous events of Jesus' career. Matthew appropriately comes first because of its length and close relation to the immediately preceding Old Testament. (Matthew often cites the Old Testament and begins with a genealogy that reaches back into the Old Testament.) After the gospels comes the triumphant aftermath of Jesus' life and ministry in the Acts of the Apostles, a stirring account of the successful upsurge and outreach of the church in Palestine and throughout Syria, Asia Minor, Macedonia, Greece, and as far as Rome, Italy. (Literarily, Acts followed up Luke to form the second volume in a two-volume work, Luke-Acts.) So far the historical books of the New Testament.

The epistles and Revelation (or the Apocalypse) explain the theological significance of the foregoing redemptive history and spell out implications for Christian conduct. Among the epistles, Paul's stand first and within that group the order is one of decreasing length, first for the subgroup of those addressed to churches, then for the subgroup of those addressed to individuals. The longest of the non-Pauline epistles, Hebrews (author unknown), comes next, then the Catholic or General Epistles by James, Peter, John, and Jude. Finally, the book which looks forward to Christ's return, Revelation, draws the New Testament to a fitting climax.

But why study such ancient documents as the New Testament contains? The historical reason is that in the New Testament we find an explanation for the phenomenon of Christianity. The cultural reason is that the influence of the New Testament has permeated Western and, increasingly, global civilization to such an extent that one cannot be well-educated without knowing what the New Testament says. The theological reason is that the New Testament consists of divinely inspired accounts and interpretations of Jesus' redemptive mission in the world and forms the standard of belief and practice for the church. The devotional reason is that the Holy Spirit uses the New Testament to bring people into a living and growing personal relation with God through his Son Jesus Christ. All reasons enough!

PART I

Political, Cultural, and Religious Antecedents

1

Intertestamental and New Testament Political History

- ❖ *What happened in the Middle East from the end of the Old Testament period through the intertestamental and New Testament periods?*

- ❖ *How did the Jews fare?*

- ❖ *What cultural developments took place?*

- ❖ *What factions among the Jews did the political pressures, cultural changes, and religious questions produce?*

- ❖ *Who were the leaders in these developments, and what did they contribute to the sweep of this history?*

The Greek Period

Old Testament history closed with the Assyrian exile of the northern kingdom of Israel, the subsequent Babylonian exile of the southern kingdom of Judah, and the return to Palestine of some of the exiles under Persian rule in the sixth and fifth centuries B.C. The four centuries between the end of Old Testament history and the beginning of New Testament history make up the intertestamental period (sometimes called "the four hundred silent years" because of the gap in the biblical record and the silencing of the prophetic voice). During this hiatus Alexander the Great became master of the Middle East by inflicting successive defeats on the Persians at the battles of Granicus (334 B.C.), Issus (333 B.C.), and Arbela (331 B.C.).

Alexander the Great

The Greek culture, called *Hellenism*, had been spreading for some time through Greek trade and colonization, but Alexander's con-

Hellenization

quests provided far greater impetus than before. The Greek language became the *lingua franca*, or common trade and diplomatic language. By New Testament times Greek had established itself as the street language even in Rome, where the indigenous proletariat spoke Latin but the great mass of slaves and freedmen spoke Greek. Alexander founded seventy cities and modeled them after the Greek style. He and his soldiers married Oriental women. Thus the Greek and Oriental cultures mixed.

When Alexander died in 323 B.C. at the age of thirty-three, his leading generals divided the empire into four parts. Two of the parts are important for New Testament historical background, the Ptolemaic and the Seleucid. The Ptolemaic Empire centered in Egypt. Alexandria was its capital. The rulers who succeeded each other in governing that empire are called the *Ptolemies*. Cleopatra, who died in 30 B.C., was the last of the Ptolemaic dynasty. The Seleucid Empire centered in Syria. Antioch was its capital. A number of its rulers were named *Seleucus*, several others *Antiochus*. Together, they are called the *Seleucids*. When Pompey made Syria a Roman province in 64 B.C., the Seleucid Empire came to an end.

Alexander the Great, a brilliant soldier and conqueror, was also a mystic. He gave the world a new conception of the unity of humankind.

Because it was sandwiched between Egypt and Syria, Palestine became a victim of rivalry between the Ptolemies and the Seleucids, both of whom wanted to collect revenues from its inhabitants and make it a buffer zone against attack from the other. At first the Ptolemies dominated Palestine for 122 years (320–198 B.C.). Generally, the Jews fared well during this period. Early tradition says that under Ptolemy Philadelphus (285–246 B.C.) seventy-two Jewish scholars began to translate the Hebrew Old Testament into a Greek version called the Septuagint. Translation of the Pentateuch came first, remaining sections of the Old Testament later. The work was done in Egypt, apparently for

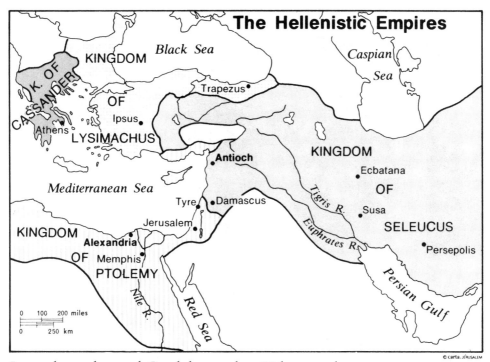

The Hellenistic Empires

© carta, JERUSALEM

Jews who understood Greek better than Hebrew and, contrary to the tradition, probably by Egyptian rather than Palestinian Jews. For parts of the translation betray a knowledge of Hebrew so inadequate as to favor that the translators themselves had less familiarity with Hebrew than with Greek, as would be probable if they lived, not in Palestine, but in Egypt. The Roman numeral LXX (seventy being the nearest round number to seventy-two) has become the common symbol for this version of the Old Testament.

The Seleucids

Seleucid attempts to gain Palestine, both by invasion and by marriage alliance, repeatedly failed. But success finally came with the defeat of Egypt by Antiochus III (198 B.C.). Among the Jews two factions developed, "the house of Onias" (pro-Egyptian) and "the house of Tobias" (pro-Syrian). Antiochus IV or Epiphanes (175–163 B.C.) replaced the Jewish high priest Onias III with Onias's brother Jason, a Hellenizer who started making Jerusalem into a Greek city. A gymnasium and an adjoining race track were built. There, to the outrage of pious Jews, Jewish lads exercised in the Greek fashion— nude. Track races opened with invocations to pagan deities. Even Jewish priests attended these events. Such Hellenization also

23

Antiochus IV (Epiphanes) is portrayed on this coin as himself (left) and as the god Zeus (right), a deliberate attempt to identify the cult of the king with the cult of Zeus.

included attendance at Greek theaters, adoption of Greek dress, surgery to remove the marks of circumcision, and exchange of Hebrew for Greek names. Jews who opposed this paganization of their culture were called *Hasidim*, or *Hasideans*, "pious people," roughly equivalent to "Puritans."

Before launching an invasion of Egypt, Antiochus Epiphanes replaced his own appointee in the high priesthood, Jason, with Menelaus, another Hellenizing Jew, who had offered to collect for Antiochus higher tribute from his subjects in Palestine. Menelaus may not have even belonged to a priestly family. Naturally, pious Jews resented the selling of their most sacred office of high priest to the highest bidder, especially when the money was to come from their own pockets.

Despite initial successes, Antiochus's attempt to annex Egypt failed. Ambitious Rome did not want the Seleucid Empire to increase in strength. Outside Alexandria, therefore, a Roman envoy drew a circle on the ground around Antiochus and demanded that before stepping out of the circle he promise to leave Egypt with his troops. Antiochus had learned to respect Roman power during twelve earlier years as a hostage in Rome; so he acquiesced.

Meanwhile, a false rumor reached the displaced high priest Jason that Antiochus had been killed in Egypt. Jason immediately returned to Jerusalem from his refuge in Transjordan and with his supporters seized control of the city from Menelaus. The embittered Antiochus, stung by his diplomatic defeat at the hands of the

Romans, interpreted Jason's action as a revolt and sent soldiers to punish the rebels and put Menelaus back into the high priestly office. In so doing, they ransacked the temple and slaughtered many Jerusalemites. Antiochus himself returned to Syria. Two years later, in 168 B.C., he sent his general Apollonius with an army of 22,000 to collect tribute, outlaw Judaism, and enforce paganism as a means of consolidating his empire and replenishing his treasury. The soldiers plundered Jerusalem, tore down its houses and walls, and burned the city. Jewish men were killed, women and children enslaved. It became a capital offense to practice circumcision, observe the Sabbath, celebrate Jewish festivals, or possess scrolls of Old Testament books. Many such scrolls were destroyed. Pagan sacrifices became compulsory, as did processional marching in honor of Dionysus (or Bacchus), the Greek god of wine. An altar to the Syrian high god, identified as Zeus, was erected in the temple. Animals abominable according to the Mosaic law were sacrificed on the altar, and "sacred prostitution" was practiced in the temple precincts.

Persecution by Antiochus Epiphanes

The Maccabean Period

Jewish resistance came quickly. In the village of Modein (or Modin, as it is also spelled) a royal agent of Antiochus urged an elderly priest named Mattathias to set an example for the villagers by offering a pagan sacrifice. Mattathias refused. When another Jew stepped forward to comply, Mattathias killed him, killed the royal agent, demolished the altar, and fled to the mountains with his five sons and other sympathizers. Thus the Maccabean Revolt began in 167 B.C. under the leadership of Mattathias's family. We call this family the *Hasmoneans*, after Hasmon, great-grandfather of Mattathias, or the *Maccabees*, from the nickname "Maccabeus" ("the Hammer") given to Judas, one of Mattathias's sons.

Maccabean Revolt

Judas Maccabeus led the rebels in highly successful guerilla warfare until they were able to defeat the Syrians in pitched battle. The Maccabean Revolt also triggered a civil war between pro-Hellenistic and anti-Hellenistic Jews. The struggle continued even after the death of Antiochus Epiphanes (163 B.C.). Ultimately, the Maccabees expelled the Syrian troops from their citadel in Jerusalem, regained religious freedom, rededicated the temple, and conquered Palestine.

Archaeological remains of the tombs of the Maccabees at Modein. Modein was the birthplace of the Jewish war of independence. Mattathias and his sons lived here, and it was in Modein where they rebelled against Antiochus Epiphanes.

Maccabean Independence

After Judas Maccabeus was killed in battle (160 B.C.), his brothers Jonathan and then Simon succeeded him in leadership. By playing claimants to the Seleucid throne against each other, they were able to gain concessions for the Jews. Jonathan began to rebuild the damaged walls of Jerusalem and its other structures. He also assumed the high priestly office. Simon gained recognition of Judean independence from Demetrius II, a contestant for the Seleucid throne, and renewed a treaty with Rome originally made under Judas. Proclaimed as "the great high priest and commander and leader of the Jews," Simon officially united in himself religious, military, and political headship over the Jewish state.

The subsequent history of the Hasmonean dynasty (142–37 B.C.) tells a sad tale of internal strife caused by ambition for power. The political aims and intrigues of the Hasmoneans alienated many of their former supporters, the religiously minded Hasidim, who split

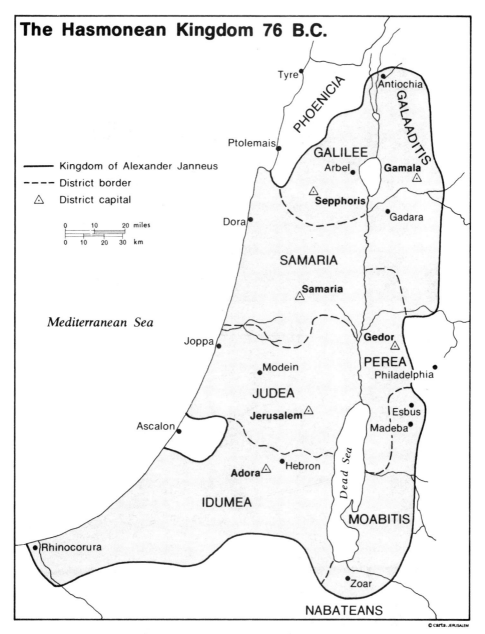

The Hasmonean Kingdom 76 B.C.

Kingdom of Alexander Janneus
District border
△ District capital

PHOENICIA
GALAADITIS
Tyre
Antiochia
Ptolemais
GALILEE
Arbel
Gamala △
Sepphoris △
Dora
Gadara
SAMARIA
Samaria △
Mediterranean Sea
Joppa
Gedor △
PEREA
Modein
Philadelphia
JUDEA
Jerusalem △
Esbus
Ascalon
Madeba
Adora △ Hebron
IDUMEA
Dead Sea
MOABITIS
Rhinocorura
Zoar
NABATEANS

© carta. JERUSALEM

into the Pharisees and the Essenes. Some of the Essenes produced the Dead Sea Scrolls from Qumran.[1] The aristocratic and politically minded supporters of the Hasmonean priest-kings became the Sadducees. Finally, the Roman general Pompey subjugated Palestine

1. See pages 71, 75–76.

Roman Forum

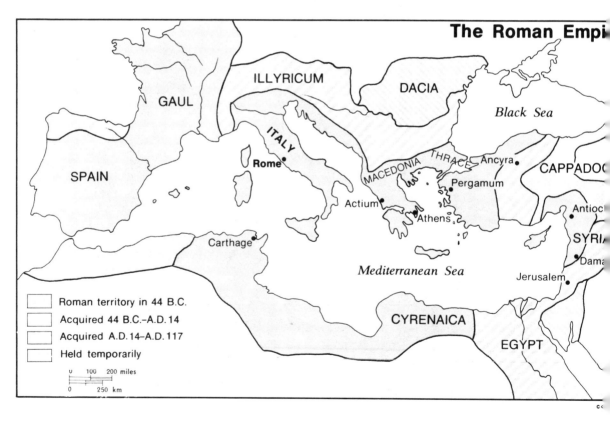

The Roman Empi

ILLYRICUM

GAUL

DACIA

Black Sea

ITALY

Rome

MACEDONIA

THRACE

Ancyra

CAPPADOC

SPAIN

Pergamum

Actium

Athens

Antioc

SYRI

Carthage

Dama

Mediterranean Sea

Jerusalem

Roman territory in 44 B.C.

Acquired 44 B.C.–A.D.14

Acquired A.D.14–A.D.117

Held temporarily

CYRENAICA

EGYPT

0   100   200 miles

0   250 km

(63 B.C.). During the New Testament period, then, Roman power dominated Palestine.

The Roman Period

The eighth century B.C. saw the founding of Rome, and the fifth century B.C. the organization of a republican form of government there. Two centuries of war with the North African rival city of Carthage ended in victory for Rome (146 B.C.). Conquests by Pompey in the eastern end of the Mediterranean Basin and by Julius Caesar in Gaul (roughly equivalent to modern France) extended Roman domination. After Julius Caesar's assassination in the Roman senate, Octavian, later known as Augustus, defeated the forces of his rival Antony and the Ptolemaic queen Cleopatra in a naval battle off the coast of Actium, Greece (31 B.C.), and became the first Roman emperor. Thus Rome passed from a period of expansion to a period of peace, known as the Pax Romana. The province of Judea broke

Roman Expansion

An inner relief on the Arch of Titus in Rome, showing captured Jews carrying through the streets of Rome the ark of the covenant and the Menorah from the temple.

the peace with major revolts that the Romans crushed in A.D. 70 and 135. Nevertheless, the prevailing unity and political stability of the Roman Empire facilitated the spread of Christianity when it emerged.

Roman Administration

Augustus set up a provincial system of government designed to keep proconsuls from administering foreign territories for their own aggrandizement. There were two kinds of provinces, senatorial and imperial. Proconsuls answered to the Roman senate, which appointed them over senatorial provinces, usually for terms of only one year. Alongside the

Augustus Caesar, a systematic and efficient ruler, initiated an era of peace and stability.

proconsuls stood procurators, appointed by the emperor, usually over financial matters. Propraetors governed the imperial provinces. Also appointed by the emperor, they answered to him and exercised their civil and military authority by means of standing armies.

Roman Emperors

Touching the New Testament story at various points are the following Roman emperors, who do not make up a complete list even for the first century:

- *Augustus* (27 B.C.–A.D. 14), under whom occurred the birth of Jesus, the census connected with his birth, and the beginning of emperor-worship
- *Tiberius* (A.D. 14–37), under whom Jesus publicly ministered and died
- *Caligula* (A.D. 37–41), who demanded worship of himself and ordered his statue placed in the temple at Jerusalem, but who died before the order was carried out
- *Claudius* (A.D. 41–54), who expelled Jewish residents from Rome, among them Aquila and Priscilla (Acts 18:2), for civil disturbance
- *Nero* (A.D. 54–68), who persecuted Christians, probably only in Rome, and under whom Peter and Paul were martyred

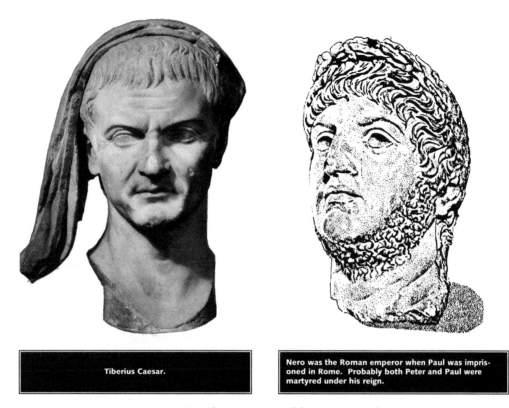

Tiberius Caesar.

Nero was the Roman emperor when Paul was imprisoned in Rome. Probably both Peter and Paul were martyred under his reign.

- *Vespasian* (A.D. 69–79), who as a general began to crush a Jewish revolt, returned to Rome to become emperor, and left completion of the military task to his son Titus, whose army destroyed Jerusalem and the temple in A.D. 70
- *Domitian* (A.D. 81–96), whose persecution of the church may have provided a background for Revelation, written to encourage oppressed Christians

The Romans allowed native vassal rulers in Palestine. One was Herod the Great, who ruled the country under the Romans (37–4 B.C.). His father Antipater, having risen to power and favor with the Romans, had thrust him into a military and political career. The Roman senate approved the kingship of Herod, but he had to gain control of Palestine by force of arms. Because of his Idumean (Edomite) ancestry, the Jews resented him.[2] Scheming, jealous, and

Herod the Great

---

2. *The Idumeans, or Edomites, descended from Esau, the elder brother and rival of Jacob, also called Israel, an ancestor of the Jews and father of the twelve sons from whom the twelve tribes of Israel descended and took their names.*

cruel, he killed two of his own wives and at least three of his own sons. According to Matthew, Herod had the infants in Bethlehem slaughtered shortly after Jesus' birth there. Augustus once said that it was better to be Herod's pig than his son (a wordplay, since the Greek words for pig, *hus*, and for son, *huios*, sound very much alike).

But Herod was also an efficient ruler and clever politician who managed to survive struggles for power in the higher echelons of Roman government. For example, he switched allegiance from Mark Antony and Cleopatra to Augustus and successfully convinced Augustus of his sincerity. Secret police, curfew, and high taxes, but also free grain during famine and free clothing in other calamities, characterized the administration of Herod. Among many building projects, his greatest contribution to the Jews was a beautification of the temple in Jerusalem. This beautification did not represent his sharing of the Jewish faith (he did not share it), but an attempt to conciliate his subjects. The temple, decorated with white marble, gold, and jewels, became proverbial for its splendor: "Whoever has not seen the temple of Herod has seen nothing beautiful." Herod

Herodian masonry in the southern wall of the Temple Mount in Jerusalem.

Caesarea, now seafront ruins, was constructed by Herod the Great. The city became the Roman center of administration in Palestine.

the Great died of intestinal cancer and dropsy in 4 B.C. He had commanded a number of leading Jews to be slaughtered when he died, so that although there would be no mourning *over* his death, at least there would be mourning *at* his death. But the order died with him.

Lacking their father's ability and ambition, the sons of Herod ruled separate parts of Palestine. Archelaus became ethnarch of Judea, Samaria, and Idumea; Herod Philip tetrarch of Iturea, Trachonitis, Gaulanitis, Auranitis, and Batanea; and Herod Antipas tetrarch of Galilee and Perea.[3] John the Baptist rebuked Antipas for divorcing his wife to marry Herodias, the wife of his half brother. When in retaliation Herodias induced her dancing daughter to demand the head of John the Baptist, Antipas yielded to the grisly request (Mark 6:17–29; Matt. 14:3–12). Jesus called him "that fox" (Luke 13:32) and later stood trial before him (Luke 23:7–12).

Herod's Dynasty

---

3. See the map on page 36.

Masada as seen from the air. In this mountaintop fortress Jewish rebels held out against the Romans. Notice the assault ramp built on the right by the Romans.

Herod Agrippa I, grandson of Herod the Great, executed James the Apostle and son of Zebedee and imprisoned Peter (Acts 12). Herod Agrippa II, great-grandson of Herod the Great, heard Paul's self-defense (Acts 25–26).

Roman Governors   The misrule of Archelaus in Judea, Samaria, and Idumea led to his removal from office and banishment by Augustus (A.D. 6). According to Matthew 2:21–23, this same misrule had influenced Joseph to settle with Mary and Jesus in Nazareth of Galilee when they returned from Egypt. Except for brief periods, Roman governors ruled Archelaus's former territory. One of those governors, Pontius Pilate, sat in judgment on Jesus. The governors Felix and Festus heard Paul's case (Acts 23–26). And Florus's raiding the temple treasury ignited the Jewish revolt of A.D. 66–74, which reached a climax with the destruction of Jerusalem and the temple in A.D.

70. Mopping-up operations lasted till the capture of Masada, a fortress on the west side of the Dead Sea, where the last rebels and their families, numbering more than nine hundred, committed mass suicide just before the Romans entered. The Jews had suffered even greater loss of life at the destruction of Jerusalem. Both that destruction and the capture of Masada were preceded by long sieges. Apart from such events and in spite of the Herods and the Roman governors, however, Jewish priests and Jewish courts controlled most local matters of daily life.

Worship at the temple and its sacrificial system ceased with the destruction of Jerusalem in A.D. 70. As a substitutionary measure Jewish rabbis established a school in the Mediterranean coastal town of Jamnia (or Yavneh) to expound the Torah, the Old Testament law, more intensively. Unsettled conditions continued in Palestine until Emperor Hadrian erected a temple to the Roman god Jupiter where the Jewish temple had stood. He also prohibited the rite of circumcision. The Jews revolted again, this time under the leadership of Bar Cochba,[4] hailed by many of them as the Messiah (A.D. 132). The Romans crushed this uprising in A.D. 135, rebuilt Jerusalem as a Roman city, and banned Jews from entering the city. Thus the Jewish state ceased to exist until its revival in 1948.

From First Jewish War to Second

---

4. *The second part of Bar Cochba's name appears in a variety of English spellings, the most common of which, besides Cochba, is Kokhba.*

The house of Herod. After A.D. 6 the territory formerly alloted to Archelaus was governed by successive Roman procurators.

The Herodian Kingdoms

SYRIA

Mediterranean Sea

Tyre

Caesarea Philippi

ITUREA

PHOENICIA

TRACHONITIS

GAULANITIS

Ptolemais

GALILEE

Julias

BATANEA

Tiberias

Sepphoris

To Syria

AURANITIS

Caesarea

Scythopolis

Pella

Gerasa

Sebaste

SAMARIA

Joppa

Phasaelis

PEREA

Philadelphia

Archelais

Livias

To Syria

Jerusalem

JUDEA

N A B A T E A N S

Ascalon

Gaza

To Syria

Dead sea

I D U M E A

Under Archelaus

Under Herod Philip

Under Herod Antipas

Under Salome

0   10   20 miles

0 10 20 30 km

© carta, JERUSALEM

A LIST OF ROMAN GOVERNORS OVER JUDEA
From the Banishment of Archelaus in A.D. 6
To the Destruction of Jerusalem in A.D. 70

(The names of those who appear in the New Testament are capitalized.)

6_____

       Coponius

10_____

       M. Ambivius

13_____

       Annius Rufus

15_____

       Valerius Gratus

26_____

       PONTIUS PILATE

36_____

       Marcellus

38_____

       Maryllus

                [Herod Agrippa I ruled as king over
                Judea and all Palestine, A.D. 41–44.]

44_____

       Cuspius Fadus

46_____

       Tiberius Alexander

48_____

       Ventidius Cumanus

52_____

       M. Antonius FELIX

59_____

       Porcius FESTUS

61_____

       Albinus

65_____

       Gessius Florus

70_____

REVIEW CHART OF LATE OLD TESTAMENT,

CENTURY	DOMINANT POWER	IMPORTANT EVENTS
B.C. 8th (700s)	Assyria	Exile of the northern kingdom of Israel with the destruction of the capital city of Samaria in 721 B.C.
7th (600s) 6th (500s)	Babylonia	Exile of the southern kingdom of Judah with the destruction of Jerusalem in 586 B.C.
	Persia	Return of some Jews to Palestine to rebuild their nation, temple, and Jerusalem from 537 B.C. onward
5th (400s)		
4th (300s)	Greece-Macedonia	Conquest by Alexander the Great and upsurge of Hellenization throughout the Middle East
		Death of Alexander the Great in 323 B.C. and the division of his empire
	Egypt	Ptolemies' domination of Palestine, 320–198 B.C.
3d (200s)		Beginning of the Septuagint with translation of the Pentateuch from Hebrew into Greek
2d (100s)	Syria	Seleucids' domination of Palestine, 198–167 B.C.
		Development of Hellenistic and Hasidic parties within Jewry
		Failure of Antiochus Epiphanes' attempt to annex Egypt
		Antiochus Epiphanes' violent attempt to force complete Hellenization, or paganization, on the Jews in 168 B.C.
		Outbreak of the Maccabean Revolt in 167 B.C. and the gaining of Jewish independence under the successive leadership of Mattathias, Judas Maccabeus, Jonathan, and Simon
	Jewish independence	Hasmonean dynasty, 142–37 B.C.
1st (99–1)		Internal strife
		Development of Jewish sects: Sadducees, Pharisees, and Essenes
	Rome	Subjugation of Palestine by the Roman general Pompey in 63 B.C.
		Rise to power in Palestine of Antipater and his son Herod the Great

INTERTESTAMENTAL, AND NEW TESTAMENT HISTORY

Century	Dominant Power	Important Events
		Assassination of Julius Caesar
		Augustus's rise to Roman emperorship (27 B.C.–A.D. 14) at the expense of Mark Antony and Cleopatra
		Birth of Jesus c. 6 B.C.
		Death of Herod the Great in 4 B.C.
A.D. 1st (1–100)	Rome	Tiberius's emperorship (A.D. 14–37); Pilate's governorship
		Public ministry, death, and resurrection of Jesus (A.D. 29–33)
		Beginnings of the Christian church under the leadership of Peter, Paul, and others
		Caligula's and Claudius's emperorships (A.D. 37–41 and 41–54)
		Expansion of the Christian church
		Beginnings of the New Testament literature
		Nero's emperorship (A.D. 54–68)
		Persecution of Christians on a limited scale
		Martyrdoms of Peter and Paul (A.D. 64–68)
		First Jewish War (A.D. 66–74)
		Short-lived emperorships of Galba, Otho, and Vitellius (A.D. 68–69)
		Vespasian's emperorship (A.D. 69–79)
		Destruction of Jerusalem and the temple by Titus in A.D. 70
		Titus's emperorship (A.D. 79–81)
		Domitian's emperorship (A.D. 81–96)
		Reconstitution of Judaism at Jamnia with almost total emphasis on the Torah because the temple had been destroyed
		Final production of New Testament literature with the Johannine writings
		Beginnings of further Roman persecution of the church
2d (100s)		Nerva's and Trajan's emperorships (A.D. 96–98 and 98–117)
		Hadrian's emperorship (A.D. 117–138)
		Second Jewish War under the rebel leader Bar Cochba (A.D. 132–135)
		Rebuilding of Jerusalem as a Roman city with a ban against Jewish entrance

A PARTIAL GENEALOGICAL CHART OF THE HERODIAN FAMILY*

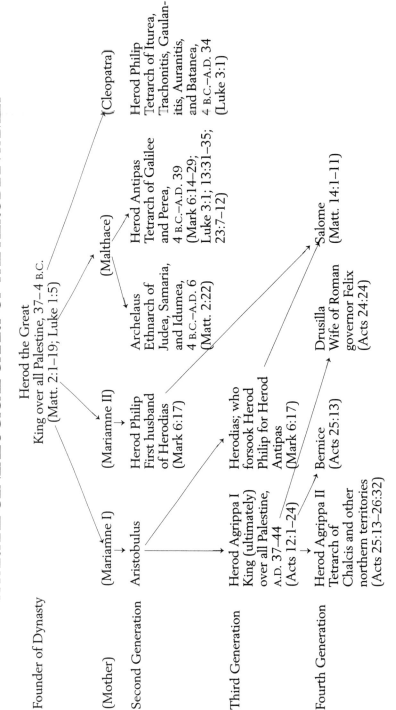

Founder of Dynasty

Herod the Great
King over all Palestine, 37–4 B.C.
(Matt. 2:1–19; Luke 1:5)

(Mother)

(Mariamne I)

(Mariamne II)

(Malthace)

(Cleopatra)

Second Generation

Aristobulus

Herod Philip
First husband
of Herodias
(Mark 6:17)

Archelaus
Ethnarch of
Judea, Samaria,
and Idumea,
4 B.C.–A.D. 6
(Matt. 2:22)

Herod Antipas
Tetrarch of Galilee
and Perea,
4 B.C.–A.D. 39
(Mark 6:14–29;
Luke 3:1; 13:31–35;
23:7–12)

Herod Philip
Tetrarch of Iturea,
Trachonitis, Gaulan-
itis, Auranitis,
and Batanea,
4 B.C.–A.D. 34
(Luke 3:1)

Third Generation

Herod Agrippa I
King (ultimately)
over all Palestine,
A.D. 37–44
(Acts 12:1–24)

Herodias; who
forsook Herod
Philip for Herod
Antipas
(Mark 6:17)

Salome
(Matt. 14:1–11)

Fourth Generation

Herod Agrippa II
Tetrarch of
Chalcis and other
northern territories
(Acts 25:13–26:32)

Bernice
(Acts 25:13)

Drusilla
Wife of Roman
governor Felix
(Acts 24:24)

* Because it covers only that part of the Herodian family which touches the New
Testament story, the chart contains numerous omissions. For example, only four of
Herod the Great's ten wives appear above.

In what providential ways did the events of the intertestamental period prepare for the coming of Christ and the rise of the church?

What parallels may be drawn between the controversy of the Hasidim with the Jewish Hellenists and similar controversies in church history, especially recent church history?

FOR
FURTHER
DISCUSSION

(Primary materials)

FOR
FURTHER
INVESTIGATION

Barrett, C. K. *The New Testament Background: Selected Documents.* 2d ed. San Francisco: Harper & Row, 1987. Especially pp. 1–22, 135–76, 269–75, 290–98, 306–8.

Kee, H. C. *The Origins of Christianity.* Englewood Cliffs, N.J.: Prentice-Hall, 1973. Especially pp. 10–53.

1 & 2 Maccabees. In *The New Oxford Annotated Apocrypha.* Edited by B. M. Metzger and R. E. Murphy. New York: Oxford University Press, 1991.

Josephus. *Jewish Antiquities.* 7 vols. Loeb Classical Library. Cambridge, Mass.: Harvard University Press, 1930–65.

Josephus. *The Jewish War.* 2 vols. Loeb Classical Library. Cambridge, Mass.: Harvard University Press, 1927–28.

Polybius. *Histories* 29.27. On the meeting between Antiochus Epiphanes and the Roman envoy outside Alexandria.

Yadin, Y. *Herod's Fortress and the Zealots' Last Stand.* New York: Random, 1967. For archaeological discoveries confirming Josephus's dramatic account of the Zealots' last stand at Masada toward the close of the first Jewish revolt.

———. *The Finds from the Bar Kokhba Period in the Cave of Letters.* Jerusalem: Israel Exploration Society, 1963. For technical description of an archaeological dig and discoveries in a cave that yielded letters from Bar Cochba during the second Jewish revolt.

(Modern treatments)

Avi-Yonah, M. *The Holy Land. From the Persian to the Arab Conquests (536 B.C. to A.D. 640). A Historical Geography.* 2d ed. Grand Rapids: Baker, 1970.

Bruce, F. F. *New Testament History.* Garden City, N.Y.: Doubleday, 1972.

Gowan, D. E. *Bridge Between the Testaments.* Pittsburgh: Pickwick, 1976.

Hengel, M. *Judaism and Hellenism.* 2 vols. Philadelphia: Fortress, 1974.

Jewish People in the First Century, The. Vol. 1. Edited by S. Safrai et al. Philadelphia: Fortress, 1974.

Lohse, E. *The New Testament Environment.* Nashville: Abingdon, 1976.

Niswonger, R. L. *New Testament History.* Grand Rapids: Zondervan, 1988.

Russell, D. S. *Between the Testaments.* London: SCM, 1960.

Schürer, E. *The History of the Jewish People in the Age of Jesus Christ (175 B.C.–A.D. 135).* Vol. 1. Revised and edited by G. Vermès and F. Millar. Edinburgh: T. & T. Clark, 1973.

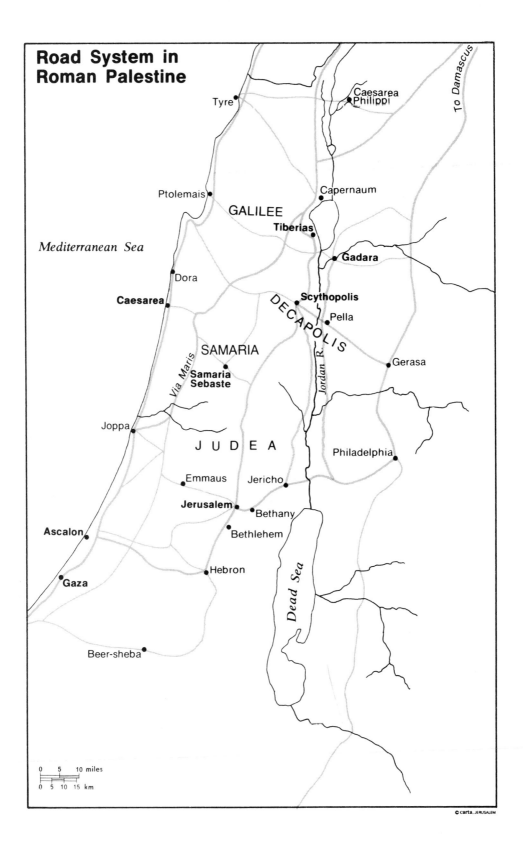

Road System in Roman Palestine

Tyre

Caesarea Philippi

To Damascus

Ptolemais

GALILEE

Capernaum

Mediterranean Sea

Tiberias

Gadara

Dora

Scythopolis

Caesarea

Pella

DECAPOLIS

SAMARIA

Gerasa

Samaria Sebaste

Via Maris

Joppa

JUDEA

Jordan R.

Philadelphia

Emmaus

Jericho

Jerusalem

Bethany

Ascalon

Bethlehem

Hebron

Dead Sea

Gaza

Beer-sheba

0   5   10 miles

0 5 10 15 km

2

The Secular Settings of the New Testament

❖ *How did people in the first century live, think, speak, work, eat, dress, travel, learn, and entertain themselves?*

❖ *What differences existed between daily life inside Palestine and daily life outside Palestine?*

Jewish Population

It has been estimated that more than four million Jews lived in the Roman Empire during New Testament times, perhaps seven percent of its total population. But scarcely seven hundred thousand of these Jews called Palestine home. More Jews lived in Alexandria, Egypt, than in Jerusalem; more in Syria than in Palestine. Even in parts of Palestine (Galilee, where Jesus grew up, and the Decapolis) Gentiles outnumbered Jews.

Languages

Latin was the legal language of the Roman Empire, but was used mainly in the West. In the East, Greek predominated. Besides Greek, Palestinians spoke Aramaic and Hebrew; so Jesus and the first disciples were probably trilingual.

Transportation, Commerce, and Communication

In transportation, commerce, and communication Palestine was relatively undeveloped. Nevertheless, several main roads deserve mention. One led southwest from Jerusalem past Bethlehem to Gaza and northeast from Jerusalem to Bethany and Jericho, up the Jordan Valley and the west side of the Sea of Galilee, and on to Damascus.

Paul was traveling this road when he received his transforming vision of Christ. A second branched off the first below the Sea of Galilee and led up the west side of that lake to Capernaum. To avoid Samaria, Jews often traveled this road in going between Galilee and Judea. But a third main road led from Jerusalem straight up through Samaria to Capernaum, and along this road Jesus talked with a Samaritan woman by Jacob's well. A fourth main road went up the Mediterranean coast from Gaza to Tyre. A branch, on which the risen Jesus conversed with two disciples, went from the southern coast past Emmaus to Jerusalem. Finally, a main road led from the northern coast past Nazareth through Capernaum to Damascus.[1]

Although the Palestinian road system was comparatively poor, throughout much of the Roman Empire the roads were justly famous. They were as straight as possible and durably constructed. Early Christian missionaries used them to full advantage, and the imperial post carried governmental dispatches over them. Private businesses had their own couriers to carry messages. People traveled by foot, by donkey, by horse or mule, and by carriage or litter. Because roadside inns were usually squalid, people of better means depended on friends for lodging. One could buy tourist maps in manuscript form, and even guidebooks for tourists.

Water offered the primary means of commercial transport. Since Egypt served as breadbasket for the Roman Empire, Alexandria provided the main port and outlet for Egyptian grain. Alexandrian ships reached almost 200 feet in length, had sails, and carried oars for emergencies. One large ship could transport several hundred passengers in addition to cargo. Paul was aboard an Alexandrian ship when he suffered shipwreck. Warships were lighter and faster. Galley slaves labored at the oars, of which there were two to five banks, sometimes as many as ten. Barges plied the rivers and canals.

Roads, rivers, and the Mediterranean Sea supplied lines of communication. Papyrus, ostraca (broken bits of pottery), and wax tablets were used as writing materials for letters and other documents. For important manuscripts, leather or parchment was used. Most news was spread by word of mouth, by town criers, and by public notices posted on bulletin boards.

---

1. See the map on p. 42.

Paved Roman roads throughout much of the empire were straight as possible and durably constructed. Early Christian missionaries used them to full advantage.

A Roman warship (bireme) with two banks of oars, as depicted in a first-century B.C. relief.

Public Conveniences

Alexandria had a well-developed school system. The city library contained well over half a million volumes. Excavations have shown that the city of Antioch, Syria, had two and one-half miles of streets colonnaded and paved with marble and a complete system of night lighting. Serving major cities of the empire were underground sewage disposal systems. Public baths for all: admission, one cent. At first people took one bath per day, but later some were taking four to seven baths daily. Shower baths had been invented by the Greeks long before New Testament times.

Homes

Houses in the western part of the Roman Empire were built of brick or concrete, at least in cities. Poorer sections and rural areas had frame houses or huts. In the eastern part of the empire, houses usually consisted of stucco and sun-dried brick. Few windows opened onto the street, because cities lacked proper police forces to keep thieves from roaming the streets at night and breaking into houses through windows. More expensive homes had double-door front entrances, sometimes with knockers. A vestibule led to the door, beyond which lay a large central court called the *atrium*. Roofs were tile or thatch. In the kitchen an open hearth, or an earthen or stone oven, served for cooking. Oil lamps provided lighting. Plumbing and heating were well developed. A central furnace heated some houses, pipes conveying the warm air to different parts of the house. Many Roman lavatories featured running water, and Pompeian houses had at least one toilet convenience, sometimes two. Murals decorated walls. In larger cities lower- and middle-class people often rented flats in apartment houses.

Palestinian towns and homes differed somewhat from their Greco-Roman counterparts and were comparatively backward. One entered a town through a gate in the wall. Inside the gate an open square provided a public place for trade and for social and legal interchange. Jesus must have preached often in these town squares. The houses were low and flat-roofed, sometimes with a guest chamber perched on top. The building material for these homes was usually bricks made of mud and straw baked in the sun. The typical low-class Palestinian had an apartment in a building containing many apartments, all on ground level. An apartment might have only one room. If so, part of the room was on a slightly higher level than the rest. Beds, chests for clothes, and cooking utensils were located on the higher level. Livestock and other domestic animals inhabited the lower level; or, when the animals were outside, children played there. Branches laid across rafters and plastered with mud formed the flat roofs. Rain caused leakage; so after each rain the mud had to be rolled to seal the holes. A parapet around the edge of the roof kept people from falling off, and a flight of stairs on the outside of the house led up to the roof. The housetop was used for sleeping in hot weather, drying vegetables, ripening fruit, and, in devout homes, for praying. The floors consisted of the hard earth or, in better houses, of stone. The beds were merely a mat or a coverlet laid on the floor. Only well-to-do homes had bedsteads. People slept in their day garments.

Food

Romans ate four meals a day. An average diet consisted of bread, porridge, lentil soup, goat's milk, cheese, vegetables, fruit, olives, bacon, sausage, fish, and diluted wine. Jews ate only two meals a day, one at noon, another in the evening. The Jewish diet consisted mainly of bread, fruits, and vegetables. Meat, roasted or boiled, was usually reserved for festival days. Raisins, figs, honey, and dates supplied sweetening, since sugar was unknown. Fish often substituted for meat. At formal meals people reclined on cushions; for informal meals they sat.

Clothing and Styles

Men wore tunics, shirt-like garments extending from the shoulders to the knees. A belt or sash, called a "girdle" in the New Testament, was worn around the waist, coarse shoes or sandals on the feet, and a hat or a scarf on the head. In cold weather a mantle or heavy cloak worn over the tunic gave additional warmth. These garments were usually white in color. Women wore a short tunic as an undergarment and a sometimes brightly colored outer tunic extending to the feet. The more fashionable used cosmetics lavishly, including lipstick, eye shadow, and eyebrow paint, and for jewelry wore earrings and nose ornaments. Women's hair styles changed constantly, though Palestinian women wore veils covering the head (but not the face). Men wore their hair short and shaved with straight razors. Dandies had their hair curled and used large amounts of hair oil and perfume. Both men and women dyed their hair, often to cover up the gray. False hair added to the coiffure, and both sexes wore wigs. In Palestine men grew beards and let their hair grow somewhat longer, but still not so long as portrayed in traditional pictures of biblical people. Generally, Palestinian styles leaned toward conservatism for both sexes.

Typical Palestinian housing of Bible times is still common today, such as these houses in Kafr Yasif in western Galilee.

Social Classes

In pagan society, class strata were sharply defined. Aristocratic landowners, government contractors, and others lived in luxury. A strong middle class did not exist, because slaves did most of the work. Now dependent on government support, the more or less middle class of previous times had become homeless, foodless mobs in the cities. The leveling influence of Judaism reduced stratification in Jewish society, but the chief priests and the leading rabbis helped form an upper class. Farmers, artisans, small businessmen, and their families made up most of the population.

Among the Jews, tax collectors, traditionally called *publicans*, became special objects of class hatred. Other Jews despised these tax collectors or, more accurately, toll collectors, because they handled currency with blasphemous pagan inscriptions and iconography and cooperated with Roman overlords. These overlords auctioned the job of collecting tolls to the lowest bidder, i.e., to the one who bid the lowest rate of commission for a five-year contract. A toll collector would gather not only the toll and his commission, but also whatever he could pocket illegally. Bribery of toll collectors by the rich increased the financial burden on poor people. As a result, the masses deeply resented toll collectors.

Slaves may have outnumbered free people in the Roman Empire. It was common to condemn criminals, debtors, and prisoners of war to slavery; and many of Jesus' sayings and parables assume that slavery existed in the Jewish culture of his time. Paul's letters reflect the presence of slaves in Christian households. Many of the slaves—doctors, accountants, teachers, philosophers, managers, clerks, copyists—had greater skill and education than their masters had. Some slaves bought their freedom or were set free by their masters.

Originally, slaves who had turned criminal were the only ones to be executed by crucifixion. Later, however, free people who had committed heinous crimes also suffered this fate. During the siege of Jerusalem in A.D. 70, Titus crucified as many as five hundred Jews in a day just outside the city walls, in plain view of the people still inside.[2] Execution by burning at the stake was occasionally practiced. At other times condemned men were forced to fight as gladiators in the arena. Whole groups might kill one another in staged warfare.

The Family

As would be expected, the family formed the basic unit of society. Some factors tended to break down the family, however, such as the numerical preponderance of slaves and the training of children by slaves rather than by parents. The typical Greco-Roman family had a low birth rate. To encourage larger families, the government offered special concessions to parents of three or more children. Bachelorhood appears to have been taxed.

In Palestine, large families were common. There was joy at the birth of a boy, disappointment at the birth of a girl. On the eighth day a Jewish male child was circumcised and named. The naming of a girl could wait a month. Families had no surnames; so people with the same name were distinguished by the mention of their father ("Simon

---

2. Josephus, The Jewish War 5.11.1 §§446–51.

The clothing of this Palestinian merchant resembles the attire of men living in Palestine in New Testament times.

the son of Zebedee"), their religious or political conviction ("Simon the Zealot"), their occupation ("Simon the tanner"), or their place of residence ("Joseph of Arimathea"). At the death of a person the surviving family performed formal acts of grief, such as rending their garments and fasting, and also hired professional mourners, usually flutists and women skilled at wailing. In addition, the family could enlist the services of a professional undertaker.

Morals

In the New Testament epistles, sexual sins usually head a list of prohibited vices. Every conceivable kind of immorality was attributed to the pagan gods and goddesses. Sexual intercourse with temple "virgins" formed an integral part of pagan religious rites. Prostitution by both men and women was a well-recognized institution. Slave girls often fell victim to this debauchery. To gain money, some men prostituted their own wives and children. Most of society accepted pederasty and other homosexual behavior. As we know from excavations at Pompeii, obscene pictures and carvings often decorated the exterior walls of houses.

Divorce was easy, frequent, and acceptable. In fact, divorce documents are among the most numerous of papyrus remains. Murder was common. Parents often "exposed" their infants, i.e., abandoned them in the city forum, on a hillside, or in an alley. One letter from a husband to his wife reads, "Should you bear a child, if it is a boy, let it live. If it is a girl, expose it."[3] Often, exposed girls were picked up to be reared as prostitutes. In fairness it should be added that despite the prevalence of low morality, decent people were not wholly lacking in the Greco-Roman world.

Entertainment

A risqué stage reflected the immorality of the day, but not all entertainment had sunk into sensuality. The Olympic Games had long provided sporting pleasure of a wholesome sort. Worthy music and literature uplifted the human spirit. Children amused themselves with toys, such as baby rattles, dolls with movable limbs, miniature houses with furniture, balls, swings, and games similar to hopscotch, hide and seek, and blindman's buff.

Chariot races corresponded to modern automobile races. Betting was common. Naturally, the public idolized winning charioteers. But gladiatorial shows provided the most spectacular form of entertainment. Gladiators might be slaves, captives, criminals, or volunteers. Once a whole arena was flooded and a naval battle staged. As many as ten thousand died in a single performance. The sand in the arena became so soaked with blood that it had to be replaced several times during the day.

Such shows often featured beasts. On one occasion three hundred lions were killed. At the opening of Titus's amphitheater five thousand wild beasts and four thousand tame beasts were slaughtered. Elephants, tigers, panthers, rhinoceri, hippopotami, crocodiles, and snakes fought each other.

---

3. *P. Oxy. 744 (1 B.C.). See* C. K. Barrett, The New Testament Background: Selected Documents, *2d ed. (San Francisco: Harper & Row, 1987), 40–41.*

Roman terracotta relief, made in Italy (late first century A.D.), illustrating a chariot race.

Roman theater in Amman, Jordan. Partially restored, the lower wings are now offices for the Jordanian Department of Antiquities.

Business and Labor

Trade guilds with patron deities foreshadowed modern labor unions. The trade guilds engaged in politicking, extended aid to members in distress, and gave benefits to widows and orphans of deceased members. In Palestine they regulated days and hours for working.

Industry was limited to small, local shops because the transportation of goods to distant places was prohibitively expensive. Besides, caravans were slow and subject to plunder; and shipping on the Mediterranean Sea could take place only during the summer months of calm weather.

In some respects agriculture was surprisingly advanced. Farmers practiced seed selection according to size and quality and soaked grain seeds in chemical mixtures to protect them from insect pests. They also used different kinds of fertilizer and practiced crop rotation.

Private companies carried on banking much as it is done today with borrowing, lending, discounting of notes, exchanging of foreign currency, and issuing of letters of credit. The ordinary interest rate varied from four to twelve percent.

Science and Medicine

Though Jews had little interest in science during the New Testament period, science had already made a beginning. In the third century B.C., for example, Eratosthenes, librarian at Alexandria, taught that the earth is spherical and calculated its size at 24,000 miles in circumference (only 800 miles short of the modern estimate) and the earth's distance from the sun at 92 million miles (the modern estimate: 93 million miles). He also conjectured the existence of the American continent.

Medicine, or at least surgery, had advanced more than we might have guessed—a relevant bit of information since one of the New Testament writers, Luke, acted as Paul's private physician. Surgeons performed operations on the skull, tracheotomies (incisions into the windpipe), and amputations. Knowledge and use of anesthetics were limited, however, so that the qualifications for a surgeon went as follows:

> A surgeon ought to be young, or, at any rate, not very old; his hand should be firm and steady, and never shake; he should be able to use his left hand as readily as his right; . . . he should be so far subject to pity as to make him desirous of the recovery of his patient; but not so far as to suffer himself to be moved by his cries; he should neither hurry the operation more than the case requires,

nor cut less than is necessary but do everything just as if the other's screams made no impression on him.[4]

A variety of medical instruments was used, such as lancets, stitching needles, an elevator for lifting up depressed portions of the skull, different kinds of forceps, catheters, spatulas for examining the throat, and ratcheting instruments to dilate passages in the body for internal examination. Dental work included the filling of teeth with gold. False teeth came from the mouths of deceased people or animals. People sometimes used tooth powder for brushing and polishing their teeth.

Thus, a sampling of the first-century Greco-Roman world shows that though they lived before the age of modern science and technology, the people of New Testament times, no less intelligent and gifted than we, had developed a society and culture in many respects surprisingly close to our own. This similarity was less in Palestine, where Christianity began, but greater outside Palestine, where Christianity rapidly spread.

FOR FURTHER DISCUSSION

What cultural preparation for the coming of Christ and the rise of the church can you see in the Greco-Roman world?

Why did Palestinian Jewry tend to be culturally backward? Does the Christian church likewise tend to be culturally backward? If so, is it for similar or for different reasons? If not, why not, in view of the fact that Christianity arose out of Judaism?

FOR FURTHER INVESTIGATION

Bailey, A. E. *Daily Life in Bible Times.* New York: Scribner's, 1943.

Barrett, C. K. *The New Testament Background: Selected Documents.* 2d ed. San Francisco: Harper & Row, 1987. Especially pp. 38–50 for quotations from primary sources.

Bouquet, A. C. *Everyday Life in New Testament Times.* New York: Scribner's, 1953.

Corswant, W. *A Dictionary of Life in Bible Times.* Completed and illustrated by E. Urech. New York: Oxford University Press, 1960.

Daniel-Rops, H. *Daily Life in the Times of Jesus.* New York: Mentor, 1964.

Everyday Life in Bible Times. Edited by M. B. Grosvenor. National Geographic Society, 1967.

Jewish People in the First Century, The. Vol. 2. Edited by S. Safrai et al. Philadelphia: Fortress, 1976.

---

4. *Quoted from p. 171 of A. C. Bouquet's* Everyday Life in New Testament Times, *a source for much of the material in this chapter.*

Jones, C. M. *New Testament Illustrations*. New York: Cambridge University Press, 1966.

Malina, B. J. *The New Testament World: Insights from Cultural Anthropology*. 2d ed. Louisville: Westminster/John Knox, 1993.

Matthews, V. H. *Manners and Customs in the Bible*. 2d ed. Peabody, Mass.: Hendrickson, 1991.

Miller, M. S. and J. L. *Encyclopedia of Bible Life*. New York: Harper, 1944.

Thompson, J. A. *Handbook of Life in Bible Times*. Downers Grove, Ill.: Inter-Varsity, 1986.

Wight, F. H. *Manners and Customs of Bible Lands*. Chicago: Moody, 1953.

3

The Religious and Philosophical Settings of the New Testament

❖ **What were the religious be-liefs and practices—esoteric, mythological, superstitious, philosophical—among pa-gans in the Greco-Roman period?**

❖ **How did Jewish religious institutions and beliefs**

develop from Old Testament to New Testament times?

❖ **In what way did pagan and Jewish religious settings contribute to the birth of Christianity?**

Paganism

Mythology Atop the Greek pantheon or hierarchy of gods sat Zeus, son of Cronus. According to myth, Cronus, who had seized government of the world from his father Uranus, ordinarily devoured his own chil-dren as soon as they were born. But the mother of Zeus saved her infant by giving Cronus a stone wrapped in baby blankets to swal-low. On reaching adulthood, Zeus overthrew his father and divided the dominion with his two brothers, Poseidon, who ruled the sea, and Hades, who ruled the underworld. Zeus himself ruled the heav-ens. The gods had access to earth from their capital, Mount Olympus in Greece.

Zeus had to quell occasional rebellions by the gods, who exhib-ited the human traits of passion and lust, love and jealousy, anger and hate. In fact, the gods excelled human beings only in power, in-telligence, and immortality—certainly not in morality. A very popu-lar god was Apollo, son of Zeus and inspirer of poets, seers, and

The Tholos (round temple) of Delphi in Greece was erected early in the fourth century B.C.

prophets. He played many other roles as well. At Delphi, Greece, a temple of Apollo stood over a cavern, out of which issued vapors thought to be his breath. A priestess seated on a tripod over the opening inhaled the fumes and in a trance muttered words which were written and vaguely interpreted by priests in answer to inquiring worshipers.

Roman state religion incorporated much of the Greek pantheon and mythology. Roman gods came to be identified with Greek gods: Jupiter with Zeus, Venus with Aphrodite, and so on. The Romans also added new features, such as a priesthood in which the emperor himself acted as *pontifex maximus* (chief priest). The all-too-human traits of the gods destroyed many people's faith in the Greco-Roman pantheon, but for others this faith persisted through the New Testament period.

State Religion

Following the long-established practice of ascribing divinity to rulers, the Roman senate started the emperor cult by deifying, after

Emperor Worship

57

their decease, Augustus and subsequent emperors who had served well. Having long regarded their living rulers as divine, enthusiastic loyalists in the eastern provinces sometimes anticipated this postmortem deification. The first-century emperors who claimed deity for themselves while still alive—Caligula, Nero, and Domitian— failed to receive the senatorial honor at death. The insane Caligula (A.D. 37–41) ordered his statue erected for worship in the temple of God at Jerusalem. Fortunately, the more sensible Syrian legate delayed carrying out the order. He knew the Jews would have revolted. Meanwhile, Caligula was assassinated. Domitian (A.D. 81–96) made the first concerted attempt to force worship of himself. The refusal of Christians to participate in what most others considered a patriotic duty and unifying pledge of allegiance to the emperor as a god brought increasing persecution.

Mystery Religions   Much has been written about the widespread popularity and influence of Greek, Egyptian, and Oriental mystery religions in the first Christian century—the cults of Eleusis, Mithra, Isis, Dionysus, Cybele, and many local cults. These promised purification and immortality of the soul and often centered on myths of a goddess whose lover or child was taken from her, usually by death, and later restored. The mysteries also featured secret initiatory and other rites involving ceremonial washing, blood-sprinkling, sacramental meals, intoxication, emotional frenzy, and impressive pageantry by which devotees were supposed to gain union with the deity. Social equality within the mysteries helped make them attractive to the lower classes.

On the other hand, not until the second, third, and fourth centuries of the Christian era do we get detailed information concerning the beliefs held by devotees of the mysteries. Therefore, though nobody doubts the pre-Christian existence of mystery religions, their pre-Christian beliefs remain largely unknown. Where their later beliefs look slightly similar to Christian beliefs, the direction of borrowing may have gone from Christianity to the mystery religions[1] rather than vice versa, especially since pagans were notoriously assimilative (see the following discussion of "Syncretism") and early Christians exclusivistic. Besides, similarities are often more apparent than real, and even where real they do not necessarily imply borrowing in either direction.

---

1. *Compare the following comments on "Gnosticism."*

For example, the myths of dying and rising gods do not really correspond to the New Testament accounts of Jesus' death and resurrection. In the first place, the deaths of the gods were not thought to purchase redemption for human beings. Furthermore, the story of Jesus' death and resurrection had to do with a recent historical figure; the myths usually had to do with personifications of vegetational processes (the annual dying and renewal of plant life) and thus did not move on the plane of history at all, much less recent history. Finally, the mythological gods did not rise in full bodily resurrection, but revived only in part or merely in the world of the dead. When the fourteen parts of Osiris's body were reassembled, for example, he became king of the dead in the underworld. All that Cybele could obtain for the corpse of Attis was that it should not decay, that its hair should continue to grow, and that its little finger should move—yet the story of Cybele and Attis, who purportedly died by self-castration, is sometimes cited as a significant parallel to the story of Jesus' death and resurrection. As a matter of fact, the very thoughts of death by crucifixion and of physical resurrection were abhorrent to ancient pagans, who associated crucifixion with criminals and often thought of the body as a prison for the soul and as the seat of evil. If Christians had borrowed their beliefs from popular mystery religions, one wonders why the pagans widely regarded the Christian gospel as foolish, incredible, and deserving of persecution.[2]

Superstition and Syncretism

Superstition had a stranglehold on most people in the Roman Empire. Use of magical formulas, consultation of horoscopes and oracles, augury or prediction of the future by observing the flight of birds, the movement of oil on water, and the markings on a liver, and the hiring of professional exorcists (experts at casting out demons)—all these superstitious practices and many more played a part in everyday life. Jews numbered among the most sought-after exorcists, largely because it was thought that they alone could correctly pronounce the magically potent name *Yahweh* (Hebrew for "LORD"). Correct pronunciation, along with secrecy, was considered necessary to the effectiveness of an incantation. In a practice known as *syncretism* common people simply combined various religious beliefs and superstitious practices. Household idol shelves were filled

---

2. See J. G. Machen, The Origin of Paul's Religion *(Grand Rapids: Eerdmans, 1947), chaps. 6–7; J. S. Stewart,* A Man in Christ *(New York: Harper, n.d.), 64–80.*

Fragment of an Assyrian amulet (late eighth century B.C.) designed to exorcise demons from the sick. Upper register contains seven demons, each with a different animal's head. The second register shows the horned demon Lamashtu holding a serpent in her hand. To the left is a bed for the sick; to the right is a smaller demon and demonic head.

with the images of birds, dogs, bulls, crocodiles, beetles, and other creatures.

Gnosticism

Plato's dualistic contrast between the invisible world of ideas and the visible world of matter formed a substratum of first-century Gnosticism, which started to take shape late in the first century and which equated matter with evil, spirit with good. Out of this equation came two opposite modes of conduct: (1) asceticism, the suppression of bodily passions because of their connection with evil matter, and (2) libertinism or sensualism, the indulgence of bodily passions because of the transience and consequent unimportance of matter. In both modes, Oriental religious notions mixed with Platonic philosophy. Physical resurrection seemed abhorrent so long as matter was regarded as evil. Immortality of the spirit seemed desirable, however, and attainable through the knowledge of secret doctrines and passwords by which at death one's departing spirit could elude hostile demonic guardians of the planets and stars on its flight from earth to heaven. Under this view the human problem does not consist in guilt, which needs forgiveness, so much as in ignorance, which needs replacement with knowledge. In fact, *Gnosticism* comes from *gnosis*, the Greek word for *knowledge.* To keep the realm of supreme deity pure, later Gnostics separated it from the material and therefore evil universe by a series of lesser divine beings called "aeons." Thus an elaborate angelology developed alongside demonology.

Gnostic ideas seem to stand behind certain heresies attacked in later New Testament literature; but the contents of a Gnostic library discovered in the 1940s at Nag Hammadi, Egypt, give evidence that full-blown Gnostic mythology did not yet exist at the time Christianity arose. In the first century, Gnosticism was still developing out of an aggregate of loosely related philosophical and religious ideas and had yet to turn into a highly organized system of doctrine.

The intelligentsia were turning to purer forms of philosophy. *Philosophies* *Epicureanism* taught pleasure (not necessarily sensual) as the chief good in life. *Stoicism* taught dutiful acceptance of one's fate as determined by an impersonal Reason which rules the universe and of which all human beings are a part. The *Cynics*, who have a number of modern counterparts, regarded the supreme virtue as a simple, unconventional life in rejection of the popular pursuits of comfort, affluence, and social prestige. The *Sceptics* were relativists who

Books from the Nag Hammadi library.

abandoned belief in anything absolute and succumbed to doubt and conformity to prevailing custom. These and other philosophies did not determine the lives of very many people, however. Superstition and syncretism characterized the masses. Thus, Christianity entered a religiously and philosophically confused world. The old confidence of classical Athens had run out. The enigmatic universe defied understanding. Philosophy had failed to provide satisfactory answers. So also had the traditional religions. People felt helpless under the fate of the stars, which they regarded as angelic-demonic beings. Gloom and despair prevailed.

Judaism

The Synagogue More important for New Testament study than the pagan religious and philosophical milieu is the Judaism out of which Christianity arose. Judaism as it was in the first century originated toward the close of the Old Testament period during the Assyro-Babylonian exile. The prophets had predicted exile as punishment for the idolatry practiced by the people of Israel. Fulfillment of the prediction permanently cured them of idolatry. Temporary loss of the temple during the Exile gave rise to increased study and observance of the Old Testament law (the Torah)[3] and at least ultimately to establishment of the synagogue as an institution. It is debatable whether synagogues originated during the Exile, during the restoration, or during the intertestamental period. But a reasonable conjecture is that since the Babylonian conqueror Nebuchadnezzar had destroyed the first temple (Solomon's) and deported most of the Jews from Judea, they established local centers of worship called synagogues ("assemblies") wherever ten adult Jewish men could be found. Once established as an institution, synagogues remained and multiplied even after the rebuilding of the temple under Zerubbabel's leadership.[4]

At first not very elaborate, the typical synagogue consisted of a rectangular room perhaps having a raised speaker's platform behind which rested a portable chest or shrine containing Old Testament scrolls. The congregation sat on stone benches running along two or three walls and on mats and possibly wooden chairs in the center of the room. In front, facing the congregation, sat the ruler and elders

---

3. The Hebrew word torah *has a wider meaning than "law." It also connotes instruction, teaching, and divine revelation in toto, and refers variously to the Ten Commandments, the Pentateuch, the whole Old Testament, and the oral law or traditional interpretations of the Old Testament by rabbis.*

4. *See Ezra 3–6; Haggai; Zechariah 1–8 for the rebuilding of the temple.*

A complete scroll of Isaiah in Hebrew was discovered at Qumran. The parchment scroll measures twenty-four feet in length.

of the synagogue. Singing was unaccompanied. To read from an Old Testament scroll, the speaker stood. To preach, he sat down. For prayer, everyone stood. The typical synagogue service consisted of the following:

- Antiphonal recitations of the Shema (Deut. 6:4ff., the "golden text" of Judaism)[5] and of the Shemone Esreh (a series of praises to God)[6]
- Prayer
- Singing of psalms
- Readings from the Hebrew Old Testament law and prophets interspersed with a Targum, that is, a loose oral translation into Aramaic (or Greek), which many Jews understood better than Hebrew
- A sermon (if someone competent at preaching was present)
- A blessing or benediction

5. "Hear, O Israel: The LORD our God is one LORD" (Deut. 6:4), later expanded by verses 5–9; 11:13–21; Numbers 15:37–41. Shema is the Hebrew word behind "Hear."

6. Shemone Esreh means "eighteen," but in fact the exact number of benedictions has varied from time to time.

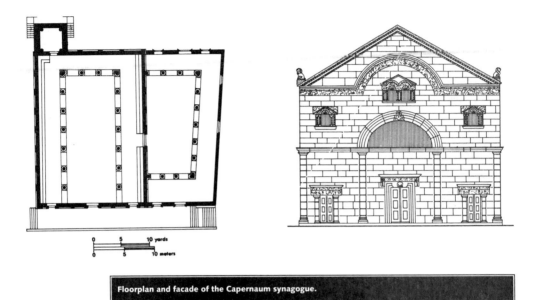

Floorplan and facade of the Capernaum synagogue.

There was freedom in the wording of the liturgy. The whole congregation joined in an "Amen" at the close of prayers. The elected head, or ruler, of the synagogue presided over meetings, introduced strangers, selected different members of the congregation to lead recitations, read Scripture, and preach. Qualified visitors were likewise invited to speak, a practice which opened many opportunities for Jesus and Paul to preach the gospel in synagogues. The synagogue attendant (*hazzan*) took care of the scrolls and furniture, lighted the lamps, blew a trumpet announcing the Sabbath day, stood beside readers to ensure correct pronunciation and accurate reading of the sacred texts, and sometimes taught in the synagogue school. A board of elders exercised spiritual oversight of the congregation. Erring members faced punishment by whipping and excommunication. Alms taken into the synagogue were distributed to the poor. Early Christians, mainly Jews, naturally adopted synagogal organization as a basic pattern for their churches.

The synagogue was more than a center for religious worship every Saturday. During the week it became a center for administration of justice, political meetings, funeral services, education of

The ruins of the synagogue at Capernaum, situated on the shore of the Sea of Galilee.

Jewish lads, and study of the Old Testament. This study tended to obscure the importance of offering sacrifices in the temple. As a result, the rabbi, or teacher of the law, began to upstage the priest.

The Mosaic law prescribed that sacrifices could be offered only at a central sanctuary. The second temple continued to be important, therefore, until its destruction in A.D. 70. The urging of the prophets Haggai and Zechariah had spurred its building during the Old Testament period of restoration from the Exile. Plundered and desecrated by Antiochus Epiphanes in 168 B.C., it had been repaired, cleansed, and rededicated by Judas Maccabeus three years later. Then, at much expense, Herod the Great beautified it even beyond the glory of the first temple, which had been built in grand style more than nine hundred years earlier by King Solomon, son of King David.

The Temple The temple proper stood in the middle of courts and cloisters covering about twenty-six acres. Gentiles could enter the outer court, but inscriptions in Latin and Greek warned them on pain of death not to enter the inner courts, reserved for Jews alone. Just outside the temple proper stood an altar for burnt offerings and a laver or tub full of water which the priests used for washing. Inside the first room or holy place, curtained from the outside with a heavy veil, stood a seven-branched golden lampstand that burned olive oil mixed with other substances, a table stocked with bread representing God's providential presence, and a small altar for the burning of incense. Another heavy veil curtained off the innermost room, the Holy of Holies, into which the high priest entered but once a year, alone, on the Day of Atonement. The ark of the covenant, the only piece of furniture placed in the Holy of Holies during Old Testament times, had long ago disappeared in the upheavals of invasion and captivity. Besides private sacrifices, daily burnt offerings for the whole nation were sacrificed at midmorning and midafter-

Herod's Temple, from the reconstructed model of Jerusalem at the Holyland Hotel.

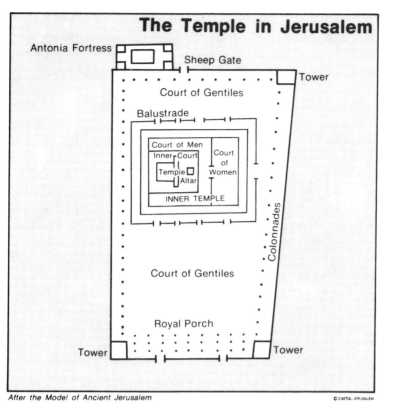

The Temple in Jerusalem

Antonia Fortress

Sheep Gate

Tower

Court of Gentiles

Balustrade

Court of Men

Inner Court

Court of Women

Temple

Altar

INNER TEMPLE

Colonnades

Court of Gentiles

Royal Porch

Tower

Tower

After the Model of Ancient Jerusalem

© carta, JERUSALEM

Floorplan of the Temple.

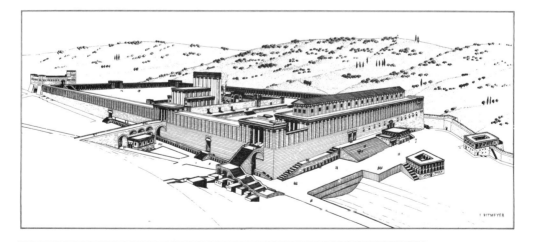

Reconstruction of the Temple Mount during the Second Temple Period.

67

noon in conjunction with the burning of incense and with prayers, priestly benedictions, pouring out of wine as a libation (liquid offering), blowing of trumpets, and chanting and singing by choirs of Levites accompanied with harps, lyres, and wind instruments. Sabbaths, festivals, and other holy days featured additional ceremonies.

The Religious Calendar   Closely related to worship in the temple were the religious festivals and holy days of the Jews. Their civil year began approximately in September–October, their religious year approximately in March–April (see the Jewish religious calendar, p. 69). The Mosaic law prescribed the first six items on the calendar (Passover–Tabernacles).[7] The remaining two (Hanukkah and Purim) arose later and apart from scriptural command. Pilgrims thronged to Jerusalem from elsewhere in Palestine and also from foreign countries for the three main festivals: Passover-Unleavened Bread, Pentecost, and Tabernacles.

The Literature of Judaism: Old Testament   The Old Testament existed in three linguistic forms for Jews of the first century: the original Hebrew, the Septuagint (a Greek translation), and the Targums (oral paraphrases into Aramaic, which were just beginning to be written down). The Targums also contained traditional, interpretive, and imaginative material not found in the Old Testament itself.

Apocrypha   Written in Hebrew, Aramaic, and Greek and dating from the intertestamental and New Testament periods, the apocryphal books of the Old Testament contain history, fiction, and wisdom. The Jews and later the early Christians did not generally regard these books as sacred Scripture. Thus *apocrypha*, which originally meant "hidden, secret" and therefore "profound," came to mean "noncanonical." The apocryphal books include the following:

> 1 Esdras
> 2 Esdras (or 4 Ezra, apocalyptic in content; see the next paragraph on the nature of apocalyptic)
> Tobit
> Judith
> Additions to the Book of Esther
> Wisdom of Solomon
> Ecclesiasticus, or the Wisdom of Jesus the Son of Sirach
> Baruch
> Letter of Jeremiah
> Prayer of Azariah

---

7. See *Leviticus 23:4–43* for details.

THE JEWISH RELIGIOUS CALENDAR

Feast of		Dates[8]
Passover and Unleavened bread,	Commemorating the Exodus from Egypt and marking the beginning ("first fruits") of the wheat harvest	Nisan (Mar.–Apr.) 14 15–21
Pentecost, or Weeks,	Marking the end of the wheat harvest	Iyar (Apr.–May) Sivan (May–June) 6 Tammuz (June–July) Ab (July–Aug.) Elul (Aug.–Sept.)
Trumpets, or Rosh Hashanah	Marking the first of the civil year and the end of the grape and olive harvests	Tishri (Sept.–Oct.) 1–2
Day of Atonement, or Yom Kippur,	For national repentance, fasting, and atonement (not called a "feast")	10
Tabernacles, or Booths, or Ingathering	Commemorating the Israelites' living in tents on their way from Egypt to Canaan—a joyous festival, during which the Jews lived in temporary shelters made of branches	15–22
Lights, or Dedication, or Hanukkah,	Commemorating the rededication of the temple by Judas Maccabeus, with brilliant lights in the temple precincts and in Jewish homes	Heshvan (Oct.–Nov.) Kislev (Nov.–Dec.) 25– Tebet (Dec.–Jan.) 2 or 3
Purim,	Commemorating the deliverance of Israel in the time of Esther, with public readings of the Book of Esther in synagogues	Shebet (Jan.–Feb.) Adar (Feb.–Mar.) 14

Song of the Three Young Men
Susanna
Bel and the Dragon
Prayer of Manasseh
1 Maccabees
2 Maccabees

Other Jewish books dating from the same era are labeled *pseudepigrapha* ("falsely inscribed"), because some of them were written under the falsely assumed names of long-deceased Old Testament figures to achieve an air of authority. Some pseudepigraphal writings

Pseudepigrapha and Apocalyptic

---

8. *Because of differences in calendrical systems, the equivalents in our months are only approximate.*

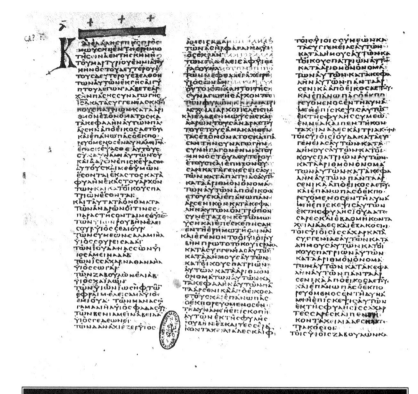

Portion of Greek Septuagint showing a page from the book of Numbers, included in the Codex Vaticanus from the fourth century.

also fall into the class of apocalyptic[9] literature, which describes in highly symbolic and visionary language the end of present history with the coming of God's kingdom on earth. By promising the soon arrival of that kingdom, apocalyptists encouraged the Jewish people to endure persecution. Repeated disappointment of the hopes built up in this way eventually stopped the publication of apocalyptic literature.

The pseudepigraphal literature, which has no generally recognized limits, also contains anonymous books of legendary history, psalms, and wisdom.[10] A list of well-known pseudepigraphal books follows:

---

9. From the Greek word apokalypsis, meaning "revealing," here with reference to the true course of history and especially to future events.

10. Roman Catholics call the pseudepigrapha the apocrypha, and the apocrypha the deutero-canonical books. Others call the pseudepigrapha "the outside books," since not all of them bear false names and almost no one regards them as canonical. (The canon of the Ethiopic church includes 1 Enoch and Jubilees.)

1 Enoch
2 Enoch
2 Baruch, or the Apocalypse of Baruch
3 Baruch
Sibylline Oracles
Testaments of the Twelve Patriarchs
Testament of Job
Lives of the Prophets
Assumption of Moses
Martyrdom of Isaiah
Paralipomena of Jeremiah
Jubilees
Life of Adam and Eve
Psalms of Solomon
Letter of Aristeas
3 Maccabees
4 Maccabees

In addition, the Qumran scrolls discovered in caves near the Dead Sea include literature similar to the traditional pseudepigrapha: *Dead Sea Scrolls*

Damascus (or Zadokite) Document (fragments of which were known before)
Rule of the Community, or Manual of Discipline
War Between the Children of Light and the Children of Darkness
Description of the New Jerusalem
Temple Scroll
Thanksgiving Hymns (*Hodayoth*)
Psalms of Joshua
Pseudo-Jeremianic literature
Apocryphal Danielic literature
Various commentaries (*pesherim*) on the Psalms, Isaiah, Hosea, Micah, Nahum, Habakkuk, and Zephaniah
Various books of laws, liturgies, prayers, blessings, mysteries, wisdom, and astronomical and calendrical calculations

Rabbinic case decisions about interpretative questions stemming from the Old Testament law formed a memorized oral tradition in New Testament times. This tradition grew during the succeeding centuries until the Jewish Talmud enshrined it in writing. A Palestinian edition came out in the fourth century; a Babylonian edition, about three times longer and encyclopedic in length, in the fifth century. Chronologically, the Talmud consists of the Mishnah, *Talmud*

Qumran caves, where the scrolls were discovered, are located in the cliffs below the Qumran community ruins.

or oral law, developed by rabbis up through the second century, plus the Gemarah, which contains comments on the Mishnah by rabbis living from the third through the fifth centuries. Topically, the Talmud consists of the *halakah*, or strictly legal portions, and the *haggadah*, or nonlegal portions (stories, legends, explanatory narratives). Eventually asserting that the oral law dates back to Moses at Mount Sinai, the rabbis elevated their conflicting interpretations of the Old Testament to a position of greater practical importance than the Old Testament itself. Two famous schools of rabbinic interpretation existing already in the first century were the usually moderate school of Hillel and the usually strict school of Shammai, though even the moderate school seems very strict by prevailing modern standards.

Despite its intensely nationalistic spirit, Judaism attracted large numbers of Gentile proselytes, who were full converts,[11] and God-fearers, who were Gentiles willing to practice Judaism in part but unwilling to undergo circumcision and observe the stricter Jewish taboos. These Gentiles found Jewish theology superior to pagan polytheism and superstition, for the Jews emphasized their monotheistic belief in one God and opposed idolatry even in their own temple. Unconverted pagans, on the other hand, could not comprehend a temple without an idol. Why build a temple if not to house an idol? The Jewish emphasis on moral behavior also appealed to the conscience of Gentiles offended by the immorality of the pantheon as described in pagan mythology and of the devotees of those gods and goddesses.

Proselytes and God-fearers

Jewish beliefs sprang from the acts of God in history as recorded in a collection of sacred books (the Old Testament) and not, as in paganism, from mythology, mysticism, or philosophic speculation. The Old Testament emphasized the fate of Israel the nation; hence, the doctrine of individual resurrection did not appear often. The intertestamental period saw an increased emphasis on the fate of the individual and therefore on the doctrine of individual resurrection. Nationalism and the awareness of being God's chosen people had by no means died out, however.

The Theology of Judaism

Jews were looking for the Messiah to come. Indeed, some of them awaited a variety of messianic figures—prophetic, priestly, and royal. But they did not expect the Messiah to be a divine as well as human being, or to suffer, die, and rise from the dead for their salvation from sin.[12] Instead, they looked for God to use a purely human figure in bringing military deliverance from Roman domination. Or God himself would deliver his people, they thought, and then introduce the Messiah as ruler.[13] "This present age," evil in

Messianic Hope

---

11. *Male proselytes had to get circumcised. All had to baptize themselves in the presence of witnesses and go to the temple in Jerusalem, if possible, to offer a sacrifice there. It may be that self-baptism was a later requirement—after the destruction of the temple—in lieu of offering a sacrifice.*

12. *A fragment among the Dead Sea Scrolls has been interpreted by some to indicate a belief at Qumran in the Messiah's suffering, but this interpretation is neither the only one possible nor the most likely one.*

13. *It is probable that higher characterizations of the Messiah as a preexistent divinity of some sort, as in the "Similitudes" of 1 Enoch and in 2 Esdras, postdate the rise of Christianity and developed out of the Jewish troubles with Rome during A.D. 66–135 and perhaps also in imitation of the high Christian view of Jesus.*

character, was to be followed by the utopian "days of the Messiah" or "day of the Lord," indeterminate or variously calculated as to length. Afterwards, "the coming age," or eternity, would begin. Occasionally in Jewish thinking, the messianic kingdom merged with the eternal age to come.

Sects and Other Groups Within Judaism: Pharisees

The Pharisees ("separated ones" in a ritualistic or a derogatory sense) originated shortly after the Maccabean revolt as an outgrowth of the Hasidim, who had objected to the Hellenization of Jewish culture.[14] Middle-class laymen for the most part, Pharisees made up the largest of Jewish religious sects but still numbered only about six thousand in the time of Herod the Great. They scrupulously observed the rabbinic as well as the Mosaic laws. A Pharisee could not eat in the house of a "sinner" (a flagrant violator of the law), but might entertain a sinner in his own house. He had to provide clothes, however, lest the sinner's own clothes be ritually impure.

Observance of the Sabbath was similarly scrupulous. Some rabbis in the Pharisaical tradition forbade spitting on the bare ground during the Sabbath lest the action disturb the dirt and thus constitute plowing, which would break the prohibition of working on the Sabbath. A woman should not look in the mirror on the Sabbath lest she see a gray hair, be tempted to pluck it out, yield to the temptation, and thereby work on the Sabbath. It became a moot question whether one might lawfully eat an egg laid on a festival day. Were such eggs tainted even though hens lack an awareness of festival days?

But Pharisaically minded rabbis devised legal loopholes for their and others' convenience. Though a man should not carry his clothes in his arms out of a burning house on the Sabbath, he could put on several layers of clothing and bring them out by wearing them. One should not travel on the Sabbath more than three-fifths of a mile from the town or city where he lived. But if he wished to go farther, on Friday he might deposit food for two meals three-fifths of a mile from his home in the direction he wished to travel. The deposit of food made that place his home-away-from-home, so that on the Sabbath he could travel yet another three-fifths of a mile. Jesus and the Pharisees repeatedly clashed over the artificiality of such legalism. Nevertheless, average Jews admired Pharisees as paragons of virtue; indeed, they considered them the mainstays of Judaism.

---

14. See pages 26–27. "Pharisee" may originally have meant "Persianizer," a taunting designation which the Pharisees reinterpreted to mean "separated one."

The aristocratic Sadducees were heirs of the intertestamental *Sadducees*
Hasmoneans. Though fewer than the Pharisees, they wielded more
political influence because they controlled the priesthood.[15] Their
contacts with foreign overlords tended to diminish religious devotion and carry them further in the direction of Hellenization. Unlike
the Pharisees, they regarded only the first five books of the Old
Testament (the Pentateuch, Mosaic law, or Torah) as fully authoritative and denied the oral law of the nonpriestly rabbis. They did
not believe in divine foreordination, angels, spirits, or the immortality of the soul and resurrection of the body, as did the Pharisees.
Though strict, the Pharisees were in one sense progressive; for they
kept applying the Old Testament law to new and changing circumstances of daily life. But the comfortably situated Sadducees wanted
to maintain the status quo and therefore resisted any contemporiz-
ing of the law lest they lose their favored positions of affluence and
wealth. Because the center of priestly power, the temple, was destroyed in A.D. 70 along with large numbers of the Sadducees themselves, the Sadducean party disintegrated. The Pharisees survived to
become the foundation of orthodox Judaism in later centuries.

A small sect of Essenes numbered about four thousand. Like the *Essenes*
Pharisees, they evolved from the Hasidim who became disgruntled
with the increasingly political aims of the Hasmoneans. Some of
the Essenes lived in monastic communities, such as the one at
Qumran, which produced the Dead Sea Scrolls. Admission required
a two- or three-year probation and relinquishment of private property and wealth to a communal treasury. Either the more strict re-
frained from marriage, or they all stopped cohabiting with their
wives after several years of marriage. Their punctilious legalism ex-
ceeded that of the Pharisees. For this reason it is doubtful that they
contributed significantly to the rise of Christianity, as has been suggested by some modern writers. If Jesus denounced Pharisaic legalism, he certainly could not have owed very much to the even more
rigid Essenes. Moreover, his mingling with sinners contrasted sharply
with Essene withdrawal from society.

---

15. *The prevalent view that the Sadducees were the party of the priesthood has been challenged by V. Eppstein in* Zeitschrift für die Neutestamentliche Wissenschaft 55 *(1964):
50–54 and in* Journal of Biblical Literature 85 *(1966): 213–224. "Sadducees" may originally
have meant "members of the supreme council," reinterpreted by the Sadducees to mean "righteous
ones." Others relate the term to Zadok, priest under David and Solomon.*

The ruins of Qumran, an Essene settlement by the Dead Sea.

The Essenes did not offer animal sacrifices in the temple at Jerusalem, because they regarded it as polluted by a corrupt priesthood. To symbolize their own purity they wore white robes. The sect regarded itself as the elect remnant living in the last days. They looked for the appearance of several eschatological figures—a great prophet, a royal messiah, and a priestly messiah—and prepared themselves for a forty years' war which they expected to culminate in the messianic kingdom. A former leader called the "Teacher of Righteousness" exerted a profound influence on their beliefs and practices but hardly occupied the position of divine and redemptive prominence given to Jesus in Christian doctrine.

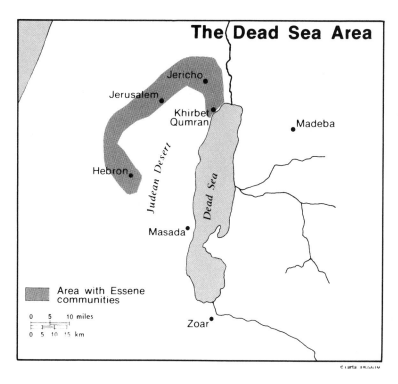

The **Herodians** seem to have been a small minority of influential Jews—probably centered in Galilee, where Herod Antipas ruled—who supported the Herodian dynasty and, by implication, the Romans, who had put the Herods in charge. Contrasting with the Herodians were revolutionaries dedicated to the overthrow of Roman power. They refused to pay taxes to Rome, regarded acknowledgment of loyalty to Caesar as sinful, and sparked several uprisings, including the Jewish revolt which led to the destruction of Jerusalem in A.D. 70. During that revolt some of them came to be known as "**Zealots**" (formerly a nonpolitical designation—Acts 21:20; 22:3; compare Luke 6:15; Acts 1:13). Modern scholars have sometimes identified these Zealots with the Sicarii ("assassins"), who carried concealed daggers; but the Sicarii may have formed a branch of Zealotry or an originally separate group that fused with the Zealots.

The **scribes** were neither a religious sect nor a political party, but a professional class. "Lawyer," "scribe," and "teacher (of the law)" are synonymous terms in the New Testament. To these must be added "rabbi" (literally, "my great one"), a term of respect for teach-

Herodians and Zealots

Scribes

77

ers. Originating with Ezra, according to tradition, the scribes interpreted and taught the Old Testament law and delivered judicial
pronouncements on cases brought to them. Application of the law
to daily life necessitated their interpretative task. What constituted
Disciples working on the Sabbath, for example? The disciples ("learners") of
the scribes followed behind them wherever they went and learned
by observation and rote memory the minutiae of the Old Testament
and of rabbinic lore. The scribes taught in the temple precincts and
synagogues and occasionally debated in the presence of their disciples.

By Jesus' time most of the scribes probably belonged to the
Pharisaical sect, though not all Pharisees possessed the theological
expertise required of scribes. Since scribal activity was gratuitous,
scribes depended on a trade to support themselves. For example,
Paul, who had received rabbinic training, made tents (Acts 18:3).
Though he lacked formal theological education, Jesus was called
"Rabbi" and gathered disciples around himself. He regularly taught
in easy-to-remember rhythmic structure, sententious sayings, and
vivid parables. His teaching carried the weight of his own authority
("Truly I say . . ."; compare Matt. 7:28–29). In contrast, the scribes
endlessly quoted opinions of past rabbis.

Sanhedrin The Romans allowed Jews to handle many of their own religious
and domestic matters. As a result, numerous local courts existed.
Outranking them all was the Jewish supreme court, the Great
Sanhedrin, which met daily, except for Sabbaths and other holy
days, in Jerusalem. This Sanhedrin even commanded a police force.
The high priest presided over seventy other members of the court,
who came from both the Pharisaical and the Sadducean sects. The
New Testament refers to the Sanhedrin by the terms "council,"
"chief priests and elders and scribes," "chief priests and rulers," and
simply "rulers."

"People of the In Palestinian Jewry the masses of common people, called "the
Land" people of the land," remained unaffiliated with the religious sects
and political parties. Because of their ignorance of and indifference
to the fine points of the Old Testament law and rabbinic regulations,
the Pharisees held these people in contempt; but they criticized
Jesus most of all for mingling with others known for flagrant viola-
tions of the Mosaic law.

Outside Palestine the Jews of the Diaspora ("Dispersion") fell *Diaspora*
into two classes: (1) Hebraists, who retained not only their Judaistic
faith but also their Jewish language and customs and thereby incurred Gentile hatred for their stand-offishness, and (2) Hellenists,
who adopted the Greek language, dress, and customs while retaining
their Judaistic faith in varying degrees. An outstanding example of
Hellenistic Judaism was Philo, a first-century Jewish philosopher
and resident of Alexandria. He combined Judaism and Greek philosophy by allegorizing the Old Testament, making it teach Greek
philosophy in symbolic form. Doubtless, Judaism outside Palestine
tended to be less strict and more influenced by Gentile modes of
thinking than was Judaism in Palestine. But we must not overdraw
the differences, for Hellenistic influences had so pervaded Palestine
that Judaism there was much more variegated than the Talmud,
which represents a later and more monolithic stage of Judaism,
might lead us to believe. After the failure of revolts against Rome in
A.D. 70 and 135, Palestinian Judaism consolidated itself increasingly
around a deapocalypticized Phariseeism emphasizing the Torah; for
the Sadducees had lost their base of influence in the temple and the
Romans had defeated the hopes of smaller, apocalyptically minded
sects such as the Essenes.

Jewish children received their first lessons in Hebrew history and *Jewish*
religion, practical skills, and perhaps also reading and writing from *Education*
their parents. The Mosaic law and Proverbs in the Old Testament
contain many injunctions concerning this parental responsibility,
which included the employment of physical punishment for failure
to learn properly. Jewish boys entered local synagogue schools at
about six years of age. There they used the Old Testament as a textbook for reading and writing. Lessons also included simple arith-
metic, extrabiblical Jewish tradition, and complicated religious
rituals. Besides this narrow academic training, every Jewish boy
learned a trade. To become an advanced scholar in the Old
Testament, a Jewish young man attached himself as pupil to a rabbi.
Before his Christian conversion, for example, Paul studied under
the famous rabbi Gamaliel (Acts 22:3).

By contrast, Greco-Roman education was liberal in its scope. *Greco-Roman*
Slaves supervised boys in their earlier years by giving them their *Education*
first lessons and then leading them to and from private schools until

they graduated into adulthood with a great deal of ceremony. As young men they could then attend universities at Athens, Rhodes, Tarsus, Alexandria, and other places to study philosophy, rhetoric, law, mathematics, astronomy, medicine, geography, and botany. Or they could attend the lectures of peripatetic philosophers, so called because these philosophers dispensed their wisdom as they walked around. The high degree of literacy evidenced by papyrus remains shows that education was widespread. People commonly carried small notebooks for jotting down grocery lists, appointments, and other memoranda. Even shorthand was used.

In conclusion, a wide range of literature, including extrabiblical writings as well as the New Testament, helps us reconstruct the pagan and Jewish religious and philosophical backgrounds necessary for a reasonably complete understanding of the New Testament. The Judaism out of which Christianity arose was a monotheistic faith with cross currents of religious and political thought and with various religious and cultural institutions.

FOR FURTHER DISCUSSION

In the times just before the New Testament what religious and philosophical developments prepared for the coming of Christ and the rise of Christianity?

Do modern people hold to mythological, superstitious, and syncretistic beliefs and practices? If not, why not? If so, what are those beliefs and practices—and why has modern scientism failed to banish them?

What parallels as well as differences may be drawn between Gnosticism and current philosophies of education?

What counterparts to the Pharisees, Sadducees, Essenes, Herodians, and Zealots might you find in Christendom today?

To which of those groups would you have joined yourself, and why? If to none of them, give your reasons.

In what ways have educational practices in Western culture combined traits characteristic of both Jewish and Greco-Roman educational practices?

FOR FURTHER INVESTIGATION

(Primary materials)

Barrett, C. K. *The New Testament Background. Selected Documents.* 2d ed. San Francisco: Harper & Row, 1987. Especially pp. 31–38, 51–134, 157–62, 177–268, 279–89, 298–349.

Dupont-Sommer, A. *The Essene Writings from Qumran*. Oxford: Blackwell, 1961.

Foerster, W. *Gnosis*. 2 vols. Oxford: Clarendon, 1972–74.

Kee, H. C. *The Origins of Christianity*. Englewood Cliffs, N.J.: Prentice-Hall, 1973. Especially pp. 54–261.

New Oxford Annotated Apocrypha, The. Edited by B. M. Metzger and R. E. Murphy. New York: Oxford University Press, 1991.

Old Testament Pseudepigrapha, The. Edited by J. H. Charlesworth. 2 vols. Garden City, N.Y.: Doubleday, 1986.

Robinson, J. M., et al. *The Nag Hammadi Library in English*. 2d ed. San Francisco: Harper & Row, 1990.

Vermès, G. *The Dead Sea Scrolls in English*. 2d ed. Baltimore: Penguin, 1988.

(Modern treatments)

Bruce, F. F. *Second Thoughts on the Dead Sea Scrolls*. Revised and enlarged edition. Grand Rapids: Eerdmans, 1961.

Coss, T. L. *Secrets from the Caves*. New York: Abingdon, 1963.

Eastwood, C. C. *Life and Thought in the Ancient World*. Philadelphia: Westminster, 1965.

Glover, T. R. *The Conflict of Religions in the Ancient Roman Empire*. Boston: Beacon, 1960.

Grant, R. M. *Gnosticism*. New York: Harper & Row, 1961.

Jeremias, J. *Jerusalem in the Time of Jesus*. Philadelphia: Fortress, 1969.

Jonas, H. *The Gnostic Religion*. 2d ed. Boston: Beacon, 1963.

LaSor, W. S. *The Dead Sea Scrolls and the New Testament*. Grand Rapids: Eerdmans, 1972.

Mansoor, M. *The Dead Sea Scrolls*. Grand Rapids: Eerdmans, 1964.

Moore, G. F. *Judaism*. 3 vols. Cambridge, Mass.: Harvard University Press, 1927–30.

Neusner, J., W. S. Green, and E. S. Frerichs. *Judaisms and Their Messiahs at the Turn of the Christian Era*. New York: Cambridge University Press, 1987.

Rose, H. J. *Religion in Greece and Rome*. New York: Harper & Row, 1959.

Rudolph, K. *Gnosis*. San Francisco: Harper & Row, 1987.

Sanders, E. P. *Jewish Law from Jesus to the Mishnah*. London: SCM; Philadelphia: Trinity, 1992.

Schürer, E. *The History of the Jewish People in the Age of Jesus Christ (175 B.C.–A.D. 135)*. Vol. 2, revised by G. Vermès et al. Edinburgh: T. & T. Clark, 1979.

Vermès, G. *The Dead Sea Scrolls. Qumran in Perspective*. Philadelphia: Fortress, 1981.

Yamauchi, E. M. *Pre-Christian Gnosticism*. Grand Rapids: Eerdmans, 1973.

Some of these entries are only representative of numerous volumes on the Dead Sea Scrolls. For a full account of their discovery, see J. C. Trever, *The Untold Story of Qumran* (Westwood, N.J.: Revell, 1965).

PART II

Literary and Historical Materials

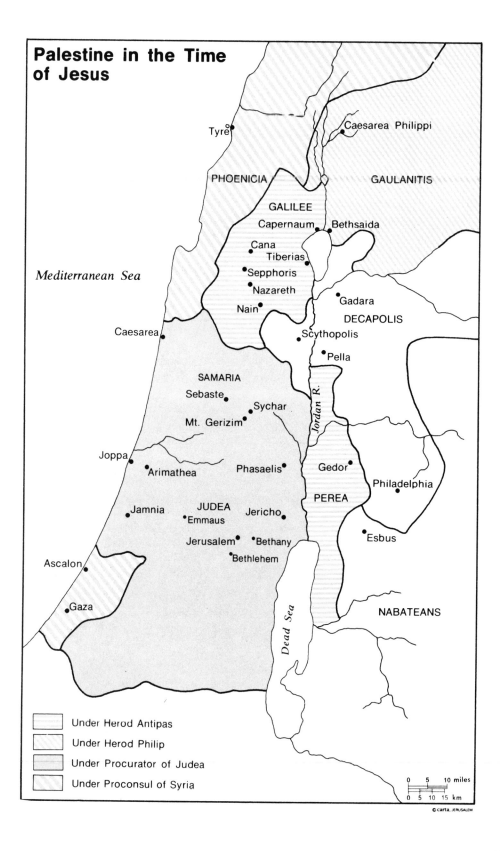

Palestine in the Time of Jesus

Tyre

Caesarea Philippi

PHOENICIA

GAULANITIS

GALILEE

Capernaum • Bethsaida

Cana
Tiberias
Sepphoris
Nazareth

Mediterranean Sea

Nain

Gadara

DECAPOLIS

Caesarea

Scythopolis

Pella

SAMARIA

Sebaste

Sychar

Mt. Gerizim

Jordan R.

Joppa

Arimathea

Phasaelis

Gedor

Philadelphia

PEREA

Jamnia

JUDEA

Jericho

Emmaus

Jerusalem • Bethany

Bethlehem

Ascalon

Esbus

Gaza

Dead Sea

NABATEANS

Under Herod Antipas

Under Herod Philip

Under Procurator of Judea

Under Proconsul of Syria

0   5   10 miles

0 5 10 15 km

© carta, JERUSALEM

4

The Canon and Text of the New Testament

❖ *How did the early church manage at first without the New Testament?*

❖ *How did the New Testament then come to be considered by the church as an authoritative collection of books?*

❖ *How do we know that our New Testament represents a substantially accurate version of what its authors originally wrote?*

The Canon

The New Testament canon consists of books accepted by the early church as divinely inspired Scripture. The term *canon* originally meant "measuring reed" but developed the metaphorical meaning "standard" (compare the literal and metaphorical meanings of *yardstick*). As applied to the New Testament, canon refers to those books accepted by the church as the standard that governs Christian belief and conduct.

At first, Christians did not have any of the books contained in our New Testament. They depended therefore on the Old Testament, on oral tradition about Jesus' words and deeds, and on messages from God spoken by Christian prophets. Even after having been written, many of the New Testament books were not distributed geographically throughout the church. And before they were gathered into the New Testament, Christian writers had produced still other books—some good, some inferior. Books such as Paul's epistles and the gospels received canonical recognition quickly. Uncertain authorship caused other books, such as Hebrews, to be questioned for a while. The early church hesitated to adopt 2 Peter because its Greek style differs from that in 1 Peter and thus raised doubts about its claim to authorship by the apostle Peter. Because of their brevity and limited circulation, some books simply did not become known widely enough for rapid acceptance into the Canon.

Quotations of New Testament books as authoritative by the early church fathers help us recognize what books they regarded as canonical. Later, the church compiled formal lists, or canons. An early Gnostic heretic named Marcion seems to have played a provocative role. He taught that a harsh God of the Old Testament and Judaism and a loving God oppose each other, that Jesus came as a messenger of the loving God, that Jesus was killed at the instigation of the harsh God, that Jesus entrusted to the twelve apostles his message from the loving God, that they failed to keep it from corruption, and that Paul turned into the sole preacher of the uncorrupted message. To support this teaching Marcion selected only those books that he considered free from and contrary to the Old Testament and Judaism: Luke (with some omissions) and most of Paul's epistles. This canon dates from about A.D. 144. The violent reaction of orthodox Christians against its omission of other Christian books now in the New Testament shows that the church as a whole had already accepted or was in the process of accepting those books that Marcion rejected. By the fourth and fifth centuries all our New Testament books were generally recognized and others excluded. Church councils of those centuries merely formalized existing belief and practice concerning the New Testament canon.

The idea of a canon implies that God guided the early church in its evaluation of various books so that truly inspired ones gained acceptance as canonical and those not inspired, whatever of lesser value they might offer, did not gain acceptance as canonical. The process of canonization took time, and differences of opinion arose. But we may be grateful that the early church did not accept books without evaluation and, at times, debate. Most readers who will compare the subapostolic writings[1] and the New Testament

---

1. *So called because they were written in the age immediately following that of the apostles by the "apostolic fathers." Books belonging to this class are 1 and 2 Clement, the Epistles of Ignatius, the Epistle of Polycarp to the Philippians, the Didache or Teaching of the Twelve Apostles, the Epistle of Barnabas, the Shepherd of Hermas, the Martyrdom of Polycarp, the Epistle to Diognetus, and the writings of Papias (of which we have only fragments).*

apocrypha[2] with the canonical books of the New Testament will heartily endorse the critical judgment of the early Christians.

Various criteria for canonicity have been suggested, such as edifying moral effect and agreement with the oral tradition of apostolic doctrine. But some edifying books failed to achieve canonical status. So also did some books that carried forward the oral tradition of apostolic doctrine. More important—in fact, crucial—was the criterion of apostolicity, which means authorship by an apostle or by an apostolic associate and thus also a date of writing within the apostolic period.

Mark associated with both of the apostles Peter and Paul. Luke accompanied Paul. And whoever authored Hebrews exhibits close theological contacts with Paul. James and Jude were half or stepbrothers of Jesus and associates of the apostles in the early Jerusalem church. Traditionally, all other authors represented in the New Testament were themselves apostles: Matthew, John, Paul, and Peter. Modern criticism casts doubt on some of the traditional ascriptions of authorship. Such questions receive individual attention in later sections of the present book. But even under negative critical views it is usually affirmed that books not written by apostles were at least written in the apostolic tradition by followers of the apostles.

Jesus himself affirmed the full authority of the Old Testament as Scripture[3] but made his own words and deeds equally authoritative[4] and promised the apostles that the Holy Spirit would remind them of his ministry and teach them its significance (John 14:26; 16:12–15). The canon of the New Testament consists, then, of the authoritative record and interpretation of God's self-revelation through Jesus Christ—an interpretative record predictively authenticated by Jesus himself, whose view of his own words and deeds, now written and expounded by the apostles and their associates, did not fall behind his view of the Old Testament as God's Word. The

---

2. These fanciful and sometimes heretical books differ from the Old Testament apocrypha and have not gained acceptance as canonical by any branch of the church.

3. For example, Matthew 5:17–19a: "Do not think that I have come to abolish the law and the prophets; I have not come to abolish, but to fulfill. For truly, I say to you, till heaven and earth pass away, not one iota or one stroke will pass from the law till all has happened. Whoever then relaxes one of these least commandments and teaches people so will be called least in the kingdom of heaven"; John 10:35b: "the Scripture cannot be broken."

4. See, for example, the statements, "You have heard that it was said to the ancients, [there follows an Old Testament quotation or paraphrase] . . . . But I say to you . . . ," in the Sermon on the Mount (Matt. 5:21, 27, 31, 38, 43; compare Mark 1:22, 27; Luke 4:32, 36).

closing of the Canon by limiting it to apostolic books arose out of a recognition that God's revelation in Christ needs no improvement.

The Text

Papyrus supplied the writing material for most, and perhaps all, books of the New Testament. Again most and perhaps all New Testament authors used scrolls, though a few may have used codices (plural of codex, a book with pages bound together in the modern style). Commonly, an author dictated to a writing secretary, called an *amanuensis*. Sometimes the author gave the amanuensis greater or lesser freedom in the choice of words.[5]

The original documents, none of which are extant, go by the term *autographs*. At first, copies were made one by one when private individuals and churches wanted them. But as demand increased, a reader dictated from an exemplar to a roomful of copyists. Gradually, errors of sight and sound, inadvertent omissions and repetitions, marginal notes, and deliberate theological and grammatical "improvements" slipped into the text. Concern for textual purity led to the checking of some manuscripts against other manuscripts. Nevertheless, the number of errors kept multiplying.

As the church grew richer and increasingly regarded the text of the New Testament as sacred, more durable writing materials, such as vellum (treated calfskin) and parchment (treated sheepskin), came into use. Earlier manuscripts were usually written all in capital (*uncial*, or *majuscule*) letters, later manuscripts in cursive, small (*minuscule*) letters. Word divisions, punctuation marks, and chapter and verse divisions were lacking at first—in fact, these did not come until much later.[6] The earliest manuscripts in the possession of modern scholars date from the second century.[7] Most of the variant readings, or differences, in early manuscripts have to do with spelling, word order, the presence or absence of "and" and "the," and other relatively inconsequential items.

Making up our primary sources for determining the original text of the New Testament are Greek manuscripts, early versions (that is, ancient translations, especially Syriac and Latin), and quotations in

---

5. *See E. R. Richards,* The Secretary in the Letters of Paul *(Tübingen: Mohr, 1991), and compare page 343 here.*

6. *Stephen Langton (d. 1228) divided the text into chapters, R. Stephanus into verses in his printed edition of 1551.*

7. *The very earliest, the Rylands Fragment of John, dates from about A.D. 135.*

the writings of the early church fathers and in lectionaries (readings from the New Testament in ancient liturgies). By comparing these, scholars can usually decide among variant readings with a fair degree of certainty. Among their most important rules for evaluation are preference for the reading in the oldest and most carefully copied manuscripts and versions, preference for the reading that best explains the development of other readings, preference for the more difficult reading (since it is more probable that copyists made an expression easier to understand than harder to understand), and preference for the shorter reading (because copyists were more liable to add to the text than to delete, except where the omission appears to have been accidental). For example, since angels regularly speak but eagles do not, an original

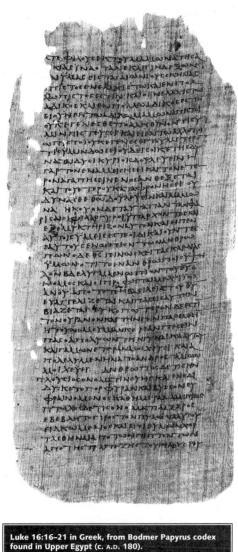

Luke 16:16–21 in Greek, from Bodmer Papyrus codex found in Upper Egypt (c. A.D. 180).

"eagle" would explain a shift in some texts to "angel" at Revelation 8:13; but for the same reason a shift from "angel" to "eagle" would hardly have occurred. With regard to God's granting of prayer requests, some texts of Mark 11:24 read the present tense "you receive" or the future tense "you will receive" (compare Matt. 21:22) because the past tense of the original "you received" seemed too bold. Some texts add "paralytics" at the end of John 5:3, apparently because the self-description of the man whom Jesus is about to heal

makes one think of paralysis. In 1 Corinthians 10:19 some texts seem to have accidentally skipped from the first "is" to the second "is" and thus omitted Paul's question whether an idol is anything.

Materials for determining the original text of the New Testament are far more numerous and ancient than those for the study of any of the old classical writings. Thanks to the labors of textual critics, remaining uncertainties about the text of the Greek New Testament are not serious enough to affect our understanding of its fundamental teachings.

So far as English versions of the New Testament are concerned, John Wycliffe produced his translation from Jerome's Latin Vulgate in 1382, and William Tyndale did a translation from the original Greek in 1525. Following a succession of further English Bibles, the Roman Catholic Douay Version appeared in 1582 and the King James (or Authorized) Version in 1611. But the earliest and best manuscripts of the New Testament had not yet been discovered, and the following centuries saw great advances in scholarly knowledge concerning the kind of Greek used in the New Testament. A large contribution has come from the study of numerous papyri found during the last hundred and fifty years. As a result, numerous

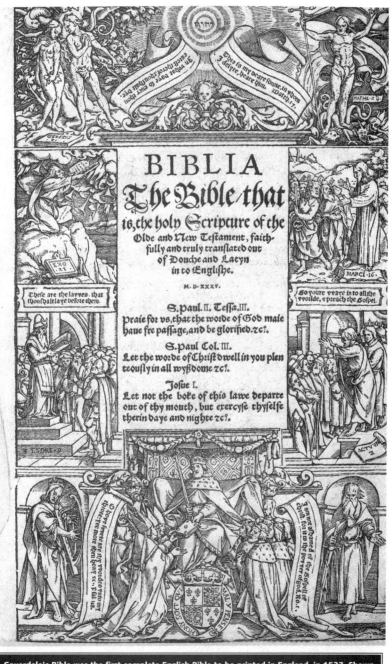

Coverdale's Bible was the first complete English Bible to be printed in England, in 1537. Shown here is the title page.

versions have appeared in recent times, for example, the English Revised Version (1881), the American Standard Version (1901), the Revised Standard Version (1946), the New English Bible (1961), the New American Standard Bible (1963), the Jerusalem Bible (1966), Today's English Version (1966), and the New International Version (1978), plus updates of some of these versions and various individual efforts.

FOR FURTHER DISCUSSION

Try to reconstruct a typical church service as it was before the New Testament was formed as a basis for preaching and teaching. Also reconstruct an early Christian's private devotional life without the New Testament.

What evidences of continuing Marcionism are still apparent?

How and why are Christian classics such as Augustine's Confessions, *John Bunyan's* Pilgrim's Progress, *and some of Charles Wesley's hymns to be distinguished from the canonical books of the New Testament?*

Why did the church close the canon? Or is it still open? If an apostolic book—say, a long lost epistle of Paul to the Corinthian church besides the epistles to that church that we already have—came to light and was verified as apostolic, should the church add it to the New Testament?

For practical purposes, does translation of Scripture take away the benefit of inspiration by removing readers one step from the original text?

What are the advantages and disadvantages of a single accepted translation of the New Testament and of many different translations?

FOR FURTHER INVESTIGATION

(Primary materials containing translations of the subapostolic writings and New Testament apocrypha)

Grant, R. M., et al. *The Apostolic Fathers.* 6 vols. New York: Nelson, 1964–68. With extensive introductions and notes.

Hennecke, E. *New Testament Apocrypha.* Edited by W. Schneemelcher. 2d ed. 2 vols. Louisville: Westminster/John Knox, 1993. With technical introductions and notes.

James, M. R. *The Apocryphal New Testament.* New York: Oxford University Press, 1924.

Lake, K. *The Apostolic Fathers.* 2 vols. Loeb Classical Library. New York: Putnam's, 1930. With Greek text as well as English translation.

Lightfoot, J. B., J. R. Harmer, and M. W. Holmes. *The Apostolic Fathers.* Grand Rapids: Baker, 1989.

(Modern discussions of the Canon)

Bruce, F. F. *The Canon of Scripture.* Downers Grove, Ill.: InterVarsity, 1988.

Cross, F. L. *The Early Christian Fathers.* Naperville, Ill.: Allenson, 1960. Chapter 5.

McDonald, L. M. *The Formation of the Biblical Canon.* Nashville: Abingdon, 1988.

Metzger, B. M. *The Canon of the New Testament.* New York: Oxford University Press, 1992.

Ridderbos, H. N. *Authority of the New Testament Scriptures.* Nutley, N.J.: Presbyterian & Reformed, 1963.

(Modern surveys of textual criticism)

Aland, K., and B. Aland. *The Text of the New Testament.* 2d ed. Grand Rapids: Eerdmans; Leiden: Brill, 1990.

Fee, G. D. "The Textual Criticism of the New Testament." In *Biblical Criticism: Historical, Literary and Textual,* G. D. Fee et al. Grand Rapids: Zondervan, 1978. Pp. 127–55

Holmes, M. W. "Textual Criticism." In *New Testament Criticism and Interpretation.* Edited by D. A. Black and D. S. Dockery. Grand Rapids: Zondervan, 1991. Pp. 101–34.

Metzger, B. M. *The Text of the New Testament: Its Transmission, Corruption and Restoration.* 3d ed. New York: Oxford University Press, 1991.

(The English New Testament)

Bruce, F. F. *History of the Bible in English.* 3d ed. New York: Oxford University Press, 1978.

5

The Study
of Jesus' Life

❖ *Are there literary sources for the life and teaching of Jesus outside the New Testament? If so, what are they and what is their value?*

❖ *Are the gospels independent or interdependent? If interdependent, what are their relationships?*

❖ *What sources, if any, lie behind the gospels?*

❖ *From the standpoint of historical criticism, how reliable is the information about Jesus in the gospels?*

❖ *How did the gospels come to be written, and what are the main modern understandings of their portraiture of Jesus?*

Sources

Extrabiblical History Though not the first documents of the New Testament to have been written (some of the epistles were written first), the gospels of Matthew, Mark, Luke, and John fittingly stand first as our main sources for reconstructing the life of Jesus. The few notices concerning him in non-Christian sources—the first-century Jewish historian Josephus (with later insertions by Christian copyists), the Babylonian Talmud, and the Roman writers Pliny the Younger, Tacitus, Suetonius, and Lucian—are so brief as to be almost valueless for a reconstruction. They do confirm, however, that Jesus lived, became a public figure, and died under Pontius Pilate, and that within

First page of the Gospel of Thomas, from the Nag Hammadi library.

a dozen years of his death the worship of him had spread as far as Rome.

Agrapha

There are sayings of Jesus recorded outside the four gospels. For example, Paul quotes a dominical[1] saying otherwise unknown: "It is more blessed to give than to receive" (Acts 20:35). These *agrapha*, as they are called, differ from Jesus' sayings in the gospels, but are quoted by early Christian writers and are sometimes placed in the margins of ancient manuscripts of the New Testament. *Agrapha* is Greek for "unwritten." These sayings were written down, of course (otherwise we would not know them), but not in the text of the canonical gospels—hence the designation "unwritten."

Collections of Sayings

Most notable among other records of Jesus' sayings outside the four canonical gospels are the Oxyrhynchus papyri and the Gospel of Thomas. The Gospel of Thomas, discovered at Nag Hammadi, Egypt, in about 1945, is not really a gospel; for it does not contain a narrative thread. Nor did the apostle Thomas write it. Both this so-called gospel and the Oxyrhynchus papyri offer sizeable collections of Jesus' sayings. Some of the sayings look almost exactly like those recorded in the canonical gospels. Others obviously stem from canonical sayings but have undergone changes of various sorts. Still

---

1. From the Latin *dominicus*, *"lord, master," often used for what pertains to the Lord Jesus.*

95

others differ wholly from anything found in the New Testament.[2] Concerning their relationship to the New Testament, three possibilities present themselves: (1) the noncanonical records draw from the canonical gospels; (2) the noncanonical records represent an independent tradition of Jesus' sayings; (3) both relationships hold true in a mixed way. With the exception of scholars who deeply distrust the reliability of the canonical gospels, it is generally agreed that the Oxyrhynchus papyri and the Gospel of Thomas reflect a largely corrupted tradition concerning the words of Jesus.

Apocryphal Gospels

Luke 1:1 mentions numerous accounts written about Jesus and antedating the third gospel, but none of these except Mark and probably Matthew have survived. Postapostolic apocryphal gospels did survive, however; and they present a motley picture of heretical beliefs and pious imagination, especially in filling out the details of Jesus' childhood and the interval between his death and resurrection, about which the canonical gospels are largely silent.[3]

Source Criticism of the Gospels

Synoptic Problem: Oral Tradition

As students of Jesus' life we must go first to our primary sources, the canonical gospels. Immediately the "synoptic problem" confronts us: Why are the first three (or synoptic) gospels very much alike? (*Synoptic* comes from two Greek words meaning, "a seeing together.") According to the theory of oral tradition, resemblances derive from rapid crystallization of the tradition about Jesus in a more or less fixed oral form, which later came to be written down. But most modern scholars doubt that transmission by word of mouth could have retained so many and such minute verbal resemblances as exist among the synoptics, especially in narrative, which is not so

---

2. *Here are examples of extracanonical sayings varying in degree of similarity to canonical sayings (from* The Gospel According to Thomas, *Coptic text established and translated by A. Guillaumont et al. [New York: Harper, 1959]):*

Logion 54: *Jesus said: Blessed are the poor, for yours is the Kingdom of Heaven.*

Logion 46b: *But I have said that whoever among you becomes as a child shall know the Kingdom, and he shall become higher than John.*

Logion 82: *Jesus said: Whoever is near to me is near to the fire, and whoever is far from me is far from the Kingdom.*

See further Joachim Jeremias, Unknown Sayings of Jesus, *2d English ed. (London: SPCK, 1964).*

3. *See M. R. James,* The Apocryphal New Testament *(Oxford: Clarendon, 1924); or E. Hennecke,* New Testament Apocrypha, *ed. W. Schneemelcher, 2 vols. (Louisville: Westminster/ Knox, 1993). The latter work contains extensive technical introductions and notes in addition to translations.*

96

likely to have been memorized verbatim as possibly the words of Jesus were memorized.[4]

W. R. Farmer has recently led an attempt to revive the synoptic theory of an eighteenth-century German scholar named J. J. Griesbach. According to this theory, Matthew wrote first. Then Luke used Matthew. Finally, Mark wrote an abbreviated combination of Matthew and Luke. Most contemporary scholars think that the order of narrative materials in the synoptics might be explained fairly adequately in this way but that Luke's disrupting the order of teaching materials in Matthew and detailed changes of wording do not receive an adequate explanation under this theory.[5]

Griesbach Hypothesis

The Mark-Q documentary hypothesis has gained the greatest favor: Matthew and Luke based most of their narrative on Mark, drew most of Jesus' sayings, or teaching, from a lost document designated Q,[6] and added distinctive material of their own. Scholars marshal a number of arguments for the priority of Mark. Luke 1:1–4 states the utilization of earlier documents. This statement at least opens the possibility that Mark provided one of the documents behind Luke. More specifically, Matthew incorporates nearly all of Mark, and Luke about one-half. Both Matthew and Luke often carry the exact words of Mark, even in minute details. Furthermore, Matthew and Luke usually carry Mark's sequence of the events in Jesus' life; they do not depart *together* from that sequence, as one would have expected them to do at least occasionally if they had not both been drawing on Mark.[7] And it often appears that Matthew and Luke changed the wording of Mark to clarify his meaning,[8] to omit material the meaning of which might be mis-

Marcan Priority

---

4. *Two Scandinavian scholars, H. Riesenfeld* (The Gospel Tradition and Its Beginnings *[London: Mowbray, 1957]) and B. Gerhardsson* (Memory and Manuscript: Oral Tradition and Written Transmission in Rabbinic Judaism and Early Christianity *[Uppsala: Gleerup, 1961] and* Tradition and Transmission in Early Christianity *[Uppsala: Gleerup, 1964]) have revived the theory of oral tradition. Their emphasis on the importance of memory in ancient Jewish culture supports an estimate of the gospels as trustworthy but does not explain the literary interrelationships of the synoptics, particularly in narrative material.*

5. *W. R. Farmer,* The Synoptic Problem: A Critical Analysis *(New York: Macmillan, 1964; reprinted by Western North Carolina Press, 1976).*

6. *The designation Q is usually connected with the German word* Quelle, *meaning "source."*

7. *In other words, it appears that Mark is the anchor that keeps Matthew and Luke from drifting very far away (and never at the same time) from the order of events contained in Mark. Occasional, independent differences in sequence arise because topical considerations sometimes override chronology in the concerns of the evangelists (a technical term for the writers of the gospels).*

8. *For example, compare Mark 2:15 and Luke 5:29 as to whose house was the scene of a banquet.*

taken,[9] to delete material unnecessary for their own purposes,[10] and to smooth out awkward grammar (a matter of style, not of accuracy)[11]—all phenomena which indicate a utilization of Mark.

Q Hypothesis   Since similarities in *narrative* material appear to rise from common use of the document Mark by Matthew and Luke, similarities between Matthew and Luke in *sayings* material not contained in Mark have led to the positing of a second document, Q, thought to be an early collection of Jesus' sayings with a minimum of narrative. Q would be something like the Gospel of Thomas and the Oxyrhynchus collection of Jesus' sayings or, better yet, like Old Testament prophetical books that contain the account of a prophet's call, extensive records of his preaching, sometimes bits and pieces of narrative, but no account of the prophet's death. Thus Q might be thought to begin with the baptism and temptation of Jesus (his "call"), to continue with his preaching, but to lack any account of his suffering, death, and resurrection.

As to be expected especially for a hypothetical document, Q raises some questions. For instance, why does the degree of agreement between Matthew and Luke in sayings material vary widely? Did Matthew and Luke use or make different Greek translations of an originally Aramaic Q, use different editions of a Greek Q, or use the same Greek Q? Should we doubt the very existence of Q (Why did it not survive as such?) and adopt for the sayings material a theory of many short documents, or the theory of oral tradition (easier to believe for sayings than for narrative), or a combination of the two? Some believe that Luke used Matthew for much of the sayings material; but if so, why did Luke often rearrange Matthew's order of that material? Or could it be that in the main, Luke used Mark and Q, but that he also used Matthew, only subsidiarily (a theory that would explain the so-called minor agreements of Matthew and Luke against Mark)?[12]

---

9. For example, Matthew and Luke omit Mark's story that Jesus' family thought he had gone mad, perhaps because their audiences might put a wrong interpretation on the incident and infer too much.

10. For example, Matthew 8:14 and Luke 4:38 omit the names of Andrew, James, and John in Mark 1:29 and retain only Peter's name.

11. For example, Mark 2:7 (literally translated), "Who can forgive sins except one, God?" becomes, "Who can forgive sins except God alone?" in Luke 5:21. Mark has a rough and ready style—forceful, but not elegant.

12. Proposing a four-document hypothesis, B. H. Streeter added M for the sayings of Jesus distinctive to Matthew, and L for most of the matter distinctive to Luke. He also advanced the

Marcan priority enjoys considerable favor. About Q there is more uncertainty. Perhaps we should think of it as a body of loose notes jotted down by Matthew. His gospel often arranges and collects the sayings of Jesus topically instead of chronologically, as do also the other gospels, but to a lesser degree. In contrast with Matthew, Luke may have used Mark as a supplement rather than as the backbone of his narrative; but this possibility falls far short of certainty. It does not follow that where Matthew and Luke used Mark or another common source, such as Q, their testimony is historically inferior. Rather, they wanted to preserve the unity of the apostolic tradition about Jesus because that tradition was anchored in history and deserved a united testimony in its favor. Where they change Mark or any other earlier source, they do so not in misleading ways but in ways that combat misinterpretation of the earlier accounts, add further details, omit others, and elaborate so as to bring out a variety of theological implications.

Form Criticism of the Gospels

Task

The earliest Christians did not have any of the four gospels, much less all four. In the first decades of the twentieth century, therefore, German scholarship set for itself the ambitious task of inferring by literary analysis (*Formgeschichte*, "form history") what the oral tradition about Jesus was like before it came to be written down in the gospels. For example, from the beginning of Christianity the story of Jesus' arrest, trial, and crucifixion (the Passion) must have been told and retold at the Lord's Supper and in sermons. Then, as the need for instruction in Christian doctrine and conduct arose, isolated bits of tradition about the words and deeds of Jesus were recalled as an authoritative pattern for such doctrine and conduct. Should Christians marry? Divorce? Pay taxes? The oral tradition about Jesus was kept alive in the answering of these and similar questions.

Method

Form critics try to determine the nature and content of the oral tradition by classifying individual units of the written gospel material[13] according to their form and usage in the early church. The

Proto-Luke theory: the first edition of Luke's gospel consisted only of Q + L, to which Luke later added a preface and the birth stories of John the Baptist and Jesus and interspersed Marcan material. There is no general agreement on Streeter's proposals (B. H. Streeter, The Four Gospels [New York: St. Martin's, 1951], part 2; compare V. Taylor, The Formation of the Gospel Tradition [New York: St. Martin's, 1960], appendix A).

13. The technical term for an individual unit, or section, of the gospels—such as the story of Jesus' healing a leper or the record of a parable—is pericope (pĕ rĭ́ kō pē).

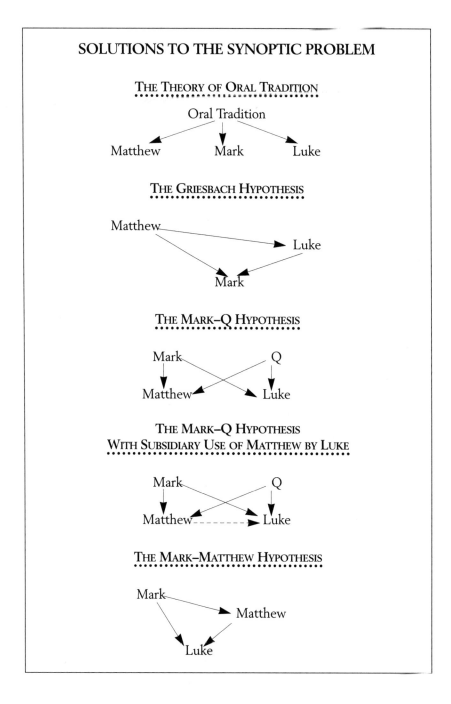

common categories are (1) apothegms, paradigms, or pronouncement stories (stories climaxing in a saying of Jesus), used for sermon
illustrations; (2) miracle stories, used as models for the activities of
Christian healers; (3) sayings and parables, used for catechetical instruction; (4) legends, used to magnify the greatness of Jesus (with
perhaps a core of historical truth, but greatly exaggerated); and (5)
the passion story, used in celebrations of the Lord's Supper and in
evangelistic preaching. In its more sceptical expression, this approach assumes that early Christians modified the information
about Jesus greatly and invented stories and sayings to meet the
needs which arose out of missionary preaching, catechetical instruction, sermonizing, formation of liturgies, doctrinal controversies,
and questions of church discipline. As a result, the gospels tell us
more about the *Sitz im Leben* ("situation in life") of the early church
than about that of Jesus. To determine the truth about Jesus, form
critics typically think that they must strip away editorial accretions,
such as geographical and chronological notations, miraculous features, and doctrinal elements supposedly dating from a period later
than Jesus.

Development

The Old Testament scholar J. Wellhausen fostered form criticism
of the gospels. M. Dibelius popularized it. K. L. Schmidt convinced
many that the geographical and chronological framework in Mark
came by Mark's own invention. And R. Bultmann (best known of
the form critics) concluded after detailed analysis that almost all
the gospel tradition was fabricated or highly distorted. A characteristic line of reasoning is that since Christians believed in the deity of
Jesus, they justified their belief by concocting stories in which he
performed a miracle. We should, thought Bultmann, "demytholo-
gize" the gospels (take away the myths) to make the Christian message palatable to modern people, who from their naturalistic
standpoint can no longer accept the supernatural claims of the
gospels on Jesus' behalf.[14]

Evaluation

Form criticism has placed salutary emphasis on literary analysis as
a means toward reconstructing the oral gospel tradition and on the
continuing relevance of Jesus' words and deeds for the life of the
early church. His openness toward Gentiles, for example, must have

---

14. See R. Bultmann et al., Kerygma and Myth, *ed. H. W. Bartsch; rev. ed. by R. H. Fuller
(New York: Harper, 1961), 1–44; Bultmann,* The History of the Synoptic Tradition, *2d ed.
(New York: Harper & Row, 1968); and numerous other writings by Bultmann and others
about his method and theology.*

helped the entrance of Gentiles into the church. But utility was not the only factor. Form critics have not allowed enough room for the sheer biographical interest that early Christians must have had in Jesus. If those Christians really did appeal to his words and deeds to justify their beliefs and practices—as form critics themselves admit, indeed, emphasize—then the strongest motives existed for remembering him. Even Paul, who apparently had not known Jesus, could quote no higher authority (see, for example, 1 Cor. 7:10–11).

Nor have form critics allowed for the possibility that the gospel tradition was preserved because it was true as well as useful for Christian evangelism, teaching, and liturgy. The single generation between Jesus and the writing of the gospels did not allow enough time for extensive fabrication of myths concerning him. Mythology does not normally develop in less than half a century. Yet the early Christians were proclaiming Jesus as a risen and exalted Savior-God almost immediately after his death. Moreover, during the first decades of church history the hope of Jesus' soon return burned brightly, so that the early Christians would not have felt much need to fabricate more information about him than was already available.

Form critics seem also to have forgotten that both Christian and anti-Christian eyewitnesses of Jesus' career must have deterred wholesale fabrication and distortion of information. Throughout the New Testament numerous references indicate that early Christians valued highly the factor of eyewitness in establishing testimonial reliability. For examples, see Luke 1:1–4; John 1:14; 20:30–31; 1 Corinthians 15:5–8; 1 John 1:1–4. Not only would both friendly and unfriendly eyewitnesses have provided a restraining influence, but also their recollection of Jesus' teaching and example would have been mined for solutions to ecclesiastical and doctrinal problems, for answers to inquiries from prospective converts, and for apology in the face of malicious charges. There is more than one reason, then, not to underestimate the factor of eyewitness.

Nor must we think that all ancient people gullibly accepted every tale of the supernatural they heard. Scepticism in the Greco-Roman world was widespread. Even among the disciples evidence had to overcome doubt, as in the case of Thomas, who at first disbelieved the report of Jesus' resurrection. Had Jesus not been the arresting figure portrayed in the gospels, why the great stir about him? Why was he crucified? Why did people follow him and continue to believe in him and proclaim him as Savior, even and quickly after he had died the death of a criminal? Would they have been willing to suffer and die, as they did, for a false tradition of their own making? And especially, why did Jews, trained from childhood to worship only the one invisible God, feel constrained to worship a human being whom they had known? If the gospels are not reliable, we draw a blank at the beginning of Christianity. But the dramatic upsurge of Christianity demands an explanation equal to the phenomenon.

Very early in the second century, probably in its first decade, the church father Papias passed on a tradition that Mark wrote down Peter's reminiscences of Jesus. There are not sufficient reasons to doubt this tradition or the reliability of the gospels in general. On the contrary, the texts of the four gospels contain numerous indications of authenticity. Realistic details abound—references to places, names, and customs unnecessary to the overall story—just as one expects in accounts deriving from eyewitnesses. Descriptions of legal practices and social conditions in Palestine vis-à-vis the Hellenistic world exhibit an amazing accuracy.[15] Later Christians would have glorified the twelve apostles (as in later Christian literature) rather than unflatteringly portraying them as often bumbling, thickheaded, unbelieving, and cowardly. Why would sayings of Jesus embarrassingly difficult to interpret have been invented?[16] Their very difficulty implies authenticity. It is also doubtful that wholesale distortion and fabrication would have produced the large amount of Semitic poetry evident in Jesus' teaching as recorded by the evangelists.[17] The same thing is true concerning other traits of its Semitic style, which shines through even though the gospels were written in Greek, a non-Semitic language.

The absence of parables from the epistles of the New Testament shows that early Christians did not use parables as a pedagogical device and are therefore unlikely to have created them in the gospels. Similarly, the absence in the epistles of the Christological title "Son

---

15. See A. N. Sherwin-White, Roman Society and Roman Law in the New Testament (Oxford: Clarendon, 1963), chap. 6 and pp. 186ff.

16. For examples, see Matthew 10:23; Mark 9:1; 13:32.

17. The poetic form of parallel statements, as in the Hebrew poetry of the Old Testament, is not apparent in most English translations of the gospels. But here is an example of Semitic poetic parallelism in Jesus' teaching:

Ask, and it will be given to you;

Seek, and you will find;

Knock, and it will be opened to you (Luke 11:9).

of man" (frequent in the gospels) shows it to be distinctive and thus characteristic of Jesus. Conversely, the failure of the gospels to say anything about many of the burning issues reflected in Acts and the epistles (such as whether or not Gentile converts should be circumcised) shows that the early Christians did not read their own later developments of doctrine wholesale into Jesus' mouth. Paul provides a good example: he separated his own pronouncements on marriage and divorce from the Lord's (1 Cor. 7:6, 7, 8, 10, 12, 17, 25, 26, 28, 29, 32, 35, 40). Only a positive assessment of the gospel tradition adequately explains the beginnings of Christianity and the literary features of the gospels and epistles.

The Kerygma

The prominent British scholar C. H. Dodd offered an alternative to sceptical form criticism by noting a common pattern in the sermons of the early chapters in Acts (especially 10:34–43) and in the epistles of Paul where Paul occasionally summarizes the gospel (for example, Rom. 1:1–4; 10:9; 1 Cor. 11:23ff.; 15:3ff.):

- Jesus has inaugurated the fulfillment of messianic prophecy.
- He went about doing good and performing miracles.
- He was crucified according to God's plan.
- He was raised and exalted to heaven.
- He will return in judgment.
- Therefore repent, believe, and be baptized.

This pattern Dodd called the *kerygma* (Greek for "proclamation" or "preaching"). Gradually, the bare outline of this kerygmatic pattern came to be filled with stories, sayings, and parables from Jesus' life. As eyewitnesses began to die off, the gospels were written for a permanent record. Also, as the gospel spread geographically far from Palestine to places where eyewitnesses were not available for confirmation, the need arose for trustworthy written records to be utilized by Christians in their preaching about Jesus' words and deeds. Thus, the gospel of Mark is an expanded *kerygma* in written form.[18]

---

18. C. H. Dodd, The Apostolic Preaching and Its Development *(London: Hodder & Stoughton, 1936). In addition, Dodd distinguished* didache, *"teaching" for Christian life and faith, from* kerygma, *designed to make converts. It is increasingly recognized that the distinction is hard to maintain. Indeed, the outline of the* kerygma *itself may not have been so rigid as Dodd's reconstruction.*

A common idea is that at first the Christians did not even think of writing about the life of Jesus, because they expected him to return in the immediate future. When decade after decade he failed to do so, it dawned on them that more formal and fixed accounts were needed to fill the ever-widening gap. This idea may contain some truth. Nevertheless, the expectation of a nearly immediate return of Jesus is easily overestimated. Closer scrutiny of relevant texts in the New Testament shows that early Christians looked for the Second Coming as a possibility within their lifetimes, but not as a certainty. The books of the New Testament do not stem from embarrassment over the delay in Jesus' return. They exude far too much confidence for us ever to think so.

Redaction Criticism (Redaktionsgeschichte)

After World War II scholars began to analyze the gospels as unified compositions carefully edited (redacted) by their authors to project distinctive theological views. A well-known example of this approach is H. Conzelmann's hypothesis that Luke reinterpreted Jesus' ministry to be, not the final stage of history (as Conzelmann alleges early Christians believed), but the midpoint of history with the age of the church and the Second Coming to follow—hence, Luke's addition of the book of Acts to his gospel.[19] Usually, the particular theological standpoint of the evangelist is attributed to an entire school of thought within the church. The contribution of redaction criticism consists in its identifying ways in which the evangelists tailored earlier materials about Jesus to the needs of their own times; thus his words and deeds do not appear as fossils of dead history, but as applications to contemporary life (as form critics say was already being done with individual units of tradition in the preceding oral stage). The danger of redaction criticism lies in a tendency to neglect the importance of earlier traditions as such, an importance seen in the fact that the evangelists saw those traditions as worth incorporating, tailoring, and applying.

Other Kinds of Higher Criticism

Other kinds of higher criticism jostle for attention, too, though none of them has attained the prominence of the foregoing. Composition

---

19. H. Conzelmann, *The Theology of St. Luke (London: Faber & Faber, 1960). We might question Conzelmann's conclusion that Luke's view of history represents a shift from an expectation that Jesus would return almost immediately.*

criticism pays attention to editorial arrangements of and additions to tradition (and as such is scarcely distinguishable from redaction criticism). Narrative criticism tries to establish the story line of a gospel. Tradition criticism traces the origin and development of theological themes present in the gospels. Rhetorical criticism considers the implications of persuasive art on the presentation of dominical tradition. Literary criticism studies the impact of style on the message of the gospels. Genre criticism, looking for the significance of larger literary forms, asks, What is a gospel? How does it differ from other comparable books? Why does it differ? Canon criticism stresses the effect on the meaning of a gospel had by its association with other biblical books. *Tendenzkritik* (tendency criticism) keeps an eye on the influence of theological conflicts in the early church. Sociological criticism studies the influence of societal oppositions— wealth versus poverty, freedom versus slavery, honor versus shame, city versus country, and so forth—on Christian life and belief as represented by the gospels. Anthropological criticism seeks to initiate modern readers into the culturally different ways of thinking and acting that the gospels reflect. Reader response criticism examines the efforts of readers to make their own sense of the gospels and pays special attention to reading between lines where the evangelists have left matters unexpressed or vague. Structural criticism examines modes of thought underlying the gospels and common to human expression. Deconstruction tries to show that in and of itself the text of a gospel contains no meaning. These kinds of criticism have application outside the gospels, too.

The Study of Jesus' Life

Most contemporary scholars agree that a full-scale biography of Jesus is impossible, because the gospels are very selective in the amount and kind of information they present about him. But during the nineteenth century, before this restriction was felt so keenly, several outstanding biographies of Jesus appeared. A sceptical treatment by the German scholar D. F. Strauss (1835) concluded that most of the material in the gospels is mythological. E. Renan's life of Christ (1863) became famous for its literary beauty. This French author portrayed Jesus as an amiable carpenter who turned into an apocalyptist. In 1883 Alfred Edersheim, a converted Jew, produced his widely used and conservative *Life and Times of Jesus the Messiah* from a background of acquaintance with rabbinic literature. At the turn of the century a typically liberal view, outstandingly represented by the German scholar, A. von Harnack, saw in Jesus a good example of sacrifical service to fellow human beings and a teacher of lofty ethical ideals, but not a divine-human redeemer.

In 1906, Albert Schweitzer shook the theological world with his *Quest of the Historical Jesus*. As indicated by the original German title, *Von Reimarus zu Wrede*, it was a critical survey of some modern studies of Jesus' life. Schweitzer argued that liberal treatments rested more on preconceived notions than on data in the gospels. According to him, Jesus thought that God's kingdom was about to arrive on earth and that God would install him as the Messiah. In fact, Jesus told the twelve disciples that God would send him as the Son of man (a superhuman messiah) to establish the kingdom before they completed a preaching mission throughout Galilee (Matt. 10:23). When this expectation failed, Jesus became increasingly convinced that he would have to die for God to bring the kingdom.

Meanwhile, Jesus revealed the secret of his messiahship to Peter, James, and John at the Transfiguration. Peter then betrayed this secret to the rest of the Twelve on the occasion of his great confession (Mark 8:27–30; Matt. 16:13–20; Luke 9:18–20). (To achieve this reconstruction Schweitzer had to switch the order of Peter's confession and Jesus' transfiguration as given in the synoptics.) Judas then betrayed the secret to the Jewish authorities, who set in motion the events which culminated in Jesus' death. Jesus himself courageously but foolishly thought that God would raise him from the dead and immediately reveal him to the world on the clouds of heaven to establish the kingdom on earth. Such an event did not happen, of course; so for Schweitzer, Jesus became a tragic and mysterious figure, hard for moderns to understand but worthy of imitation in his selfless dedication.

Schweitzer's portrayal of Jesus has not received general acceptance. He laid too much stress on Matthew 10:23, which can be interpreted in other ways. He disregarded statements by Jesus that God's kingdom had already arrived. He failed to explain adequately why Jesus gave large amounts of ethical teaching. Someone who believed and proclaimed that God's kingdom was going to arrive in the next few weeks or months would hardly have felt the need for instructing people at length how to behave in present evil society. Schweitzer's great contribution lay, rather, in his forcing a reconsideration of the eschatological[20] teaching of Jesus and the messianic implications of his ministry, both of which were being passed over lightly by most liberal scholars and even now are being negated again by such scholars.

In the present state of research on the life of Jesus, disparate opinions clamor for recognition. The lingering influence of Bultmann causes many to reject most of the gospel tradition. Some of Bultmann's former students, dubbed "post-Bultmannians," have accepted a bit more as authentic.[21] Mediating scholars accept a somewhat larger proportion as authentic but reject the rest. While some have revived the quest of the historical Jesus, others have forsaken it altogether in favor of literary, political, sociological, and psychological concerns. Conservative scholars find good historical and theological reasons for full acceptance of the gospel records. Such acceptance does not imply that the evangelists always quoted Jesus verbatim and never elaborated the tradition of his words and deeds interpretatively. On the contrary, differences among the gospels imply editorial arrangement, paraphrasing, and interpretative elaboration, all of which can be perfectly legitimate ways to convey someone else's meaning and significance. Nor do conservative scholars insist on a complete and always chronological account of Jesus' activities. But measured by the purpose for which the gospels were written—to proclaim the good news about him for evangelism and church life—the gospels merit our trust.

FOR
FURTHER
DISCUSSION

How do literary interrelationships, differences among the gospels in wording and order, and the use and revision of source materials affect belief in the divine origin and inspiration of the Bible?

To what extent, if any, should the gospels be made palatable or acceptable to modern ways of thinking (a major question raised by Bultmann's program of demythologization)?

What is a "myth"? What is its relation to historicity? To universal human experience? According to definitions, does the Bible contain myths?

---

20. Eschatological *means "having to do with the 'end' of history."*

21. *See J. M. Robinson,* A New Quest of the Historical Jesus *(Naperville, Ill.: Allenson, 1959).*

For further investigation, consult the books cited in the footnotes to the preceding chapter and the bibliography at the close of the following chapter. For evangelical treatments of some of the issues here discussed, see also the following:

FOR FURTHER INVESTIGATION

Althaus, P., et al. *Jesus of Nazareth, Saviour and Lord.* Edited C. F. H. Henry. Grand Rapids: Eerdmans, 1966.

Black, D. A., and D. S. Dockery, eds. *New Testament Criticism and Interpretation.* Grand Rapids: Zondervan, 1991.

Bruce, F. F. *The New Testament Documents: Are They Reliable?* 5th ed. Grand Rapids: Eerdmans, 1966.

Ladd, G. E. *The New Testament and Criticism.* Grand Rapids: Eerdmans, 1966.

McKnight, S., ed. *Introducing New Testament Interpretation.* Grand Rapids: Baker, 1989.

Marshall, I. H. *I Believe in the Historical Jesus.* Grand Rapids: Eerdmans, 1977.

———, ed. *New Testament Interpretation.* Grand Rapids: Eerdmans, 1977.

Other works worth consulting include:

Beardslee, W. A. *Literary Criticism of the New Testament.* Philadelphia: Fortress, 1970.

Dunn, J. D. G. *The Evidence for Jesus.* Philadelphia: Westminster, 1985.

Gerhardsson, B. *The Origins of the Gospel Tradition.* Philadelphia: Fortress, 1979.

Güttgemanns, E. *Candid Questions Concerning Form Criticism.* Pittsburgh: Pickwick, 1979.

Holmberg, B. *Sociology and the New Testament: An Appraisal.* Minneapolis: Fortress, 1990.

Horsley, R. A. *Sociology and the Jesus Movement.* New York: Crossroad, 1989.

Kee, H. C. *Christian Origins in Sociological Perspective.* Philadelphia: Westminster, 1980.

———. *Jesus in History.* 2d ed. New York: Harcourt, Brace, Jovanovich, 1977.

———. *Knowing the Truth: A Sociological Approach to New Testament Interpretation.* Minneapolis: Fortress, 1989.

Krentz, E. *The Historical-Critical Method.* Philadelphia: Fortress, 1975.

McKnight, E. V. *What Is Form Criticism?* Philadelphia: Fortress, 1969.

Malina, B. J. *Christian Origins and Cultural Anthropology.* Atlanta: John Knox, 1985.

———. *The New Testament World: Insights from Cultural Anthropology.* Atlanta: John Knox, 1981.

Malina, B. J., and R. L. Rohrbaugh. *Social-Science Commentary on the Synoptic Gospels.* Minneapolis: Fortress, 1992.

Patte, D. *Structural Exegesis for New Testament Critics.* Minneapolis: Fortress, 1990.

Perrin, N. *What is Redaction Criticism?* Philadelphia: Fortress, 1969.

Petersen, N. R. *Literary Criticism for New Testament Critics.* Philadelphia: Fortress, 1978.

Pilch, J. J. *Introducing the Cultural Context of the New Testament*. New York–Mahwah: Paulist, 1991.

Powell, M. A. *What Is Narrative Criticism?* Minneapolis: Fortress, 1990.

Rohde, J. *Rediscovering the Teaching of the Evangelists*. Philadelphia: Westminster, 1969.

Sanders, E. P., and M. Davies. *Studying the Synoptic Gospels*. London: SCM; Philadelphia: Trinity, 1989.

Soulen, R. N. *Handbook of Biblical Criticism*. 2d ed. Atlanta: John Knox, 1985.

Theissen, G. *Sociology of Early Palestinian Christianity*. Philadelphia: Fortress, 1978.

In general terms compare *The Life of Apollonius* by Philostratus, parts of which are quoted in C. K. Barrett, *The New Testament Background: Selected Documents*, 2d ed. (San Francisco: Harper & Row, 1987), pp. 82–84, with the portraits of Jesus given in the gospels; also H. C. Kee, *The Origins of Christianity* (Englewood Cliffs, N.J.: Prentice-Hall, 1973), pp. 211–29; D. R. Cartlidge and D. L. Dungan, *Documents for the Study of the Gospels* (Cleveland: Collins, 1980); F. F. Bruce, *Jesus and Christian Origins Outside the New Testament* (Grand Rapids: Eerdmans, 1974).

To appreciate some of the issues debated by source, form, and redaction critics, carefully compare Matthew's and Luke's accounts of the Sermon on the Mount/Plain (chaps. 5–7 and 6:20–49, respectively), the different accounts of the Last Supper (Matt. 26:20–35; Mark 14:17–31; Luke 22:14–38; John 13–17; 1 Cor. 11:23–26), or almost any other part of the gospel tradition.

6

An Introductory Overview of Jesus' Public Life and Ministry

- ❖ **What were the dates of Jesus' public life?**

- ❖ **What were the general developments and the ultimate outcome of his ministry?**

- ❖ **Where were the origins of**

- ❖ **his teaching and how did he go beyond them?**

- ❖ **What were the framework and primary motifs of his preaching?**

The dates of Jesus' public ministry remain somewhat obscure, *Dates* partly because of uncertainty concerning the way in which Luke figured the beginning of Tiberius's reign (Luke 3:1). But the three-and-one-half-year period leading up to A.D. 33 is as likely as any, though many scholars prefer A.D. 30. Traditionally, this span of time has been divided into a year of obscurity, a year of popularity, and a year of rejection.

The year of obscurity began with the heralding ministry of John *Obscurity* the Baptist. He may have grown up in the Essene community at Qumran (compare Luke 1:80), but on his appearance in public he looks to be a lone, hermit-like prophet whose preaching to crowds and baptizing of people in preparation for the coming of God's kingdom differ from the social withdrawal of those Essenes. By the time of John it may have been required of Gentile proselytes that they baptize themselves as a rite of initiation into Judaism; but John

Jesus' Trial, Judgment, and Crucifixion

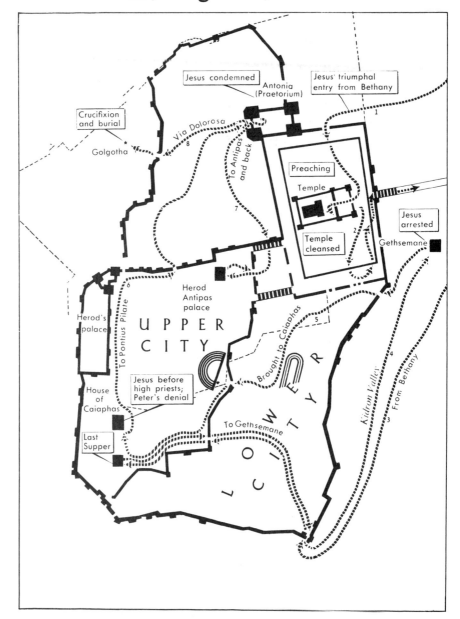

required baptism for Jews as a sign of repentance from sins. Or if proselyte baptism had not yet come into Judaism (the evidence is disputed), John may have borrowed the practice of ritual self-washings from the Essenes and endowed it with new significance.[1] Under either theory of origin, John innovated by administering the rite himself—therefore the phrase, "baptism of John." Jesus received this baptism. Satan tested him. And having passed this test, Jesus made his first disciples, started preaching, teaching, and performing miracles and exorcisms here and there, mainly in Galilee but occasionally also on pilgrimages to Jerusalem.

The message of both John and Jesus focused on "the kingdom." *The Kingdom* Often the two phrases "of God" and "of heaven" modify this term. The phrases are synonymous. Parallel usage occurs within the same passage. For example, Jesus says in Matthew 19:23–24 that it is difficult for a rich man to enter the kingdom *of heaven*, so difficult, in fact, that it is easier for a camel to go through the eye of a needle than for a rich man to enter the kingdom *of God*. The phrases also alternate in parallel accounts of different gospels. For example, "to such [children] belongs the kingdom of God" (Mark 10:14) becomes ". . . of heaven" in Matthew 19:14. Only the gospel of Matthew has "kingdom of heaven," because Matthew, it is usually thought, reflects the growing Jewish custom of avoiding divine names for fear of desecrating them. On the other hand, Matthew does not hesitate to use God's name elsewhere; so perhaps "kingdom of heaven" reflects Daniel 2:44 and accents universality—just as heaven arches over the whole earth, so also the kingdom encompasses it—as in that Old Testament passage. Jesus may have used both phrases, his choice depending on the audience and on the emphasis he wished to give. Or Matthew's "kingdom of heaven" represents Jesus' phrase, which the other evangelists translated into "kingdom of God" for Gentiles who might not understand the use

---

1. See the note by C. S. Mann in J. Munck, The Acts of the Apostles, *rev. W. F. Albright and C. S. Mann (Garden City: Doubleday, 1967), 281–83, and C. H. H. Scobie,* John the Baptist *(Philadelphia: Fortress, 1964), 95ff. For an opposite view, see H. H. Rowley, "The Baptism of John and the Qumran Sect," in* New Testament Essays: Studies in Memory of T. W. Manson, *ed. A. J. B. Higgins (Manchester: Manchester University Press, 1959), 218–29. We know that in the second century a Gentile who offered himself for baptism was asked why he did so, in view of anti-semitism. If he answered with a sense of unworthiness to share in the sufferings of Israel, he received instruction in some aspects of the Mosaic law. Then he dipped himself into the water as two scholars of the Torah recited commandments from the Old Testament. See G. F. Moore,* Judaism *(Cambridge, Mass.: Harvard University Press, 1950), 1:332–35.*

of "heaven" for "God." Or, most likely, Jesus regularly used "kingdom of God," and Matthew substituted "kingdom of heaven."

The term *kingdom* carries two meanings: (1) a sphere of rule and (2) the activity of ruling. Because of the verbal idea in this second meaning, many scholars prefer the translation, "the rule (or reign) of God." Both meanings are present in the New Testament use of *kingdom*. Context determines which of the two predominates. The activity of ruling includes the delivering of its subjects from oppression and the bringing to them of blessing as well as the exercise of authority over them.

Realized Eschatology

John the Baptist and Jesus said that the kingdom was "at hand [near]" and that people must prepare for it by repenting (Matt. 3:2; 4:17; Mark 1:14–15). Once his ministry got under way, Jesus said that the kingdom had indeed come: "If I cast out demons by the Spirit of God, then the kingdom of God has come upon you" (Matt. 12:28 par. Luke 11:20; compare Matt. 11:12–13 par. Luke 16:16; 17:20–21). In other words, God's rule was invading the world in the person and activity of Jesus. One must therefore enter the kingdom by faith in him (John 3:3). Emphasis on an arrival of the kingdom in his appearance and ministry is called "realized eschatology," a phrase associated with C. H. Dodd.

Consistent Eschatology

In another vein, Jesus also spoke about the kingdom's arrival when the present evil age comes to an end: ". . . until that day when I drink it anew in the kingdom of God" (Mark 14:25); "many will come . . . and recline . . . in the kingdom of heaven" (Matt 8:11 par. Luke 13:28–29). The petition which Jesus taught his disciples in the Lord's Prayer, "Thy kingdom come," also implies that the kingdom is yet to come. Emphasis on an arrival of the kingdom in the future, particularly in the near future, is called "consistent eschatology," a phrase associated with Albert Schweitzer. He himself did not hold to consistent eschatology, of course; but he argued that Jesus held to it.

Mystery of the Kingdom

Both realized and consistent eschatology receive strong support from passages such as those just mentioned. So evidence is convincing that Jesus taught both present and future forms of the kingdom. The "mystery" of the kingdom then becomes that before God fully imposes his rule on earth when Jesus comes back, believers enjoy its future blessings in advance.

Through his preaching, Jesus brought God's rule to the Jews, but on the basis of repentance and faith rather than on a politico-military basis. By rejecting Jesus, most of the Jews, especially their official leaders, rejected God's rule. Consequently, God transferred it to the church (Matt. 21:42–43; compare Acts 8:12; 28:23, 28–31; Rom. 14:17; Col. 1:13) until the restoration of Israel (Matt. 19:28 par. Luke 22:28–30).[2]

Parables

Jesus put much of his teaching about the kingdom into parables. These were more or less extended figures of speech, often in story form. Interpreters used to assign allegorical meanings to every detail in the parables. The scholarly world then veered toward Adolf Jülicher's insistence that each parable contains but one didactic point, other details being solely for realism.[3] Currently, it is coming to be recognized that no hard and fast distinction exists between a parable with a single point and a multifaceted parable. Allowance must then be made for some allegorism in parables, especially in the longer ones.

Miracles

The miracles of Jesus raise a question of the supernatural, to which people who consider themselves scientifically minded often object. But if there is a God who has acted in history, especially by revealing himself through Jesus Christ, how else may we expect him to have acted than supernaturally? If he had not, we could point to a lack of historical evidence that it really was God acting. The very fact that other religions often lay claim to the supernatural shows that people really do expect the divine to show itself in ways not subject to naturalistic explanations.

A truly scientific attitude will keep open the possibility of supernaturalism and test the claims to supernatural events in past history by searching questions: Were there eyewitnesses? If so, was their number sufficient and their character and intelligence trustworthy? How tenaciously did they maintain their testimony under pressure? Are there early written records, or only late records written long after myth-making could have corrupted oral tradition? Questions like these put the claims of other religions to supernatural events in a poor light, the claims of Christianity in a favorable light. For Jesus' career there were many eyewitnesses. Those who allied themselves

---

2. See further the three books by G. E. Ladd, The Gospel of the Kingdom (Grand Rapids: Eerdmans, 1959); The Presence of the Future (Grand Rapids: Eerdmans, 1974); and Crucial Questions About the Kingdom of God (Grand Rapids: Eerdmans, 1952); and, for a broader purview, A. J. McClain, The Greatness of the Kingdom (Grand Rapids: Zondervan, 1959).

3. A. Jülicher, Die Gleichnisreden Jesu, 2 vols. (Tübingen, 1910). For a wealth of information concerning the background of Jesus' parables, see J. Jeremias, The Parables of Jesus, 2d ed. (New York: Scribner's, 1971).

with him endured ostracism, torture, and even death for what they proclaimed concerning him—and they felt constrained to make proclamation even at such costs. They could have saved themselves by admitting falsehood in their testimony or simply by ceasing to testify.

Furthermore, the records of Jesus' ministry began to be written well within half a century after he lived. The very extravagance of the stories from a naturalistic point of view makes it unlikely that they were fabricated and accepted during the period when eyewitnesses were still living.[4] Thus the claim of other religions to the miraculous does not at all undercut Christianity's similar claim when both are tested by the tools of historical research in an open-minded way.[5]

Popularity The activities of preaching, teaching, and performing miracles and exorcisms continued in Jesus' year of popularity. Increasingly large crowds attended him, so much so that he sought privacy for *Rejection* himself and his disciples, not always successfully. The year of rejection may be something of a misnomer, for large crowds kept flocking to Jesus. When able to gain some privacy, he devoted himself to teaching the disciples. Sometime during this period Peter, speaking for the rest of them, confessed the messiahship of Jesus; and Jesus began predicting his death and resurrection. The Transfiguration occurred. The last journey to Jerusalem began. According to the fourth gospel, Jesus' raising of Lazarus from the dead convinced members of the Sanhedrin that they should eliminate Jesus and with him what they thought to be the threat of a messianic revolt. According to the synoptic gospels, which do not mention the raising of Lazarus, Jesus' cleansing of the temple after the Triumphal Entry on Palm Sunday made the Sanhedrin determine to eliminate him. Judas arranged to betray him.

Last Supper The Last Supper, a Passover meal, took place on the following Thursday evening. The Passover liturgy included a blessing, the passing of several cups of wine around the table, a recital of the Exodus story by the host, an eating of the roasted lamb, unleavened bread

---

4. *Similarly concerning apostolic miracles, Paul would hardly have dared to argue from miracles which he had performed among the Galatians if they had never seen him do any (see Gal. 3:5).*

5. *See further C. S. Lewis,* Miracles *(New York: Macmillan, 1947); and for representative technical discussions, E. L. Mascall,* The Secularization of Christianity *(New York: Holt, Rinehart & Winston, 1966); H. van der Loos,* The Miracles of Jesus *(Leiden: Brill, 1965); I. Sabourin,* The Divine Miracles Discussed and Defended *(Rome: Catholic Book Agency, 1977).*

and bitter herbs, and the singing of psalms. In line with the Jewish expectation of a messianic banquet, Jesus had already compared the kingdom of God to a supper. He had also described his suffering as a cup to be drunk. Furthermore, the Passover commemorated God's redeeming Israel from Egyptian slavery by virtue of the sacrifice of a Passover lamb. But Jesus had intimated that Israel was now rejected. Therefore he instituted the Lord's Supper to commemorate the redemption of a new people of God, the disciples, from slavery to sin by virtue of his own sacrificial death.

The arrest and Jewish trial of Jesus took place Thursday night,[6] the Roman trial early Good Friday morning, the Crucifixion from midmorning to midafternoon, and the burial in late afternoon. Jesus' sayings spoken from the cross are called "The Seven Last Words" (Matt. 27:46 par. Mark 15:34; Luke 23:34, 43, 46; John 19:26–27, 28, 30). The Resurrection occurred very early on Sunday, and Jesus appeared to his disciples a number of times during forty days of postresurrection ministry. Finally, he ascended little more than a week before the outpouring of the Holy Spirit on the Day of Pentecost.

Death and Resurrection

Excursus on the Resurrection of Jesus

That Jesus really did rise from the dead is supported by the short-comings of alternative possibilities. One is that Jesus only appeared to die, that he lapsed into a coma and later revived for a while. But his death is indicated by the brutal beating he endured, by the six hours of hanging on a cross, by the thrusting through of his abdomen with a spear and the resultant gushing out of watery fluid and blood, by his partial embalming and being wrapped up in grave clothes, and finally by his being sealed in a tomb.

---

6. *In capital cases, later (and possibly earlier) Jewish trial procedure required that a trial begin during the daytime; that if unfinished it be adjourned during nighttime; that a majority of only one sufficed for acquittal, but that a majority of at least two was necessary for conviction; that a verdict of acquittal might be given on the very first day, but that a verdict of guilty must be delayed until the next day so that the judges might carefully weigh a condemnatory decision overnight; that therefore no trial should be held on the eve of a Sabbath or festival day; and that the accused not be forced to witness against themselves or convicted on their own testimony (Babylonian Talmud, Sanhedrin 4.1.3–5a; 5:1, quoted in C. K. Barrett, The New Testament Background: Selected Documents, 2d ed. [San Francisco: Harper & Row, 1987], 213–15). It is possible that the Sadducees, who dominated the Sanhedrin in Jesus' time, lacked the consideration for accused people which characterized the later Sanhedrin, dominated by Pharisees. On the other hand, the danger which members of the Sanhedrin thought Jesus posed may well have led them to violate their normal rules of trial procedure.*

Others suggest that the disciples stole Jesus' corpse. But to do so they would have had to overpower the Roman guards, an unlikely event, or bribe them, equally unlikely, since the guards knew they would be subject to capital punishment for failing to protect Jesus' body from theft. That the graveclothes lay undisturbed (not even unwrapped) and the turban still twirled up and set to one side militates against a hasty removal of the corpse by theft. Thieves do not usually take time to tidy up. Here they would probably have taken the body along with its wrappings.

The surprise, even unbelief, of the disciples at Jesus' resurrection further shows that they did not steal his corpse, unless their surprise and unbelief were fabricated to make the story look convincing. But such a fabrication seems too clever. It also seems unlikely that stories would have been fabricated in which the apostles are first portrayed as unbelievers in the Resurrection, for the early church soon began to revere the apostles.

Yet others think that the disciples experienced hallucinations. But the New Testament gives evidence of Jesus' appearances in different locations at different times to different parties numbering from one to more than five hundred. In 1 Corinthians 15, Paul as much as challenges doubters to ask the eyewitnesses. The appearances were too many and too varied to have been hallucinations. Furthermore, the disciples were psychologically unprepared for hallucinations, since they did not expect Jesus to rise and actually disbelieved the first reports that he had risen. All that unbelieving Jews would have had to do when the report of Jesus' resurrection began circulating was to produce the corpse. But they never did.

The same objection militates against a suggestion that Jesus' disciples came to the wrong tomb. Why did unbelieving Jews fail to produce his corpse from the right tomb? They must have known where it was, for they had induced Pilate to put a guard there.

Still others explain that the disciples modeled Jesus' resurrection after the dying and rising of gods in pagan mythology. But the differences loom far greater than the similarities. History does not provide a framework for the myths as it does for the accounts of Jesus' resurrection. The New Testament draws no connection with the annual dying and reviving of nature, as in the pagan myths, associated as they are with the agricultural cycle and fertility. The matter-of-fact style of reporting in the gospels contrasts sharply with the fantasies that abound in myths. And accounts of the resurrection appear immediately in the early church, without the lengthy interim required for evolution of detailed mythology. Paul's triumphant statement that most of the more than five hundred people who saw Jesus at the same time and place were still alive, and therefore could be asked, looks unbelievably audacious if the whole story came by way of mythological development (1 Cor. 15:6).[7]

Something unique must have made the first Jewish disciples change their day of worship from the Sabbath to Sunday. Either they were deceived—then again the unbelieving Jews could have stopped Christianity by producing Jesus' corpse—or they foisted a hoax on the world—then it looks psychologically incredible that they willingly suffered hardship, torture, and death for what they knew to be false. It also looks inconceivable for the ancient world that fabricators would have made women the first witnesses of the risen Jesus, for the testimony of women was distrusted.

One does not have to treat the New Testament as inspired by God to feel the force of the historical evidences for Jesus' resurrection. The gospel accounts and other evidence need explanation even when they are not regarded as divinely authoritative. Making up one's mind beforehand that such a thing could not have happened forms the chief obstacle to faith in the Resurrection.[8]

Because Jesus did rise, there is a human being in heaven interceding for those who believe in him as the sacrifice for their sins. His resurrection also provides power for Christian living and guarantees both his return and the resurrection and eternal life of those who believe in him.

Teaching

The style of Jesus' speech was colorful and picturesque. Figures of speech abounded. He often created epigrams, not easily forgotten, and delighted in puns, which usually fail to come through in trans-

---

7. See pages 101–4.

8. For the historicity of the resurrection and criticisms of alternative theories, see J. N. D. Anderson, "The Resurrection of Jesus Christ," Christianity Today, 29 March 1968, 4[628]–9[633], with the dialogue and overcomment in Christianity Today, 12 April 1968, 5[677]–12[684]; F. Morison, Who Moved the Stone? (London: Faber & Faber, 1944); J. Orr, The Resurrection of Jesus (London: Hodder & Stoughton, 1908); D. P. Fuller, Easter Faith and History (Grand Rapids. Eerdmans, 1965); G. E. Ladd, I Believe in the Resurrection of Jesus (Grand Rapids: Eerdmans, 1975); M. J. Harris, Raised Immortal (Grand Rapids: Eerdmans, 1985); idem, From Grave to Glory (Grand Rapids: Zondervan, 1990).

lation. Many sayings are set in the parallelistic forms of statement characteristic of Semitic poetry. His use of parables was masterly.

In the content of his teaching Jesus built on the Old Testament foundation of ethical monotheism, that is, of belief in one God of love and righteousness who acts redemptively and judgmentally in history according to his covenantal relations with human beings. By declaring sins forgiven, claiming to be the judge of everyone's eternal destiny, demanding utter allegiance to himself, making astounding "I am . . ." statements, and introducing many sayings in a tone of ultimate authority with *amen* (translated "truly" or "verily"), Jesus put himself forward as a unique person. But he reluctantly accepted *Christy* and used the term "Christ," or "Messiah," because of its dominantly political and militaristic overtones in first-century Judaism. He pre-*Son of Man* ferred to speak of himself as "the Son of man" whom Daniel saw in a vision as a superhuman figure coming from heaven to judge and rule the whole world (Dan. 7:9–14). But Jesus also associated the suffering of the Servant of the LORD (Isa. 52:13–53:12) with himself as the Son of man. Significantly, the designation "Son of man" occurs for Jesus almost exclusively on his own lips. Among the Jews it was largely or entirely unused in a messianic sense. As a result, Jesus *Son of God* could build up his own definition. The additional term "Son (of God)" occurs both in his claims for himself and in the words of others about him.

Jesus' consciousness of uniquely divine sonship expressed itself *Abba* also in his use of the Aramaic word *abba*, "Father," which originated as a child's stammering "Dadda" or "Daddy." Nevertheless, this address escaped oversentimentality in that children continued to use it after they had grown up. Jesus also taught his disciples to address God as *abba* because of their relation to God through him. In earlier times God had been viewed largely as father of the Israelite nation as a whole. Thus the frequency, warmth, and individualistic emphasis with which Jesus spoke of God's fatherhood mark a distinctive feature of his teaching.

Love   Loving God and one's neighbor compose the two main ethical imperatives, according to Jesus. His view of righteous living emphasized inward motivation as opposed to outward show. The Golden Rule, which occurs in its positive form, helps define what he meant by loving.

Framing all that Jesus taught was his proclamation that the time of God's kingdom had dawned. He himself represented that kingdom, but he also foresaw his rejection and redemptive death and resurrection. Beyond those events lay the time when his disciples would evangelize the world. Then he would return to judge the human race and establish God's kingdom fully and forever.[9]

How would a modern biographer differ from the evangelists in presenting the life of Jesus? What might he omit, add, emphasize, and de-emphasize? Why do the evangelists in some respects not write as a modern biographer would write?

What aspects of Jesus' life and teaching do modern people tend to find unacceptable—intellectually, esthetically, and socially—in comparison with ancient people, and why?

How do the startling claims of Jesus for himself square with his teaching about humility, his demand for personal allegiance with his teaching about unselfish service toward others, and his egocentricity with his very sanity? Or is it right to speak of his egocentricity (some would even say megalomania)?

FOR
FURTHER
DISCUSSION

(From a conservative standpoint)

FOR
FURTHER
INVESTIGATION

Guthrie, D. *Jesus the Messiah*. Grand Rapids: Zondervan, 1972.

Harrison, E. F. *A Short Life of Christ*. Grand Rapids: Eerdmans, 1968.

Ridderbos, H. *The Coming of the Kingdom*. Philadelphia: Presbyterian & Reformed, 1962.

Stein, R. H. *The Method and Message of Jesus' Teachings*. Philadelphia: Westminster, 1978.

Vos, G. *The Self-Disclosure of Jesus*. Grand Rapids: Eerdmans, 1954.

(From a moderate standpoint)

Barclay, W. *Jesus as They Saw Him*. New York: Harper, 1963.

———. *The Mind of Jesus*. New York: Harper, 1961.

Hunter, A. M. *The Work and Words of Jesus*. Philadelphia: Westminster, 1950.

Schweizer, E. *Jesus*. Richmond: John Knox, 1971.

Stauffer, E. *Jesus and His Story*. New York: Knopf, 1960.

Taylor, V. *The Life and Ministry of Jesus*. Nashville: Abingdon, 1955.

Turner, H. E. W. *Jesus, Master and Lord*. 2d ed. Naperville, Ill.: Allenson, 1954.

(From a liberal standpoint)

Bornkamm, G. *Jesus of Nazareth*. New York: Harper, 1960.

Braun, H. *Jesus of Nazareth*. Philadelphia: Fortress, 1979.

---

9. See pages 113–15 for greater detail about the kingdom of God.

Bultmann, R. *Jesus and the Word*. New York: Scribner's, 1960.

Conzelmann, H. *Jesus*. Philadelphia: Fortress, 1973.

Crossan, J. D. *The Historical Jesus: The Life of a Mediterranean Jewish Peasant*. San Francisco: Harper, 1991.

Schillebeeckx, E. *Jesus*. New York: Seabury, 1979.

PART III

The Four Canonical Gospels and Acts

7

Mark:
An Apology for the Crucifixion of Jesus

❖ *Who wrote the gospel of Mark?*

❖ *How do we determine its authorship?*

❖ *How close did its author stand to the eyewitness tradition of Jesus' life and teaching?*

❖ *When was this gospel written, and what indications do we have of its date?*

❖ *For what audience, from what standpoint, and with what purpose did the author write?*

❖ *What features and emphases characterize this gospel?*

❖ *What overall plan determines its movement?*

The books called *gospels* deal with the life and ministry of Jesus. Unlike modern biographies, however, they lack contemporary historical background, analysis of character and personality, and probing of the inner thoughts of the hero. Nor do the gospels resemble Hellenistic narratives which celebrate the real or supposed acts of ancient miracle workers. There is much more than narration of miracles in the gospels. Nor do the gospels present us with simple memoirs; rather, with proclamations and instructions written from theological standpoints.

    The author of a gospel is called an *evangelist,* which means a proclaimer of good news. Since titles were probably added to the gospels not until some time after the original writing, we depend on

Gospels

Evangelists

early tradition and internal evidence to answer questions of authorship. The first gospel to have been written takes its name from John Mark, who appears as the companion of Paul, Barnabas, and Peter in Acts and the epistles.

Mark and Peter

Very early in the second century the church father Papias passed on an even earlier tradition that Mark accurately wrote down in his gospel the reminiscences of Peter concerning Jesus' life and teachings, yet not with the result of a complete or close-knit account; for Peter gave his reminiscences in the form of anecdotes told here and there on various occasions.[1] The early church fathers Irenaeus, Clement of Alexandria, Origen, and Jerome also support authorship by Mark in association with Peter.

Action

With little exception, Mark's gospel is one of action instead of lengthy discourse. In quick-moving narrative, signaled especially by the adverb "immediately" and its synonyms (all going back to the same Greek word), he relates Jesus' activities as the mighty and authoritative Son of God.

Arrangement

Though the order of Mark's material appears in general to be chronological, catch words and similarity of subject matter sometimes form the principle of arrangement for individual stories and sayings. For example, Mark 2:1–3:6 contains stories about Jesus' authority to forgive sins, to eat with toll collectors, to let his disciples refrain from fasting, to let them pluck and eat grain on the Sabbath, and himself to heal on the Sabbath. Apparently Mark strings these stories together because they all deal with Jesus' authority.

Purpose

Modern scholars have suggested a number of different purposes behind the writing of Mark. For example, some think that the evangelist writes to give new converts catechetical instruction. But his failure to give very much of Jesus' teaching undermines this view. Others think that Mark writes his gospel for liturgical use in church services. But the arrangement and style lack the smoothness and symmetry which one would expect in a liturgical document. Still others think that Mark writes to cover up a failure by Jesus to proclaim himself the Messiah and that Mark subtly removes this embarrassment to Christian belief by inventing the messianic secret, that is, by putting into Jesus' mouth prohibitions against public revelation of his messiahship to make it appear that Jesus really did teach in private that he was the Messiah though he actually did

---

1. Quoted by Eusebius, Ecclesiastical History 3.39.15. Compare the special mention of Peter in Mark 16:7: "Go tell his disciples and Peter . . . ."

not.[2] Others think oppositely that by inventing a messianic secret Mark was trying to soften the political offensiveness to Roman authorities of a ministry that was overly messianic. Both of the views which stress a messianic secret depend on hyperscepticism toward Mark's accuracy of reporting. Most readers will not gain the impression that he is embarrassed either by too little or by too much messianism in the tradition about Jesus. As we will see, moreover, Jesus' suppressions of publicity seem to have reasons that differ from one occasion to another, none of those reasons pertinent to the situation of Mark and his audience. Or perhaps Mark writes to encourage persecuted Christians by showing them that Jesus, too, suffered and died. But why then does Mark devote the bulk of his gospel to Jesus' miracles and exorcisms and to the authority with which he teaches and debates, and why does Mark depress and counteract as much as possible the element of suffering in the narrative of Jesus' arrest, trial, and crucifixion?

Apology Crucifixion was reserved mostly for criminals and slaves and had all the connotations of a modern electric chair or gas chamber. It makes best sense to think that Mark writes for the purpose of counteracting the shame of the manner in which Jesus died. This counteraction takes the form of stressing the power of Jesus to work miracles, to cast out demons, to teach astonishingly, to best his opponents in debate, to attract crowds, to predict the future, including his own fate, and to rise from the dead. As an apology, then, Mark's gospel is designed to convert non-Christians despite the shame of the Cross.

Date Early Christian tradition shows some uncertainty whether Mark wrote his gospel before or after the martyrdom of Peter (A.D. 64–67) but generally favors the earlier period. Modern scholars dispute the date of Mark's writing. Those who regard "the abomination of desolation" in 13:14 as a back reference to the destruction of Jerusalem in A.D. 70 necessarily date the gospel after that event. But this method of dating presumes that Jesus did not make a genuine prediction of the destruction and overlooks that a number of details in Mark 13 do not match Josephus's account of the destruction. Data is lacking to answer firmly the question of date. But if one accepts the phenomenon of predictive prophecy, no compelling reasons exist to deny an early date, say, A.D. 45–60. In fact, if Luke ends

---

2. W. Wrede, The Messianic Secret *(Cambridge: Clarke, 1971). Wrede attributes this motivation to the predecessors of Mark, whose material he used.*

his book of Acts without describing the outcome of Paul's trial in Rome because the trial has not yet taken place, then Acts must be dated about A.D. 63, its preceding companion volume, the gospel of Luke, somewhat earlier, and—if Luke's gospel reflects Mark—Mark still earlier in the fifties or late forties.

Audience and Provenance

Mark probably writes for a Roman audience. He translates Aramaic expressions for their benefit (3:17; 5:41; 7:34; 14:36; 15:34). Even more indicatively, he explains Greek expressions by their Latin equivalents (12:42; 15:16) and uses a number of other Latin terms. Confirmation comes from the mention in 15:21 of a Rufus, who according to Romans 16:13 lives in Rome (unless the two texts refer to different men with the same name). In addition, the presence of Mark in Rome (symbolically called "Babylon") according to 1 Peter 5:13, the combination of Papias's statement that Mark was Peter's interpreter with the early tradition of Peter's martyrdom in Rome, the indication in the anti-Marcionite prologue to Mark[3] that Mark wrote his gospel in Italy, and further statements by Clement of Alexandria and Irenaeus add external testimony favoring a Roman origin and address for the gospel of Mark.

Outline

No outline of Mark has commanded widespread agreement, probably because the gospel reflects a desultoriness in Peter's telling of anecdotes concerning Jesus. The most that we can detect with confidence is a loose arrangement of materials governed mainly by the initiatory character of John the Baptist's ministry and its locale in the wilderness at the Jordan River, by the charismatic character and Galilean locale of the bulk of Jesus' ministry, by the transitional character and Transjordanian route of his journey to Jerusalem, and by the finality of his death and resurrection and their locale at Jerusalem.

An Outline of Mark

INTRODUCTION (1:1–13)
- A. The ministry of John the Baptist (1:1–8)
- B. The baptism of Jesus (1:9–11)
- C. The temptation of Jesus (1:12–13)

I. THE ACTIVITIES OF JESUS IN AND AROUND GALILEE (1:14–9:50)
- A. Jesus' first preaching and call of Simon, Andrew, James, and John (1:14–20)

---

3. *Anti-Marcionite prologues are early manuscript introductions supposed to have been directed against Marcionism, a brand of the Gnostic heresy (compare p. 86).*

B. A group of miracles (1:21–45)
  1. An exorcism in the synagogue at Capernaum (1:21–28)
  2. The healing of Peter's mother-in-law and others (1:29–39)
  3. The cleansing of a leper (1:40–45)
C. A group of controversies (2:1–3:6)
  1. The forgiveness and healing of a paralytic (2:1–12)
  2. The call of Levi and Jesus' eating with toll collectors and sinners (2:13–17)
  3. A question about fasting (2:18–22)
  4. The plucking and eating of grain on a Sabbath (2:23–27)
  5. The healing of a withered hand on the Sabbath (3:1–6)
  6. Jesus' withdrawal and choice of the Twelve (3:7–19a)
  7. The charges that Jesus is insane and possessed by Beelzebul (3:19b–35)
D. A group of parables (4:1–34)
  1. The seeds and the soils (4:1–20)
  2. The lamp (4:21–25)
  3. The seed growing by itself (4:26–29)
  4. The mustard seed and others (4:30–34)
E. More miracles (4:35–5:43)
  1. The stilling of a storm (4:35–41)
  2. The exorcism of Legion from a demoniac (5:1–20)
  3. The healing of a woman with a constant flow of blood and the raising of Jairus's daughter (5:21–43)
F. Rejection at Nazareth (6:1–6)
G. The mission of the Twelve throughout Galilee (6:7–13)
H. The beheading of John the Baptist (6:14–29)
I. The feeding of five thousand (6:30–44)
J. Jesus' walking on the water (6:45–52)
K. Ministry at Gennesaret with controversy over ceremonial defilement (6:53–7:23)
L. More miracles (7:24–8:26)
  1. The exorcism of a demon from the daughter of a Syro-Phoenician woman (7:24–30)
  2. The healing of a deaf mute (7:31–37)
  3. The feeding of four thousand (8:1–10)

      4. The demand of Pharisees for a sign (8:11–21)

      5. The healing of a blind man (8:22–26)

  M. Peter's confession of Jesus' messiahship (8:27–30)

  N. Peter's notion of Jesus' messiahship and discipleship, corrected by Jesus' prediction of suffering, death, and resurrection (8:31 9:1)

  O. The Transfiguration (9:2–13)

  P. The exorcising of a demon from a boy (9:14–29)

  Q. Another prediction by Jesus of his death and resurrection (9:30–32)

  R. Jesus' making a child an example for his disciples (9:33–50)

II. The Activities of Jesus on His Way to Jerusalem Through Transjordan and Judea (10:1–52)

  A. The question of divorce (10:1–12)

  B. Jesus' blessing of children (10:13–16)

  C. A rich man (10:17–31)

  D. Another prediction by Jesus of his death and resurrection (10:32–34)

  E. The request of James and John for places of honor and Jesus' reply concerning self-sacrificial service (10:35–45)

  F. The healing of blind Bartimaeus (10:46–52)

III. The Activities of Jesus in and Around Jerusalem During the Week of His Passion, Death, and Resurrection (11:1–16:8)

  A. The Triumphal Entry (11:1–11)

  B. The cursing of a barren fig tree (11:12–14)

  C. The cleansing of the temple (11:15–19)

  D. The withering of a fig tree (11:20–26)

  E. Debates in the temple (11:27–12:44)

      1. The demand for a sign from Jesus (11:27–33)

      2. The parable of a vineyard (12:1–12)

      3. A question of paying taxes to Caesar (12:13–17)

      4. A question about resurrection (12:18–27)

      5. A question about the most important commandment (12:28–34)

      6. Jesus' question about the Messiah's Davidic descent and lordship (12:35–37)

    7. Jesus' warning against the scribes (12:38–40)
    8. A widow's mite versus large gifts from the rich (12:41–44)
  F. The Olivet Discourse (13:1–37)
  G. The Sanhedrin's plot against Jesus (14:1–2)
  H. The anointing of Jesus by Mary of Bethany (14:3–9)
  I. The bargain of Judas Iscariot to betray Jesus (14:10–11)
  J. The Last Supper (14:12–31)
  K. Jesus' praying in Gethsemane (14:32–42)
  L. The arrest of Jesus (14:43–52)
  M. The trial of Jesus (14:53–15:20)
    1. The hearing before the Sanhedrin, with Peter's denials (14:53–72)
    2. The hearing before Pontius Pilate, with the release of Barabbas (15:1–20)
  N. The crucifixion, death, and burial of Jesus (15:21–47)
  O. The resurrection of Jesus (16:1–8)

Because Mark depends on Peter's reminiscences and Peter did not associate with Jesus until Jesus' ministry, Mark's gospel picks up at the start of that ministry. "The beginning of the good news of Jesus Christ, God's Son" refers to John the Baptist's introduction of *John the Baptist* Jesus onto the public stage and identifies Jesus as the Son of God as well as Christ. "Christ" (Greek for the Hebrew or Aramaic "Messiah") means "anointed" in the sense of one chosen by God for a special task, in this case for the bringing of God's kingdom. As will become clear, "God's Son" connotes deity. *Read Mark 1:1–8.* Isaiah's "I" and "my" represent God. "You" and "your" represent Jesus. The messenger crying out in the wilderness represents John the Baptist. His preparing the way of the Lord represents his getting people ready for the appearance of the Lord Jesus. This readiness consists in repentance from sin, shown by John's baptizing them in water as a sign of moral cleansing. The dress and diet of John mark him as a man of the wilderness, where he preaches and baptizes in accordance with the locale predicted by Isaiah. Powerful though John's magnetism is, he predicts the coming of someone yet more powerful, who will baptize people in an element far superior to water: Holy Spirit.

Jordan River, traditional site of Jesus' baptism.

Now it comes out that John is baptizing in the Jordan River, *Jesus'*
which flows through the wilderness of Judea. There Jesus comes, *Baptism*
gets baptized, and receives the Spirit by which he will now baptize
others. This anointing with the Spirit resonates with Mark's having
called Jesus "Christ." The heavenly origin of the Spirit and of the
voice which assures Jesus that he is the beloved, well-pleasing Son
likewise resonates with Mark's having called Jesus "God's Son." *Read
Mark 1:9–11.* Jesus' seeing the heavens torn apart and the Spirit like
a dove (regarded as a divine bird in the Hellenistic world) descend-
ing into him and the direct address of the voice to him make him
aware of his power, so that he will shortly begin to exercise it.

But first the Spirit drives Jesus into the wilderness surrounding *The*
the Jordan River. *Read Mark 1:12–13.* The immediacy of the Spirit's *Temptation*
driving Jesus into the wilderness confirms his reception of the Spirit.
No emphasis falls on Satan's temptation as such. Mark neither details the temptation nor says whether Jesus resisted it. Emphasis
falls instead on its length of time, forty days. That none less than
Satan, the archdemon himself, tempted Jesus for so long, that even
wild beasts did him no harm throughout the period he was with
them, and that angels were serving him all constitute acknowledg-
ments of Jesus' status as Christ, God's Son, by the demonic, animal,
and angelic worlds in addition to the preceding declaration by God.

Read Mark 1:14–20. Mark will explain John the Baptist's arrest in *Preaching*
a kind of footnote at 6:17–29, but now he turns his attention to
Jesus' activity of preaching and calling the first disciples. "The good
news of God" consists in the announcement that God's kingdom, or
rule, has arrived. This rule demonstrates itself in the powerful effect
of Jesus' call on Simon, Andrew, James, and John: they immediately *First Disciples*
drop their occupational activities to follow the Son of God, who is
bringing God's rule. The fulfillment of Jesus' prediction that he will
make Simon and Andrew "fishers of human beings" will interpret
that figure of speech to mean getting people to repent, healing the
sick, and casting demons out of the possessed (3:13–19; 6:7–13,
30).

Jesus continues to demonstrate his power as God's Son in the as- *Exorcism*
tounding authority with which he teaches and casts out a demon,
here called from the Jewish point of view "an unclean spirit" (unclean in a ritualistic sense). *Read Mark 1:21–28.* The spirit's expressing a knowledge of Jesus' personal name and especially of his
title "the Holy One of God" (in contrast to the uncleanness of the

spirit) indicates an attempt at self-defense. Jesus' silencing this expression overcomes the attempt, and the convulsing of the possessed man and inarticulate outcry of the spirit give visual and auditory proofs of Jesus' victory.

Healing Next, Jesus demonstrates his power to heal the sick as well as to exorcise demons. *Read Mark 1:29–34.* The healing of Simon's mother-in-law is proved by her serving those present. People bring their sick and demon-possessed not until after sundown because the Sabbath goes from sundown Friday to sundown Saturday, not from midnight to midnight, so that they would be breaking the Sabbath (which means "rest") had they done the work of bringing the needy before Saturday evening. But they bring them as soon as possible, so great is Jesus' magnetism. "Many" describes as numerous the "all" whom he delivers; it does not leave out some of the "all." Again, his silencing the demons thwarts their attempt to defend themselves by expressing a knowledge of his identity.

Cleansing a Leper So great is Jesus' magnetism that now if he wants to pray he must get up before light and go out to a deserted place. But he also widens the sphere of his powerful activity by going to towns and synagogues throughout Galilee. *Read Mark 1:35–45.* The cleansing of a leper emphasizes Jesus' ability to do what only God can do, and this with a mere touch and simple word. The immediacy of the cleansing enhances the demonstration of Jesus' ability. The immediacy and forcefulness of his thrusting out the cleansed leper emphasize the instruction to have a priest confirm the cleansing in order that the ensuing sacrifice might testify to people that a cleansing has taken place (compare Leviticus 13–14). But the ex-leper does better than this instruction: he goes out and himself spreads the word, with the result that people throng to Jesus even in formerly deserted places.

Authority A series of stories now display Jesus' authority to forgive sins (2:1–12), to eat with toll collectors and sinners (2:13–17), to let his disciples dispense with fasting (2:18–22), to let them pluck grain on the Sabbath (2:23–28), and to heal on the Sabbath (3:1–6). *Read Mark 2:1–3:6.* The four who bring a paralytic to Jesus can dig through the roof because it is made of mud-plastered branches spread over rafters. The healing of the paralytic demonstrates Jesus' authority to forgive the sins of the paralytic. But Jesus has this authority, a divine one, as "the Son of man" (a phrase apparently adapted from Dan. 7:13: "one like a son of man," that is, a figure like a human being in contrast with beasts) and "on earth" (as opposed to "the clouds of heaven" with which the Danielic figure comes). To keep themselves ritually pure, Pharisees do not eat with toll collectors and sinners, those known to flout the law. But in great numbers Jesus attracts even such wicked people. His defending table fellowship with them silences the Pharisaical scribes. His presence makes his disciples so joyous that they cannot join in the fasting of John the Baptist's disciples and of the Pharisees, though the disciples of Jesus will fast in sorrow on the day of his removal. Just as an old garment could not help but rip if a patch of unshrunken cloth were to shrink after the next washing of the garment, just as old wineskins, already stretched to their limits, could not help but burst if new wine were to swell in them, so the authority of Jesus' words and deeds proves irresistible. As he does not dispute, plucking heads of grain counts as work; hence the Pharisees' question why his disciples are breaking the Sabbath.[4] He answers with the example of David that the Old Testament itself teaches violation of the law in a case of human need (1 Sam. 21:1–6); and in any case, as Lord of the Sabbath Jesus the Son of man can let his disciples break it if he wants. And he has both the power to heal a withered hand and the authority to do so on the Sabbath, as he does despite the Pharisees' watching for such a violation, which he defends so convincingly that they plot with the Herodians against his life.

Magnetism

Contrasting with that plot is the thronging to Jesus of a huge, admiring crowd, so that he tells the disciples to ready a boat for a hasty getaway if the crowd starts crushing him. To keep the crowd from increasing yet more at danger to his life and limb, he also orders unclean spirits to stop publicizing his divine sonship. As usual, they are trying to defend themselves; but he is concerned about the possibility of being crushed. *Read Mark 3:7–19.*

The Twelve Apostles

Jesus' magnetism has drawn so many that he now chooses twelve through whom he will multiply his ministry to the ever-increasing throng. Going up on a mountain, summoning "whom he wills," and exercising the prerogative of naming continue the emphasis on his authority. "Apostles" connotes being sent to act with the sender's own authority (compare 6:7–13). Though the number twelve corresponds to the number of Jacob's sons, ancestors of the twelve tribes of Israel, and thus suggests an intention to renew the people of God, the absence of an explanation leaves the emphasis on Jesus' authority.

---

4. *Deuteronomy 23:25 allows the plucking of grain while going through a field; so stealing is not the question.*

135

Holy Spirit vs. Beelzebul But where does this authority come from? *Read Mark 3:20–35.* Jesus has the Holy Spirit, not the unclean spirit Beelzebul (another name for Satan), and therefore has authority to form a new family for himself rather than having to submit to search and seizure by his natural family. The latter are probably the ones who say that he has gone berserk. Paralleling their statement is the scribes' accusation that he uses the chief demon to cast out other demons, an accusation which Jesus parabolically reduces to personal, political, domestic, and physical absurdities. It is also an accusation which, he warns, constitutes an unpardonable sin. (Note: by definition, believers in Jesus would never attribute his power to Satan rather than to the Holy Spirit.)

Read Mark 4:1–34. Here Jesus wields his authority by teaching a huge crowd, made up of outsiders as well as his new family ("the ones around him with the Twelve"; compare the phraseology in 3:31–35). His sitting in a boat represents the usual posture of an ancient Jewish teacher, but the boat is unusually necessitated by the size of the crowd (compare 3:9–10). Though capable of many nuances, "parable" basically means "comparison." The parable of the *Parables* seeds and soils is a parable about parables which compares the rejection of Jesus by some people and the acceptance of him by others to certain agricultural phenomena. But why does he speak in parables at all? The answer divides in two: (1) to obscure the truth judgmentally from outsiders, who have not responded in faith to his plain speech, and (2) with interpretation to clarify the truth rewardingly for insiders, who *have* responded in faith to his plain speech. The mystery that God is bringing his kingdom, his rule, with words, not weapons, with deeds of mercy, not acts of violence, requires clarification; so the insiders get it in private through Jesus' interpretation, an interpretation that will help them understand the other parables, too. According to this interpretation, God's rule is established in people who accept Jesus' message immediately, deeply, and exclusively, rather than delaying, accepting it only superficially, and letting other concerns stifle it.[5] The shining of a lamp represents Jesus' clarification. Nothing is hidden in a parable from outsiders

---

5. To understand the parable of the seeds and soils, one needs to know that for lack of a sufficiently extensive road system villagers often beat pathways through fields, that Palestinian farmers often sow their seeds before plowing the soil, that seeds from last year's thorns lie hidden in some soil, that rocks lie hidden beneath other soil, and that seed sown in thin soil sprouts first because heat absorbed by the rocks underneath speeds up germination and because the seed has only one direction in which to develop very much. A yield of thirty times more seeds of grain harvested than sown is average, a yield of sixtyfold good, and of one hundredfold extraordinary (compare Gen. 26:12).

that will not be revealed by him to insiders. People get what they deserve. Believers, who already have some understanding, are therefore enriched with more understanding, whereas unbelievers, who have no understanding, sink deeper into ignorance—just as in the world of investment it takes money to make money, and lack of money prevents the making of any. The message of Jesus enlightens and enriches believers with humanly incomprehensible power, just as a seed grows to fruition in an incomprehensible way. And what a large result from an infinitesimal beginning—like a mustard shrub grown big enough to give birds shade, though the shrub started as the smallest of seeds! Jesus continues to speak in such parables so long as allowed by the crowd's attention-span, and true to his promise he gives private explanations of all those parables to insiders, his disciples.

Miracles

Now Mark switches from a series of Jesus' parables to a series of Jesus' deeds. The first, a nature-miracle, demonstrates his power over wind and sea, representing the deathly powers of chaos. The second, an exorcism, demonstrates his power over a whole horde of demons who have made their victim dwell in the realm of death, a graveyard, and self-destructively lacerate himself. The third and fourth, a healing and a raising, demonstrate Jesus' power over the uncleanness and inevitability of death. *Read Mark 4:35–5:43.* "The other side of the sea" is the east side of the lake called the Sea of Galilee. The onset of evening and Jesus' sleeping imply an overnight voyage. It would seem that the accompanying boats carry the crowd *Stilling* of his new family, those who do God's will, the twelve apostles *a Storm* being in the same boat with Jesus (compare 3:32–35; 4:10, 34). The details of the storm magnify his power in stilling it. The fear and unbelief of the disciples contrastively magnify his divine self-confidence. The disciples believe in him and his message in general, of course; but even his past miracles have not given them faith for such a threat as the present one. Fear gives way to awe, however, when wind and wave give way to utter calm.

Legion

Arrival on the other side brings Jesus and his disciples into heavily Gentile territory.[6] The notation of earlier failures to tame a demo-

---

6. *Early manuscripts, versions, and church fathers disagree on whether Mark writes about the country of the Gerasenes, of the Gergasenes, or of the Gadarenes. The quality of the support for "Gerasenes" is best, but Gerasa is located about thirty miles from the nearest shoreline. Gadara is about five miles from the nearest shoreline. Gergasa is just offshore, and nearby is a steep slope such as the succeeding part of the story mentions. Furthermore, going away to preach in the Decapolis (5:20) may favor Gergasa, for Gerasa and Gadara belong to the Decapolis (a league of ten cities), whereas Gergasa does not.*

A Galilean boat, before being moved to its conservation site.

niac who meets Jesus makes the later exorcism performed by Jesus all the more impressive. The attempt to ward off Jesus by displaying a knowledge of his personal name ("Jesus") and title ("Son of the Most High God") provides for readers of Mark an answer to the disciples' recent question, "Who then is this one, that even the wind and the sea obey him?" (4:41). He does not succeed in the exorcism until discovery that he is dealing, not with one unclean spirit, but with many, called "Legion." They would rather have pigs as hosts than be sent out of the territory. The presence of pigs confirms its heavily Gentile character, for the Mosaic law prohibits pigs for Jews. The drowning of the pigs when Jesus lets Legion inhabit them escalates the exorcism to a destruction. The fear of the neighbors who come and see the ex-demoniac and the contrast between his present civility and his past ferocity highlight Jesus' power. So also do the contrast between the ex-demoniac's present plea to be with Jesus and his past attempt to ward Jesus off, and the ex-demoniac's going beyond Jesus' command to report home by going away and preaching in the Decapolis.

A Woman and Jairus's Daughter   The intertwined miracles of healing and raising take place back on the more Jewish west side of the Sea of Galilee. The surreptitious behavior of the woman suffering from a chronic flow of blood is due to her ritual uncleanness according to the Mosaic law.[7] Heightening the power of Jesus in her healing is the worsening of her malady under the care of many physicians (she has been following the oriental custom of calling all available physicians in hope that at least one of them might cure her) and the effectiveness of mere physical contact with his clothes. Her faith has magnified his power. He calls on Jairus to exercise such faith on arrival of the news that Jairus's daughter has just died. Jesus' statement to the mourners that she is not dead but sleeping anticipates his bringing her back to life shortly, so that her death will turn out to have been a kind of nap. The mourners' scornful laughter only puts him in a better light when he proves them wrong, himself right. Her standing up and walking around demonstrate that he has brought her back to life. The command not to tell anyone but to feed her has the purpose of allowing him to get away from the large crowd outside that have been accompanying him and crushing him (5:24, 31). If they hear that he has just brought the girl back to life, in their eagerness they are liable to crush him to death.

Back in his home town of Nazareth, Jesus teaches in the synagogue. The townspeople marvel at his wisdom and at the miracles that take place "through his hands." They cannot bring themselves to admit that a local-boy-made-good has himself performed the miracles, and they question the source and character of his wisdom and miracles. Jesus explains their reaction as an example of the rule that familiarity breeds contempt. Mark takes care to note that their lack of faith, not any lack of power on Jesus' part, makes him able to perform only a few miracles there. Yet even those few cause such astonishment among the townspeople that he is amazed at their refusal to believe. *Read Mark 6:1–6a.*

Nazareth

While teaching in the villages roundabout, Jesus now extends his powerful activity through the twelve apostles, whom he summons and sends in pairs—in pairs because Deuteronomy 19:15 says that a sufficient testimony requires at least two witnesses. That they carry his authority with them is shown by their having to take no baggage: others will have to provide for the apostles as though the apostles were Jesus himself. Nonwelcome will bring judgment. The apostles go out and exercise the authority of Jesus by doing what he has been doing: preaching, exorcising, and healing. Herod Antipas hears

Mission of the Twelve

---

7. *The woman cannot enter the temple or take much other part in the Jewish religion, nor is she supposed to touch other people. Leviticus 15 even requires separation from her husband.*

and is so impressed as to conclude that Jesus is John the Baptist
risen from the dead. *Read Mark 6:6b–29.* The flashback to John's
martyrdom makes the point that stupendously mighty powers must
be at work in Jesus to push the ruler into identifying him with a
man whose head the ruler himself saw delivered on a platter to his
own dining room, and then to his wife's dining room, and whose
corpse was then interred in a different location. John had accused
the ruler, not of breaking the law against adultery (though he had),
but of breaking the law against marrying your brother's wife (Lev.
18:16; 20:21).

Beheading of John the Baptist

Back to the present, Jesus takes the apostles away for some rest
when they return with a report of their mission; but his magnetism,
now multiplied by that mission, makes their vacation no vacation at
all. *Read Mark 6:30–44.* The contrast between the reasonableness of
the disciples' suggestion to send the crowd away for purchase of
food nearby and the unreasonableness of Jesus' command that they
give the crowd something to eat highlights the miracle of feeding so
vast a crowd as five thousand with only five loaves and two fish. "In
groups of hundreds and fifties" probably means that the crowd sit in
rows which taken together form a rectangle: longways, each row
contains one hundred; sideways, fifty (100 x 50 = 5,000). The
twelve baskets of leftovers show the superabundance of Jesus'
power.

Feeding of the Five Thousand

Bethsaida lies just east of the Jordan River on the north shore of
the Sea of Galilee. *Read Mark 6:45–56.* Not as when Jesus stilled a
storm (4:35–41), the adverse wind poses no danger, only difficulty.
Walking on the sea exhibits divine power (see Job 9:8; 38:16; Ps.
77:19); so Jesus' intending to walk past the disciples is an intending
to parade his deity before them (compare Ex. 33:19, 22; 34:5–7;
1 Kings 19:11). Their terror makes him get into the boat, however.
It is the fourth watch, the last quarter, of the night. Now that Jesus
has embarked, the wind dies down to provide him easy boating just
as the water has provided him firm footing. The disciples are aston-
ished because they did not even recognize a miracle in the feeding
of the five thousand (note the absence of any statement of admiration at the close of 6:30–44). But Jesus' power keeps overflowing
with further healings in the region of Gennesaret, located off the
northwest shore of the Sea of Galilee. Apparently, the adverse wind
changed the direction of the voyage, which originally aimed northeast toward Bethsaida.

Walking on Water

140

The next story displays the authority of Jesus in his putting down the Pharisees and some of the scribes from Jerusalem on a question of ritual purity, and in his pronouncing all foods clean (that is, ritually allowable to eat) despite the prohibition of some foods by the Mosaic law (Leviticus 11). *Read Mark 7:1–23.* The washing here in view does not have to do with personal hygiene, but with ritual purity, and not with the Mosaic law, but with traditional practices established by more recent Jewish teachers. These traditional practices, Jesus acidly notes, allow disobedience to God's command through Moses to honor your father and mother. You only have to mark an item that might be useful to them as destined for offering to God—and in the meantime keep on using the item yourself. Changing the law should run in the opposite direction, from ritual to morality. Jesus changes it that way. He has the right to.

Cleansing All Foods

Even in foreign territory Jesus' fame does not allow him privacy. During a trip through the region of Tyre, an ancient Phoenician port on the Mediterranean coast north of Galilee, a Gentile woman accosts him with a request to cast a demon out of her little daughter. To avoid publicity, he tries to put her off with a statement comparing Jews, particularly his disciples, with children, and Gentiles, particularly the woman's daughter, with puppies. Jews of this period regularly called Gentiles "dogs," but Jesus says "little dogs," that is, puppies, to suit the smallness of the woman's daughter. Undeterred, the woman latches onto his use of the term for puppies instead of fullgrown dogs and conceives that the deliverance of her daughter might count as a mere crumb of mercy which a puppy would eat under the table. In admiration of her wit, Jesus announces the demon's departure. As the woman will find out on her return home (the daughter has not accompanied her), he exorcises the demon at a distance and without a word. *Read Mark 7:24–30.*

Syro-Phoenician Woman

A circuitous route looping north, east, and south brings Jesus back to the sea of Galilee by way of Sidon and the Decapolis. *Read Mark 7:31–37.* The extraordinary difficulty of healing a deafmute is indicated by Jesus' seeking privacy, using physical means, looking heavenward, groaning, and speaking a curative word. Sticking fingers into the ears mimics and thereby aids an opening of the ears to hear; and spitting, as though getting rid of something in your mouth that keeps you from talking plainly, mimics and thereby—along with the application of saliva from Jesus' well-functioning tongue to the deafmute's bonded tongue—aids a loosening of the bond. So

Healing a Deafmute

astonishing is the miracle that despite Jesus' ordering them to tell no one, the people who brought the deafmute publicize it.

Feeding of the Four Thousand

Another feeding miracle takes place, but this time at a distance from towns where food might be bought; and the loaves are seven rather than five, the fish a few rather than two, the crowd about four thousand rather than five thousand, and the leftovers seven baskets full rather than twelve baskets full (contrast 6:30–44). *Read Mark 8:1–9.* Note again the lack of stated admiration for the miracle. Nobody seems to notice that a miracle has occurred.

Jesus' going with his disciples by boat to Dalmanutha poses somewhat of a puzzle, for Dalmanutha is not otherwise known. Since they started from the Decapolitan (that is, east) side of the Sea of Galilee, the boat trip is likely to have brought them to the

No Sign from Heaven

Galilean (that is, west) side. Wherever the exact location, Jesus meets a challenge by the Pharisees that he produce a sign from heaven, apparently not an earthly miracle performed by himself, for they can attribute his miraculous power to Satan (3:22–30), but a heavenly display put on by God. Jesus meets this challenge, not by producing such a sign, but with a pronouncement the sheer force of which shuts down the challenge. His groaning in his spirit, the rhetorical character of his question, the emphatic introduction to his refusal ("Truly I say to you"), and a strongly negative Hebraistic idiom in Mark's Greek text ("if to this generation a sign will be given," with the implication, "Out of the question!") all stress this force. *Read Mark 8:10–21.* On the return voyage eastward, Jesus' warning against "the yeast of the Pharisees and the yeast of Herod" makes the disciples think that Jesus is alluding to their failure to bring more than one loaf of bread. They are mistaken; but Mark does not indicate what Jesus did mean, for his words turn in another direction. Jesus exposes another failure of the disciples: to understand that he miraculously provided a superabundance of bread at the feedings of the five thousand and four thousand. So they should not imagine that their having only one loaf for the thirteen of them concerns him in the least.

Healing a Blind Man

Now they arrive at Bethsaida, a voyage to which was earlier thwarted by an adverse wind (6:45–56). Here Jesus confronts a case of blindness similar in difficulty to the earlier case of deafmuteness (7:31–37). Again he seeks privacy and uses saliva as a kind of salve to perform the cure. The difficulty of this case comes out also in its taking place in two stages: (1) At first the patient can see only indistinctly; people in the distance look to him like trees whose many branches and leaves are hard to distinguish from one another, especially when waving in the wind as the people are milling about. (2) A further application of Jesus' hands brings clear sight even at a distance. The command to go home rather than into the village is designed to demonstrate that a healing has occurred: the man no longer needs the villagers to lead him home; he can see for himself. *Read Mark 8:22–26.*

Close to Caesarea Philippi, considerably north of the Sea of Galilee and different from Caesarea on the Mediterranean coast, Peter (at first called Simon—see 1:16 with 3:16) identifies Jesus as the Christ. Peter is representing the view of his fellow disciples, too. Jesus orders them not to tell anyone. The crowds have almost crushed him to death even when thinking that he is only John the Baptist, Elijah, or one of the prophets come back to earth. What might they do if convinced that he is none less than the Christ? *Read Mark 8:27–9:1.* The human things thought by Peter consist in expectations that Jesus will not suffer but rule as the Christ. The things of God which Peter fails to think consist in the necessities that Jesus will first undergo death and resurrection. The severity of Jesus' rebuke to Peter shows the strength of these divine necessities. In correspondence with them, Jesus calls on people to take up their own cross and follow him. "Cross" does not mean a whole cross, which would be too heavy to carry, but the cross-beam which victims often have to carry to their place of execution as crowds lining the way hurl abuse at them. So taking one's cross and following Jesus means exposing oneself to abuse by open discipleship. To the prediction of his own death and resurrection, which shows his divine foreknowledge, Jesus adds predictions of what will happen to those who answer his call and to those who do not. These added predictions provide reasons to answer. Finally comes a prediction that some standing right there will not die until they see, despite appearances to the contrary in the suffering of Jesus and his disciples, that God's rule has come with power.

Read Mark 9:2–13. The transfiguration of Jesus fulfills his immediately foregoing prediction that some standing there at the time would see before they die that God's rule has come with power. The glistening of Jesus' clothes and the conversation with him of Elijah and Moses show that the upcoming suffering of Jesus and his disciples does not negate the presence of God's powerful rule.

Peter's Confession

Passion Prediction

Transfiguration

Indicating this lack of negation are the locale on a high mountain, the glistening of Jesus' clothes, the conversation with him of Elijah and Moses (the only Old Testament figures to see God on a mountain), the disciples' terror, and the voice of God the Father declaring Jesus to be his beloved Son and telling the disciples to listen to Jesus. Jesus' ordering the disciples not to tell what they have seen until after his resurrection is again designed to avoid the danger of being mobbed. Because Malachi 4:5 says that Elijah will come back before the Day of the LORD and because resurrection was expected to take place on that day, the scribes say that the return of Elijah will precede the resurrection. So the disciples perceive a possible disagreement with the prediction that Jesus will rise, apparently before Elijah's return. Jesus answers both that Elijah has already returned in the person of John the Baptist and that Elijah is yet to come, but not before Jesus suffers; for he would not have to suffer if Elijah had already restored all things, that is, introduced the world into a perfect state.

The astonishment of a crowd who see Jesus on his descent from the Mount of Transfiguration suggests an afterglow on his clothes.

Exorcism *Read Mark 9:14–29.* The special difficulty of the exorcism in this story is shown by the disciples' failure, by the extensively described effects of the demonic possession, by the seizure on the spot, by the length of possession and the frequency of seizures, by the length of Jesus' exorcistic command, and by his saying that only prayer can effect an exorcism of this kind of demon. So strong is Jesus, however, that he has exorcised it without prayer. The shriek and severe convulsion, leaving the victim seem dead until Jesus raises him, do not add to the difficulty of the exorcism so much as they demonstrate its success and finality.

Another prediction by Jesus of his death and resurrection exhibits his divine foreknowledge. The ignorance of the disciples is a foil to that foreknowledge, and their fear is a testimony to Jesus' awesomeness. *Read Mark 9:30–32.*

Back at Capernaum, the divine authority of Jesus is on display in his shattering of accepted norms. He equates greatness with servanthood, firstness with lastness, believing children with himself and God. He affirms the possibility of allegiance to himself and to the disciples apart from following them. Better to be drowned at sea than cause a believing child to sin. Better a maimed body in heaven *Fire and Salt* than a whole one in hell. The fire of judgment will rain down on

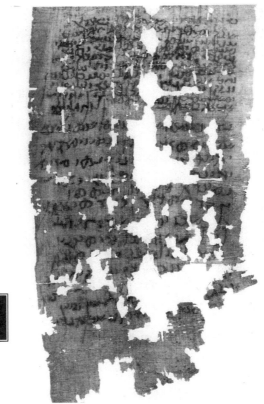

Divorce certificate from the Dead Sea Scrolls.

everybody like salt out of a salt shaker; so be sure to have the better salt of peaceful relations as opposed to rivalry with your fellow disciples. There is no possibility of finding peace outside the community of disciples. *Read Mark 9:33–50.*

While going to Judea through Transjordan, Jesus continues to display his authority as God's Son through the shattering of accepted norms. *Read Mark 10:1–12.* What the Pharisees call a Mosaic permission of divorce Jesus calls a command, but he upsets this command by calling it an accommodation to the Pharisees' hardheartedness and by going behind Moses to God's original intention at the Creation. According to that intention, a man should not break the marital union that God has established. Thus, as Jesus later explains to his disciples, divorce followed by marriage to another constitutes adultery, which means having sex with another person's spouse. In Jewish society, only a man could divorce his wife, not a wife her husband; and a man would commit adultery against the other woman's husband, since she was considered his

Divorce and Remarriage

145

property, not against his own wife, also mere property. But the explanation to disciples elevates the status of his own wife by directing the adultery against her and reflects (but does not defend) the right of Gentile women to divorce their husbands.

Yet again Jesus upsets norms with his authoritative pronouncements: adults should imitate children in coming to Jesus and accepting God's rule; wealth makes it next to impossible to enter the kingdom of God; leaving one's home and family for the sake of Jesus and the gospel will bring a hundred times more now as well as in eternity; he will be killed in Jerusalem, toward which he and other pilgrims are headed, and then rise; and his serving others by giving his life for their ransom sets an example of service that will displace his disciples' vying for prominence. *Read Mark 10:13–45.*

Children Some children are brought to Jesus for a touch of blessing, not of healing. "Except one, [that is] God" (10:18) echoes 2:7, where Jesus acted as God in forgiving sins, so that here as well Jesus is implying his deity by relating the goodness attributed to him to the exclusivity of God's goodness. That God alone is good prepares for the inadequacy of keeping even God's commandments if one wants *Wealth* eternal life. For that, the rich man must sell all his possessions, give the proceeds to poor people, and follow Jesus. Jewish rabbis forbid selling all your possessions lest you become dependent on charity. The disciples are puzzled because they, like most people, view wealth as a blessing from God, not as a roadblock against entry into God's kingdom (see, for example, Job 1:10; Prov. 10:22). A camel loaded with burdens cannot go through a narrow gate, much less a needle's eye; and riches are burdens that only God can unload from their victims. The community of disciples and their homes make up the hundredfold new houses, brothers, sisters, and so on of those who leave all to follow Jesus. The amazement and fear of those who are following him to Jerusalem enhance Mark's portrayal of him as the Son of God as well as Christ. He has the divine fore-*Cup and* knowledge to predict his disciples' destiny as well as his own. "Cup" *Baptism* and "baptism" stand for suffering and death. As a ransom, Jesus' suffering and death will liberate "many."

From Jericho the road west and a little south will lead up to Jerusalem. Usually the crowds want to see Jesus perform a miracle, but now they seem eager for him to arrive in Jerusalem for a reestablishment of the Davidic kingdom (compare 11:9–10). Surely his going ahead of them toward Jerusalem means that he is about to declare war, crush the Romans, and sit on David's throne (compare 10:32a). *Read Mark 10:46–52.* Following Jesus on the road contrasts with sitting on the edge of the road and offers proof that Bartimaeus is no longer blind or begging. He was begging for money from others but wanted healing from Jesus—and got it.

Read Mark 11:1–10. The Mount of Olives stands just across the Kidron Valley to the east of Jerusalem. So the route of Jesus and other pilgrims from Galilee takes them across that mountain past Bethany, on the south slope, and Bethphage, probably on the west slope facing Jerusalem. In the finding of a colt Jesus' divine foreknowledge becomes prominent: he predicted the discovery in delicious detail. His deity gives him the prerogative of requisitioning the colt; and his sitting on the colt while others walk suits that deity. So also the saddle of donated garments, the paving of the road with such garments and with straw, and the acclamation by the crowd. Originally "hosanna" meant "save now," a prayer, but it has come to mean "Hurrah!" Even highest heaven joins in this acclamation. *The Triumphal Entry*

Now Jesus enters Jerusalem and the temple to inspect them. It is too late to do anything about what he sees, and he knows the hostility in Jerusalem toward him (see 10:33–34); so he exits with the apostles and stays overnight in Bethany. *Read Mark 11:11–25.* The season for figs (June for early figs, then August–October) has not yet arrived, but fig trees in leaf at Passovertide (Mark–April) might well be expected to have edible buds, eaten by Palestinians even in modern times. Thus Jesus' cursing of the fig tree: no buds now, no fruit in June or ever after. Back in the temple he exercises his authority by driving out the traffickers who have turned the outer court, to be used for prayer by Gentiles, into an emporium for the buying of animals and doves certified as fit for sacrifice. This act and the popularity of Jesus make the Sanhedrin, who have charge of the temple, determined to kill him. Discovery next morning that the fig tree has withered, not as usually from the foliage down, but from the roots up, illustrates the power of Jesus' curse only the previous day and the impossibility of the fig tree's revival. He uses this startling development to startle the disciples further with statements about the power of faith and prayer and about the necessity of forgiveness. "This mountain" refers to the Mount of Olives, over which they are walking; and "the sea" refers to the Dead Sea, visible in the distance on a clear day. Ancient people thought that mountains reach down to the very foundation of the earth. *Cursing and Withering of a Fig Tree*

Cleansing of the Temple

147

A wild donkey and her young colt in the Judean hills.

A fig branch in leaf.

The denarius of Caesar Augustus was possibly the tribute money used to challenge Jesus. Both sides of the coin glorify Caesar.

Now Jesus outwits members of the Sanhedrin, who challenge his authority to have cleansed the temple. Their challenge comes in two questions. He answers with a single question, which puts them in such an embarrassing dilemma that he then takes the initiative to tell them an accusatory parable. *Read Mark 11:27–12:12.* The vineyard stands for the Jewish people (compare Isa. 5:1–7), the planter for God, the tenant farmers for the Sanhedrin, the slaves for past prophets, the planter's son for Jesus the Son of God, the murder of the son for the coming murder of Jesus, the destruction of the tenant farmers for God's judgment on the Sanhedrin (compare 13:1–2 and the destruction of Jerusalem and the temple in A.D. 70), the transfer of the vineyard to others for a shift of leadership from the Sanhedrin to Jesus and his disciples, and the rejected stone's becoming the cap- or cornerstone to Jesus' exaltation after the Resurrection. *Parable of the Wicked Tenant Farmers*

The battle of wits continues. To the amazement of some Pharisees and Herodians, Jesus escapes from the horns of a dilemma into which they have put him; and he exposes the ignorance of Sadducees who try to nonplus him. *Read Mark 12:13–27.* For general circulation in Palestine the Romans mint copper coins without an imperial image. But the tax to Caesar, a poll tax, has to be paid in a Roman silver coin stamped with his image and with a legend proclaiming his supposedly divine ancestry; yet the law of Moses prohibits images (Ex. 20:4–6; Deut. 5:8–10), and monotheism has become the central feature of Judaism (compare Deut. 6:4). So here is the dilemma: Saying that it goes against God's law to pay the *Taxation* tax would make it possible for the Herodians, supporters of Roman rule by way of the family of Herod, to charge Jesus with the teaching of rebellion. Saying that it does not go against the law of God to pay tax to Caesar would enable the Pharisees, whom the Jewish crowds respect, to undermine Jesus' popularity; for the crowds naturally resent paying the tax, and about A.D. 6 the levying of this tax provoked an outright rebellion led by Judas the Galilean (Acts 5:37). Jesus' loss of popularity would enable the Sanhedrin to arrest him without fear of the crowds' rising up on his behalf. A charge of rebellion would trigger the taking of action against him by Roman authorities. His answer divides the things of God from the things of Caesar. The fact that God's rule has not yet come in a political way leaves intact Caesar's authority to tax. Jesus' asking for the kind of coin with which the tax is paid embarrasses the Jews: by producing it they demonstrate their tacit acceptance of Caesar's dominion, since it is generally acknowledged that a king's domain extends as far as his coins circulate.

Resurrection   A question of the Sadducees rests on the Mosaic law of levirate marriage, according to which a surviving brother should marry the widow of his brother if that brother dies childless and, if possible, produce through her an heir for him (see Deut. 25:5–10 with Gen. 38:8). But if a woman has not given birth by seven successive brothers, whose wife will she be in the resurrection? The question is supposed to make the very idea of resurrection absurd, since—polygamy being unthinkable for a woman—she will hardly be the wife of seven brothers at one and the same time. To defend the doctrine of resurrection, Jesus might have appealed to later passages in the Old Testament, for example, Daniel 12:2–3; but the Sadducees accept only the Pentateuch, which contains nothing explicit on the doctrine. So after pointing out the Sadducees' failure to consider the power of God in deducting marriage from life after resurrection, Jesus appeals to a passage in the Pentateuch (Ex. 3:6) and infers the resurrection from it. His statement that the resurrected will be "like angels in heaven" (that is, unmarried) sarcastically alludes to the Sadducees' disbelief in angels on account of angels' nonappearance in the Pentateuch (apart from the angel of the Lord, an alter ego of God).

The Son of David   The next two paragraphs deal with scribes and a widow such as scribes take advantage of. First, a scribe comes to recognize the truth of Jesus' teaching. Then, having weathered all questions successfully, Jesus asks his own question, based on Psalm 110:1: How can the scribes call the Christ "the son of David" when that designation never appears in the Old Testament for Christ and though David himself calls the Christ "Lord" rather than his son? In the following warning against scribes, they appear to sponge off the limited resources of widows impressed by their religiosity. Contrastively, a poor widow gives her last two pennies for the upkeep of divine services in the temple. "The treasury" refers to a hall in the temple where such gifts are deposited in thirteen receptacles shaped like trumpets. Jesus' putting a higher estimate on the widow's gift than on coins of much higher value and number shows him at the business of upsetting popular norms once again. *Read Mark 12:28–44.*

The Widow's Mite

Now Mark displays Jesus' ability to predict the fates of the temple, of the world, and of the elect (God's chosen, the disciples of Jesus) and his own return at the end of history as presently known. *Read Mark 13:1–37.* This speech is known as the Olivet Discourse, sometimes as the Little Apocalypse because of its similarity to the Book of Revelation, also called the Apocalypse. Jesus predicts the destruction of the temple, as happened in A.D. 70, but quickly leaves that topic behind to warn his disciples not to think of the end as near merely because of false christs, wars, earthquakes, persecution, and such like. Not until they see the abomination of desolation, a sacrilege that causes religious Jews to stop going to the temple and thus to leave it desolate, deserted of worshipers,[8] will the end be near. Then disciples living in the populated areas of Judea should immediately flee to the nearby wilderness of Judea, a mountainous region full of caves long used as hideaways.[9] Pregnancy, nursing, and winter weather would hamper flight. Happily, the Lord will cut short this horrible period, known as the Great Tribulation, to save the lives of the elect. When the smoke of battle has darkened the sun and moon and meteorites have showered the earth, Jesus will

The Olivet Discourse

---

8. *Originally, the abomination of desolation referred to an altar to Zeus and perhaps his statue, erected in the temple by Antiochus Epiphanes (Dan. 9:27; 11:31; 12:11). As a result, pious Jews refused to worship there until Judas Maccabeus captured, cleansed, and rededicated the temple.*

9. *"In the mountains" does not fit Pella, a town at the base of foothills in Transjordan to which Christians fled from Jerusalem some time before A.D. 70, according to Eusebius, Ecclesiastical History 3.5.2–3. Nor does "the abomination of desolation" fit the setting up in the temple precincts of Roman standards with images of the supposedly divine Caesar affixed to them. That took place at the destruction in A.D. 70. By then it was too late for flight. Compare 2 Thessalonians 2:4; Revelation 13:11–18 for worship of the Man of Lawlessness, Beast, or Antichrist and his image.*

come with great power and glory. The angels' gathering of the elect, scattered by persecution, will spell salvation. A parable teaches that those who see the abomination of desolation can be sure that Jesus is about to come, just as those who see a fig tree bud after losing its leaves for the winter know that summer is near. But exactly how near nobody knows but God the Father, for he has kept secret the amount of time that he will lop from the preceding tribulation. So all Jesus' disciples should stay alert.

Now begins the fulfillment of predictions that Jesus has made concerning the Passion (his suffering and death) and Resurrection. *Read Mark 14:1–11.* "Not during the festival" (14:2) should probably read "not in the festal assembly." The members of the Sanhedrin do not want to risk a riot on behalf of Jesus by arresting him in a crowd of his fellow Galilean pilgrims; rather, apart from the crowd if they can catch him in such a situation. Judas Iscariot will provide them with that kind of opportunity. In anticipation of his resultant *Anointing* death, Jesus interprets the perfuming of his head by a woman in the *of Jesus* house of Simon the leper as an advance preparation of his body for burial. (But there is no need to suppose that she herself understood the deed as anything more than an act of devotion.) Three hundred denarii amount to the annual wage of a fully employed manual laborer, and the perfume lavished on Jesus is worth even more: a tribute to his status and an amelioration of the shame of his coming crucifixion.

Last Supper The Thursday before Good Friday has arrived. *Read Mark 14:12–31.* The story of making preparation for the Passover, an evening meal commemorating the Exodus of Israel from Egypt (Ex. 12:1–51; Lev. 23:4–8), serves the purpose of highlighting Jesus' divine foreknowledge with respect to two of the disciples' finding a man carrying a jar of water (as only women usually do) and finding a large upper room furnished and ready. The story of the Passover meal itself, traditionally called the Last Supper, likewise serves the purpose of highlighting Jesus' divine foreknowledge. He predicts that one of the Twelve will hand him over to his enemies. He predicts the violence of his death by separating his body and blood in the symbols of bread and a cup of wine and interpreting the violence as sacrificial on behalf of many people. He predicts his coming abstinence followed by victorious celebration at the messianic banquet when God's rule takes over fully. With a quotation of Zechariah 13:7, he predicts that the disciples will desert him. He predicts that after his resurrection he will go ahead of them into Galilee. And he predicts Peter's denials of him. The fulfillments of these predictions will help overcome the shame of crucifixion and enhance Mark's portrayal of Jesus as Christ, God's Son. The antiphonal singing of Psalms 113–118, constituting a hymn called the Hallel, brings the Passover liturgy to a close.

Now the fulfillment of Jesus' predictions comes to full flower. *Gethsemane* Judas Iscariot betrays him by enabling the Sanhedrin to arrest him apart from the crowd. The rest of the disciples flee. The Sanhedrin judges him deserving of death. And Peter denies him. *Read Mark 14:32–72.* Mark describes the emotional distress of Jesus to excite sympathy for him, and mentions his submission to God the Father's will to excite admiration for Jesus. "Abba" is Aramaic for "Father" and indicates his sense of sonship to God. "The hour" is the hour of his betrayal (see 14:41 with 14:35), and "this cup" his death (10:38–39; 14:23–24). His strength in staying awake contrasts with the weakness of even his three closest disciples in falling asleep. Judas displays perfidy in a show of affectionate homage; and mem- *Arrest* bers of the Sanhedrin, Jesus sarcastically notes, by arresting him in secret rather than in public as they have often had opportunity to do, also display an evil purpose. Many have identified the young man who flees naked with John Mark, author of this gospel; but no identification is given. Whoever he is, then, his escape seems to symbolize in advance the resurrection of Jesus, who will be buried in a linen cloth such as the young man has been wearing (15:46) and whose resurrection a young man will announce in the empty tomb (16:5–7). The Sanhedrin's finding it impossible to obtain valid testi- *Trial Before* mony against Jesus implies his innocence. The false testimony that *the Sanhedrin* he said he would destroy the man-made temple and in three days build another, God-made temple sounds like a mishmash of his predictions that the temple would be destroyed (though not by him) and that he would rise from the dead in three days. The judgment that he speaks capital blasphemy in answer to the high priest has to do with Jesus' prediction that at the Second Coming they will see him sharing the throne of God (reverentially called "the Power") just before he starts to return. Ironically, he is challenged to prophesy right as his earlier predictions are coming true. The details of the mockery to which he is subjected and of Peter's three denials this *Denials* very night before the second crow of a rooster underline the exacti- *by Peter* tude of Jesus' divine foreknowledge.

Coin from A.D. 221 showing the Roman Emperor Elagabalus wearing a radiant crown.

Trial before Pilate   The parade of fulfillments continues. The Sanhedrin take Jesus to Pilate, the Roman governor, just as Jesus said they would "hand him over to the Gentiles" (10:33). Pilate does not care whether or not Jesus has blasphemed the God whom Jews worship, but he does care whether Jesus might claim to be a king rivaling the Caesar whom he the governor serves. "Are you the King of the Jews?" implies that the religious charge of blasphemy under which the Sanhedrin condemned Jesus has given way to a political charge of insurrectionism. His answer, "You yourself are speaking," admits "the King of the Jews" as a designation given to him but rejects it as a self-designation; in other words, Jesus denies that he is an insurrectionist.

Barabbas   *Read Mark 15:1–20a.* Barabbas, not Jesus, is an insurrectionist—a murderer as well. Since the Sanhedrin arrested and tried Jesus in secret and brought him to Pilate early in the morning, the crowd who ask Pilate to follow his custom of releasing a prisoner to them must not have Jesus in mind.[10] It is Pilate who insinuates Jesus into the request of the crowd to find out whether Jesus' popularity is of a political sort that really does threaten the rule of Caesar, as the Sanhedrin have claimed. If the crowd want Jesus released as their king, the Sanhedrin will have been proved correct. If not, Pilate will. When the crowd asks for Barabbas, Pilate knows himself to be correct in his opinion that the Sanhedrin is merely envious of Jesus' popularity, but his attempt to release Jesus wilts before the

---

10. *On the one hand, the yearly custom of releasing a prisoner has scant support outside this story. On the other hand, the fabricating of such a custom seems unlikely in view of the well-documented fact that Romans released prisoners occasionally—all that would be needed in the case of Jesus and Barabbas.*

onslaught of the crowd's demand. Pilate is looking out for his own political future; he does not want the Sanhedrin to lodge a complaint with Caesar that he, Pilate, has let go a rival king. Thus the coming crucifixion of Jesus is shown to be a miscarriage of justice. Further mockery, this time by soldiers, returns to the fulfillment of Jesus' predictions (see 10:34). The praetorium, where it takes place, is Pilate's official residence, or palace, when he visits Jerusalem from Caesarea, where he normally resides. The soldiers design the mock crown of thorns also as an instrument of torture shaped like a laurel wreath with some of the spikes pointing inward toward Jesus' head, or solely as an instrument of mockery with the spikes pointing outward in imitation of the rays of the sun.

All along, Mark has been counteracting the shame of Jesus' coming crucifixion by noting its fulfillment of Jesus' own predictions, its benefit to others, its stemming from the will of God the Father and at the same time from a miscarriage of human justice. In the narrative of the Crucifixion itself, Mark carries forward this program by noting that Jesus does not have to carry his own cross; that he is offered wine mixed with myrrh (a delicacy); that to stay awake with

Crucifixion

The Church of the Holy Sepulchre is the traditional site of Jesus' crucifixion and burial. Archaeological evidence indicates that this location was probably outside the city wall in New Testament times.

full sensibility, as in Gethsemane, he refuses the mixture; that his clothes become objects of desire; that he occupies a central position when crucified; that further mockery continues to fulfill his predictions (10:33–34); that he hangs on the cross only six hours (whereas victims of crucifixion normally hang there much longer, as long as several days); that for the last three hours a supernatural darkness hides him from the leering of those who blaspheme him; that he does not weaken bit by bit and lapse into unconsciousness before dying, but dies with a loud shout; that with this shout the gigantic veil of the temple is torn in two, from top to bottom to indicate supernatural action;[11] that the way Jesus dies makes the centurion overseeing the crucifixion declare that truly Jesus must have been God's Son; that a large number of women who followed and served him in Galilee saw the events which evoked the centurion's declaration; and that Jesus' corpse gets a dignified burial by none less than a respected, pious, and brave member of the Sanhedrin, and this despite the Roman prohibition of such a burial for those executed like Jesus under the charge of high treason. *Read Mark 15:20b–47.*

"The father of Alexander and Rufus" (15:21) probably implies that these sons of Simon of Cyrene were known to Mark's original audience. A rough similarity between "Eloi" and "Elian" ("Elijah," 15:34–36) makes some bystanders think that Jesus is calling for help from the Old Testament prophet Elijah. Jesus does not take the sour wine offered him: he has already died with a loud shout. The shout derived from Psalm 22:1 and referred to God's abandoning him to die. Mark does not specify the outer rather than inner veil of the temple, but the centurion's observation requires the outer and favors the Mount of Olives, just opposite the veiled end of the temple, as the site of the Crucifixion rather than the traditional site, out of eyeshot as well as on the wrong side. "Preparation" (15:42) means

Burial Friday as the day of preparing to rest on Saturday, the Sabbath. Rolling a stone against the door of Jesus' tomb shields his corpse from the indignity of ravage by predators.

Read Mark 16:1–7. Because of the very large size of the stone, the

Resurrection women who come to Jesus' tomb wonder who will roll it away for them only to find it already rolled away and his corpse, which they intended to honor with the application of spices (whereas Jews ordi-

---

11. *The veil of the temple is said to have measured 60 feet by 30 feet, and in thickness to have matched the width of a human palm (about five inches).*

This tomb with a round stone for closing its entrance was found on the back (eastern) slopes of the Mount of Olives. The tomb is still in usable condition.

narily applied mere oil to a corpse), absent. "A young man" recalls the young man of 14:51–52, but "clothed in a white robe" distinguishes this one, apparently an angel, from the earlier one, a human being. Sitting on the right augurs well, for the right side is the side of favor. It augurs well indeed, for the young man announces the resurrection of Jesus and the disciples' seeing of him in Galilee, so that his prediction at the Last Supper (14:28) will reach fulfillment.

The best textual tradition stops with Mark 16:8. Inferior traditions add 16:9–20, called the long ending, and a shorter, unnumbered ending, both generally recognized as inauthentic.[12] Many think

Mark's Ending

---

12. *This textual question does not affect any major doctrine of the Christian faith. Biblical inspiration is certainly not at issue, only what was the original text of the Bible as opposed to later additions by copyists. The earliest and most trustworthy manuscripts of the New Testament had not yet been discovered in 1611; so the translators of the King James Version, which contains the long ending, did not know that the long ending was textually doubtful.*

that Mark intended his gospel to end with 16:8. If so, the women's trembling and amazement, dumbfoundedness and fear, bring the gospel to a close on the note of awe, as appropriate to Mark's portrayal of Jesus as Christ, God's Son. On the other hand, Mark's narrating the fulfillments of all Jesus' other predictions insofar as those fulfillments have occurred during Jesus' time on earth favors that Mark went on to narrate a fulfillment of the disciples' seeing Jesus in Galilee and that the two inauthentic endings arose out of awareness that such an original ending was lost. *Read Mark 16:8.*

FOR FURTHER DISCUSSION

For what sort of situation is the gospel of Mark most pertinent today?

What kind of contemporary audience might find the gospel of Mark appealing, and why?

FOR FURTHER INVESTIGATION

Anderson, H. *The Gospel of Mark.* 2d ed. Grand Rapids: Eerdmans, 1981.

Guelich, R. A. *Mark 1–8:26.* Dallas: Word, 1989. Advanced.

Gundry, R. H. *Mark: A Commentary on His Apology for the Cross.* Grand Rapids: Eerdmans, 1993. Advanced.

Hooker, M. D. *The Gospel According to St. Mark.* Peabody, Mass.: Hendrickson, 1992.

Hurtado, L. W. *Mark.* Peabody, Mass.: Hendrickson, 1989.

8

Matthew: Handbook for a Mixed Church Under Persecution

- ❖ *Who wrote the gospel of Matthew?*

- ❖ *How do we determine its authorship?*

- ❖ *When was this gospel written, and what indications do we have of its date?*

- ❖ *For what audience, from what standpoint, and with*

- *what purpose did the author write?*

- ❖ *What features and emphases characterize this gospel?*

- ❖ *What overall plan determines its movement?*

Papias

Papias's tradition, which says that Mark wrote down Peter's reminiscences, also says that Matthew wrote *logia* (Greek for "oracles") in Hebrew or Aramaic, and that others interpreted them as they were able.[1] In context, *logia* most naturally refers to a gospel. But we do not possess a gospel from the pen of Matthew in either of the Semitic languages Hebrew and Aramaic, only the present Greek gospel, which appears not to have been translated from a Semitic original. For example, why would Matthew give the Semitic originals and Greek translations of just a few terms, such as "Immanuel" (1:23), if his whole gospel were a translation from Hebrew or Aramaic? Some have thought that the tradition refers to a collection of messianic proof texts drawn up by Matthew in

---

1. *Quoted by Eusebius*, Ecclesiastical History 3.39.16.

Hebrew or Aramaic and later incorporated in Greek translation into his gospel, or to an earlier Semitic edition of Matthew not directly related to our present Greek edition. Others have thought that *logia* refers to Q.[2] According to yet another understanding, Papias's tradition refers to our present Greek Matthew as written in the Hebrew or Aramaic style rather than language and as presenting Matthew's interpretation of Jesus' life alongside Mark's interpretation. If so, there is no reference to any translation of Matthew from a Semitic original.

Authorship   Modern scholars usually deny that the apostle Matthew wrote the gospel bearing his name. Following the equation of Papias's *logia* with Q, some have suggested that Matthew wrote Q and that his name became mistakenly attached to the first gospel (in the order of our New Testament) because the unknown writer of the first gospel utilized so much of Q. But if there was a Q, adequate reasons do not exist for denying that Matthew might have written both, especially if Q was a body of loose notes on Jesus' teaching taken by Matthew and incorporated into his gospel. It is argued to the contrary that an apostle like Matthew would not have borrowed narratives of Jesus' deeds from a nonapostle like Mark. But while adding his own material, Matthew may simply be corroborating the Petrine and therefore apostolic tradition recorded by Mark. Regardless of stature, ancient authors regularly borrowed from previous writers; no one thought that by doing so they were plagiarizing material or demeaning themselves. Modern attitudes did not apply. Early church tradition unanimously ascribed the first gospel to Matthew, and false ascription to a relatively obscure apostle like Matthew seems unlikely until a later date when all the apostles became canonized in Christian imagination.

The skillful organization of this gospel agrees with the probable interests and abilities of a toll collector such as the apostle Matthew had been. So also does the fact that this is the only gospel to contain the story of Jesus' paying the temple tax (17:24–27). The account of Matthew's call to discipleship uses the apostolic name "Matthew"[3] rather than the name "Levi," used by Mark and Luke, and omits "his," used by Mark and Luke, in describing the house where Matthew entertained Jesus at dinner (9:9–13; compare Mark 2:13–17; Luke 5:27–32). These incidental details may well give tell-

---

2. *Compare pages 97–99.*

3. *See the lists of apostles in Matthew 10:2–4; Mark 3:16–19; Luke 6:13–16; Acts 1:13.*

tale indications of Matthean authorship and thus support the early church tradition.

If Matthew utilized Mark and Mark dates from the period A.D. *Date* 45–60, Matthew probably dates from slightly later in or after that period. Denial of predictive prophecy by Jesus and generally more sceptical presuppositions will force a later date in the eighties or nineties,[4] though a number of conservative scholars prefer this later date because of other considerations, such as the argument that Matthew's interest in the church (he is the only evangelist to use the term, and that twice) betrays a later period when the doctrine of the church was assuming more importance as a result of the delay in Jesus' return. But the doctrine of the church already plays an important role in Paul's epistles, all written well before the eighties and nineties. And if Matthew wrote for Jews,[5] it seems less likely that he wrote late, after the breach between church and synagogue widened, than early, when Christian Jews still dominated the church and prospects for converting other Jews seemed brighter.

Matthew writes his gospel for the church as the new chosen na- *Structure* tion, which at least for the time being has replaced the old chosen nation of Israel. The gospel starts with the nativity of Jesus (chaps. 1–2). The rest of the gospel takes up primarily Marcan narrative (usually condensed) and inserts five discourses of Jesus (though some of the material in these discourses comes from Mark). The discourses consist of more or less lengthy "sermons," to which isolated sayings of Jesus have been added in appropriate places. Each discourse ends with the formula, "And it came to pass when Jesus had finished . . . ."

The fivefold structure of these discourses suggests that for the *Jewishness* benefit of his Jewish audience Matthew is portraying Jesus as a new and greater Moses. Like Moses, Jesus speaks part of his law from a mountain. The number of his discourses corresponds to the books of Moses, called the Pentateuch because they are five in number (Genesis, Exodus, Leviticus, Numbers, and Deuteronomy). By omitting the story of the "widow's mite," Matthew even welds the denunciation of the scribes and Pharisees (chap. 23) and the Olivet

---

4. *Those who balk at predictive prophecy think that the phraseology of 22:7 ("The king . . . sent his troops . . . and burned their city") clearly points back to the destruction of Jerusalem in A.D. 70, that is, takes a later vantage point. But the phraseology may point back to the destruction of Jerusalem in 586 B.C. and reflect Isaiah 5:24–25.*

5. *The point is disputed, but this is the natural and general impression most readers will gain from the gospel.*

Discourse (chaps. 24–25) into a single unit to gain this fivefold arrangement (contrast Mark 12:38ff.; Luke 20:45ff.)

Matthew's comparison of Jesus with Moses shows itself elsewhere, too, as in the borrowing of phraseology from the story of Moses to describe Jesus' nativity and transfiguration (compare Matt. 2:13, 20–21; 17:2, 5 with Ex. 2:15; 4:19–20; 34:29; Deut. 18:15). In the Sermon on the Mount according to Matthew, Jesus himself sets his teaching alongside the Mosaic law in a series of statements, "You have heard that it was said to the ancients [there follows a quotation or paraphrase of the Pentateuch] . . . . But I say to you . . ." (Matt. 5:21, 27, 31, 33, 38, 43; contrast Luke 6:27–35).

Besides the fivefold structure of the discourses, there are many other indications of Matthew's penchant for organization. He favors groupings of three and seven. For example, he divides the genealogy of Jesus into three sections (1:17) and gives from Jesus' teaching three examples of righteous conduct, three prohibitions, and three commandments (6:1–7:20). There are seven parables in chapter 13 and seven woes against the scribes and Pharisees in chapter 23. Even though some of these numerical groupings may go back to Jesus himself and to the events themselves, their frequency in Matthew shows his fondness for them above that of the other evangelists.

Purpose   The editorial organization of Jesus' teaching, its strongly ethical content, and its emphasis on discipleship have led to the views that Matthew writes his gospel to provide a catechetical manual for new converts or a scholastic manual for church leaders, or that he designs his gospel for liturgical and homiletical reading in early church services. But the gospel gives a much stronger impression of having been written to strengthen Christian Jews in their suffering of persecution, to warn them against laxity and apostasy, and to urge them to use their persecution as an opportunity for the evangelism of all nations.

Matthew's recurring stress on Jesus' fulfillment of the Old Testament law and messianic prophecy ("Such and such happened in order that what was spoken by so-and-so the prophet might be fulfilled") and his tracing of Jesus' genealogy from Abraham, father of the Jewish nation, through the beloved King David also indicate a Jewish bent. By way of contrast, Mark did not trace the ancestry of Jesus at all; his mainly Gentile readers (like most modern readers) would have little concern for it.

Still other Jewish features appear in the characteristically Jewish designation of God as the "Father in heaven" (fifteen times in

Matthew, only once in Mark, and not at all in Luke), in the substitution of "heaven" for God's name (especially in the phrase "kingdom of heaven," where the other evangelists have "kingdom of God"), in the typically Jewish interest in eschatology (Matthew extends the Olivet Discourse by a whole long chapter, as compared with Mark and Luke), in frequent references to Jesus as the "son of David," in allusions to Jewish customs without explanation (23:5, 27; 15:2; contrast the explanation in Mark 7:2–4), in the story of Jesus' paying the temple tax (17:24–27, lacking in the other gospels), and in statements by him that have a specially Jewish flavor (for example, "I was sent only to the lost sheep of the house of Israel" [15:24]; "Go nowhere among the Gentiles, and enter no town of the Samaritans, but go rather to the lost sheep of the house of Israel" [10:5b–6]; see also 5:17–24; 6:16–18; 23:2–3). In telling the nativity story (chaps. 1–2), Matthew stresses that Jesus was born into a Davidic family and from that standpoint, therefore, has a legitimate claim to the Jewish throne. Matthew also counters the Jewish charge that the disciples of Jesus stole away his body (28:11–15).

On the other hand, universality also characterizes the gospel of Matthew, which reaches a climax in the Great Commission that Jesus' followers make disciples of all nations (28:18–20). Toward the beginning of the gospel, the Magi (wise men) worship the infant Christ—they are Gentiles (2:1–12). Jesus is quoted as saying that "many will come from the east and west and sit at table with Abraham, Isaac, and Jacob in the kingdom of heaven while the sons of the kingdom will be thrown into the outer darkness" (8:11–12). The field is "the world" in the parable of the wheat and tares (13:38). According to the parable of the vineyard, God will transfer his kingdom from Israel to others (21:33–43). And Matthew is the only evangelist to use the word "church" (16:18; 18:17). We must describe his gospel, then, as Jewish Christian with a universal outlook. *Universality*

Its Jewish character suggests that Matthew wrote in Palestine or Syria, most probably Antioch, to which many of the original Palestinian disciples had migrated (Acts 11:19, 27). Its remarkable concern for Gentiles supports Antioch, a city with the church that sent Paul on his Gentile missions. In agreement with this view stands the fact that our oldest witness for a knowledge of Matthew's gospel is an early bishop of the church in Antioch: Ignatius (first quarter of the second century; *Epistle to the Smyrnaeans* 1:1). *Provenance*

An Outline of Matthew, Showing Concentric Structure of Narrative and Discourse (A-B-C-D-E-F-E'-D'-C'-B'-A')

A. NARRATIVE (1:1–4:25)
1. Jesus' genealogy (1:1–17)
2. The birth of Jesus (1:18–25)
3. The worship of Jesus by the Magi (2:1–12)
4. The flight into Egypt for protection from Herod the Great (2:13–18)
5. The return and residence in Nazareth (2:19–23)
6. The preparatory ministry of John the Baptist (3:1–17)
   a. His preaching (3:1–12)
   b. His baptism of Jesus (3:13–17)
7. The temptation of Jesus by Satan (4:1–11)
8. Beginnings of messianic preaching and miracle-working in Galilee, with the call of Simon Peter, Andrew, James, and John (4:12–25)

B. DISCOURSE: THE SERMON ON THE MOUNT (5:1–7:29)

C. NARRATIVE (8:1–9:34)
1. The cleansing of a leper (8:1–4)
2. The healing of a centurion's servant (8:5–13)
3. The healing of Peter's mother-in-law and others (8:14–17)
4. Two would-be disciples (8:18–22)
5. The stilling of a storm (8:23–27)
6. The deliverance of two demoniacs (8:28–34)
7. The forgiveness and healing of a paralytic (9:1–8)
8. The call of Matthew and Jesus' eating with toll collectors and sinners (9:9–13)
9. A question about fasting (9:14–17)
10. The healing of a woman with a chronic flow of blood and the raising of a ruler's deceased daughter (9:18–26)
11. The healing of two blind men (9:27–31)
12. The deliverance of a dumb demoniac (9:32–34)

D. DISCOURSE: THE COMMISSION AND INSTRUCTION OF THE TWELVE (9:35–11:1)

E. NARRATIVE (11:2–12:50)
  1. The testimony of Jesus to John the Baptist (11:2–15)
  2. Jesus' condemnation of the unrepentant (11:16–24)
  3. His thanksgiving to the Father and invitation to the weary (11:25–30)
  4. His lordship over the Sabbath (12:1–14)
     a. His defense of the disciples' plucking and eating grain on the Sabbath (12:1–8)
     b. His healing a withered hand on the Sabbath (12:9–14)
  5. His withdrawal and further healings (12:15–21)
  6. His delivering a blind and dumb demoniac and defense of his exorcisms (12:22–37)
  7. His refusal to give any sign except that of Jonah, condemnation of self-righteousness, and identification of his true spiritual kindred (12:38–50)

F. DISCOURSE: A PARABLE ABOUT PARABLES, PLUS SIX PARABLES ABOUT THE KINGDOM (13:1–52)
  1. The sower (13:1–9)
  2. Reasons for parabolic teaching (13:10–17)
  3. An interpretation of the sower (13:18–23)
  4. The wheat and the tares (13:24–30)
  5. The grain of mustard seed (13:31–32)
  6. The yeast and fulfillment of Scripture by the parabolic method (13:33–35)
  7. An interpretation of the wheat and the tares (13:36–43)
  8. The buried treasure (13:44)
  9. The costly pearl (13:45–46)
  10. The dragnet with good and bad fish, and a final statement about understanding the parables (13:47–52)

E'. NARRATIVE (13:53–17:27)
  1. The rejection of Jesus at Nazareth (13:53–58)
  2. The death of John the Baptist (14:1–12)
  3. The feeding of five thousand (14:13–21)
  4. Jesus' and Peter's walking on water (14:22–36)
  5. Ritual versus moral defilement (15:1–20)
  6. Deliverance of the demonized daughter of a Canaanite woman and other healings (15:21–28)

7. The feeding of four thousand (15:29–39)
8. Another refusal to give any sign except that of Jonah (16:1–4)
9. A warning against Phariseeism and Sadduceeism (16:5–12)
10. Peter's confession of Jesus' messiahship and Jesus' blessing of Peter (16:13–20)
11. A prediction by Jesus of his suffering, death, and resurrection; a rebuke of Peter for trying to dissuade him; and a call to cross-taking discipleship (16:21–28)
12. The transfiguration of Jesus (17:1–13)
13. The healing of a demonized boy (17:14–21)
14. Another prediction by Jesus of his death and resurrection (17:22–23)
15. Paying the temple tax, or "Peter's Penny" (17:24–27)

D'. Discourse: humility and forgiveness among Jesus' disciples (18:1–35)

C'. Narrative (19:1–22:46)

1. Questions of divorce and marriage (19:1–12)
2. Jesus' blessing the children (19:13–15)
3. The rich young man and the cost and reward of discipleship (19:16–30)
4. The parable of an employer and laborers (20:1–16)
5. Another prediction by Jesus of his death and resurrection (20:17–19)
6. A request for positions of honor by the mother of James and John for her sons (20:20–28)
7. The healing of two blind men near Jericho (20:29–34)
8. The Triumphal Entry (21:1–11)
9. The cleansing of the temple (21:12–17)
10. The cursing and withering of a fig tree (21:18–22)
11. A challenge to Jesus' authority (21:23–27)
12. The parable of an obedient son and a disobedient one (21:28–32)
13. The parable of some wicked tenant farmers (21:33–46)
14. The parable of a royal marriage feast and wedding garment (22:1–14)

15. A question about paying taxes to Caesar (22:15–22)
16. A question of the Sadducees about the resurrection (22:23–33)
17. A question about the greatest commandment (22:34–40)
18. Jesus' question about the Messiah's Davidic descent and lordship (22:41–46)

B'. DISCOURSE: DENUNCIATION OF THE SCRIBES AND PHARISEES AND THE OLIVET DISCOURSE (23:1–25:46)
1. Denunciation of the scribes and Pharisees (23:1–39)
2. The Olivet Discourse (24:1–25:46)
   a. A preview of events leading up to and including the return of Christ (24:1–31)
   b Exhortations to watchfulness, with parables of the fig tree, the thief, the faithful and unfaithful servants, the ten virgins, and the talents (24:32–25:30)
   c. The judgment of the sheep and the goats (25:31–46)

A'. NARRATIVE (26:1–28:20)
1. Another prediction by Jesus of his death, the plot of the Sanhedrin, and the anointing of Jesus in Bethany, with a resultant bargain by Judas Iscariot to betray Jesus (26:1–16)
2. The Last Supper (26:17–35)
3. Jesus' praying in Gethsemane (26:36–46)
4. The arrest (26:47–56)
5. The trial (26:57–27:26)
   a. The hearing before Caiaphas, with Peter's denials (26:57–75)
   b. The condemnatory decision of the Sanhedrin (27:1–2)
   c. The hearing before Pontius Pilate, with the suicide of Judas and the release of Barabbas (27:3–26)
6. The crucifixion and death of Jesus (27:27–56)
7. The burial (27:57–66)
8. The Resurrection (28:1–15)
9. The Great Commission (28:16–20)

Excursus on New Testament
Quotations of Fulfilled Old Testament Passages

Matthew's emphasis on fulfilled messianic prophecy makes appropriate here a consideration of the fulfillment motif throughout the New Testament. The writers of the New Testament and Jesus himself saw in the coming of God's rule a fulfillment of what we would distinguish in the Old Testament as conscious predictions and unconscious typology. (Typology refers to historical events, persons, and institutions divinely intended to be prefigurative, quite apart from whether or not the authors of the Old Testament were aware of the predictive symbolism.)

Fulfillment Themes   Here is a summary of the main themes of both direct and typological fulfillment in Matthew and the rest of the New Testament: Jesus fulfilled the activities of the LORD himself as described and predicted in the Old Testament (Matt. 1:21; 3:3–4 par.; 11:5 par.; 13:41; 24:31 par.; 27:9–10). Jesus was the foretold messianic king (Matt. 1:23; 2:6, 23; 3:17 par.; 4:15–16; 21:5; 22:44 par.; 26:64 par.), the Isaianic Servant of the LORD (Matt. 3:17 par.; 8:17; 11:5 par.; 12:18–21; 1 Peter 2:22–25), and the Danielic Son of man (Matt. 24:30 par.; 26:64 par.; 28:18). He brought to a climax the line of prophets (Matt. 12:39–40 par.; 13:13–15 par., 35; 17:5 par.; 1 Cor. 10:2; 2 Cor. 3:7–18), the succession of righteous sufferers since Old Testament times (Matt. 21:42 par.; 27:34–35 par., 39 par., 43, 46 par., 48 par.), and the Davidic dynasty (Matt. 12:42 par.). He reversed the work of Adam, who plunged the human race into sin (Matt. 4:1ff. par.; Rom. 5:12; 1 Cor. 15:21–22, 45–49; Heb. 2:5–9; compare Luke 3:38). He fulfilled God's promise to Abraham (Gal. 3:16). Since he was the ideal Israelite, his own personal history recapitulated the national history of Israel (Matt. 2:15, 18; 4:4, 7, 10 par.).

Melchizedek prefigured the priesthood of Christ, as did also, in an inferior and sometimes contrasting way, the Aaronic priesthood (Heb. 7–10). The paschal lamb and other sacrifices symbolized his redemptive death (John 1:29, 36; 19:36; Rom. 3:25; 1 Cor. 5:7; Eph. 5:2; Heb. 9–10; 1 Peter 1:19–21; Rev. 5:6–14), as well as Christian devotion and service (Rom. 12:1; 15:16; Phil. 2:17). Jesus is life-giving bread like the manna (John 6:35; 1 Cor. 10:3), the source of living water like the rock in the desert during Israel's journey from Egypt to Canaan (1 Cor. 10:4; compare John 7:37), the serpent lifted up in the wilderness (John 3:14), and the tabernacle and temple of God's abode among human beings (John 1:14; 2:18–22; compare Col. 1:19).

John the Baptist was the predicted prophetic forerunner of Jesus (Mark 1:2–3). Jesus inaugurated the foretold eschatological period of salvation (John 6:45) and established the new covenant (Heb. 8:8–12; 10:16–17). Judas Iscariot fulfilled the role of the wicked opponents of Old Testament righteous sufferers (Acts 1:20). The church is, or individual Christians are, the new creation (2 Cor. 5:17; Gal. 6:15; Col. 3:10), the spiritual seed of Abraham by incorporation into Christ (Rom. 4:1–25; 9:6–33; Gal. 3:29; 4:21–31; Phil. 3:3), the new Israel (Rom. 9:6–33; 11:17–24; 2 Cor. 6:16; 1 Peter 2:9–10), and the new temple (1 Cor. 3:16; 6:19; 2 Cor. 6:16; Eph. 2:20–22). The Mosaic law prefigured divine grace both positively and negatively (John 1:17; Col. 2:17; Galatians). The Deluge (Noah's flood) stands for the Last Judgment (Matt. 24:37–39 par.) and for baptism (1 Peter 3:20–21). The passage through the Red Sea and the rite of circumcision foreshadowed baptism (1 Cor. 10:2; Col. 2:11–12). Jerusalem stands for the celestial city (Gal. 4:26; Heb. 12:22; Rev. 21:1–22:5). Entrance into Canaan prefigures the entrance of Christians into spiritual rest (Heb. 3:18–4:13). And proclamation of the gospel to all people fulfills God's promise to Abraham and prophetic predictions of Gentile salvation (Acts 2:17–21; 3:25; 13:47; 15:16–18; Rom. 15:9–12, 21).

Text-Plots and Testimony Books

It is worth noting that the pursuit of these themes kept New Testament writers from atomizing the Old Testament. C. H. Dodd pointed out that they drew most of their fulfillment-quotations from a rather limited set of Old Testament passages ("text-plots") considered especially relevant to the new age.[6] Perhaps the early Christians also drew up manuals of Old Testament proof texts, called "testimony books" by modern scholars. Something like a testimony book has appeared among the Dead Sea Scrolls, but of course it is not Christian in orientation. Apparently the early church learned a new and holistic way of interpreting the Old Testament from Jesus himself (compare Luke 24:27).

Textual Traditions

The Septuagint provided a textual base for most of the Old Testament quotations, but variations are often evident. Matthew in particular appears to have utilized the Hebrew text of the Old

6. C. H. Dodd, According to the Scriptures *(London: Nisbet, 1961).*

Testament, the Targums, and other textual traditions in addition to the Septuagint.[7]

Historicity   Sometimes it is argued that the early Christians massively invented incidents in the life of Jesus to obtain "fulfillments" of supposed messianic prophecies. It is true that the evangelists often borrow Old Testament phraseology in describing the events of Jesus' career. But the allusions to Old Testament texts are usually far too fleeting for those texts to have formed the basis of free invention of dominical tradition. Furthermore, many of the quoted Old Testament passages are so obscure that they could hardly have been the source for corruption of that tradition. The Old Testament quotations appear to be later additions to the tradition concerning Jesus. The tradition came first, the recognition of correspondences to ancient prophecy and typology later.

Jesus'
Genealogy   Matthew appeals to his Jewish Christian reading audience by starting his gospel with a genealogy of Jesus which reaches back into the Old Testament, highlights Abraham, father of the Jewish people, and King David, prototype of the messianic king expected by the Jews, leads through David's royal descendants, and emphasizes the identity of Jesus as the Christ. *Read Matthew 1:1–17.* Comparison with the Old Testament shows that Matthew deliberately omits three generations of Davidic kings to get three sets of fourteen generations each. These fourteens put a triple emphasis on David as prototype of the messianic king, Jesus, because David appears in fourteenth place on the genealogical list and because the numerical values of the Hebrew consonants in his name add up to fourteen: d (4) + v (6) + d (4) = D[a]v[i]d (14). (Matthew writes before the invention of Arabic numerals and before the introduction of vowels into written Hebrew.) The third set of fourteen numbers only thirteen unless one counts Mary the mother of Jesus as well as Joseph his foster father, as is perhaps intended because Jesus was born of Mary, with Joseph providing the legal but not the biological lineage. (In Jewish society of the time, legal rights passed through a father, even a foster father, not through a mother, even a biological mother.) The unusual appearance of four women on the list prior to Mary supplements its Jewishness with a Gentile element, for three

---

7. *See* K. Stendahl, The School of St. Matthew and Its Use of the Old Testament *(Philadelphia: Fortress, 1968);* R. H. Gundry, The Use of the Old Testament in St. Matthew's Gospel *(Leiden: Brill, 1967), for technical studies.*

of them were Gentiles (Tamar, Rahab, and Ruth) and the fourth the wife of a Gentile (and thus called "the wife of Uriah" rather than by her Jewish name "Bathsheba"). This Gentile element points forward to the discipling of all nations at the end of Matthew (28:18–20).

Matthew tells the nativity story from the standpoint of Joseph. *The Nativity* Mary conceives Jesus by the Holy Spirit during her engagement to Joseph. In Jewish culture of the time, engagement was so binding that people called the engaged couple husband and wife, only divorce or death could break the engagement, and in case of death the survivor became a widow or widower. So on learning of Mary's pregnancy, Joseph resolves to divorce her privately; but a message from an angel of the Lord leads him to marry her instead. As a result and because of Joseph's descent from David, Jesus is born into a Davidic family and considered legally qualified to inherit David's throne. Joseph's naming Jesus indicates an acceptance of Jesus as his legal son. *Read Matthew 1:18–25.* "By the Holy Spirit" (1:18) echoes phrases used of women in 1:3, 5 (twice), 6, 16 and therefore shows that in contrast to pagan myths, according to which male gods have sexual intercouse with human mothers-to-be, the Holy Spirit does *Virgin Birth* not play the sexual role of a male: there is no carnal intercourse. Nor does Joseph have intercourse with Mary until after she gives birth to Jesus. It is disputed whether Joseph resolves to divorce Mary because he thinks her unfaithful and wants to obey the law (compare Deut. 22:23–24) or because he knows her to have conceived by the Holy Spirit and wants not to intrude. Favoring suspicion is the angel's telling him that she has conceived by the Holy Spirit, as though Joseph has not known this fact before. In either case, Matthew portrays him as a model of righteousness, mercy, and obedience. By popular etymology, "Jesus," Greek form of the Hebrew name "Joshua," means "Yahweh (the LORD) is salvation." The peo- *Immanuel* ple whom Jesus will save from their sins are those who in the words of Isaiah 7:14, which Matthew quotes as fulfilled, will call his name "Immanuel," that is, who will recognize that he is "God with us" (compare 28:18–20).

The story of the Magi portrays these astrologers from the East, *The Magi* probably Persia, as the vanguard of many other Gentiles who will acknowledge Jesus as the Christ (again compare 28:18–20, but also 8:10–12). *Read Matthew 2:1–12.* Bethlehem comes into the picture as the town of Jesus' birth, just as it was the town of David's origin. In accordance with Micah 5:2, the messianic king is born in the town of King David. And whatever the astronomical or nonastronomical truth (a conjunction of planets or of a planet and a star, a comet, a supernova, etc.), the star of the messianic king recalls the star of David (Num. 24:17). Herod the Great fears a rival in the making; Jerusalem sides with him in anticipation of Jesus' later rejection in that city. The Magi's worshiping Jesus and offering him gifts suit his being "God with us." The three kinds of gifts they offer do not necessarily indicate the number of the Magi.

The Slaughter of the Innocents and the Flight to Egypt

Read Matthew 2:13–23. Herod's attempt to kill the infant Christ anticipates the actual killing of the adult Christ. Herod was infamous for his cruelty. The flight to Egypt and return fulfill Hosea 11:1, which originally referred to Israel's Exodus from Egypt, where God had treated them as his son by preserving them from famine, just as now God treats Jesus as his Son by preserving him there. Traditionally called "The Slaughter of the Innocents," the killing of male children under two in and around Bethlehem fulfills Jeremiah 31:15, which originally referred to the weeping of Jewish mothers on seeing their offspring taken to exile in Babylon. The residence of the holy family in Nazareth fulfills various prophecies that call the Messiah a branch or shoot, one Hebrew word for which is *netzer*,

Nazareth–Nazarene

which sounds something like "Nazareth" (Isa. 11:1; also Jer. 23:5; 33:15; Zech. 3:8). The Babylonian exile cut the tree of David's dynasty down to a stump; but out of that stump of a dynasty grows a branch or shoot, reviving the dynasty in the Messiah descended from David. The very name *Nazareth* encodes this outgrowth.

The Baptist's Preaching

Read Matthew 3:1–17. "Those days" (3:1) refers to the days of residence in Nazareth (2:23). Matthew emphasizes John the Baptist's preaching of repentance and of judgment. In the phrase "kingdom of heaven," which appears often in Matthew but nowhere else in the New Testament, "heaven" substitutes for "God" to put an accent on majesty and universality (compare Dan. 4:1–37). Wheat means kernels of wheat and stands for repentant people. Chaff means husks and straw and stands for the unrepentant. After the treading of oxen on a threshing floor has loosened the wheat from the husks and ground up the straw, a farmer scoops up the mixture, throws it into the air, and lets wind blow the chaff to one side. The gathering of wheat into a granary represents salvation by baptism in the Holy Spirit. The burning of chaff with unquenchable fire represents judgment by baptism in fire. Because of Jesus' superiority as

An aerial view of Nazareth. Located in lower Galilee, Nazareth was the hometown of Joseph and Mary, and it was here that Jesus spent his childhood and grew up to manhood.

the baptizer in the Holy Spirit and fire, John tries not to baptize Jesus; but Jesus' insistence makes him an example for his disciples to follow in baptism—without delay ("now," 3:15; compare 28:19); for baptism is the entirely right thing to do (the meaning of "fulfills all righteousness"). "This is my beloved Son, in whom I am well pleased" confirms to John that it was the right thing: God has taken pleasure in Jesus because of his baptism.

Jesus' Baptism

Matthew details three temptations of Jesus by the devil. The first two urge Jesus to take personal advantage of his being God's beloved Son, as stated in the preceding story. But Jesus resists these temptations, and the third temptation as well, by citing Scripture. Thus he becomes the model of postbaptismal obedience to the law (compare 28:19). *Read Matthew 4:1–11.* "Devil" is Greek for the Hebrew "Satan." The terms mean "accuser" with respect to bringing before God accusations against his people. The devil tempts in the

The Temptation

hope of being able to accuse. To tempt is to test, sometimes with hardship, at other times with enticement, and at yet other times with both. The first temptation rests on a similarity in appearance between stones and loaves of bread. The second temptation, located in Jerusalem, urges a publicity stunt; for the wilderness has many precipices off which Jesus might have jumped but for the lack of onlookers. "The pinnacle of the temple" may refer to the southeast corner of the temple courts dropping off into the Kidron Valley, to the lintel atop the temple gate, or to the roof of the temple proper. The devil's quotation of Psalm 91:11–12 omits "to guard you in all your ways" because that phrase points to accidental stumbling over a stone in one's path rather than to a deliberate throwing of oneself from a high perch, as the devil is tempting Jesus to do. Given Jesus' identity as "God with us" (1:23), the devil can only leave when at the close of the third temptation Jesus tells him to be gone.

Jesus withdraws to Galilee on hearing of John the Baptist's arrest and then starts to preach, teach, heal, and make disciples in this region known for its Gentiles, which means "nations," in addition to its Jewish population. The withdrawal makes Jesus a model of fleeing persecution so as to preach and make disciples elsewhere, as his disciples are to do among all the nations (see 10:23 with 28:18–20). *Read Matthew 4:12–25.*

Sermon on the Mount Now Jesus ascends a mountain, takes the seated position of a teacher, and teaches his disciples. Since he is "God with us" (1:23) and human beings are to live "on every word that comes out of the mouth of God" (4:4), what comes out of Jesus' mouth when he opens it is the very words of God, like the law of God given through Moses on Mount Sinai, only perfecting that law. *Read Matthew 5:1–16.* The series of statements beginning with the word "blessed" are known as the Beatitudes. "Blessed" does not mean "happy," as is sometimes said mistakenly; for those who mourn are not happy. Otherwise they would not be mourning. "Blessed" means "congratulations to" and reflects God's estimate rather than human emotion. The Beatitudes promise compensation at the Last Judgment for disciples inwardly desperate, mournful, nonretaliatory, longing for divine vindication, merciful, pure, peacemaking, and righteous in the *Salt* face of persecution. "The salt of the earth" means salt used in carefully measured amounts to fertilize soil and symbolizes the witness given to the world by the good works of Jesus' disciples, though the

Judean wilderness southeast of Jerusalem.

failure of false disciples to persevere in such works brings irreversible judgment, like the throwing away of salt that has lost its saltiness through adulteration or leaching. "The light of the world" means the sun, here an additional symbol, along with a lamp, for the witness given to the world by the good works of Jesus' disciples. *Light*

After affirming the complete validity of the Law and the Prophets, the two sections of the Old Testament read in synagogues every Sabbath, Jesus contrasts his teaching with that of the Old Testament, not by way of denying that teaching, as the traditional designation "Antitheses" implies, but by way of escalating it to a level toward which it was already tending. The prohibition of murder escalates to a prohibition of anger and abusive speech and a command to reconciliation; the prohibition of adultery to a prohibition of lust; the command to give a divorced wife a certificate of divorce (to protect her from the false charge of desertion) to warnings against making a divorcee commit adultery in marrying another man out of economic necessity and against committing *The Antitheses*

View from the Sea of Galilee toward the Horns of Hattin. This traditional site of the Sermon on the Mount is generally known as the Mount of Beatitudes.

adultery by marrying a divorcee; the command to avoid false vows and keep oaths to a prohibition of all oaths; the command that penalties suit rather than exceed crimes (the *lex talionis,* or law of retaliation: "an eye for an eye . . ." in contrast with ancient law codes that imposed severe penalties for minor crimes) to a requirement of meekness and helpfulness; and the command to love your neighbor and hate your enemy (see Ps. 139:21–22 for the latter) to a command to love your enemies and pray for your persecutors. *Read Matthew 5:17–48.* The exception of immorality in 5:32 allows a man to divorce his wife if she has had sex with another man, for then the divorce arises out of immorality instead of issuing in it.[8] Being forced to go one mile in 5:41 reflects the practice of the

8. *Some think that immorality here means incest, such as the Mosaic law prohibits (Lev. 18:6–18) but Gentiles sometimes practice.*

Romans, especially Roman soldiers, in requisitioning their subjects to carry baggage for them.

Comparisons with the Old Testament now fade into the distance and Jesus teaches as a sage. He warns against showiness in religious practice, particularly in giving charity, praying, and fasting. *Read Matthew 6:1–18*. The reward of human praise is all the reward that those who seek such praise will get. Not letting your left hand know *Charity* what your right hand does in giving charity means slipping a gift to a beggar unobtrusively with the right hand alone rather than offering it with both hands extended so as to attract the attention of onlookers. The Lord's Prayer, or *Pater Noster* (Latin for the first words of *The Lord's* the prayer: "Our Father"), stands here as an example of praying *Prayer* with an economy of words as opposed to the heaping up of empty phrases in pagan prayers. "Our debts" are moral debts owed to God, that is, our sins. Forgiving our debtors may refer to forgiving financial debts at the Year of Jubilee (Lev. 25:8–55). "Do not lead us into temptation" does not ask to avoid temptation, but means, "Do not let us succumb to temptation." The last petition should probably read, "but deliver us from the evil one," in reference to Satan. The familiar doxology, "For thine is the kingdom and the power and the glory forever," does not appear in the earliest and best manuscripts. By pouring ashes over their heads the hypocrites make their faces disappear to appear to others as fasting (so the wordplay in Matthew's Greek). Ancient Jews do not wash their faces and oil their heads daily for hygienic and cosmetic reasons, but only occasionally for joyous occasions. So Jesus says to mask your fasting, not your face, with the appearance of joy, not with a somber look.

The next section prohibits the building up of earthly wealth and commands the building up of heavenly wealth, because your heart will follow your wealth. This is not to say that building up earthly wealth is wrong if you have a wrong attitude toward it; rather, building it up is wrong because it will in fact produce a wrong attitude. By contrast, building up heavenly wealth draws your heart to heaven. *Read Matthew 6:19–34*. A healthy eye, sparkling like a lighted lamp, stands for generosity; an unhealthy eye, dull with disease, stands for stinginess. "Mammon" (6:24) is Aramaic for *Mammon* "wealth." Since God's righteousness (6:33) contrasts with your (the disciples') righteousness (5:20; 6:1), the righteousness of God that Jesus' persecuted disciples are to seek does not consist in their own good works but in God's doing the right thing by them, that is, caring for them now and rewarding them at the end (compare 5:6).

In 7:1–12 Jesus finishes his description of the righteousness that surpasses that of the scribes and Pharisees (note how "the Law and the Prophets" in 7:12 harks back to "the Law or the Prophets" at the start of this description in 5:17). His prohibition of judgment has to do with respect for other people's profession of discipleship (7:1–5), his prohibition of giving sacrificial meat to dogs and of throwing pearls before pigs with the danger of letting into the community of disciples people who do not even profess discipleship (7:6), and his command to keep the Golden Rule ("Do for others whatever you want others to do for you") with helping one another within that community (7:7–12). *Read Matthew 7:1–12.* Judging means taking it on oneself to declare a fellow disciple false. Only God can make that judgment, and he will make it against those hypocrites who do it themselves without noticing that their own faults exceed the faults of those they are judging. On the other hand, self-criticism will turn an otherwise condemnatory judgment into a kindly act of restoration. In the world of the New Testament most dogs were vicious street-roamers. Therefore, just as such dogs would turn on you if you whetted their appetite with a taste of sacrificial meat carelessly given them, and just as pigs would trample under foot any pearls foolishly thrown before them, so would the imprudent admission of nondisciples into your community expose you to persecution from within. So do not let the nonjudgmentalism necessary to good community go so far as to break down that community by erasing the boundary between it and the world of nondisciples. And God's doing good for you by answering your prayers demands that you do good for one another.

The Sermon on the Mount concludes with warnings not to heed false prophets, but to obey the teachings of Jesus. *Read Matthew 7:13–29.* A narrow mountain road leads to the City of Salvation, impregnable atop its peak. The only way to enter is through a gate easily defended because it is narrow. The narrow road and narrow gate represent the strictures of superior righteousness such as Jesus demands of his disciples. A broad road leads to the City of Destruction, situated on an open plain. Its wide gate accommodates many, but by the same token beckons invaders. The broad road and wide gate represent the lax behavior taught by false prophets and practiced by false disciples. The wise man represents

Golden Rule

Narrow and Broad

178

true disciples. The foolish man represents false disciples. Building on the rock represents obedience to Jesus' teachings. Building on the sand represents disobedience to them. And the storm represents the Last Judgment conducted by Jesus on his disciples. So although lax behavior may exempt you from persecution now, it will subject you to destruction hereafter; but though superior righteousness may expose you to persecution now, it will exempt you from destruction hereafter. *Rock and Sand*

Now Matthew shifts from the teachings of Jesus to three of Jesus' miracles that add the authority of his deeds to that of his words. *Read Matthew 8:1–15.* In cleansing leprosy, Jesus fulfills the law. In healing a centurion's servant, he pronounces believing Gentiles, like the centurion,[9] admitted to the endtime banquet of salvation (the messianic feast), but unbelieving Jews ("the sons of the kingdom" are those who should inherit the kingdom of heaven because they belong to the chosen nation) are thrown out of the banquet hall into the surrounding darkness of judgment. In healing Peter's mother-in-law, Jesus takes the initiative, uses a mere touch, and becomes the object of her service. *Miracles*

Next comes an interlude consisting of a summary, an Old Testament quotation, and two dialogues on discipleship. *Read Matthew 8:16–22.* Jesus' healings fulfill Isaiah 53:4. "Another of his disciples" (8:21) implies that the preceding "scribe" was a disciple, too (see 13:52 for a scribe as a disciple). The first disciple shows his genuineness by expressing a determination to follow Jesus wherever Jesus goes—in an itinerant ministry, as Jesus notes. The second disciple shows his falsity by asking to go and bury his father before starting to follow. Jesus' reply, "Follow me, and let the dead bury their dead," rejects even the most sacred of filial duties (burying your father) in favor of immediate allegiance to Jesus. The dead's burying their dead is not meant to make sense (How could dead people bury one of their own?), but to dismiss the problem of burial altogether. *Discipleship*

A second trio of miracles now comes into view. The first miracle demonstrates Jesus' authority over the natural elements, the second over demons, and the third his authority to forgive sins, an authority he shares with his disciples. *Read Matthew 8:23–9:8.* Matthew identifies the region in which the exorcism takes place by *More Miracles*

---

9. *In the Roman army a centurion commanded one hundred soldiers.*

the name of a city about five miles southeast of the shoreline. The second demoniac is missing in the parallel accounts at Mark 5:1–20; Luke 8.26–39. Do they omit a less obtrusive demoniac, or does Matthew introduce a second demoniac from the story in Mark 1:21–28; Luke 4:31–37, otherwise omitted by him? "The men" to whom 9:8 says God has given authority to forgive sins are "the men," that is, the disciples, who were in a boat with Jesus when he stilled a storm (8:27). Thus they declare sins forgiven and heal people to substantiate the forgiveness just as Jesus does. He is their model of forgiving and healing (compare 16:17; 18:18; John 20:23).

Call of Matthew   Matthew's becoming a disciple and Jesus' instructions on fasting provide another interlude. *Read Matthew 9:9–17.* Some think that Matthew changes "Levi" (Mark 2:14; Luke 5:27, 29) to "Matthew" to gain an apostolic name (compare Matt. 10:3), others that one man bore both names, as sometimes happened. In either case, Jesus' citation of Hosea 6:6, "I [God] want mercy and not sacrifice," makes the call of Matthew an act of mercy toward outcasts such as toll collectors and notorious sinners. The preservation of both wine and wineskins accents the preservation of fasting once Jesus the bridegroom is taken away (compare 6:16–18).

Yet More Miracles   A third trio of miracle stories now comes into the narrative. The first story narrates a double miracle that displays Jesus' authority over the destructive effects of illness and death. The second displays his ability to heal two blind men at once. And the third displays his power to heal and deliver a man doubly afflicted with dumbness and demonic possession. *Read Matthew 9:18–34.* Comparison with Matthew 20:29–34; Mark 10:46–52; Luke 18:35–43 suggests to some that Matthew here introduces a second blind man from Mark 8:22–26, otherwise omitted by him (compare the similar possibility of his having introduced a second demoniac in 8:28–34).

Missions Discourse   Next, a short narrative introduces a long discourse. The narrative stresses Jesus' compassion. Out of this compassion he declares the harvest plentiful but the harvesters few and tells his disciples to ask the harvest master to send out harvesters. The harvest represents evangelism. The harvesters are the twelve apostles, who are to make further disciples by preaching the gospel. And the harvest master is Jesus, sender of the Twelve. In the end, however, they are not said to have gone and no description of their ministry is given (contrast Mark 6:12–13), so that Jesus' lengthy instructions, which shift in midstream from the Jewish setting in Galilee to the Gentile setting of the wider world, become relevant to the evangelistic enterprise of the later Christian church. Just as the Sermon on the Mount taught disciples how to behave, then, this Missions Discourse teaches them how to bear witness. *Read Matthew 9:35–10:42.*

In chapter 10, verses 2–4 identify the harvesters with the twelve apostles. Verses 5–15 tell them how to evangelize Jews living in Galilee. And verses 16–42 warn against persecution in a further mission that will embrace Gentiles, too. Thus, the present restriction to Jews in Galilee (10:5b–6) gives way to a future inclusion of Gentiles elsewhere (10:18), but not at the expense of discontinuing the Jewish mission (10:23). Against self-aggrandizement, Jesus prohibits acquisitions taken from ministry (10:9–10); and he prohibits moving around in a locality to find the most comfortable living quarters (10:11–15). As to persecution, Jesus says to beware of informers, not to worry about preparing statements for court, and to flee from one city to another rather than staying suicidally in a city that poses a threat to life and limb (10:16–23). He also gives reasons not to fear persecution: (1) his own sufferings (10:24–25); (2) the impossibility of hiding the truth (10:26–27); (3) the unimportance of physical martyrdom in comparison with the eternal punishment of a whole person (10:28); (4) the value God puts on Jesus' disciples (10:29–31); (5) the necessity of confessing Jesus before others if one is to be confessed by him before God the Father (10:32–33); (6) the unworthiness of anyone who shrinks back through fear of personal abuse (10:34–39); and (7) the conveying of eternal life to others through self-sacrificial witness (10:40–42).

Having quoted Jesus' warning against persecution, Matthew now *Persecution* gives examples of persecution in John the Baptist, Jesus, and the disciples (11:1–12:50). More specifically, the case of John the Baptist illustrates the violence suffered by the kingdom of heaven (11:1–24). The gentleness of Jesus toward his disciples contrasts with that violence and highlights it (11:25–30). The Pharisees plot the destruction of Jesus (12:1–21) and slander him (12:22–37), but he exposes their wickedness, pronounces judgment on them (12:38–45), and describes the disciples (those who do the will of his heavenly Father and therefore are persecuted for righteousness' sake; see also 5:10–11) as his true family (12:46–52). *Read Matthew 11:1–12:50.*

The mention of John the Baptist's imprisonment suggests that though "the works of the Christ" have excited John's hopes that Jesus is the Coming One predicted by him, the failure of Jesus to rescue him from prison has raised a doubt. Jesus' answer to his question seems to indicate that the works of the Christ are providing sufficient evidence (compare Isa. 35:5–6; 61:1). Jesus' tribute to John includes a statement that the least in the kingdom of heaven is greater than John (11:11b). Since the violence suffered by that kingdom started with the persecution of John, he belongs in the kingdom; so Jesus is not saying that leastness inside the kingdom surpasses greatness outside it. Greatness in the kingdom will be explained in terms of humility at 18:4. Hence, Jesus is saying that the humblest disciple will exceed even John, thus far the greatest human being ever born. The Jews who have responded favorably neither to John nor to Jesus are like children who stubbornly reject each suggestion concerning what game they should play: mock wedding and mock funeral (11:16–19). The parallel between "the works of wisdom" (11:19b) and "the works of the Christ" (11:2) implies that Jesus the Christ is Wisdom personified (compare Matt. 23:34 with Luke 11:49). "Babies" (11:25) represents teachable disciples in contrast with the scribes and Pharisees. Jesus' unique sonship to God the Father receives eloquent expression in 11:25–27 (paralleled in Luke 10:21–22), sometimes called "the Johannine thunderbolt" because it sounds much like statements in the gospel of John concerning the relation of Jesus to God. In what way does Jesus give rest and a light load? Not by demanding less of his disciples than do the scribes and Pharisees, for he demands more (5:20). Rather, by humbly, meekly getting under the other side of the "yoke," a figure of speech for law, and pulling with his disciples (compare 1:23; 28:20).

Johannine Thunderbolt

The priests can break the Sabbath by working in the temple, because the temple is greater than the Sabbath (Num. 28:9–10). The temple is greater than the Sabbath because the Sabbath was made for human beings, the temple for God. Jesus is greater than the temple because the temple is God's dwelling, but Jesus is God's very person with us (again see Matt. 1:23). Another quotation of Hosea 6:6 ("I want mercy and not sacrifice"; compare Matt. 12:7 with 9:13) makes the Pharisees' condemnation of the innocent disciples an instance of merciless persecution. The man with a withered hand is like a sheep fallen into a pit; mercy demands that the

Breaking the Sabbath

Full-grown mustard plant (Sinapis alba L.).

man be healed even on the Sabbath more than it demands that the sheep be lifted out of the pit on the Sabbath (12:11–12). Jesus' withdrawal to escape the Pharisees' plot shows him heeding his own command to flee persecution (10:23) and fulfills Isaiah 42:1–4: he does not seek justice for himself; he proclaims it to the nations and actualizes it for his persecuted disciples (represented by "a bruised reed" and "a smoldering wick," 12:17–21). The person who is against Jesus and scatters is a persecutor (12:30). People's words reveal their character. The Pharisees' speaking blasphemy against the Holy Spirit reveals their rottenness and seals their condemnation (12:22–37).

The sign of Jonah the prophet is Jesus' spending three days and three nights in a tomb just as Jonah spent three days and three nights in the belly of a sea monster (12:39–40). The limit of three implies the Resurrection. Jesus' dying on Good Friday and rising on Easter Sunday might seem to belie "three days and three nights," but Jews often counted part of a twenty-four-hour period as a whole such period (see Gen. 42:17–18; 1 Sam. 30:1, 12–13; 2 Chron. 10:5, 12; Est. 4:16–5:1). Thus part of Friday, all Saturday, and part of Sunday may count for three days and three nights. The last and

Sign of Jonah

Farmer plowing his field.

worst state of the man in Jesus' parable whom an unclean spirit re-possessed with seven other spirits more wicked than himself points ahead to the outburst of evil in the Pharisees' helping to engineer the Passion (21:45–46; 22:15, 34, 41; 27:62). The Father in heaven completes the family of Jesus' persecuted disciples: brother, sister, and mother.

Parabolic Discourse The bulk of chapter 13 contains the third great discourse of Jesus in Matthew, a parabolic one. If the Sermon on the Mount dealt with Christian conduct and the Missions Discourse with Christian witness, the Parabolic Discourse deals with Christian understanding. The many crowds of Jesus' audience appear to represent the mixed church of Matthew's time. The disciples among those crowds appear to represent true believers as opposed to false within that church (13:1–2). As in Mark 4:3–9, the introductory parable of the sower is a parable about parables (13:3–9). Jesus then explains that he speaks in parables because those who lack understanding—that is, false disciples—fall under the judgment of losing understanding (the parables puzzle them) and because those who have understanding—that is, true disciples—get further understanding (the parables inform them; 13:10–23). The middle six parables fall into pairs and all begin with a reference to the kingdom of heaven (13:24–50). The parable of the wheat and the tares[10] emphasizes their separation not until the harvest (13:24–30). The parables of the grown mustard tree and leavened lump of dough form a pair emphasizing magnitude: the kingdom has grown and spread throughout the world (13:31–32, 33).[11] A quotation of Psalm 78:2 as fulfilled interrupts the series of parables (13:34–35). A private explanation of the parable of the wheat and the tares identifies the wheat with true disciples, the tares with false disciples, and so on (13:36–43). Thus the true disciples out of the many crowds of Jesus' audience gain more understanding through the explanation, and also through a second pair of parables concerning a treasure and a pearl, both teaching the joyful sacrifice of everything for the kingdom (13:44, 45–46),[12] and through the sixth parable, concerning good and bad fish,[13] which pairs up with the first of the six to teach the final judgment of false disciples and the final reward of true ones (13:47–50). A concluding parable compares the fully informed, true disciple to a houseowner who pulls out of his closet

---

10. *Tares are darnels, a weed resembling wheat. Ordinarily darnels are weeded out. But here they are so numerous that their roots have intertwined with those of the wheat.*

11. *Three measures of flour amount to about fifty pounds, an immense quantity making a huge lump of dough. Jesus is using hyperbole, exaggeration for emphasis. Some have interpreted the yeast as symbolic of the evil which corrupts Christendom. It is true that elsewhere yeast often stands for evil, but association with the parable of the mustard seed favors interpretation in terms of a contrast between small beginning and large ending. Other figures of speech carry various meanings. For example, salt stands for the witness of good works (Matt. 5:13), judgment (Mark 9:49), peace (Mark 9:50), and graciousness (Col. 4:6). Here, to drive home the point that God's rule is more active and powerful than the rule of Satan, Jesus may have purposefully chosen a figure that usually has an evil connotation. Some have also thought that the birds in the parable of the mustard seed represent false teachers who invade the church. But the phraseology comes from Nebuchadnezzar's dream (Dan 4:12, 21), where the nesting of birds in the branches of a tree indubitably points to the large size of the tree.*

12. *Repeated invasions of Palestine caused fearful people to bury their treasures for safekeeping. Here, the one who buried his treasure seems to have died or been killed. As a result, the treasure is ownerless. The law allowed the discoverer of a treasure to hide it again and purchase the field so as to obtain the treasure legally.*

13. *Seine nets, used to catch fish, are either dragged between two boats or laid out by one boat and drawn to shore with two long ropes. Bad fish consist of those prohibited by the Mosaic law because they lack scales or fins, and also of other marine life considered inedible by Jews.*

treasures of new clothes (new understanding) and old clothes (old understanding, 13:51–52). *Read Matthew 13:1–52.*

Understanding   Preceding parables have stressed the contrast between understanding and lack of understanding. The following block of narratives carries on this same contrast. Jesus' fellow townspeople misidentify him as the carpenter's son, whereas he is the Son of God (2:15; 3:17 et passim). *Read Matthew 13:53–58.* Herod the tetrarch (Antipas) misidentifies Jesus as John the Baptist risen from the dead. *Read Matthew 14:1–12.* Though the disciples have little faith in the feeding of the five thousand, at least they understand that Jesus wants them to distribute the provisions on hand; and to the five thousand men are added an indeterminate number of women and children to produce a church-like throng of families—husbands, wives, and children—eating in anticipation of the Lord's Supper. *Read Matthew 14:13–21.* To the story of Jesus' walking on the water is added the episode of Peter's walking on the water temporarily. This episode reaches its climax in a confessional display of the disciples' understanding Jesus to be God's Son. *Read Matthew 14:22–33.*

On arrival in Gennesaret, Jesus grants his disciples understanding with respect to true defilement. It is not any unclean thing going into the mouth (food) that defiles a person, says Jesus, but evil things coming out of the mouth (words). Thus Jesus transmutes the dietary taboos of the Old Testament into a prohibition of evil speech. *Read Matthew 14:34–15:20.* The figures of being uprooted and of falling into a pit, applied to the Pharisees, represent judgment at the hands of God (15:13–14).

With no concern for ritual purity, Jesus withdraws from his persecutors (Pharisees and scribes from Jerusalem, 15:1) and goes into Gentile territory. There, a Gentile woman shows her understanding of Jesus' true identity by addressing him once with "Son of David" and three times with "Lord" and by worshiping him. In other words, she understands his universal deity as well as his Jewish messiahship.[14] Her understanding generates faith so strong that it surmounts the obstacles of his silence, the disciples' antagonism, the

---

14. To be sure, "Lord" sometimes carries the weak meaning of "Sir"; but in Matthew's gospel the portrayal of Jesus as "God with us" (1:23; compare 18:20; 28:20), the sandwiching of Jesus as Son between God the Father and the Holy Spirit in a baptismal formula (28:19), and the substitution of Jesus' "I" for "God" (compare 28:20 with 1:23) all demand that when applied to Jesus, "Lord" connotes deity.

limitation of his commission to the Jews, and his refusal. *Read Matthew 15:21–28.*

"And they glorified the God of Israel" (15:31) shows that the four thousand whom Jesus now feeds are Gentiles. Together then with the preceding Gentile woman and, earlier, the centurion and the Magi, they represent the great mass of Gentiles who are flocking into the church of Matthew's time. And the disciples understand Jesus' intention that they should distribute bread to the crowd. As in the feeding of the five thousand, wives and children are added to portray a church-like throng of families eating in anticipation of the Lord's Supper. *Read Matthew 15:29–39.* Magadan is obscure but apparently located on the west side of the Sea of Galilee.

Gentiles

Back in Galilee, the Pharisees and Sadducees renew their persecution of Jesus. He excoriates them for their failure to understand the signs of the times, that is, his miracles and exorcisms. Then he grants his disciples understanding of the evil teaching of the Pharisees and Sadducees. *Read Matthew 16:1–12.*

Near Caesarea Philippi, Peter displays his understanding of Jesus' identity as the Christ, the Son of the living God. Jesus attributes this understanding to a revelation by his heavenly Father to Peter. *Read Matthew 16:13–20.* Peter's "the Son of the living God" echoes the disciples' "God's Son" in 14:33. "Barjonas" means "son of Jonah" and alludes to "the sign of Jonah," that is, Jesus' death, burial, and resurrection (12:39–40; 16:4). "Flesh and blood" means human beings as characterized by ignorance, frailty, mortality, and so forth. "Peter" (*petros* in Greek) means "stone." But Jesus' wordplaying statement, "and on this rock [*petra* in Greek] I will build my church," has received a variety of interpretations. If the Aramaic "Cephas" underlies Matthew's Greek, a distinction between *petros* and *petra* may not hold, and Jesus may be saying that he will make Peter, prince of the apostles, the rock-foundation of his church (whether by himself or in conjunction with the other apostles [compare Eph. 2:20], whether for the period of his lifetime alone, or in perpetuity through papal successors). On the other hand, one might have expected to read, "You are Peter [that is, 'stone' or 'rock'], and on you I will build my church." The switch from "you" to "this rock" suggests that Peter himself is not the foundation, but that the meaning of his name points to another entity as the foundation— say, Jesus as the one whom Peter has just confessed him to be, the Christ and Son of the living God (compare 1 Cor. 3:11), or the

Peter and the Rock

truth of that confession (compare 1 Tim. 3:15), or the teachings of Jesus (see 7:24–25, where "these words of mine" form the foundation-rock [*petra*, as here] on which a wise man builds his house).

The Gates of Hades

"The gates of Hades [hell]" means the power of death. The prominence of persecution in Matthew suggests death by martyrdom: the slaying of Christians will not overpower the church. Keys represent authority to open or close; binding and loosing represent forbidding and allowing. But it is disputed what churchly activity these figures of speech refer to: (1) providing and denying entrance into the church according to people's response to the gospel; (2) providing such entrance first to Jews and then to Gentiles, as Peter did on the day of Pentecost and later in the house of Cornelius (Acts 2, 10); (3) forgiving and not forgiving sins, as in the practice of Roman Catholic priests; (4) establishing rules of conduct for church order and discipline, that is, closing the door against some behavior—binding it up as prohibited—and opening the door to other behavior—unbinding it as allowable; and (5) accepting and rejecting professing disciples who under persecution have denied Jesus and later want to reenter the church.

Binding and Loosing

Passion Prediction

Next, Jesus increases the disciples' understanding by informing them of his coming death and resurrection and of the necessity that any would-be followers risk their lives by open discipleship. *Read Matthew 16:21–28.* Even in rebuking Jesus, Peter manages to address him with "Lord" and wish him God's mercy. As toward the close of the Sermon on the Mount, Jesus portrays himself as the final judge of all humanity; and the clause, "until they see the Son of man coming in his kingdom," makes the following transfiguration of Jesus a preview of the Second Coming.

Transfiguration

In Jesus' transfiguration and a following conversation with him, the disciples Peter, James, and John gain understandings of him as the new and greater Moses and of John the Baptist as Elijah. *Read Matthew 17:1–13.* Jesus' face shines as that of Moses shone in consequence of his meeting with God on Mount Sinai (Ex. 34:29–30). But as "God with us," Jesus is greater than Moses; so his face shines "like the sun." Peter again addresses him with "Lord," and the three disciples fall on their faces in extreme fear. On the way down the mountain the disciples also show that they already understand Jesus' coming death and resurrection; and they gain new understanding that although Elijah has yet to come and restore all things after

Jesus' sufferings, Elijah has already come in the person of John the Baptist, whose sufferings previewed those of Jesus.

The disciples' increased understanding needs supplementing by *Little Faith* larger faith; so the following story of an exorcism at the base of the Mount of Transfiguration ends with Jesus' criticism of little faith. *Read Matthew 17:14–20.* Again Jesus predicts his death and resurrection. The disciples' deep grief at this prediction shows that they understand it. *Read Matthew 17:22–23.* An annual tax was levied on male Jews over nineteen years old, wherever they lived, even in the Diaspora, for upkeep of the temple and its services. *Read Matthew 17:24–27.* Peter understands that Jesus pays the tax, but gains fur- *Peter's Penny* ther understanding from him both that he and Jesus are exempt and that to avoid giving offense to other Jews he and Jesus will nevertheless pay the tax. The stater to be found in a fish's mouth is worth two double drachmas and thus sufficient to pay the tax of Peter as well as of Jesus. The argument for exemption—namely, that kings do not tax their princely sons—implies that Jesus and Peter (and other disciples) belong to the royalty of the kingdom, whose king owns the temple for which the present tax is being collected.

The fourth of Jesus' discourses in Matthew deals with Christian *Discourse on* community. The kingdom of heaven provides the framework for *Christian* this community. Entry requires childlikeness (18:1–3). Humility de- *Community* fines childlikeness (18:4). Acceptance of childlike disciples entails the acceptance of Jesus himself (18:5), but causing one of these little people (that is, childlike disciples) to stumble (that is, probably, to apostatize, to forsake the Christian faith) brings judgment on oneself (18:6–7). One also needs self-discipline to keep from stumbling oneself (again, probably, from apostatizing, 18:8–9). The heavenly Father wants straying (that is, sinning) little people in the church not to be despised, but to be restored if possible through personal reproof, church discipline, and prayer (18:10–20; compare similar rules for community life at Qumran according to the Damascus Document 9:2 and the Manual of Discipline 6:1). And a wronged disciple must forgive an offending fellow disciple, repeatedly if necessary (18:21–35). *Read Matthew 18:1–35.* "Their angels in heaven" (18:10) has been used for the doctrine of guardian angels, but such angels would seemingly need to accompany their charges rather than staying in heaven.

"Seventy seven times" (or, alternatively translated, "seventy times *Forgiveness* seven") means any number of times (contrast such forgiveness with

Double drachma, used to pay the temple tax.

the seventy-sevenfold vengeance of which Lamech boasted in Gen. 4:24). "Ten thousand" is the highest number in Greek, "talent" the highest unit of money. Ten thousand talents translates into more than fifteen years of wages for a manual laborer. The unrealism of a king's loaning so much money to a slave emphasizes the enormity of a human being's debt of sin to God and makes the proposed repayment by a mere sale of the slave's wife and children ironic (as well as shocking, for Jews prohibited the sale of wives), his promise to repay everything (given the king's patience) absurd, the king's forgiveness of the debt extravagant, and the slave's throttling and imprisoning a fellow slave to get repayment of a comparatively small debt (one hundred denarii, amounting to about four months' wages) outrageous. The torture to which the king subjects the unforgiving slave stands for eternal punishment and implies the falsity of a disciple who does not genuinely forgive a fellow disciple. "Until he should repay all the debt" implies the eternality of the punishment, since the unforgiving slave cannot hope to pay all. People are not really sorry for their own sins against God if they do not forgive the sins of others against them. Forgiveness must be worked out as well as received. Not to work it out indicates a failure not only to appreciate God's mercy, but also a failure to appropriate it.

Divorce and Remarriage   On his way to Jerusalem, Jesus now arrives in southern Transjordan where some Pharisees put him to the test on a question of interpretation disputed by their rabbis: Does the Mosaic law allow a man to divorce his wife for any reason at all (so Rabbi Hillel and his followers) or only for reason of immorality on her part (so

Rabbi Shammai and his followers; see Deut. 24:1, and especially the enigmatic phrase "something objectionable about her" [NRSV]). Whereas the Pharisees say that Moses commanded divorce, Jesus says that Moses only permitted it. *Read Matthew 19:1–12.* The disciples' reaction that Jesus' teaching makes it better not to marry at all suggests that they understand him to allow an exception for immorality only with respect to divorce, not with respect to remarriage (compare 5:31–32, where remarriage of the husband goes unmentioned though the exception of his wife's immorality is mentioned). If so and if they understand Jesus correctly, he redefines divorce as a dissolution of marriage without the right to remarry. His following statement about eunuchs—those born such, those made such by their captors or masters, and those who make themselves such— seems to describe in terms of eunuchry the single life of a man who has divorced his wife because of her immorality and, for the sake of the kingdom, has not remarried. Otherwise Jesus would be talking about self-castration.

Eunuchry

Just as the preceding narrative carried on the theme of communal life to which the discourse in chapter 18 was devoted, so again a topic of communal life comes up in narrative: the acceptance of children into the church. The disciples' rebuke of the children who come to Jesus rests on a general disdain of children in antiquity. Acting as a foil to the children who come to Jesus is a rich young man who went away from him. "If you wish to be perfect" also means "if you wish to be mature" and alludes to the rich man's youth. This perfection or maturity refers to discipleship as such, not to a higher-than-usual level of discipleship. *Read Matthew 19:13–26.*

Perfection

In contrast with the departed rich young man, notes Peter, he and his fellow disciples have left everything to follow Jesus. Then Peter asks what will be their compensation. Jesus' answer contains no rebuke, but takes Peter's note at face value and promises that at the renewal of Israel the Twelve will sit enthroned, judging the twelve tribes. *Read Matthew 19:27–20:16.* Jesus' promise to the Twelve casts them as "the first," that is, as the original Jewish disciples. "The last" would then seem to be Gentiles discipled at a later time (compare the movement in chapter 10 from Jewish mission to Gentile mission and Jesus' sending the apostles to disciple all the nations in 28:18–20). As a whole, then, this section teaches the ungrudging acceptance of Gentile latecomers into Jesus' community by Jewish

Vineyards in the hills near Jerusalem.

Laborers in a Vineyard early comers. "The third hour" in the parable of workers in the vineyard is the third after dawn (9:00 A.M.), the sixth hour the sixth after dawn (noon), and so on. Those hired at the eleventh hour (5:00 P.M.) worked for only an hour. A denarius represents the normal daily wage of a manual worker. Since every day is payday, the employer instructs his foreman to give the workers their money— but to everyone a full day's wage and in reverse order, the last being paid first. Ordinarily those who worked all day would be paid first and would leave before seeing that the latecomers are receiving an equal amount. But Jesus introduces an unrealistic feature to bring out the point of the parable in an argument that ensues: just as the employer is not being unfair to those who worked all day (they receive a full wage according to contract), but only generous to the latecomers in order that they may receive a liveable wage (any less

An aerial view of Jerusalem from the east.

would fall below subsistence), so God grants his grace to the undeserving out of sheer munificence.

The theme of Christian community proceeds with narratives concerning acceptance of the blind, the lame, and children. The section starts with Jesus' ascent to Jerusalem and ends with arrival there. He again predicts his death and resurrection (20:17–19), answers a request for special honor by pointing to his service to others (20:20–28), and exemplifies such service by giving sight to two blind men (20:29–34) and entering Jerusalem and the temple to heal the blind and the lame and to defend the children who praise him there. *Read Matthew 20:17–21:17.* With the two blind men in 20:29–34, compare those in 9:27–31. Does Matthew repeat the → *I don't think so. They are conflicting details.* story for emphasis? The earlier passage stresses Jesus' ability; the present passage, in tune with the overarching theme of Christian community, his compassion. The story of the Triumphal Entry emphasizes Jesus' gentleness—again in tune with the overarching

The Triumphal Entry

193

theme of Christian community—but also his kingship, as underscored by the quotation of Isaiah 62:11; Zechariah 9:9 as fulfilled by the doubling of the animals and by the crowd's acclaiming Jesus to be "the Son of David." There was an expectation that the messianic king would reveal himself as such at the Passover season, as here; and Zechariah 14:1–11 prophesies the LORD's establishing his kingdom from the Mount of Olives, the very starting point of the Triumphal Entry. It is as a prophet, too, that Jesus cleanses the temple and heals blind and lame people right in the temple (contrast their exclusion from the palace in 2 Sam. 5:8). The episode contains further quotations of the Old Testament, more specifically, of Psalm 118:26–27; Isaiah 56:7; Jeremiah 7:11; Psalm 8:2 (all except the last contained also in one or more of the other gospels).

Cleansing the Temple

The sandwiching of the cursing and withering of a fig tree (21:18–22) between confrontations of Jesus with members of the Sanhedrin (21:15–17; 23:1ff.) makes the fate of the fig tree symbolic of God's coming judgment on the Jewish leaders. In the following confrontation Jesus tells three parables condemning those leaders. They are like the son who says he will work for his father but does not (21:28–32), like the tenant farmers who kill the owner's son (21:33–46), and like those who refuse a wedding invitation, go about their own activities, mistreat and kill the invitation-bearers, and receive a due judgment of destruction (22:1–14). *Read Matthew 21:18–22:14.*

Cursing and Withering of a Fig Tree

The impudence of the son who at first refuses to obey comes out in his nonuse of the respectful address, "Sir," whereas the son who says he will obey uses this address. Contrasting with the ultimately disobedient son, but taking after the repentant and finally obedient one, are the toll collectors and prostitutes who are entering the kingdom (21:32).The destruction of the tenant farmers is accompanied by the transfer of God's kingdom "to another nation producing its fruits" (21:43), that is, to the church portrayed as a new chosen nation. The evil and the good people who are gathered into the wedding feast represent false and true disciples (22:10), and the man not wearing a wedding garment stands out as representative of the false. A wedding garment is probably a newly washed garment symbolizing good works as proof that one's discipleship is true. The king's inspection represents the Last Judgment. The many who are called are the masses in a large, mixed church; the few who are chosen are those found to be true.

Two Sons

Tenant Farmers

Wedding Feast

The introduction to a question of paying tax to Caesar reveals *Questions* Matthew's point of emphasis: the wicked purpose of the Pharisees to trap Jesus into saying something they can use against him. *Read Matthew 22:15–22.* The conclusion to the Sadducees' question concerning resurrection reveals Matthew's point of emphasis: the overwhelming impact of Jesus' teaching. *Read Matthew 22:23–33.* The introduction to a question of the greatest commandment in the law reveals Matthew's point of emphasis: the plotting of the Pharisees against Jesus and the Satanic role of one of their lawyers in testing (that is, tempting) Jesus (compare Mark 1:13). *Read Matthew 22:34–40.* The conclusion to a question of the Christ's Davidic sonship reveals Matthew's point of emphasis: Jesus' victory in verbal combat. *Read Matthew 22:41–46.*

Chapters 23–25 make up the fifth and last great discourse of *Last* Jesus in Matthew. It balances the first discourse, the Sermon on the *Discourse* Mount, in its length, in its association with a mountain, in Jesus' taking the seated position of a teacher (so also for the middle discourse, 13:1), in the contrast between woes here and beatitudes there, and in closing judgmental scenes, each of which includes the addressing of Jesus as "Lord" by the condemned. Throughout the present discourse runs a note of warning. The discourse starts with a prohibition of honorific titles in the church. *Read Matthew 23:1–12.* That this prohibition has to do with church life is shown by references to the Christ as sole teacher of the addressed and to them as brothers in the family of the heavenly Father. The seat of Moses is the chair in the synagogue on which scribes sat when expounding the Mosaic law. To the extent that they communicate that law, says Jesus, do what they say. But do not follow their example of disobeying the law. The heavy loads they lay on people's shoulders are not interpretations of the law, for Jesus has judged those interpretations too light (5:20; 15:3–9). The heavy loads consist of the scribes' and Pharisees' demands for recognition (23:5–7). The phylacteries which they broaden for religious show are amulets inscribed with Mosaic texts and worn on hand and forehead (compare Ex. 13:9, 16; Deut. 6:8; 11:18). The tassels which they lengthen for religious show are fringes of blue cord commanded by Moses to be sewn on the four corners of cloaks as reminders of the law (Num. 15:38–39; Deut. 22:12). As noted before, "rabbi" means "my great one."

Next come seven woes against the scribes and Pharisees for their *Woes Against Scribes* hypocrisy, which means acting in the sense of pretending, and a *and Pharisees* lament by Jesus over Jerusalem. *Read Matthew 23:13–39.* Behind the scribes' and Pharisees' teaching on oaths lies the rationale that a creditor cannot place a lien on the temple or the altar because they belong to God. They provide no surety; so if a debtor swears in the name of the temple or of the altar to pay back his creditor, the oath is meaningless. It is not in the creditor's power to seize the temple or the altar if the debtor fails to pay. But if the debtor swears by the gold that he has dedicated for future offering to the temple or the altar and does not pay his debt, the creditor can seize that gold. According to Jesus, the making of such a distinction countenances untruthful oaths. Mint, anise, and cummin are small herbs used for seasoning and medicine. Gnats and camels are the smallest and largest of Palestinian animal life, both of them ritually unclean according to the law of Moses. The Pharisees strained wine through a piece of cloth or a fine wicker basket to ensure that they did not swallow an unclean insect when drinking the wine. Here, straining out a gnat represents the doing of small duties to gain a reputation for piety; and swallowing a camel represents the neglect of large duties to avoid the sacrifice entailed by them. "Fill up then the measure of your fathers" (23:32) gives an ironic command: "Go ahead and kill me, as you are going to do. You will be imitating your murderous ancestors, not repudiating them as you now pretend to do." Since it is Jesus who sends the prophets, sages, and scribes in 23:34, they must be his disciples portrayed as such. "From the blood of Abel . . . to the blood of Zechariah . . ." means "from the first martyr in the Old Testament to the last," because the Hebrew Bible starts with Genesis, which speaks of Abel's martyrdom, but ends with 2 Chronicles, which speaks of Zechariah's martyrdom (24:20–22). "Your house" (23:38) may refer to the temple in anticipation of Jesus' leaving it and predicting its destruction (24:1–2). Galilean pilgrims shouted, "Blessed is he who comes in the name of the Lord," as Jesus rode toward Jerusalem (21:9); so the same shout by Jerusalemites is reserved for the Second Coming and may imply a happy reception (compare the regeneration of Israel in 19:28; also Rom. 11:25–27).

The Course of This Age   The narrative interruptions in 24:1, 3 are similar to those in 13:10; 18:21. *Read Matthew 24:1–14.* The disciples ask Jesus not only for the time of the destruction of the temple, but also for the sign of his coming (*parousia*, a Greek word often brought over into English for the Second Coming) and of the end of the age. His answer starts with a prediction of events that will not signal that coming and end. False Christs, wars, famines, earthquakes, and such like belong to the normal course of events. Particularly noteworthy are apostasy, treachery, laxity, and lovelessness in the church because of persecution. To save their necks, some will give up their Christian profession. Others will curry favor with persecutors by betraying fellow disciples to them. Others will live so loosely as to avoid being recognized as Christian. And mutual suspicion in the church will chill mutual love. Yet persecution will have the beneficial effect of scattering evangelists throughout the world.

Now Jesus tells what will signal his coming and the end. *Read Matthew 24:15–31.* A necessity of fleeing the abomination of desolation on the Sabbath would pose difficulty and danger in the suspension of services to travelers and in exposure to capture because of others' not traveling. To counteract the claims of false prophets to have had private contacts with Christ in the isolation of the wilderness or in the secrecy of city hideouts, emphasis falls on the universal visibility of Jesus' coming. It will take place in the sky, where people will see him as easily as they see vultures circling over a carcass. "The sign of the Son of man" (24:30) differs from the sign of his coming and of the end (24:3), which referred to the abomination of desolation (24:15), and refers to the universal visibility of Jesus at his coming.

The emphasis on visibility carries over to the seeing of events predicted to signal Jesus' coming, events compared to the leafing of a fig tree. *Read Matthew 24:32–51.* "Eating and drinking, marrying [what men do] and giving in marriage [what fathers do with their daughters]" does not refer to gluttony, drunkenness, and serial marriages, but to normal human activity that shows unawareness of Jesus' coming soon. So also with respect to men's working in the field and women's grinding at the mill. Despite the danger of incurring persecution of themselves, true church leaders will feed refugees from persecution and get an appropriate reward. False church leaders will mistreat their fellow disciples, squander resources on their own and friends' selfish pleasures, and receive an appropriate punishment.

Read Matthew 25:1–13. The bridegroom and his friends went to the bride's home to escort her to the groom's home, where the wedding festivities take place. The delay until midnight is probably due to insistence by the bride's family that the groom and his family

The Ten Virgins

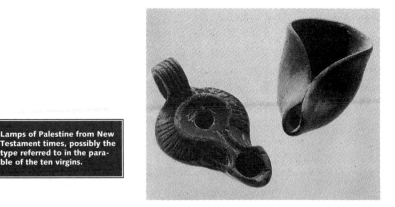

Lamps of Palestine from New Testament times, possibly the type referred to in the parable of the ten virgins.

give a larger dowry (wedding gift). Such insistence shows the reluctance of the bride's family to give up their daughter and compliments the groom for his choice of such an outstanding young woman, one who deserves the larger dowry. The lamps of the ten virgins are either torches wrapped with rags that have to be soaked repeatedly in oil, or copper fire vases filled with pitch, oil, and rags for burning, or clay bowls with spouts, a wick, and olive oil for fuel. The lamps need to be kept burning because it will not be easy to kindle them in a hurry when the procession arrives, but five of the virgins foolishly overlook the possibility of delay and run out of fuel. The ten virgins represent professing disciples, the five foolish ones false, the five wise ones true. The oil for their lamps represents the good works of discipleship which show a person to be prepared for Jesus' coming, represented by the arrival of the bridegroom. The foolish virgins' going off to buy more oil and returning too late for entrance into the wedding feast represents the hopelessness of those caught unprepared for Jesus' coming. The wedding feast itself represents final salvation.

The Talents   The following parable of the talents also teaches good works as proof of true discipleship. Here, talents are not abilities, but are the largest denomination of money (see 18:24), standing for opportunities given according to ability. *Read Matthew 25:14–30.* The slave who did not invest the one talent given him represents false disciples. His statement in 25:24 says in effect that the work of investment would not have profited him, because the master would have taken the profit as well as the principle. This slave did not consider the possibility of sharing the joy of his master (a figure of eternal reward) or of being cast out (a figure of eternal punishment).

Shepherdesses and their flock in the Negev.

The discourse closes with yet another emphasis on good works as proof of genuine discipleship. *Read Matthew 25:31–46.* On account of the wool and meat they provide, sheep are more valuable than goats. Palestinian sheep and goats graze in mixed flocks during the day and then have to be separated from each other because sheep prefer open air at night but goats need the warmth of shelter. Here, the separation of sheep from goats stands for the separation of true disciples from the rest of humanity at the Last Judgment. The charitable deeds of "the sheep" stand for care shown to Jesus' persecuted disciples, called by him "these least brothers of mine." Again, such care demonstrates genuineness of discipleship inasmuch as it exposes the carers themselves to persecution (compare 24:10–12).[15]

Sheep and Goats

Matthew's passion account starts with Jesus' declaring that the disciples understand both the arrival of Passover after two days and the delivery of him to crucifixion. Then Matthew identifies as Caiaphas the high priest in whose courtyard or palace the Sanhedrin

---

15. This passage is often interpreted in terms of general humanitarianism, ministering to anyone in need. The interpretation neglects Jesus' use of "little" and "brother" only for his disciples in 5:22, 23, 24, 47; 7:3, 4, 5; 10:21, 42; 11:11; 12:48, 49, 50; 18:6, 10, 14, 15, 21, 35; 23:8, and also Jesus' identifying himself in 10:40 only with his needy disciples, not with needy people in general.

Anointing of Jesus plotted against Jesus. *Read Matthew 26:1–5.* In the story of Jesus' anointing, Matthew identifies the questioners of the anointing as the disciples, so that the answer of Jesus adds to their knowledge and the going of Judas Iscariot to strike a bargain with the Sanhedrin turns into a reaction against Jesus' answer. In Judas's bargain to deliver Jesus to the Sanhedrin, the Sanhedrists pay Judas on the spot. *Read Matthew 26:6–16.*

Read Matthew 26:17–25. By mentioning disciples without specifying only two of them (26:17), Matthew makes the obedience of those who followed Jesus' instructions in preparing the Passover an example of discipular obedience in general. Emphasizing this obedience is 26:19a: "and the disciples did as Jesus had commanded them" (compare 21:6). On announcement that one of the Twelve will betray Jesus, the betrayer himself—Judas Iscariot—asks, "Rabbi, it isn't I, is it?" False disciple! The implied negative answer and the honorific address show his hypocrisy. The thirty pieces of silver are already jingling in his pocket. Jesus' answer, "You yourself have said it," makes Judas self-condemned.

Words of Institution *Read Matthew 26:26–29.* The commands to eat bread and drink from a cup stress the disciples' obligation and form the Words of Institution in that these commands established the Christian practice of eating the Lord's Supper, also called the holding of Communion or celebration of the Eucharist ("thanksgiving"). Jesus does not say that the disciples should drink all the wine, but that all of them should drink from the cup. The interpretation of his blood-shedding as "for forgiveness of sins" gives good reason for celebration. More particularly, the red wine in the cup represents his blood as the basis of a new covenant that contrasts with the Mosaic covenant, based on the blood of animal sacrifices capable only of covering up sins provisionally and temporarily. Jesus' blood remits sins, that is, takes them clean away.

Gethsemane For the story of Jesus in Gethsemane, Matthew concentrates on Peter by leaving James and John unnamed (contrast Mark 14:33). Matthew is making Peter a negative example of prayerlessness. By contrast, Jesus stands out as an example of prayerfulness. Matthew counts out the number of Jesus' prayers—one, two, three—and specifies the content of all three of them. Correspondingly, Peter's three failures to pray will lead him to deny Jesus three times. *Read Matthew 26:30–46.*

When Judas Iscariot approaches Jesus for the arrest, Jesus ad- *Arrest*
dresses him with "Friend," the very address used in the parable of
the wedding feast for the man without a wedding garment (22:12),
and ironically tells him to do his dirty business. Thus the falsity of
Judas's discipleship is underlined. *Read Matthew 26:47–56.*
Matthew identifies the errant swordsman as "one of those with
Jesus," and Jesus' command to put the sword away models the
teaching of nonretaliation in the Sermon on the Mount (5:38–42).
The twelve legions of angels that could be at his disposal would
provide one legion apiece for him and the eleven apostles (Judas ex-
cepted, of course). As often in Matthew, emphasis falls on the fulfillment of Old Testament prophecy.

Matthew portrays the Sanhedrin as seeking false testimony serious enough to sentence Jesus to death but as not finding any so serious. The later testimony of two witnesses (a number sufficient to
establish truth, Deut. 19:15) comes close to the words of Jesus in
John 2:19. *Read Matthew 26:57–68.* Caiaphas puts Jesus under *Caiaphas*
oath; but because Jesus prohibited oath-taking (5:33–37), he turns
back Caiaphas's question whether he is the Christ, the Son of God,
with the answer, "You have said so." Thus Jesus models his own
teaching. But Peter disobeys it by denying Jesus with an oath. *Read*
Matthew 26:69–75. Peter's threefold failure to pray in Gethsemane *Peter*
has caught up with him. In view of 10:32–33, his denying Jesus
"before them all" poses a frightful fate. No wonder the bitterness of
Peter's tears.

Back to back with the bitter weeping of Peter stands the suicide *Suicide of*
of Judas Iscariot. It warns against betrayals in the church during *Judas Iscariot*
persecution (compare 24:10). As often, Matthew notes a fulfill-
ment of Old Testament prophecy (see Jer. 19:1, 11; Zech.
11:12–13). *Read Matthew 27:1–10.* In Jesus' interrogation before *Pilate*
Pilate, Matthew emphasizes the meekness of Jesus as an example for
his disciples to follow (compare 5:5; 11:29; 21:5). *Read Matthew*
27:11–14.

Before the unjust delivery of Jesus for crucifixion, Pilate's wife, *Pilate's Wife*
declaring Jesus righteous, warns Pilate to have nothing to do with
Jesus; and Pilate responds by washing his hands and declaring his innocence of Jesus' blood in a ceremony such as Moses commanded in
Deuteronomy 21:1–9. All the people, who have demanded Jesus'
crucifixion, accept responsibility for it and include their children
with themselves. Anti-Semites have taken this acceptance as

The Valley of Hinnom, the traditional place of Judas's suicide, viewed from Mount Zion.

grounds for persecuting the Jews, but such persecution goes against Jesus' prohibition of using a sword on his behalf (26:52–54). *Read Matthew 27:15–26.*

Crucifixion   Matthew's account of the Crucifixion highlights the indignities done to Jesus as a victim of persecution and his kingship and divine sonship. Though his enemies mock the kingship and sonship, Matthew presents their mockery as ironically true: not only the robing of Jesus and the crowning of him with thorns, but also the putting of a reed in his right hand and the kneeling before him; not only the hailing of him as "King of the Jews," but also the wording of the inscription, "This is the King of the Jews," and of the gibe, "He is the King of Israel," plus two occurrences of "God's Son." *Read Matthew 27:27–44.* The spitting mocks Jesus' robe; the hitting of his head with a reed mocks his crown. The mixing of wine with gall gives the wine a bitter taste and insults Jesus with a drink that at first seems merciful but turns out cruel (compare Ps. 69:21, especially in the LXX [69:22]). The crucifixion itself is subordinated to the division of his garments.

As Jesus is dying, some bystanders thwart the effort of one of their number to aid him with a drink. Jesus dies with a second loud outcry. An earthquake splits rocks and opens tombs, so that many resurrections occur. These resurrections encourage Christians to endure persecution to the death, if necessary; for as Jesus was thus persecuted but then raised from the dead, so will his followers be raised (compare Ezek. 37:7, 12–13; Dan. 12:2). Not only does the centurion confess Jesus' divine sonship; so also do his fellow soldiers. Together they, like the Magi of the Nativity, represent the many Gentiles who later become disciples of Jesus. *Read Matthew 27:45–61.* The ministry of women to Jesus on his way to Jerusalem provides a model of the way disciples are to care for fellow disciples under persecution; the characterization of Joseph of Arimathea as a disciple of Jesus makes his burial of Jesus' corpse an act of loving remembrance, as further comes out in descriptions of Jesus' linen shroud as "clean" and of the tomb as "new" and Joseph's own.

Resurrections of Saints

Burial of Jesus

"The next day, which is after Preparation" means "the Sabbath, which follows Friday." *Read Matthew 27:62–28:20.* The reliability of Jesus' predictions of the Resurrection stands in contrast with the deceitfulness of the chief priests and of the Pharisees, who not only bribe the guards at the tomb to say that the disciples of Jesus stole his body but also promise to bribe Pilate into exercising leniency should he hear that the guards slept on duty, a dereliction punishable by death. What the chief priests and Pharisees call "the first deception" is belief in Jesus as the Christ and Son of God (27:64).

Bribing of the Guards

As at the Resurrection in 27:51–53, an earthquake occurs, only this time a big one befitting the identity of Jesus as the Christ and Son of God. Also befitting it is the descent of an angel of the Lord to roll away the stone and the shaking of the guards with fear. For the women disciples, however, great joy mingles with fear until an appearance of the risen Jesus erases the fear. Their taking hold of his feet confirms his resurrection, and their worship of him again befits his identity. So also does that of the Eleven, except for some doubters who exemplify the danger of little faith in a persecuted church. Matthew has not mentioned Jesus' designation of a mountain before; so the inclusion of a mountain here combines with the mention of Jesus' commandments to suggest the mountain on

Resurrection of Jesus

The Great Commission

which he gave commandments, that of the Sermon on the Mount. His universal authority makes all the nations the proper field of the disciples' mission, which is to last until the end of the age. In the meanwhile, his promise to be always with the disciples recalls "Immanuel, God with us" (1:23) and gives courage to endure the persecution incurred through carrying out the Great Commission.

FOR FURTHER DISCUSSION

How might Matthew's gospel apply to contemporary megachurches? To Christians whose profession is mainly formal, inherited, or lapsed? To Christians suffering for their profession?

How might Matthew's gospel apply to contemporary questions of multi-culturalism in the church?

FOR FURTHER INVESTIGATION

Davies, W. D., and D. C. Allison, Jr. *A Critical and Exegetical Commentary on the Gospel According to Saint Matthew*. Vols. 1 and 2. Edinburgh: T. & T. Clark, 1988, 1991 (Vol. 3 forthcoming). Advanced.

France, R. T. *Matthew*. Grand Rapids: Eerdmans, 1985.

Gundry, R. H. *Matthew: A Commentary on His Handbook for a Mixed Church Under Persecution*. 2d ed. Grand Rapids: Eerdmans, 1993. Advanced.

Hagner, D. A. *Matthew 1–13*. Dallas: Word, 1993 (Vol. 2 forthcoming). Advanced.

Luz, U. *Matthew One–Seven*. Philadelphia: Fortress, 1989. Advanced.

Meier, J. P. *Matthew*. Wilmington: Glazier, 1980.

Morris, L. *The Gospel According to Matthew*. Grand Rapids: Eerdmans, 1992.

Ridderbos, H. N. *Matthew*. Grand Rapids: Zondervan, 1987.

9

Luke: A Promotion of Christianity in the Greco-Roman World at Large

- ❖ *Who wrote the gospel of Luke?*

- ❖ *How do we determine its authorship?*

- ❖ *How did the author go about writing?*

- ❖ *When was this gospel written, and what indications do we have of its date?*

- ❖ *For what audience, from what standpoint, and with what purpose did the author write?*

- ❖ *What features and emphases distinguish this gospel?*

- ❖ *What overall plan determines its movement?*

The author of the third gospel begins with a reference to pre- *Sources* vious narratives of Christian beginnings based on reports of *and Purpose* "eyewitnesses and ministers of the word" (1:1–2). He then defines his project as "an orderly account" of that tradition and states a purpose to convince his audience of its reliability (1:3–4).

The gospel of Luke and the Acts of the Apostles must come *Authorship* from the same author, for they both begin with dedications to Theophilus and exhibit common interests and a common style of writing. Moreover, Acts refers back to the "first book" (Acts 1:1). Since Luke and Acts must come from the same author, we deduce Luke's authorship of Luke-Acts from the fact that he is the only one of Paul's traveling companions mentioned in the epistles who could have written the "we"-sections of Acts. All others are excluded by the impossibility of harmonizing their geographical movements according to the epistles with the geographical movements in the "we"-sections of Acts.[1] Furthermore, early tradition confirms Lucan authorship.[2]

Luke was probably a Gentile (or at least a Hellenistic Jew) and may have been converted at Antioch in Syria.[3] His name is Greek. In the farewells of Colossians 4:10–14 Paul seems to distinguish him from Jews, perhaps Hebraistic ones, and links him with Gentiles. His facility in using the Greek language also suggests that he was a Gentile (or a Hellenistic Jew), more at home in the Greek language than most Jews would have been. The Greek style of Luke, together with that in the Epistle to the Hebrews, is the most refined in the New Testament. Exceptions occur where Luke appears to have been following Semitic oral or written sources, or adopting a Semitic style of Greek to sound "biblical," that is, Septuagintal. On the other hand, both of the books authored by Luke begin with a formal dedication in Greco-Roman literary style—the only New Testament books to do so. In Colossians 4:14, Paul calls Luke "the beloved physician," a description supported by Luke's more than usual interest in sickness and by his frequent use of medical terms[4]—though these features of his writings should not be over-stressed.

Theophilus and Gentile Audience

Luke dedicates his work to Theophilus, perhaps a potential or recent convert or a patron who sponsored the circulation of Luke-Acts, and slants both of his books toward Gentiles, especially those who have open-minded interest in the historical origins of Christianity—most probably proselytes and especially God-fearers who have renounced idolatry and immorality and attend Jewish synagogues. Luke's concern is to establish the religious piety, moral purity, and political innocence of Jesus and his followers.[5] He shows

---

1. See pages 295–96.

2. *The Muratorian Canon; the anti-Marcionite prologue to Luke; Irenaeus,* Against Heresies *3.1.1, and later writers.*

3. *Compare the anti-Marcionite prologue to the third gospel and "we" in Codex D at Acts 11:28, dealing with Antioch. The majority of scholars regard Luke as a Gentile. For defenses of his Jewishness, see E. E. Ellis,* The Gospel of Luke *(London: Nelson, 1966), 52–53; W. F. Albright, in Johannes Munck's* The Acts of the Apostles *(Garden City, N.Y.: Doubleday, 1967), 264–67; B. Reicke,* The Gospel of Luke *(Richmond: Knox, 1964), 12–23. On the contrary, see J. A. Fitzmyer,* The Gospel According to Luke (I–IX) *(Garden City, N.Y.: Doubleday, 1981), 41–47.*

4. *See, for example, Luke 14:1–6.*

5. *See especially Luke's account of Jesus' trial before Pilate, where the Roman governor repeatedly absolves Jesus of guilt (23:1–25).*

that the gospel is universal, that Jesus has broken down the barrier between Jews and Gentiles and inaugurated a world-wide community in which the old inequalities between slaves and free and between men and women no longer exist. Because of his Gentile audience, he does not exhibit a narrowly Jewish interest in fulfilled messianic prophecy, as Matthew does, but a broader interest in God's historical plan as revealed by the Old Testament and in the continuity of Christianity with Judaism. He also modifies peculiarly Jewish expressions and allusions to Jewish customs in order that Gentiles may better understand.[6]

There are many specific indications of Luke's promotion of *Universality* Christianity in the Greco-Roman world at large, indications largely missing in the other gospels. Special interest attaches to dating Jesus' career by the events of secular history (1:5; 2:1; 3:1–2). Jesus is "a light . . . to the Gentiles" (2:32). A quotation of Isaiah 40 includes "all flesh shall see the salvation of God" (3:6). The genealogy of Jesus goes back, not just to Abraham, father of the Jewish nation (as in Matt. 1:1–2), but to Adam, father of the whole human race, and ultimately to God himself (3:23–38). Jesus calls attention to Elijah's staying with a Phoenician widow instead of an Israelite and to Elisha's healing a Syrian leper (Naaman) rather than an Israelite (4:25–27). In common with Matthew, Luke contains the Great Commission to evangelize "all nations" (24:47; compare Matt. 28:19–20). But Matthew's is a universality in which Jewish Christianity has shed its parochialism, whereas Luke's is a Hellenistic universality which never knew Jewish parochialism.

Lucan universality includes not only Gentiles, but also social outcasts, such as the immoral woman who anointed Jesus' feet (7:36–50), Zacchaeus the toll collector (19:1–10), the repentant criminal who died alongside Jesus (23:39–43), the prodigal son (15:11–32, parabolic), the repentant toll collector (18:9–14, parabolic), Samaritans, and poor people. James and John draw rebuke for wanting to call down fire from heaven on a Samaritan village (9:51–56). The good Samaritan of a parable appears in favorable light (10:29–37). The one leper out of ten who returns to thank Jesus for healing is a Samaritan, designated "this foreigner" (17:11–19). At Nazareth, Jesus preaches "good news to the poor" (4:16–22). Mary says that God "has exalted the lowly, filled the

---

6. For example, "the abomination of desolation" (Mark 13:14 par. Matt. 24:15) becomes the encircling of Jerusalem with armies (Luke 21:20).

hungry with good things, and sent away the rich empty" (1:52b–53). The beatitude on the poor lacks Matthew's qualification "in spirit" (6:20; contrast Matt. 5:3), as also the beatitude on the hungry lacks Matthew's qualification "for righteousness" (6:21; contrast Matt. 5:6). And Luke balances the beatitudes on the poor and hungry with woes against the rich and full (6:24–25). He is the only evangelist to include Jesus' words: "When you give a dinner or a banquet, do not invite your friends or your brothers or your relatives or rich neighbors . . . . But when you give a feast, call poor people, crippled people, lame people, blind people" (14:12–13). It is Luke who calls the Pharisees "lovers of money" (16:14) and gives us the parables of the rich fool, the dishonest manager who acted charitably (and therefore shrewdly), and the rich man and Lazarus (12:13–21; 16:1–13, 19–31).

Lucan universality shows itself also in the special attention paid to women: Mary, Elizabeth, and Anna in the nativity story (chaps. 1–2), the widow of Nain (7:11–17), the women who supported Jesus financially (8:1–3), the immoral woman (7:36–50), Mary and Martha (10:38–42), the poor widow (21:1–4), and the women who lamented Jesus (23:27–31), watched the crucifixion (23:49), and intended to embalm him but witnessed the empty tomb instead and reported the Resurrection (23:55–24:11).

Luke thus portrays Jesus as a cosmopolitan Savior with broad sympathies, one who mingles with all sorts of people, socializes with both Pharisees and toll collectors (5:27–32; 7:36; 11:37; 14:1; 19:1–10), and concerns himself with victims of personal calamity (7:11–17; 8:40–56; 9:37–43). Where Matthew concentrates on Jesus and the kingdom, Luke concentrates on Jesus and people, with resultant character sketches that are quite vivid.

Prayer On numerous occasions Jesus appears as a man of prayer: at his baptism (3:21), after ministering to crowds (5:16), before choosing the Twelve (6:12), before Peter's confession and Jesus' prediction of his own death and resurrection (9:18), at the time of his transfiguration (9:28–29), on the return of the seventy-two from their mission (10:21), before teaching the disciples to pray (11:1), in Gethsemane (22:39–46), and twice on the cross (23:34, 46). Almost all these references to Jesus' prayers are distinctive of Luke's gospel. Only Luke records two parables of Jesus about prayer (11:5–13; 18:1–8) and informs us that Jesus had prayed especially for Peter (22:31–32).

Luke similarly emphasizes the work of the Holy Spirit. He tells *Holy Spirit* us that John the Baptist was to be filled with the Holy Spirit even from his mother's womb (1:15). The Holy Spirit comes on Mary in order that she may miraculously give birth to the Son of God (1:35). When Mary visits Elizabeth, Elizabeth is filled with the Holy Spirit to say, "Blessed are you among women, and blessed is the fruit of your womb" (1:41–42). When John the Baptist is born and then named, his father Zacharias (Zechariah) is filled with the Holy Spirit and prophesies (1:67). The Holy Spirit rests on Simeon, informs him that before dying he will behold the Christ, and leads him to the temple to see the Christ child (2:25–27). After receiving the Spirit at his baptism, Jesus is "full of the Holy Spirit" and "led by the Spirit" in the wilderness (4:1). Following his temptation, he returns to Galilee "in the power of the Spirit" (4:14). When the seventy-two disciples return from their successful mission, he rejoices "in the Holy Spirit" (10:21). And before his ascension he promises that the Spirit will clothe the disciples "with power from on high" (24:49). Consequently, the gospel of Luke (as later the book of Acts) throbs with the thrill of an irresistible movement of God's Spirit in human history.[7] Luke writes with supreme confidence in the inevitably successful advance of the gospel inaugurated by Jesus "the Lord" (a favorite designation of Jesus in Luke) and carried on by his disciples in the energy of the Holy Spirit.

Nothing prevents a fairly early date for the third gospel, slightly *Date* after that of Mark under the assumption that Luke utilized Mark. Many scholars think that Luke's changing the abomination of desolation (Mark 13:14) to the siege of Jerusalem (Luke 21:20) proves that he wrote after A.D. 70. But this line of reasoning again overlooks or denies the possibility that Jesus really did predict the siege and destruction of Jerusalem. Luke may have omitted to mention the abomination of desolation simply because he knew that his Gentile audience would not understand it. If he was conforming Jesus' words to the events in and around A.D. 70, why did he retain the command, "Flee to the mountains" (21:21), despite the fact that during the siege of Jerusalem Christians fled to Pella in an *unmoun-*tainous part of Transjordan (if they fled to Pella at all—the evidence is disputed)?

---

7. *See the references to joy in 1:14, 44, 47; 6:21, 23; 10:21; 15:5–7, 9, 10, 23–25, 32; 24:52–53.*

Acts closes with Paul's awaiting trial in Rome, probably because events had progressed no further at the time of writing.[8] If so, Acts dates from some time before A.D. 64–67, the most likely period of Paul's martyrdom. Then if Luke wrote his gospel before Acts, as would seem likely, the gospel must likewise date from a slightly earlier time.[9] The place of writing might be Rome, where Luke was staying with Paul during Paul's imprisonment (though early tradition is divided between Greece and Rome for the place of writing).

Plan and Materials   The gospel of Luke is the most comprehensive of the synoptics. Indeed, it is the longest book of the New Testament. In the first two chapters Luke begins with a prologue and stories concerning Jesus' birth and boyhood. The baptism, genealogy, and temptation of Jesus follow in 3:1–4:13, the Galilean ministry in 4:14–9:50, the last journey to Jerusalem in 9:51–19:27, and finally Passion Week, the Crucifixion, the Resurrection, the post-Resurrection ministry, and the Ascension in 19:28–24:53. The last journey to Jerusalem makes the most distinctive contribution of Luke to our knowledge of Jesus' career. In that section he presents the ministry of Jesus in Perea, gives many of the most famous parables not elsewhere recorded (the Good Samaritan, the Rich Fool, the Prodigal Son, Dives and Lazarus, the Pharisee and the Toll Collector, and others), and emphasizes the significance of Jerusalem as the goal of Jesus' ministry. (Later, in Acts, Jerusalem will turn into the place from which Christian witnesses go out to evangelize the world.) The nativity story in Luke contains much information not found in Matthew, including several hymns and an account of John the Baptist's birth as well as Jesus' birth. Finally, Luke gives material concerning Jesus' resurrection quite different from that in the other gospels and becomes the only evangelist to describe the ascension of Jesus.

An Outline of Luke

PROLOGUE: DEDICATION TO THEOPHILUS AND STATEMENT OF PURPOSE TO WRITE AN ORDERLY ACCOUNT OF HISTORICAL TRUSTWORTHINESS (1:1–4)

I. THE NATIVITY AND CHILDHOOD OF JOHN THE BAPTIST AND JESUS (1:5–2:52)

---

8. See pages 297–98.
9. See pages 127–28.

A. The annunciation of John the Baptist's birth to Zacharias and Elizabeth (1:5–25)
B. The annunciation of Jesus' birth to Mary (1:26–38)
C. The visit of Mary to Elizabeth and Mary's Magnificat (1:39–56)
D. The birth, circumcision, and naming of John the Baptist, and the Benedictus of Zacharias (1:57–79)
E. John the Baptist's growing up in the wilderness (1:80)
F. The birth of Jesus (2:1–7)
G. The visit of the shepherds (2:8–20)
H. The circumcision and naming of Jesus (2:21)
I. The presentation in the temple, with the Nunc Dimittis of Simeon and the adoration of Anna (2:22–40)
J. Jesus' visit to the temple at the age of twelve (2:41–52)

II. THE PRELUDE TO JESUS' MINISTRY (3:1–4:13)
A. The preparatory ministry of John the Baptist (3:1–20)
B. The baptism of Jesus (3:21–22)
C. The genealogy of Jesus (3:23–38)
D. The temptation of Jesus (4:1–13)

III. THE GALILEAN MINISTRY (4:14–9:50)
A. The rejection of Jesus in Nazareth (4:14–30)
B. An exorcism in the synagogue at Capernaum (4:31–37)
C. The healing of Peter's mother-in-law and further miracles and preaching (4:38–44)
D. A miraculous catch of fish and the call of Simon Peter, James, and John to discipleship (5:1–11)
E. The cleansing of a leper (5:12–16)
F. The forgiveness and healing of a paralytic (5:17–26)
G. The call of Levi and Jesus' eating with toll collectors and sinners (5:27–32)
H. Remarks about fasting (5:33–39)
I. Jesus' defense of his disciples' plucking and eating grain on the Sabbath (6:1–5)
J. The healing of a withered hand on the Sabbath (6:6–11)
K. The choice of the Twelve (6:12–16)
L. The Sermon on the Plain ("a level place," 6:17–49)

M. The healing of a centurion's servant (7:1–10)

N. The raising from the dead of a widow's son (7:11–17)

O. The question of John the Baptist and Jesus' answer and tribute to him (7:18–35)

P. Jesus' anointing by and forgiveness of a sinful woman (7:36–50)

Q. Preaching with financial support from certain women (8:1–3)

R. The parables of the seeds and the soils and of the lamp (8:4–18)

S. The attempt of Jesus' family to see him (8:19–21)

T. The stilling of a storm (8:22–25)

U. The deliverance of a demoniac (8:26–39)

V. The healing of the woman with a chronic flow of blood and the raising of Jairus's daughter from the dead (8:40–56)

W. The mission of the Twelve (9:1–6)

X. The guilty fear of Herod Antipas over the death of John the Baptist (9:7–9)

Y. The feeding of the five thousand (9:10–17)

Z. Peter's confession of Jesus' messiahship and the prediction by Jesus of his own death and resurrection, with a call to cross-taking discipleship (9:18–27)

AA. The Transfiguration (9:28–36)

BB. The deliverance of a demonized boy (9:37–45)

CC. Remarks on humility (with a child as an example) and tolerance (9:46–50)

IV. The Last Journey to Jerusalem (9:51–19:27)

A. Jesus' determination to go to Jerusalem and the inhospitality of a Samaritan village (9:51–56)

B. Remarks on discipleship to would-be disciples (9:57–62)

C. The mission of the seventy-two (10:1–24)

D. The parable of the Good Samaritan (10:25–37)

E. Entertainment of Jesus by Mary and Martha (10:38–42)

F. Teaching about prayer, including the Lord's Prayer and the parable of the host whose guest arrived at midnight (11:1–13)

G. Polemical episodes (11:14–12:12)
    1. Defense against the charge of Satanic empowerment, refusal to give any sign except that of Jonah, and the parable of the lamp (11:14–36)
    2. Exposé of the Pharisees and lawyers (11:37–54)
    3. Warning against Phariseeism (12:1–12)
H. Remarks on covetousness, anxiety, trust, and eschatological watchfulness, including the parable of a rich fool (12:13–59)
I. A call to repentance, including the parable of the fig tree (13:1–9)
J. The healing on a Sabbath of a woman bent over (13:10–17)
K. The parables of the mustard seed, leaven, and narrow door (13:18–30)
L. Jesus' refusal to be panicked in the face of Herod Antipas and a lamentation over Jerusalem (13:31–35)
M. The Sabbath healing of a man with dropsy (14:1–6)
N. A parable about invitations to a marriage feast (14:7–14)
O. The parable of a great banquet (14:15–24)
P. The parables of a tower-builder and of a king who goes to war (14:25–35)
Q. Three parables in defense of welcoming sinners (15:1–32)
    1. The parable of a lost sheep (15:1–7)
    2. The parable of a lost coin (15:8–10)
    3. The parable of the Prodigal Son and his elder brother (15:11–32)
R. Two parables about the use of money (16:1–31)
    1. The parable of the Unjust Steward, with further comments to the Pharisees (16:1–18)
    2. The parable of the Rich Man and Lazarus (16:19–31)
S. Remarks on forgiveness, faith, and a sense of duty (17:1–10)
T. The healing of ten lepers and the gratitude of one, a Samaritan (17:11–19)
U. The coming of God's kingdom and the Son of man, including the parable of a widow and an unjust judge (17:20–18:8)

V The parable of the Pharisee and the Publican (18:9–14)

W. Jesus' welcoming little children (18:15–17)

X. The rich ruler (18:18–30)

Y. Prediction by Jesus of his death and resurrection (18:31–34)

Z. The healing of a blind man near Jericho (18:35–43)

AA. The conversion of Zacchaeus (19:1–10)

BB. The parable of the pounds (19:11–27)

V. PASSION WEEK AND THE DEATH, RESURRECTION, POST-RESURRECTION MINISTRY, AND ASCENSION OF JESUS IN AND AROUND JERUSALEM (19:28–24:53)

A. Passion week and the death of Jesus (19:28–23:56)

1. The Triumphal Entry, including the cleansing of the temple (19:28–48)

2. Theological debate in the temple precincts (20:1–21:38)

a. The challenge to Jesus' authority (20:1–8)

b. A parable about the wicked tenants of a vineyard (20:9–18)

c. A question about paying taxes to Caesar (20:19–26)

d. The Sadducees' question about resurrection (20:27–40)

e. Jesus' question about the Christ's Davidic ancestry and lordship (20:41–44)

f. Warning against the scribes (20:45–47)

g. A widow's two copper coins (21:1–4)

h. Prophetic teaching (21:5–36)

i. Further teaching (21:37–38)

3. The Sanhedrin's plot to kill Jesus and the bargain with Judas Iscariot (22:1–6)

4. The Last Supper (22:7–38)

5. Jesus' praying in Gethsemane (22:39–46)

6. The arrest (22:47–53)

7. The trial (22:54–23:25)

a. A nighttime hearing in the high priest's house, with Peter's denials of Jesus (22:54–65)

b. An early morning condemnation by the Sanhedrin (22:66–71)

     c. The first hearing before Pilate (23:1–5)

     d. The hearing before Herod Antipas (23:6–12)

     e. The second hearing before Pilate, with his grudging release of Barabbas and delivering up of Jesus for crucifixion (23:13–25)

  8. The Crucifixion (23:26–49)

     a. The carrying of Jesus' cross by Simon of Cyrene and the lament of the women (23:26–31)

     b. The crucifixion and mocking of Jesus (23:32–38)

     c. The repentant criminal (23:39–43)

     d. The death of Jesus (23:44–49)

  9. The burial (23:50–56)

B. The Resurrection (24:1–12)

C. The post-Resurrection ministry (24:13–49)

  1. A walk to Emmaus with Cleopas and another disciple (24:13–35)

  2. An appearance in Jerusalem (24:36–43)

  3. Jesus' teaching about himself from the Old Testament, and the Great Commission (24:44–49)

D. The Ascension (24:50–53)

Prologue

In his prologue, Luke mentions earlier written accounts of Jesus' life, oral testimonies by eyewitnesses, his own investigation of these accounts and testimonies, and his purpose to present this tradition as reliable. *Read Luke 1:1–4.* The earlier accounts may include Mark and Matthew. The orderliness of Luke's account consists in careful arrangement, yet topical and geographical arrangements may sometimes override chronological arrangement. Though "most excellent" describes Theophilus loftily, nothing more is known about him. Perhaps he is Luke's literary patron, but other possibilities exist.

Annunciation to Zacharias

Immediately after his prologue, Luke provides a historical frame of reference: "in the days of Herod, king of Judea." There follow the annunciation to Zacharias of John the Baptist's birth, the conception of John by Zacharias's wife Elizabeth, the annunciation to Mary of Jesus' birth, and Mary's visit to Elizabeth. *Read Luke 1:5–56.* "The division of Abijah" (1:5) was one of the twenty-four platoons of priests that served at the temple twice a year, a week each time. In line with his appeal to the highest religious and moral ideals of Hellenistic culture, Luke describes Elizabeth as descended from

Bethlehem as viewed south to Manger Square and the Church of the Nativity. This was the ancestral town of Joseph.

Aaron, elder brother of Moses in the tribe of Levi, just as her husband Zacharias had to be for priestly service, and emphasizes the righteousness of both of them. A casting of lots determined which priest gained the privilege of burning incense in the temple; and once privileged to do so, a priest was disqualified in order that other priests might have a better chance. But for Luke, the choice of Zacharias by lot was due to divine providence, not chance (compare Acts 1:24–26). Again in line with Luke's appeal to the highest religious and moral ideals, the coming abstinence of John from alcoholic beverages, his filling with the Holy Spirit even before birth, his reformative ministry to Israel, and his playing the role of Elijah all emphasize a special holiness (compare Lev. 10:9; Num. 6:2–4; Judg. 13:4; 1 Sam. 1:11; Mal. 4:5). So also do the virginity of Mary, her

Annunciation to Mary

having found favor with God, her coming virginal conception by the Holy Spirit, the consequent holiness and divine sonship of her son, whom she is to name Jesus, and her believing acquiescence. Notably, Luke is telling the story from her standpoint. "The sixth month" when the annunciation to her takes place is the sixth month of Elizabeth's pregnancy (1:26). The filling of Elizabeth with the Holy Spirit gives authority to her blessing of Mary and Jesus and to her calling Jesus "Lord." Mary's hymn of praise, traditionally called the *Magnificat* (after the opening word for "magnifies" in the Latin Vulgate[10]), draws much of its phraseology from the song of Hannah (1 Sam. 2:1–10) and brings out the theme of justice for the poor, hungry, and oppressed.

Read Luke 1:57–80. The Mosaic law prescribed circumcision on the eighth day (Gen. 17:12–14; 21:4; Lev. 12:3; compare Phil. 3:5). The use of sign-language in 1:62 shows that Zacharias was struck deaf as well as dumb. His prophecy of praise is traditionally called the *Benedictus* (after the opening word for "blessed" in the Latin Vulgate) and brings out the themes of fulfillment, deliverance from oppression, forgiveness of sins, and peaceful service to God—yet again in line with the highest religious and moral ideals, and social and political ones, too.

Birth of John the Baptist

For Jesus' nativity Luke again provides an historical frame of reference, this time a much broader one suitable to the universality of the salvation brought by Jesus. *Read Luke 2:1–20.* The census of Caesar Augustus has traditionally been thought to have the purpose of levying taxes, but it may rather have had the purpose of declaring allegiance to Augustus.[11] Swaddling clothes are cloths wrapped tightly around an infant, as customarily done at the time. A manger is a feeding trough. The shepherds suit the birth of Jesus in Bethlehem, home town of David the shepherd-king. Their staying in the fields overnight disfavors winter as the season of Jesus' birth. The people for whom an angel of the Lord brings good news are the people of Israel, the Jews. The song of the angelic choir is

Nativity of Jesus

---

10. *The Latin Vulgate was a translation by St. Jerome in the fourth century and for many centuries afterward the standard text of the Bible in the Roman Catholic Church.*

11. *A problem arises out of Luke's reference to the Syrian governorship of Quirinius. According to Matthew, Herod the Great was still ruling Judea when Jesus was born. Herod the Great died in 4 B.C. (The sixth-century Christian monk Dionysius Exiguus miscalculated the year of Jesus' birth when setting up the system of dating B.C. and A.D., in which Jesus is supposed to have been born on December 25, 1 B.C., and circumcised eight days later on January 1, A.D. 1.) Outside the New Testament, Quirinius is said to have governed Syria in A.D. 6–7, but there is the possibility of an earlier governorship as well.*

traditionally called the *Gloria in Excelsis Deo* (after the opening words for "glory to God in the highest" in the Latin Vulgate). "Peace" refers to the manifold blessings of salvation, and the traditional "good will to men" refers to the good will that God directs toward his people. Mary's treasuring and pondering all these events hints that she is Luke's source (compare 2:51), and "all that they [the shepherds] had heard and seen, just as it had been told them" appeals to eyewitness testimony combined with heavenly revelation (compare 1:1–4).

Presentation in the Temple Emphasis continues to fall on the moral and religious excellence of the players in this drama of the Nativity: obedience to the angelic command to name Mary's son Jesus, obedience to the law of Moses in performing a ritual of purification (Leviticus 12), righteousness, devoutness, expectancy, enduement with the Holy Spirit, reception of divine revelation, the prophetic gift, lengthy devotion to the temple, and constant fasting and prayer—and these of women as well as men. *Read Luke 2:21–40.* The directing of salvation to the Gentiles as well as Israel (2:32) contributes to Luke's cosmopolitanism. "The fall and rise of many in Israel" (2:34) probably refers to the judgment of Jews who will reject Jesus and the salvation of those who will accept him. He himself is the sign that some will oppose (2:34). And the sword which will pierce Mary's soul may stand for the coming crucifixion of Jesus as her firstborn son (2:35), whose physical and mental development and divine favor mark him out as the ideal human being (2:40).

Visit to the Temple Luke now relates a particular instance of Jesus' precociousness and concludes with another statement of Jesus' perfect progress: mentally ("in wisdom"), physically ("in stature"), spiritually ("in favor with God"), and socially ("in human favor"). In between, Luke notes the devotion of Jesus to God his Father and his obedience to Joseph and Mary. *Read Luke 2:41–52.* Since Jewish lads assumed adult responsibilities in Judaism at the age of thirteen, this visit to the temple may have the purpose of preparing Jesus for those responsibilities.

The Baptist's Ministry For John the Baptist's ministry of preparation, Luke provides a historical frame of reference yet again. *Read Luke 3:1–20.* Luke continues the quotation of Isaiah long enough to get the universalism of "all flesh will see the salvation of God." In his preaching, John addresses the crowds; and Luke includes a section on the social ideals of charity, honesty, justice, and contentment. As a foil to these ideals stands the wickedness of John's nemesis Herod (Antipas), which according to Luke includes more than the imprisonment of John. The contrast enhances the admirability of the Christian movement, beginning as it does with John.

Luke's account of Jesus' baptism brings out the piety of Jesus: he is praying. The bodily form of the Holy Spirit that descends on him makes the descent open to eyewitness (again compare 1:1–4). The notation of Jesus' age lends a historical touch. And the tracing of Jesus' genealogy further back than Abraham, and even Adam, to God highlights the divine sonship of Jesus and the universality of the salvation he brings. *Read Luke 3:21–38.*[12]

Jesus' Baptism and Genealogy

The story of Jesus' temptation portrays him as filled with the Holy Spirit, constantly led by the Spirit, and refusing to serve himself by taking advantage of his divine sonship. *Read Luke 4:1–13.* The last placement of the temptation in Jerusalem links with Luke's emphasis on that city as the point of destination in Jesus' ministry and the starting point of Christian witness afterwards. The devil's finishing every temptation and departing from Jesus until an opportune time highlight Jesus' moral victory.

The Temptation

The power of the Holy Spirit characterizes the return of Jesus to Galilee for the start of his teaching. The results are widespread publicity and universal admiration. The customariness of his attending synagogue evidences his piety. The application to himself of Isaiah 61:1–2 carries on Luke's portrayal of him as endued with the Spirit and adds the socially admirable elements of ministry to the poor, the captive, the blind, and the oppressed. *Read Luke 4:14–30.* The question, "This is Joseph's son, isn't it?" illustrates the popular ignorance of Jesus' virgin birth (see 3:23) and leads him to anticipate ultimate rejection by his fellow townspeople. The reference to his deeds in Capernaum, when those deeds have yet to be narrated in the next paragraph, shows that Luke has advanced this visit to Nazareth to make it programmatic of Jesus' reception as a whole: admiration followed by rejection. The notation of Elijah's and Elisha's ministries to Gentiles looks forward to Gentile salvation. Strikingly, Jesus stops his scriptural reading just before a reference to "the day of vengeance" (Isa. 61:2), a central theme in the nationalistic messianism of first-century Jews, who interpreted the phrase in terms of their revenge on Gentile nations. Luke's notation of murderous rage

In the Synagogue at Nazareth

---

12. *For discussion of the many differences between the genealogies of Jesus in Matthew and Luke, see commentaries on these gospels and books on Jesus' birth.*

Cliff near Nazareth, possibly the one from which the townspeople intended to throw Jesus.

on the part of all in the synagogue attributes the rejection of Jesus to a moral fault in them, not to any in him.

In the Synagogue at Capernaum

Jesus continues to teach in the synagogue at Capernaum (compare 4:15), where a demoniac confronts him. The loudness of the demoniac's voice and his initial "Leave us alone!" (or "Ha!") heighten the conflict with Jesus. The demon's throwing of the man into the middle of the congregation makes the exorcism visible to all (compare Luke's emphasis on eyewitness testimony, 1:1–4), and the demon's doing the man no harm on exit heightens the power as well as the authority of Jesus' word of rebuke to the demon. So also the extremity of the fever of Peter's mother-in-law and the immediacy of her standing up and serving when healed heighten the power as well as the authority of Jesus' word of rebuke to her fever. Similarly with respect to the variety of the diseases afflicting others brought to Jesus and his nevertheless healing each one of them with the mere application of his hands. He displays his authority and power by even keeping the demons quiet after they have come out shouting that he is the Son of God. *Read Luke 4:31–44.* Luke uses "the Christ" as a synonym for "the Son of God" (compare 9:20; 22:67 with 70; 23:35). The crowds' searching Jesus out and trying to keep him from leaving them demonstrate his attractiveness, and his going off to preach the good news of God's rule in the synagogues of Judean cities demonstrates fidelity to his mission.

Jesus' preaching of God's word proves so attractive that a crowd presses in on him, so that he commandeers the boat of Simon (Peter) from which to teach them offshore. *Read Luke 5:1–11.* The failure of a whole night's fishing without Jesus makes the almost unmanageable success of fishing with him all the more impressive. Attraction of the crowd now transmutes into attraction of disciples; so Simon and his partners end up following Jesus instead of Jesus' departing from them, as Simon in fear has asked him to do. *Fishing*

The fullness of a man's leprosy now makes its miraculous departure so astounding that the word concerning Jesus draws crowds from increasing distances. Uncorrupted by this popularity, he continues to slip away for prayer. *Read Luke 5:12–16.* In the story of the paralytic's healing, Luke continues to emphasize the extent of Jesus' attractiveness and the power that he has from God to heal. A further emphasis on the failure to wedge through the crowd with the paralytic enhances Jesus' popularity. Letting the paralytic down through the roof tiles "in the middle" of the crowd makes the healing verifiable by eyewitnesses, as the immediacy of his standing up heightens the miracle. The glorification of God by the healed man as well as by the eyewitnesses puts on exhibit the religious validity of Jesus' activity and erases the charge that Jesus is blaspheming God by forgiving sins. *Read Luke 5:17–26.* *Healing a Leper and a Paralytic*

Levi's "leaving everything behind" to follow Jesus and making "a big banquet for him in his [own] house" magnify the attractiveness of Jesus yet again. *Read Luke 5:27–39.* The question to the disciples, "Why do you eat and drink with the toll collectors and sinners?" paints a picture of social harmony at meal which appeals to Luke's Hellenistic audience; and "to repentance" shows that underlying *Call of Levi*

The ruins of an octagonal structure (remains of a fifth-century church) cover the traditional site of Peter's house at Capernaum.

Feasting Instead of Fasting

this harmony is personal reformation. Since Jesus has answered their question to the disciples, the Pharisees and their scribes turn their questioning to Jesus. The frequency of fasting by the disciples of John the Baptist and of the Pharisees and their praying while fasting point up their social withdrawal. The eating and drinking of Jesus' disciples refers to what they are doing at the moment in Levi's house. Using the figures of a bridegroom and groomsmen (or wedding guests), Jesus tells the Pharisees and their scribes that they cannot make his disciples fast, that is, cannot make them stop eating and drinking in Levi's house. Using further figures, Jesus says that stopping the enjoyment of social harmony at meal in Levi's house would be like tearing up a new garment to get a patch for an old one, a patch that would not match the old anyway, and like losing new wine by putting it in old wineskins, which would also be lost by bursting. But like wine-drinkers, who prefer old wine to new, the Pharisees and their scribes prefer the social isolation of their frequent fasting and praying to the social harmony of the disciples' meal with repentant toll collectors and sinners.

Read Luke 6:1–11. The disciples rub the heads of wheat in their hands to separate the edible kernels from the inedible chaff. As in 5:30–31, the Pharisees direct their question to Jesus' disciples but he answers. "Except for the priests alone" (6:4) emphasizes the illegality of David's and his men's eating the bread of presence, and thus emphasizes the kindness of Jesus in using his lordship over the Sabbath to let the disciples satisfy their hunger by breaking the Sabbath. The designation of the withered hand as a right hand and therefore presumably the most needful (since the vast majority of people are right-handed) likewise emphasizes Jesus' kindness in restoring it. The fury incurred by the restoration acts as a foil to play up this kindness all the more, and the repeated reference to the patient's standing up in the middle of the synagogue congregation makes the restoration an object of eyewitness. *[The Sabbath Question]*

Read Luke 6:12–49. Luke introduces Jesus' Sermon on the Plain with the choice of the twelve apostles. Jesus' praying all night on a mountain before choosing them makes him a model of piety. His naming them apostles highlights their authority as eyewitnesses of his ministry (compare Acts 1:21–22). The great throng awaiting Jesus at the base of the mountain is a reminder of his attractiveness, and the exorcisms and other healings which occur by merely touching him are reminders of his power. Four beatitudes are balanced by four woes. Both sets deal with the economic and social conditions of Jesus' disciples and their persecutors. The following instructions tell the disciples how to live under these conditions, that is, to overcome evil with good, with love and mercy, generosity and helpfulness. *[Sermon on the Plain]*

With an eye to his Gentile audience, Luke stresses the worthiness and humility as well as great faith of a centurion (Gentile, of course) who seeks and gets from Jesus the healing of his highly esteemed slave. *Read Luke 7:1–10.* In a male-dominated society, the death of a widow's only son puts her in desperate straits (she has no man to support her); so Luke emphasizes the compassion of Jesus in raising the son of the widow of Nain and in giving him back to her. The awestruck crowd's glorification of God and recognition of Jesus as his spokesman (the meaning of "prophet") add a religious benefit to the social benefit of Jesus' miracle. *Read Luke 7:11–17.* In the episode concerning John the Baptist's question, Luke highlights Jesus' working of miracles on the spot, as John's two messengers are watching, so as to bring out the reliability of this eyewitness tradition (compare 1:1–4). Jesus' tribute to John underscores the con- *[A Centurion] [Widow of Nain] [John the Baptist]* trast between John's more-than-prophetic ruggedness and the luxurious lifestyle of self-indulgent royalty. A similar contrast between the repentant masses and toll collectors, on the one hand, and the self-righteous Pharisees and experts in the Mosaic law, on the other hand, underscores the justice of God in rejecting the latter and accepting the former, who are the children of wisdom, those who by their submission to John's baptism proved themselves to be wise in

A Sinful Woman contrast with the others. *Read Luke 7:18–35.* The story of a sinful woman's forgiveness gives a particular instance of the loving effect of Jesus' forgiveness. *Read Luke 7:36–50.* Walking on dirt paths in open sandals made the offering of water for foot-washing a courtesy. Also included among courtesies were a kiss of greeting and the rubbing of olive oil on the head so that it might glisten with the joy of the occasion. The feet of recliners on cushions at formal meals stretched out from the table; so the woman had easy access to Jesus' feet. It was customary for uninvited people to enter and watch a dinner party.

Read Luke 8:1–21. Jesus' itineration appeals to Luke's Hellenistic audience, fascinated as they are with travel. The proclamation of good news concerning God's rule strikes a happy note. Accompaniment by the Twelve provides eyewitness testimony. The

Support by Women women's support of Jesus and the Twelve exemplifies the Hellenistic ideal of sharing goods. Description of the women's prior maladies calls attention to the benefits of Jesus' ministry to women. The gathering of a crowd from one city after another exemplifies his

Parables attractiveness. In his first parable, the trampling of the seed on a path intensifies the exposure of the seed by stressing a location on the edge of the path, not beside it. "On the rock" (not "on rocky soil") stresses lack of moisture; for even thin soil holds some moisture above the underlying rocks, but a rock holds none. Identification of the seed as God's word equates it with Jesus' message (see 5:1). The issue raised by the parable is believing for salvation, as opposed to apostasy under trial and the preoccupations of worry, wealth, and pleasure. The faith which perseveres reveals a heart of moral beauty. The command to be careful how you hear therefore interprets the shining lamp and the manifest secret as the beautiful fruit of persevering faith. The inability of Jesus' mother and brothers to get to him because of the crowd comes back to his attractiveness. And hearing and doing the word of God, characteris-

Gerasa, associated with Legion.

tics that define Jesus' family of followers, come back to persevering faith in his message.

The story of Jesus' stilling a storm revives the question of faith. *Read Luke 8:22–25.* The story concerning the exorcism of Legion gives another example of Jesus' saving power, magnified by the length of time the demoniac went naked and homeless, by his falling before Jesus, by his begging Jesus, by Legion's urging Jesus not to command them to depart into the abyss (another word for hell— compare Matt. 25:41; 2 Peter 2:4; Rev. 20:3), by Jesus' permitting them to enter a herd of pigs, by the civilized condition and position of the delivered demoniac at Jesus' feet, and by the great fear that grips the local inhabitants. *Read Luke 8:26–39.* The herders' seeing (8:34) provides testimony by eyewitnesses. The ex-demoniac's proclamation provides first-person testimony throughout the whole city from which he came (compare 8:27).

Stilling a Storm and Exorcising Legion

225

Jairus's Daughter and a Woman A crowd's expectant welcome contrasts with the request in 8:37. *Read Luke 8:40–56.* That Jairus has only one daughter heightens the pathos of his request. The denial of all that they have touched Jesus, his repetition of the question who touched him, and the woman's seeing that she cannot stay hidden enhance his prophetic clairvoyance. Her declaration "before all the people" again provides both first-person and eyewitness testimony. Each in its own way, the command not to trouble Jesus and his command to stop weeping highlight the raising of the dead. So also do the breast-beating, in addition to weeping, and the mourners' knowledge that the child has died. The returning of her breath ("spirit") enables her to stand up and signals her salvation from death.

Mission of the Twelve Luke's version of the mission of the Twelve brings out the power as well as the authority that Jesus gave them, plus the elements of his sending them, which corresponds to the meaning of "apostle" (compare 6:13), and of their evangelistic and therapeutic itineration through one village after another, in accordance with the Hellenistic interest in travel. *Read Luke 9:1–6.* The doings of the Twelve come to the ears of Herod (Antipas), whose perplexity and desire to see Jesus (who gave the Twelve their power and authority) Luke uses to deride Herod, the high and mighty doer of evil (3:19–20), and to ennoble Jesus, the gracious doer of good. *Read Luke 9:7–9.* Testifying to Jesus' graciousness is his welcoming the crowds who followed him to Bethsaida even though he had retreated there for some privacy with his disciples. So also with respect to his talking to the crowds about God's rule, healing the sick, and of course feeding about five thousand men. *Read Luke 9:10–17.*

Peter's Confession Jesus' piety comes out again in his praying alone at the time of Peter's confessing him to be "the Christ of God," that is, "God's Anointed One." By equating Jesus' instruction that the disciples not tell anyone with the first passion prediction, Luke indicates that as the Christ of God, Jesus and the rule of God that he brings are not politically dangerous: Jesus comes for rejection, not for revolution. Likewise, his followers must risk their lives daily for personal gain hereafter, not for political gain here and now. *Read Luke 9:18–27.*

Transfiguration Luke's introduction to the Transfiguration, "And it happened approximately eight days after these words," makes clear the fulfillment by that event of Jesus' preceding prediction that some of the audience would not die before seeing God's rule. The specification of eight days instead of Mark's and Matthew's six days appears to reflect a Roman week of eight days, but "approximately" forestalls a contradiction of Mark and Matthew. Again the praying of Jesus evidences his piety. The glorification of Moses and Elijah as well as of Jesus and their talking about his departure, which he is about to accomplish in Jerusalem, show the kingdom of God to be a heavenly one unthreatening to the present Roman Empire; for Jesus' departure will turn out to be an ascension to heaven (9:51; 24:50–51; Acts 1:9–11). *Read Luke 9:28–36.* The linking of Peter's ill-considered suggestion with his and the other disciples' grogginess sympathetically lightens his blame. Their fear explains their later silence, and the addition of "the Chosen One" to "my Son" distinguishes Jesus from Moses and Elijah as the one the disciples should listen to.

The following episode happens "the next day" inasmuch as the disciples' sleepiness implied an overnight stay on the Mount of Transfiguration. *Read Luke 9:37–43a.* The father's begging Jesus and the son's being an only son heighten the pathos and thus the kindness of Jesus in giving the son back to his father healed from the unclean spirit. The amazement of all at God's greatness saves Jesus from any charge of self-promotion even though everybody marvels at all that Jesus is doing. Another passion prediction and the emphasis with which it is introduced also help save him from such a charge. *Read Luke 9:43b–50.* The hiddenness of Jesus' meaning again sympathetically lightens blame in the disciples' arguing who of them might be greatest. "Knowing the speculation of their hearts" shows Jesus' prophetic insight, and standing a little child "beside himself" and the following sayings make the small great. Similarly, Jesus validates an exorcist who uses Jesus' name but does not follow with the Twelve. Thus the wide-ranging appeal of Jesus in Luke.

The Strange Exorcist

Now begins a Hellenistically appealing travelogue of Jesus' journey to Jerusalem to be taken up in the Ascension. That he "sets his face" shows bravery in view of the preceding passion predictions. The sending of messengers to make advance preparations turns this journey into one of royal visitations (see especially 10:1; 19:28–38, 44c), and most of it provides a narrative framework for extensive teaching by Jesus. Even the few miracle stories issue in his teaching. *Read Luke 9:51–62.* As residents of central Palestine and offspring from intermarriages of northern Israelites not taken exile by the Assyrians and of Gentiles imported to northern Israel by those same Assyrians, the Samaritans hated Jews and vice versa—hence the refusal of a Samaritan village to receive Jesus, and James and John's

Journey to Jerusalem

question whether to call down fire from heaven to annihilate the village (see Josephus, *Antiquities of the Jews* 20.6.1 §§118–24, for an instance of Samaritans' killing Galilean pilgrims to Jerusalem, as Jesus and his disciples are here, and Jews' counterattacking). Jesus' rebuke of James and John and going to another village exhibit magnanimity. The last three episodes in the chapter emphasize itineration ("the Son of man has nowhere to lay his head"), proclamation ("come away [from your father] and announce far and wide the rule of God"), and perseverance ("no one putting his hand on a plow and looking back is useful for the rule of God").

Mission of the Seventy-Two

Since ancient Jews counted the number of nations in the world at seventy-two, Jesus' appointment and sending of seventy-two other messengers ahead of him probably symbolizes the worldwide evangelistic mission of the church (compare 24:27; Acts 1:8).[13] *Read Luke 10:1–16.* The prohibitions of greetings along the road and of moving from house to house in a locality and the command to eat what is served are due to the need for haste, for Jesus is soon to arrive. "Peace" (*shalom* in Hebrew) is a normal Semitic greeting, but here it connotes the blessings of salvation that Jesus is bringing. "A son of peace" (10:6) is a person receptive of those blessings. Because Jesus is soon to arrive, the rule of God has come near.

Read Luke 10:17–24. Jesus equates the exorcisms reported by the seventy-two with a lightning-like fall from heaven of Satan, ruler of the demons. The promise of protection has to do with travel in evangelistic endeavor (serpents and scorpions along the way), not with contrived demonstrations of supernatural power. To guard against arrogance, Jesus substitutes joy in privilege (the recording of names in heaven) for joy in performance (the exorcism of demons). Similarly, his own joy, inspired by the Holy Spirit always active in his life, lies in God the Father's revelation through him to babies in learning, such as the seventy-two, rather than to the learned. The privilege of his revelation exceeds anything enjoyed by prophets and kings.

The Good Samaritan

Next Jesus shows graciousness to a lawyer by commending his answer despite his testing of Jesus. *Read Luke 10:25–37.* The good answer of the lawyer sets out religious and social ideals. The parable of the good Samaritan robs the lawyer of his attempted self-justification by indicating that to love your neighbor obediently as you love yourself naturally, you must be a neighbor yourself rather than

---

13. *Some ancient texts of Luke read "seventy," but they tend to be inferior to those that read "seventy-two."*

defining who else is or is not your neighbor. Being a neighbor means treating any needy person near you as your neighbor without laboring over a definition, whereas laboring over the definition of a neighbor keeps you from helping the needy person. Jesus shocks the lawyer by making the helper a Samaritan. A Jew such as the lawyer would expect Jesus at most to have made the Samaritan a person in need of help, so that the lesson would run: a Jew should help even a Samaritan in need. Instead it runs: even a Samaritan helps a Jew in need. End of ethnic pride in Jesus' ideal society![14]

The travelogue continues with an episode that invites women *Martha* into the privileges of discipleship heretofore reserved for males: sit- *and Mary* ting at the feet of Jesus and listening to his words. It is unnecessary for women to serve the meal. *Read Luke 10:38–42.*

Again the piety of Jesus comes out in his praying, but this time *Prayer* his praying leads to instruction on praying. *Read Luke 11:1–13.* The Lord's Prayer, shorter here than in Matthew, tells the disciples what to pray. The following parable and sayings tell them how to pray: with perseverance. As beggars know, if you keep on asking, people will give. If you look long enough, you will find. If you do not stop knocking, the person inside will finally open the door.[15] Given a

---

14. *A knowledge of background deepens appreciation of this point. The road from Jerusalem to Jericho descends over 3000 feet in less than 15 miles, through gorges and ravines infested with bandits. The priest and the Levite may fear ritual defilement from what could well be a corpse. Such defilement would cost them the purchase of ashes of a red heifer for purification, the loss of temple privileges (such as eating from sacrifices) during a week of defilement, the arrangement of burial for the corpse, and the rending of a perfectly good garment as a sign of grief. The priest and the Levite quite clearly see in the victim a threat of personal loss and inconvenience. The Samaritan has equal reason to by-pass the injured and possibly dead man, however, because Samaritans likewise avoid defilement from the dead—and perhaps even more reason, because chances are that the victim is a detestable Jew. But not only does the Samaritan stop to investigate. He treats the wounds with wine to disinfect them and with olive oil to soothe them, tears bandages from his own turban or linen undergarment to wrap up the lesions, goes on foot as the victim rides his donkey (the slower pace exposing them to greater danger of further attack by bandits), pays enough money to an innkeeper for two weeks of convalescence, and pledges unlimited credit for any additional expense—all without hope of reimbursement, since Samaritans have no legal rights in Jewish courts. When asked to identify the true neighbor in the parable, the scribe cannot bring himself to say, "the Samaritan," but uses a circumlocution, "the one who showed him mercy."*

15. *Apparently the traveler in Jesus' parable journeyed during the evening to avoid the heat of afternoon and so arrives at midnight, very late by the standards of ancient Orientals, who retire early. The oriental "law of hospitality" causes the traveler's host to wake a neighbor for provisions of food. The three small loaves of bread for which he asks are considered a meal for one person. The reluctance of the neighbor is aggravated by the fact that Palestinian families slept close together on mats in the same room, so that to rise and unbolt the door would wake up the whole family. In the neighbor's reply, the absence of a polite address, such as "Friend" in the request to him, shows annoyance.*

fatherly relation to the disciples, how much more will God answer their persistent prayers! Both long and scaly, fish and snakes look alike. So too do eggs and scorpions if the latter have their claws and tails rolled up.

Disbelief The setting back to back of the accusation that Jesus exorcises demons by their ruler, Satan, and the demand that Jesus produce a sign from heaven exposes a disbelief unreasonable in its refusal to be satisfied by what should count as adequate evidence. *Read Luke 11:14–36.* The finger of God stands for his power, the fully armed strong man and his castle and possessions for Satan and his kingdom and demoniacs, and the stronger man and his victory for Jesus and his exorcisms. His beatitude on those who hear the Word and do it shows him to be a teacher of high morals. The condemnation of his contemporaries as evil shows him to be impatient with low morals. Coming as it does right after Jesus as the sign of Jonah, the lamp on the lampstand seems to represent Jesus. But "the lamp of your body" represents a person's perception of Jesus.

Pharisees and Lawyers Next comes some table talk such as Luke's Hellenistic audience delighted in. *Read Luke 11:37–52.* The verb usually translated "washed" in 11:38 literally means "baptized" and may refer to bodily immersion, practiced by Pharisees among others, not just to hand-washing. Ever the teacher of ethics and religion, Jesus contrasts the evil of rapacity and the good of generosity and pairs the social virtue of justice with the religious virtue of love for God. The wisdom of God that will send prophets and apostles appears to be God's wisdom personified, or perhaps a now-lost book called "The Wisdom of God," or Jesus speaking of himself as God's wisdom.

The increasing attractiveness of Jesus to thousands contrasts with the hostile reaction of a few scribes and Pharisees. *Read Luke 11:53–12:59.* To his disciples Jesus speaks about speech (12:1b–12). He warns against hypocrisy in speech (12:1b–3). Calling his disciples "my friends," an address which projects a social ideal, he warns against speaking in fear of other human beings and encourages speaking in fear of God and in dependence on the Holy Spirit, against which Spirit opponents of the disciples will blaspheme to their eternal loss (12:4–12). To a member of the crowd and then to the crowd, Jesus warns against greed (12:13–14, 15–21). To his disciples again, he warns against anxiety (12:22–32) and commands charitable giving (12:33–34) and readiness for the Second Coming (12:35–40). When Peter asks whether Jesus is speaking to the crowd as well as to the disciples, Jesus keeps right on speaking to the disciples by defining their readiness for the Second Coming in terms of civility and moderation (12:41–48), and by describing his First Coming in terms of dividing disciples from nondisciples—at great cost to himself (12:49–53). Finally turning back to the crowds, he tells them to settle up with God before time runs out (12:54–59).

To settle up with God means to repent and bear the fruit of good behavior, but time is limited. *Read Luke 13:1–9*. Nothing more is known about Pilate's having some Galilean pilgrims killed in Jerusalem as they were offering sacrifices in the temple, or about the fall of the tower in Siloam (perhaps a tower in the wall of Jerusalem near the Pool of Siloam). To those who report the first of these incidents, Jesus speaks about the need for repentance (13:1–5) and, by parable, about the limited time available for it. Fig trees deprive surrounding vines and other plants by absorbing an extraordinary amount of nourishment from the soil. Therefore the fig tree in question is given only one more year's chance to bear fruit before being chopped down (13:6–9). *Repentance*

Time for repentance is followed by time for healing. Jesus' healing a woman on the Sabbath displays both his humanitarianism, in contrast with the legalistic indignation of a synagogue ruler, and Jesus' esteem for the woman as "a daughter of Abraham." Two parables follow. These interpret the humiliation of Jesus' opponents and the whole crowd's rejoicing over all the splendid things done by him as God's rule grown large, like a mustard seed grown into a tree, and extensive, like yeast having permeated a huge lump of dough. The "therefore" which introduces the parables of a mustard seed and yeast relates them to the immediately preceding effect of Jesus' miracle. *Read Luke 13:10–21*. *Healing*

Now Luke reminds his audience of the character of the present narrative as a travelogue and relates Jesus' by-passing a question on the number of those being saved to teach the avoidance of evil as evidence of salvation, a salvation that on the grounds of such evidence will include many Gentiles, such as Luke writes for, but excludes many Jews. *Read Luke 13:22–30*. The last who will be first are Gentiles, the first who will be last are Jews. Final firstness means salvation, final lastness means damnation. *Salvation*

Herod (Antipas), too, is going to Jerusalem (see 23:8–12); but Jesus refuses to let that fact deter him from his own journey to Jerusalem. *Read Luke 13:31–35*. "That fox" is feminine in the Greek *Herod the Fox*

Frigidarium in Herod's winter palace at Jericho.

text and alludes to Herod's insignificance: a vixen is no lion and may hint at the domination of Herod by his unlawful wife Herodias.

Healing and Table Talk   At Sabbath meal in the house of a leading Pharisee, Jesus heals a man afflicted with dropsy (14:1–6). This healing again illustrates Jesus' humanitarianism (compare 13:10–17) and leads to table talk (compare 7:36–50). The first part of the table talk, entailed in the healing, shames into silence the lawyers and Pharisees present (compare 13:17). The second part deals with honor and shame in the receiving of hospitality (14:7–11) and in the giving of hospitality (14:12–14). In the third part of the table talk, the universality of the gospel issues out of the offended honor of a man whose dinner invitations were refused by those whom he invited first. They represent self-righteous Jews, such as the lawyers and Pharisees at table with Jesus. The poor, crippled, blind, and lame who are brought to the dinner represent social outcasts; and those brought in from outside town represent Gentiles. *Read Luke 14:1–24.*

A coin-bedecked headdress.

Discipleship

After reminding his audience again of Jesus' popularity and of the character of the narrative as a travelogue, Luke quotes sayings of Jesus that use the possibility of shame to spur his fellow travelers into true—that is, self-sacrificial—discipleship. *Read Luke 14:25–35.* Salt that has lost its saltiness (literally translated, "has become foolish") is subject to the shame of being thrown out as useless.

Three parables follow to defend Jesus against the grumbling of the Pharisees and the scribes that he has table fellowship with toll collectors and sinners. In all three, the element of joy over finding the lost contrasts with that grumbling; and in the third parable, the anger of an older brother represents the grumbling. *Read Luke 15:1–32.* In connection with the parable of a lost sheep, the righteous who need no repentance do not really exist. Jesus is speaking with sarcastic irony about the self-righteous who only think that they do not need to repent.

The Lost Sheep

The lost coin may belong to a coin-bedecked headdress of the kind often worn by Palestinian wives as part of the dowry given them at marriage. The woman lights a candle, not because it is nighttime, but because the typical Palestinian house lacks windows and has only one low door, which lets in very little light. Apparently the coin has fallen on the lower level of a one-room house. There it

The Lost Coin

lies hidden underneath some straw scattered over the lower level because of domestic animals. The housewife sweeps with a broom, probably a small palm branch, not to uncover the coin, but to make it tinkle on the hard earthen floor in order that she may determine its whereabouts. Her joy on discovering the coin represents "joy in the presence of the angels of God over one sinner who repents." Jesus is not referring to the joy of angels, but to the joy of God himself in the presence of the angels. Forming a stark contrast is the rabbinic saying, "There is joy before God when those who provoke him perish from the world."

The Prodigal Son   According to the law of primogeniture, a younger son receives much less by inheritance than an older son receives. "Gathering everything together" means converting into cash, presumably by sale. Since pigs are ritually unclean for Jews, feeding pigs because of employment to a Gentile and wanting to satisfy hunger with the carob pods fed to the pigs evidence the desperate straits of the prodigal son. Repentance grows out of the prodigal's sense of misery and need and makes him resolve to return home with the confession, "Father [a respectful address], I have sinned against heaven [a reverential Jewish substitute for 'God'] and in your sight [an admission of guilt first in relation to God and then in relation to the father]," and with the plea to be restored only as a hired servant. Denying any claim on his father, he will ask for mercy.

But the prodigal underestimates his father's love, just as the Pharisees and the scribes are underestimating the love of God. On seeing his son returning, the father runs to meet his son. Running is unusual and undignified for an aged oriental man; but the father's love and joy overpower his sense of decorum, as though to say that even God forgets his dignity in a burst of joy when a sinner turns in repentance to him. The father's kiss signifies forgiveness. The son begins to blurt out his prepared confession, but before he comes to the part about being taken back as a hired servant, the father interrupts with commands to clothe him with the best robe as a sign of honor, to place on his finger a signet ring for sealing legal documents as a sign of restored filial authority, to put shoes (a luxury worn only by free people) on his feet as a sign that he is no longer a hired laborer, and to kill the fattened calf for a banquet of celebration. Since meat did not form part of the daily diet, its presence on the menu denotes festivity.

Here the parable might have ended. But it is double-edged. The words of the older brother to his father are revealing. He rudely omits the respectful address, "Father." He avoids calling the prodigal his brother but refers to him as "your son." He complains that his father has never given him so much as a young goat, much less a fattened calf, for a party with his friends. (One could query how many friends such a person has.) The older brother follows a sense of duty without a balancing sense of freedom, serves his father without fellowship, and prides himself on his own merits. No wonder he feels resentful of his father's grace toward the prodigal. (There is a rabbinic parable in which a son is redeemed from slavery but brought back as a slave rather than as a son in order that obedience may be forced from him.) The father's reply to the older brother graciously begins with an affectionate "Son," reminds him that all the family estate is now deeded to him, and explains the appropriateness of festivity in that "your brother" (not "my son") was (as good as) dead and lost, but is now alive and found. What is the older brother's response? Jesus does not say, but leaves the parable open-ended because the Pharisees and the scribes and all others who trust in their own merits finish the parable themselves, either by renouncing their self-righteousness to join in the messianic feast of salvation or by shutting themselves out through maintaining their self-righteousness. Finally, the older brother shows that a person does not have to feel lost to be lost. One can be estranged from God right on home territory. But everyone is invited—both flagrant sinner and decent older brother—on the same terms, God's forgiving grace.

The Older Brother

Jesus addresses his next parable to the disciples. Like the preceding parable of the prodigal son, it illustrates the shortsightedness of squandering wealth: by trying to serve wealth as well as his master, a household manager succumbs to the love of wealth, squanders his master's estate, and loses his position just as people in general who succumb to the love of wealth squander their heavenly reward and lose their position in God's household. By way of contrast with the prodigal's foolish shortsightedness, however, the present parable also shows a prudently foresighted way to use wealth, that is, to make friends with it through generosity. *Read Luke 16:1–13.* The manager has his master's debtors dispose of their old bills and write new, smaller ones in their own handwriting. The manager hopes that if the ruse is discovered, the absence of his handwriting will keep him

The Unjust Steward

from blame. Since elsewhere Jesus compares God to an unjust judge without attributing injustice to him, and his own return to the housebreaking of a thief without attributing thievery to himself, the dishonesty of a manager does not destroy the positive point of the present comparison. Specifically, the manager uses money to help other people and thus to make friends for the period of his unemployment. Similarly, disciples of Jesus ought to use money in charitable enterprises, for such action will be to their own advantage in the eternal future. "The sons of this age" means worldly people. "The sons of light" means disciples of Jesus. "The mammon of unrighteousness" means wealth in its capacity of leading people who have it to act unrighteously, not wealth gained unrighteously; for one could hardly be "faithful" with regard to ill-gotten wealth. The making of friends with mammon points up a social ideal such as Luke uses to appeal to his Hellenistic audience.

A description of the Pharisees as lovers of money links the following section to the preceding one on wealth. Their scoffing at Jesus leads him to expose them as detested by God even though admired by their fellow human beings, in contrast with the toll collectors and sinners who, though detested by the Pharisees, are forcing their way by repentance into the kingdom of God. The Pharisees' practice of divorce and remarriage and of marrying divorcees offers an example of their violating the law through committing adultery despite their self-justification and despite the validity of the Law and the Prophets. *Read Luke 16:14–18.*

The Rich Man ("Dives") and Lazarus

Read Luke 16:19–31. The money-loving Pharisees resemble the rich man, who selfishly and shortsightedly disregards Lazarus, a helpless, poor man. The rich man is therefore the obverse of the foresighted manager in 16:1–8. "Lazarus" is Greek for the Hebrew "Eleazar," which means "God is (his) help." No one else helps him. The crumbs from the rich man's table, which Lazarus would like to eat, may be pieces of bread used as napkins to wipe the hands and then discarded beneath the table. The phrase "Abraham's bosom" implies a heavenly banquet with Lazarus as a recently arrived guest reclining on a cushion immediately in front of Abraham. The banquet scene makes appropriate the rich man's request that Lazarus dip his finger in water. The address of the rich man, "Father Abraham," appeals to his Jewish descent from Abraham. But Abraham's response, beginning with "Son," indicates that although as a Jew the rich man has enjoyed every advantage, Hebrew ancestry

A beggar in Jerusalem.

does not guarantee heavenly bliss. The closing statement that some-one's resurrection from the dead will not persuade the rich who disobey Mosaic and prophetic injunctions to help the poor hints at Jesus' resurrection.

Now Jesus turns back to the disciples and speaks about their communal relations: the inevitability that some ("stumbling blocks") will lead others ("little ones") to sin ("stumble"); the needs to rebuke a sinning fellow disciple ("your brother") and forgive a repentant one, repeatedly, if necessary; and obedience to the command to for-give as requiring only a small amount of faith and a mere sense of

Christian Community

237

obligation. A reference to the uprooting of a sycamine (or sycamore or mulberry) tree grows out of the extraordinary strength and depth of its roots. *Read Luke 17:1–10.*

The Healing of Ten Lepers

A reminder of Jesus' journey to Jerusalem renews the narrative.[16] Ten lepers' standing at a distance reflects a demand of the Mosaic law that lepers live apart from others (Lev. 13:45–46; Num. 5:2–4). Emphasis falls not so much on Jesus' healing the ten lepers, but on the glorifying of God, thanksgiving to Jesus, and saving faith of the one leper who is a Samaritan; for Luke is appealing to Gentiles. *Read Luke 17:11–19.*

Answering a question of the Pharisees, Jesus deters them from thinking that the rule of God is yet to come with observable signs. Though the Pharisees have not recognized its presence, it is already among them. Then turning to the disciples Jesus speaks of the future: the time just preceding and including his unmistakably recognizable return ("the days of the Son of man" culminating in "his day"), a time not to follow the example of Lot's wife, who turned

Lot's Wife

into a pillar of salt for looking back toward the city of Sodom when she should have been fleeing its destruction without hesitation (Gen. 19:26). For Luke, however, the important point lies in the futurity of those days (". . . you will long to see one of the Son of man's days and will not see it") and the present political innocence of the rule of God brought by Jesus: Christianity does not threaten Roman society, but improves it. *Read Luke 17:20–37.*

Continuing Jesus' speech to the disciples is a parable that teaches

The Widow and the Unjust Judge

them to pray patiently but persistently for justice at the Second Coming. *Read Luke 18:1–8.* In ancient Jewish society the marrying of girls thirteen or fourteen years old resulted in a large class of young widows. A widow's bringing her case to one judge instead of a tribunal implies a matter of money, such as an unpaid debt or part of an inheritance withheld from her. A judge's not fearing God means that he lacks honesty; his not regarding people means that he lacks sympathy. Apparently a rich and influential opponent of the widow in Jesus' parable has bribed the judge, but she is too poor to do so. Her only weapon consists in a tenacious faith that justice will be

---

16. *"Between Samaria and Galilee" contains two puzzles: (1) the border between these two regions runs east and west, whereas "the way to Jerusalem" runs from north to south; (2) going to Jerusalem would take Jesus from Galilee through Samaria, whereas Luke mentions Samaria before Galilee. Possibly but not certainly, Luke's original text read "through Samaria and Galilee" and mentioned Samaria first, not because of geographical order but out of interest in the Samaritan who figures in the following story.*

done if she exasperates the judge with her persistence. The widow represents disciples, unjustly persecuted by their enemies and therefore unsubversive of the Roman government. The delay in her reception of justice represents a delay in the Second Coming. But the delay will not last long, for God has much greater concern for justice than the judge in the parable does. The only question, then, is whether Jesus' disciples will maintain their faith during the delay.

The preceding parable dealt with praying for justice in relation to one's persecution; a follow-up parable deals with praying for justification in relation to one's sins. Directed to people who regard themselves as righteous and others as sinful, this parable teaches humility. Infants, the smallest of children, then become Jesus' example of humility. *Read Luke 18:9–17.* With the Pharisee's prayer may be compared an excerpt from the Jewish Prayer Book: "Blessed are you, O Lord our God, King of the Universe, who have not made me a Gentile . . . who have not made me a slave . . . who have not made me a woman." But modern stereotyping of the Pharisee and the toll collector has taken away the force of this parable. Pharisees served God seriously by going without food from sunrise to sunset on Mondays and Thursdays and by tithing all their possessions as well as keeping the moral and ritual commandments of the law. Common people admired them greatly. Toll collectors, on the other hand, collaborated with the hated Roman oppressors, fleeced their fellow Jews, and practiced all sorts of fraud; the common people detested them. Jesus' audience must have been shocked to hear him put the Pharisee in a bad light, the toll collector in a good light. But the very unexpectedness in the reversal of good and bad roles underscores the nature of forgiveness as God's gift, unmerited and granted solely on the basis of repentant faith.

The Pharisee and the Toll Collector (Publican)

While the self-righteous need to learn humility for entrance into God's kingdom, an extremely wealthy ruler needs to learn charity to the extent of selling all his property and distributing the proceeds to the poor, plus following Jesus. *Read Luke 18:18–30.* A second prediction of the Passion and the Resurrection (compare 9:22) puts emphasis on their carrying out prophetic passages in the Old Testament and on the hiding of Jesus' prediction from the disciples' comprehension. Luke is excusing their incomprehension so as to portray the Christian community in the most attractive light possible. *Read Luke 18:31–34.* The healing of a blind beggar issues in his glorifying God and in the eyewitnesses' giving praise to God—a religious success in addition to the therapeutic one. *Read Luke 18:35–43.*

Zacchaeus   The episodes in Luke 19 are replete with notations of Jesus' progress to Jerusalem. The travelogue is nearing completion. *Read Luke 19:1–10.* In itself, the story of Zacchaeus shows that salvation can come even to a rich man if he repents. By promising to give half his possessions to the poor and pay back those he has defrauded four times the original amount, Zacchaeus far exceeds the normal boundaries of charity and restitution; for in cases of financial fraud, such as Zacchaeus's, the Mosaic law prescribes a restitution of the original amount plus only twenty percent (Lev. 6:1–5; Num. 5:6–7). In Luke's larger picture, the excess of Zacchaeus's charity and restitution exhibits the social benefits of Christianity.

The Pounds   *Read Luke 19:11–27.* The practice of local leaders' going to Rome to gain imperial support for their claims to rulership forms the background of the parable of the pounds (or minas, each one the equivalent of about three months' wages for a manual worker). The parable shows that neither the Hellenistic world in general nor the Roman government in particular has anything to fear from Christianity; for Christians regard themselves as individually subject to strict standards of judgment by their own Lord, as required to live productively, and as awaiting God's rule, not fomenting a rebellion against Rome. The nobleman represents Jesus. His going to a distant country represents Jesus' ascension to heaven. His receiving royal power there represents Jesus' heavenly exaltation at the right hand of God (compare Acts 2:34–36). The citizens' expressed desire not to have him rule over them represents the Jewish leaders' rejection of Jesus (compare 23:13–25). His return represents the second coming of Jesus. The calling of his servants to account represents the Last Judgment. And the execution of his enemies represents final punishment of the Jewish leaders. The case of the servant who wrapped up his pound teaches the impossibility of safe discipleship. To truly follow Jesus entails the risk of life-investment as opposed to the security of life-preserving.

In the Temple   *Read Luke 19:28–48.* The episodes of the Triumphal Entry and of the cleansing of the temple show Jesus' kingship to be heavenly and peaceful, not earthly and seditious. It features miracles of healing, not acts of rebellion, and issues in joyful praise to God and in religious reformation. Jesus does not fight; he weeps. Only the corrupt chieftans of the temple oppose him; the general populace applaud his teaching.

The next two chapters, Luke 20–21, tell of Jesus' teaching, preaching the gospel, and answering questions in the temple. *Read Luke 20:1–26.* The Sanhedrin's fear that all the people will stone them if they say that the baptism of John had a merely human origin points up the success of John's Spirit-empowered testimony to Jesus. Though the parable of the vineyard refers to God (the owner), Israel (the vineyard), Jewish leaders (the tenant farmers), Old Testament prophets (the slaves), and Jesus (the beloved son), the long time for which the owner goes away would seem to remind Luke's audience that Jesus, too, has been away for a long time (compare 17:22; 19:11–12). The members of the Sanhedrin correspond to the builders who reject the cap- or cornerstone and who will therefore be broken to pieces and crushed in judgment. Their wickedness, exposed in their trying to seize Jesus "that very hour," in their fear of the people, in their watching Jesus, in their tricky sending of spies who pretend to be righteous, and in their intention to trap Jesus and hand him over to the governor—this wickedness sets Jesus by contrast in a good moral and political light.

Read Luke 20:27–44. Jesus' putdown of the Sadducees contrasts "the sons of this age" with those "considered worthy to attain that age [the coming age] and the resurrection from the dead" and brings out the immortality of those worthy ones because "they are children of God, being children of the resurrection," and their living for God. Thus Jesus' disciples as well as Jesus himself appear in a good light. The commendation of him by some of the scribes gives further testimony to the power of his putdown and prepares for his asking them a question, criticizing them in public, and contrasting their detestable behavior with the admirable behavior of a poor widow. As usual in Luke, Jesus looks the part of a good moral teacher. *Read Luke 20:45–21:4.*

Presence in the temple at or near the treasury leads some to remark the beautiful stones and votive gifts (tapestries, gold grape clusters, etc.) that decorate the temple. Jesus responds with a prediction of its destruction. When asked for the time and portent of this destruction, he stresses delay and avoidance of claims to immediacy: do not go after those who say that the time is near; wars and revolutions must take place first, and even then the end does not follow right away; persecution and Christian testimony will precede large earthquakes, plagues, famines, terrors, and great heavenly signs; and Gentiles will trample Jerusalem for a while after its destruction. The exhortation not to be terrified by wars and revolutions distances Jesus' disciples from such fighting. Irresistible wisdom will characterize their speaking, and perseverance their suffering of persecution, which will include treachery of the worst kind and will fall due to the name of Christ, not to any misbehavior on the part of his disciples. They should flee Jerusalem and the Judean countryside rather than staying and joining in rebellion. It is nondisciples who will get their comeuppance. The disciples are to avoid dissipation, drunkenness, and worldly worries, and to keep alert by praying. Nothing to fear from Christians here. Their speech and conduct will be admirable, as is that of Jesus, who draws so much admiration that everybody gets up early to hear him in the temple. *Read Luke 21:5–38.*

Passion Narrative *Read Luke 22:1–6.* The introduction to Luke's passion narrative features the Sanhedrin's fear of the people because of Jesus' popularity. Apparently the Sanhedrin fear that the people will stone them for killing Jesus just as they feared that the people would stone them for denying the heavenly origin of John's baptism (compare 20:1–8). The contrast between their fear and Jesus' popularity puts them in a bad light and him in a good light. Satan's entering Judas Iscariot makes Jesus' arrest, trial, and death due to influence from the archdemon himself rather than to any misdeed on the part of Jesus. This entry also explains how such a dastardly deed could have been done by one of the twelve apostles. Otherwise, the deed would wreck Luke's portrayal of Jesus and the disciples as an ideal community.

Passover *Read Luke 22:7–13.* The necessity of slaughtering a Passover lamb on the Day of Unleavened Bread combines with Jesus' taking the initiative in sending Peter and John to prepare the Passover meal. This combination portrays Jesus as a law-abiding Jew rather than as a renegade (compare 2:21–24, 39, 41–52). That he includes the apostles with himself as those for whom the meal is to be prepared highlights the fellowship of friends and family at table, a kind of fellowship that figures prominently in Hellenistic culture.

Read Luke 22:14–23. The apostles' reclining with Jesus renews the emphasis on table fellowship among friends and family (compare 8:19–21). So also does Jesus' saying that he has eagerly desired to eat the Passover with the apostles before he suffers. This desire is due to his coming inability to eat the Passover with the apostles until the Passover reaches its fulfillment at the messianic banquet in God's kingdom. Yet again emphasizing table fellowship are a command that the disciples divide the cup among themselves, the description of Jesus' body (represented by bread) as "given" for them, and the further command to carry on this table fellowship in memory of him while he is gone. Double emphasis on the cup and a placement of the cup after dinner as well as before make for a symposium ("drinking together," accompanied by table talk) such as followed a banquet in the Greco-Roman culture to which Luke is appealing. "Until the rule of God comes" is a reminder that the present interim poses no political threat to Rome. The setting of table fellowship makes the betrayer's presence as dastardly as possible. The going of Jesus "as it has been determined" makes his death a matter of prior plan on God's part instead of present human failure on Jesus' part. And the apostles' beginning to discuss among themselves which one of them might be the betrayer puts them in the good light of accepting Jesus' exclamation that the betrayer's hand is with him at table.

Not so flattering to the apostles is their dispute over which of them seems to be the greatest. But some comments of Jesus, which carry on the table talk at this symposium, negate the dispute immediately. *Read Luke 22:24–30.* Jesus' comments do not redefine greatness in terms of a slave's service, but tell the greatest person to become like the youngest person, the leader to become like a waiter at table, just as Jesus himself, great though he is, has become like a waiter at table. Thus the theme of table fellowship is maintained and service is taught without a denial of greatness. Again putting the apostles in a good light is Jesus' mentioning their loyalty to him in hard times and conferring on them the privilege of further table fellowship with him in his kingdom, just as God his Father has conferred rulership on him. Greatness indeed!

Read Luke 22:31–34. Sifting like wheat stands for an attempt to shake loyalty. Emphasizing that Peter's three denials of Jesus will hold the danger of apostasy are Jesus' using the old name "Simon" rather than the new name "Peter," doubling the old name "Simon," addressing Simon alone despite the plural number of "you" whom Satan has demanded to sift (see the Greek text), praying that Simon's faith not fail, and indicating the need of Simon's fellow disciples that he strengthen them. Much as in Judas's case, the use of the activity of Satan explains how Simon could be so disloyal as to verge on apostasy with his denials, how such disloyalty could show itself in the ideal community of Jesus and his disciples. The turning back of Simon to the extent of strengthening his fellow disciples illustrates the restorative possibilities in this community. Simon's response exhibits a respect of Jesus ("Lord") and expresses without any self-exalting comparison with the other apostles a readiness to travel with Jesus both to prison and to death. Though Simon will deny that he knows Jesus, he will not deny Jesus himself. Thus Luke continues to portray Christian community, as represented by the apostles, in the best possible light.

The next dialogue in this symposium indicates that the apostles should return to the taking of normal provisions now that Jesus will die the death of a criminal in fulfillment of Isaiah 53:12. By implication, he is not a criminal even though he will be treated as such; and the apostles will carry on an itinerant ministry in his absence. The presentation of two swords implies that the apostles think of defending Jesus and prepares for just such an effort in Gethsemane—even explains in advance how it can be that a disciple of the peace-loving Jesus will draw a sword and strike off the right ear of a servant of the high priest—whereas Jesus' answer, "It is enough," implies that he thinks of no such effort, much less of armed rebellion against the powers that be, but of their defending themselves from the dangers of travel. *Read Luke 22:35–38.*

The symposium has ended. Luke's account of the episode in Gethsemane, for which he substitutes a less specific reference to the Mount of Olives in accordance with 21:37, now emphasizes the disciples' need to pray just as Jesus prays. A reference to their sorrow explains their sleeping, answers in advance his question, "Why are you sleeping?" and thus puts them and their community with Jesus in the best possible light. It is highly debatable whether Luke wrote 22:43–44 or a scribe added these verses later, for most of the very best manuscripts and early versions lack the verses. If authentic, they add to Luke's emphasis on Jesus' praying. *Read Luke 22:39–46.*

Arrest   *Read Luke 22:47–53.* Judas's kiss slips from the realm of actuality to that of intention so as to leave more room for the question of armed conflict. A description of the cut-off ear as the slave's right one adds to the seriousness of the swordman's act of violence, for the righthandedness of most people makes the right more useful and favorable than the left. Jesus' answer, "Enough of this!" and healing of the ear answers the question of armed conflict negatively. From now on, governmental authorities have nothing of this sort to fear from the disciples. That the ones around Jesus see what is going to happen lends the credibility of eyewitness to the episode (compare 1:1–4). And references to the hour of his enemies and the power of darkness attribute his arrest to the most evil of influences rather than to any misbehavior on his part.

Luke goes directly to Peter's denials of Jesus in the courtyard of *Peter's Denial* the high priest's house. Jesus' turning and looking intently at Peter after the third denial and cockcrow trigger Peter's memory and bitter weeping. A description of Jesus' mockers as blaspheming, that is, *Mockery and* as engaging in slander, shows him innocent. His trial before the *Trial of Jesus* Sanhedrin takes place with the coming of day. The questions of *The Sanhedrin* christhood and divine sonship are divided. Jesus' answer to the first exposes the Sanhedrin's unbelief and fear (compare 20:3–8), projects a heavenly rule unthreatening to Caesar, and raises the second question. *Read Luke 22:54–71.*

Read Luke 23:1–5. A description of the Sanhedrin as "all their *Pilate* multitude" (literal translation in 23:1) prepares for their overwhelming of Pilate's desire to release Jesus. The claim that they have found him forbidding people to pay taxes to Caesar and calling himself Christ, a king (and therefore a rival of Caesar), spells out the ways in which he has purportedly been perverting the Jewish nation. Refusal to pay taxes is considered an act of rebellion. Luke's audience can easily see the falsity of these charges in Jesus' having said to pay taxes to Caesar (20:19–26) and in his having strictly ordered the disciples not to tell anyone that he is the Christ (9:20–21; compare 4:41), in his never having told the people himself that he is the Christ, a king (though they themselves called him a king at the Triumphal Entry, 19:38), and in his having refused to answer the Sanhedrin's own question whether he is the Christ (22:66–68). On interrogation, Pilate himself finds him innocent, but the Sanhedrin only expand their charge so as to say that in his teaching Jesus has been inciting the people to rebel all the way from Galilee to Jerusalem, whereas Luke's audience knows that Jesus has been teaching morality and religious devotion.

The Sanhedrin's mention of Galilee leads Pilate to ask whether *Herod Antipas* Jesus is a Galilean. Learning that he is one leads Pilate to send him to Herod Antipas, who has jurisdiction over Galilee. *Read Luke 23:6–12.* Herod's desire to see Jesus started as far back as 9:9.

The Pilate Inscription.

Vehemence substitutes for truth in the Sanhedrin's accusations against Jesus before Herod. In view of Jesus' innocence, the ridicule to which Herod and his soldiers subject him is supposed to draw the sympathy of Luke's audience; but in view of Acts 12:21, Herod may pridefully put a bright robe on himself rather than mockingly on Jesus.

Read Luke 23:13–25. Suddenly "the people" turn up on the side of the Sanhedrin against Jesus. Yet since they have joined the Sanhedrin in charging him with turning "the people" away from Roman rule, the people who accuse him must differ from those purportedly misled by him. Perhaps the accusatory people are the same as "the council of elders of the people" (22:66), but called simply "the people" to link up with Luke's having referred to the Sanhedrin as "all their multitude" (23:1). Pilate repeats his earlier declaration of Jesus' innocence, underlines its validity by noting that he interrogated him in the Sanhedrin's presence, adds to his own declaration a like one by Herod, and indicates that he will release Jesus after a good whipping just to teach him not to get in trouble with the Sanhedrin again. The thought of Jesus' release triggers a wholesale outcry for the release of Barabbas instead. The description of Barabbas as a prisoner who committed murder and participated in a rebellion right under the Sanhedrin's noses in Jerusalem exposes the gross injustice of the requested exchange: a life-giving pacifist for a murderous rebel. Pilate's second indication of desire to release Jesus draws forth a demand, doubled and put in the present tense for emphasis (so the Greek text), that Pilate crucify Jesus, that is, give him a criminal's death. Yet a third indication by Pilate that he will release Jesus after a good whipping because Jesus has not committed a capital crime seals the innocence of Jesus, supports the political innocence of his followers in Luke's time, and puts Roman officialdom in a comparatively good light and Jewish officialdom in an incomparably bad light. The voices of the latter prevail: insistence overcomes justice; loudness substitutes for evidence. Pilate never does declare Jesus guilty, but orders that the Sanhedrin's demand be carried out. Another mention of Barabbas's imprisonment for rebellion and murder renews attention to the gross injustice perpetrated by the Sanhedrin.

Luke now describes the leading of Jesus away as a procession in which Simon the Cyrenian carries the cross behind Jesus and a large multitude of the people and of mourning women follow. The loyalty of these people to the bitter end displays their recognition of Jesus' truly good character over against the false charges leveled at him by the Sanhedrin. Selflessly, he brushes aside a lamentation for him and warns of disasters to fall on the people. "Daughters of Jerusalem" implies that he is speaking about the destruction of Jerusalem (compare 19:41–44; 21:5–6). *Read Luke 23:26–31.* The green tree stands for a favorable time, the dry tree for an unfavorable time. Hence, if an event so bad as Jesus' crucifixion takes place during the present period of peace, how much worse will be the disaster to befall Jerusalem during the coming period of war (again compare 19:41–44). *Via Dolorosa*

Read Luke 23:32–43. The crucifixion of two criminals with Jesus further highlights the injustice of his crucifixion. The meaning of criminals, "doers of evil," contrasts with Jesus' having done good (see Acts 10:38). Luke avoids the word "bandits, revolutionaries" (so Mark and Matthew), perhaps to keep his audience from even associating Jesus with insurrection against Rome. Jesus' praying forgiveness for his enemies and excusing their injustice as due to ignorance show him pious to the end and boundlessly magnanimous. The rulers' sneering contrasts with the people's watching. So also does the soldiers' mockery. (Is Luke playing on public dislike of soldiers for their bullying, as in 3:14?) The blaspheming of Jesus by one of the criminals crucified with him forms a foil against which stands *Crucifixion*

The Repentant Thief out the statement of the other criminal that in contrast to them, Jesus has done nothing wrong. In the conversation between the second criminal and Jesus, the replacement of Jesus' kingdom with present Paradise pushes that kingdom into the future and makes Paradise a heavenly state unthreatening to earthly Rome.

Read Luke 23:44–49. Luke explains the darkness of early afternoon as due to the sun's failing to shine. Suitably to his emphasis on Jesus' piety as shown in prayer, the last word from the cross consists of a prayer, one that expresses trust in God the Father with the last breath drawn by Jesus. The centurion, an eyewitness of this event, reacts by glorifying God with an affirmation of Jesus' innocence. And all the crowds, having viewed the whole series of events, react by lamenting his death as they leave the scene. But his acquaintances and women followers stand still, seeing also things that now transpire.

Joseph of Arimathea *Read Luke 23:50–24:12.* Even in his death Jesus attracts the best: Joseph of Arimathea is good and righteous and a holdout against the Sanhedrin's machination. His interring of Jesus' body in a tomb never used before pays special tribute to Jesus' innocence (compare 19:30). *Women* The women disciples continue to play the role of eyewitnesses by following Joseph to the tomb and observing the interment. Their resting on the Sabbath after returning and preparing spices and perfumes with which to anoint Jesus' body shows them to be law-abiding Jews. Given the suspicion of novelty and the legal standing of Judaism in the Greco-Roman world, Luke stresses the linkage of Christianity with Judaism. Sunday morning, the women's finding the stone rolled away from the tomb combines with their not finding the body of Jesus inside to cause them perplexity. The standing of two men to announce his resurrection provides sufficient testimony and erases their fear. The dazzling apparel of the men enhances their testimony by pointing to its divine source (compare 9:30, 32 and the identification in 24:23 of these two men as angels, that is, messengers from God). A reminder of Jesus' having predicted the very events of passion and resurrection that have now taken place erases the women's perplexity. The nonsensical and incredible impression made by their own testimony on the eleven apostles and Peter's confirmation of the emptiness of the tomb show that the apostles will believe in Jesus' resurrection only on sure and certain grounds (compare 1:1–4).

The Emmaus Disciples The testimony of two disciples outside the circle of the eleven now supplements that of the two angels who appeared as men at

Ruins at 'Imwas, one of the possible sites of Emmaus.

the empty tomb. This new testimony arises out of a personal encounter with the risen Jesus. The occurrence of this encounter on the very day that the angels have explained the emptiness of the tomb as due to his resurrection underlines the truth of their explanation. The naming of one of the disciples (Cleopas) and of the village to which they are traveling from Jerusalem (Emmaus) and the specification of distance (sixty stadia, or about seven miles) provide circumstantial data supporting the reliability of the two disciples' testimony. By matching Jesus' habit of talking with his disciples during travel and at table, his doing the same here likewise supports the testimony of the two. Their sadness and initial failure to recognize him disfavor fabrication of the testimony out of an expectation that he will rise from the dead. His scriptural explanation to the two of his passion and resurrection again supports their testimony by linking its subject matter with a divine plan already evident in ancient tradition. Their inward feeling of warmth as he gives this explanation supplements scriptural tradition with existential impact. The opening of their eyes to recognize him makes them eyewitnesses. And an appearance of him to Simon (Peter) adds to their eyewitness testimony a second such testimony. *Read Luke 24:13–35.*

A third appearance of the risen Jesus occurs in the midst of all the disciples as the travelers to Emmaus are giving their testimony. *Read Luke 24:36–53.* Alarm, fear, and long-lasting doubt again disfavor a fabrication of the account out of an expectation that Jesus will rise ***Bodily*** from the dead. The visibility and tangibility of his body combine ***Resurrection*** with his eating of food to define the Resurrection as physical and make the disciples eyewitnesses. The reminder of his passion-and-resurrection predictions and his further explanation of the Old Testament (according to its Hebrew division into the Mosaic Law, the Prophets, and miscellaneous writings headed by the Psalms) confirm what they see and lead to his commissioning them to preach in his name to all the nations. The subject matter of their preaching—that is, repentance issuing in the forgiveness of sins—will carry on the social reform begun by John the Baptist and enlarged by Jesus. The promise of God the Father that he will "clothe" them with "power from on high" is the coming of the Holy Spirit (Acts 1:4–5; 2:1–4). No one can criticize the effect of Jesus' ap-***Ascension*** pearance, actions, words, blessing, and departure through ascension into heaven: the disciples praise God continually in the temple. Thus Luke ends volume one of his two-part work by evoking admiration for the piety of the Christian community.

FOR *To what class of people in the modern world is Luke's gospel best suited?*
FURTHER *Or is Luke's a classless gospel?*
DISCUSSION

How would you describe the personality of Jesus if you had only Luke's gospel for evidence?

Evans, C. A. *Luke*. Peabody, Mass.: Hendrickson, 1990.

Evans, C. F. *Saint Luke*. London: SCM; Philadelphia: Trinity, 1990. Advanced.

Fitzmyer, J. A. *The Gospel According to Luke*. 2 vols. Garden City, N.Y.: Doubleday, 1981, 1985. Advanced.

Marshall, I. H. *The Gospel of Luke*. Grand Rapids: Eerdmans, 1978. Advanced.

Nolland, J. *Luke 1–9:20, 9:21–18:34, 18:35–24:53*. 3 vols. Dallas: Word, 1989, 1993. Advanced.

Stein, R. H. *Luke*. Nashville: Broadman, 1992.

Talbert, C. H. *Reading Luke*. New York: Crossroad, 1984.

*FOR
FURTHER
INVESTIGATION*

10

John:
Believing in Jesus
for Eternal Life

- ❖ *Who wrote the gospel of John?*

- ❖ *How do we determine its authorship?*

- ❖ *When and where was this gospel written, and what indications do we have of its date and provenance?*

- ❖ *For what audience, from*

what standpoint, and with what purpose did the author write?

- ❖ *How does this gospel differ from the synoptics?*

- ❖ *What theological emphases stand out in it?*

- ❖ *What overall plan determines its movement?*

Authorship

Written in a simple style, the last of the gospels exhibits a theological profundity beyond that of the synoptics. Early church tradition favors that the apostle John wrote this gospel toward the close of the first century in Ephesus, a city of Asia Minor. Especially important is the testimony of Irenaeus, a disciple of Polycarp, who was in turn a disciple of the apostle John—a direct line of tradition with only one link between Irenaeus and John himself.[1]

In the past, some scholars insisted that the fourth gospel was not written until the mid-second century and therefore long after the apostle John had died. But discovery of the Rylands Fragment of John forced abandonment of that view. This papyrus fragment dates

---

1. *Irenaeus*, Against Heresies *2.22.5; 3.1.1; 3.4; Eusebius*, Ecclesiastical History *2.23.1–4; 4.14.3–8; 5.8.4; 20.4–8.*

from about A.D. 135 and requires several previous decades for the writing, copying, and circulation of John as far as the Egyptian hinterland, where the fragment was discovered. Other early papyri containing the text of John support the implication of the Rylands Fragment.

But many scholars are still unconvinced that the apostle John wrote the fourth gospel. Some suggest that a disciple of the apostle John, perhaps the elder John mentioned very early by Papias,[2] wrote it and was later confused with the apostle of the same name. But closer inspection of Papias's statement shows that he probably used the term *elder* in an apostolic sense, and so becomes a primary witness for authorship by the *apostle* John.[3]

The writer of the fourth gospel claims to have been an eyewitness of Jesus' ministry (1:14; compare 19:35; 21:24–25) and exhibits a Semitic style of writing[4] and an accurate knowledge of Jewish customs (for example, the customs of water-pouring and illumination by candelabra during the Festival of Tabernacles, presupposed in 7:37–39; 8:12) and of Palestinian topography as it was before the outbreak of the Jewish war in A.D. 66 and the destruction of Jerusalem and the temple in A.D. 70 (for example, the pool with five porches near the Sheep Gate [5:2] and the paved area outside the Praetorium [19:13], both in Jerusalem).[5] In addition, details such as one would expect from an eyewitness, yet incidental to the story,

---

2. *Quoted by Eusebius,* Ecclesiastical History *3.39.4.*

3. *"If, then, any one came who had been a follower of the elders, I questioned him in regard to the words of the elders, what Andrew or what Peter said, or what was said by any other of the disciples of the Lord, and what things Aristion and the presbyter [elder] John, the disciples of the Lord, say" (Papias, as quoted by Eusebius, according to the translation in A Select Library of Nicene and Post-Nicene Fathers of the Christian Church, 2d series, ed. P. Schaff and H. Wace, trans. A. C. McGiffert [New York: Scribner's, 1904], 1:171). Both times the name John appears in Papias's statement, it appears with both the designations "elder" and "disciple." By contrast, Aristion, even though designated a disciple, lacks the title "elder" when mentioned alongside John. This fact points toward a single individual named John. Papias wanted to make plain the single identity of John by repeating the designation "elder" just used for the apostles but omitted with Aristion, and Papias mentioned John a second time because John was the only one of the apostles still alive and speaking. Admittedly, Eusebius interpreted Papias to refer to two different men named John and even claimed a tradition of two men named John and having different tombs in Ephesus; but Eusebius wished to find a way around apostolic authorship of the book of Revelation, which he disliked. It appears, then, that from Papias's statement an elder John allegedly distinct from the apostle John has been conjured up to enable an attribution of Revelation to the elder rather than to the apostle.*

4. *Seen especially in parallel statements. This style has led to the theory, not popular, that John originally wrote his gospel in Aramaic.*

5. *Some scholars therefore date the fourth gospel three decades or so earlier than the closing years of the first century.*

appear everywhere—numbers (six water jars [2:6], three or four miles [6:19], one hundred yards [21:8], 153 fish [21:11]), names (Nathanael [1:45ff.], Nicodemus [3:1ff.], Lazarus [11:1ff.], Malchus [18:10] et al.), and many other vivid touches. These traits substantiate both the early tradition of apostolic authorship and its corollary that the gospel represents trustworthy historical tradition.

Moreover, the author writes as "the disciple whom Jesus loved," not out of egotism (he never identifies himself by name), but to emphasize that the contents of the gospel merit belief since they come from the man in whom Jesus confided. Still further, the beloved disciple repeatedly appears in close association with Peter (13:23–24; 20:2–10; 21:2, 7, 20ff.). The synoptists tell us that James and John the sons of Zebedee worked at fishing with Peter and with him formed an inner circle among the Twelve. Since James died as a martyr long before the time of writing (Acts 12:1–5) and since Peter appears as a different person from the beloved disciple, only John is left to be the beloved disciple and author of the fourth gospel. For if someone other than the beloved disciple wrote it, why did he not attach the name of John to "the disciple whom Jesus loved"? The anonymity of the beloved disciple can hardly be explained unless he himself wrote the gospel, and the process of elimination identifies him with John the apostle.

Supplementation of the Synoptics   John consciously supplements the synoptics and possibly reworks them at a number of points.[6] He emphasizes the Judean ministry of Jesus and largely omits parables and the theme of God's kingdom. Apparently John thought the synoptics had presented enough information about Jesus' Galilean ministry and the kingdom. He also supplements the synoptics by making clear that Jesus' public ministry lasted considerably longer than a reading of the synoptics alone would indicate. The synoptics mention only the last Passover, when Jesus died. But John mentions at least three Passovers and probably four during Jesus' ministry; thus it lasted at least more than two years and probably from three to three and a half years.[7]

Jesus' Speech in John   With the partial exception of Matthew, the fourth gospel contains more extended discourses by Jesus than the synoptics do. The discourses tend to curtail narrative. Questions and objections from the audiences often punctuate these discourses, and John regularly

---

6. *Others think the fourth evangelist did not know the synoptics.*

7. *See A. T. Robertson,* A Harmony of the Gospels *(New York: Harper & Row, 1950), 267–70.*

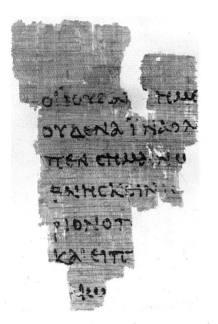

The Papyrus Rylands Greek 457, a fragment of John's gospel, dates back to the first half of the second century.

reports Jesus as speaking in a style different in many respects from that which the synoptists report. The differences may stem partly from John's way of translating into Greek the teaching which Jesus originally spoke in Aramaic and Hebrew and partly from John's habit of elaborative paraphrasing, with the result that the vocabulary, style, and theological concerns of the evangelist often appear in his record of Jesus' teaching. In the synoptics, translation is apparently more literal and elaborative paraphrasing less extensive.[8] Often, loose translation and elaborative paraphrasing can communicate the intended meaning of a speaker and the larger consequences of what he said even more effectively than direct quotation does, so that John's procedure is not at all illegitimate. On the other hand, we must not overestimate the degree of Johannine elaboration or looseness in translation, for the two famous parallel passages in Matthew 11:25–27 and Luke 10:21–22 favor that Jesus could and did speak in the style represented by the fourth gospel. Prominent in those passages are the Father-Son relationship and emphasis on divine revelation, knowledge, and election—all typical of the gospel of

---

8. *The vocabulary and style of John himself are recognizable from those parts of the fourth gospel where Jesus is not speaking and from 1–3 John. Revelation, also Johannine, is somewhat different for various possible reasons (see page 458).*

John. It is also possible that John preserves the more formal aspects of Jesus' teaching, such as sermons in synagogues and disputes with Jewish theologians.

Johannine Theology   Throughout the fourth gospel, many important theological themes appear and reappear in different combinations and often crop up in 1–3 John and Revelation as well. John expounds these themes by skillfully alternating narratives and discourses, so that the words of Jesus bring out the inner meaning of his works. Thus, *Symbolism* much of the action becomes symbolic. For example, Jesus' washing the disciples' feet represents cleansing from sin. There is also frequent irony, such as that which tinges his question, "I have shown you many good works from the Father; for which of these do you stone me?" (10:32). And just as the works of Jesus bear a symbolic *Multiple Meanings* meaning, so also his words often carry a second and even a third meaning. "Born again [or anew]" also means "born from above" (3:3ff.), and the reference to Jesus' being "lifted up" alludes not only to the means of his execution, a cross, but also to his resurrection and exaltation back to heaven (12:20–36, especially 32).

Word   The theological themes in John begin under the category of revelation. Jesus is the revelatory *Word (Logos)* of God. As such he re-*Truth* veals the *truth*, which is more than veracity. It is the ultimate reality *Witness* of God's own person and character, as *witnessed* to by Jesus, the *Light and* Father himself, the Spirit, Scripture, and others. The *light* of this *Darkness* revelation illuminates those who believe and drives back the *dark-* *Judgment* *ness* of evil. The repulsion of darkness is the *judgment* of the world. Not that Jesus came to condemn the world, but he did come to discriminate between those who belong to the light and those who belong to the darkness—and the latter stand already self-condemned *The World* by their unbelief. The *world*, human society dominated by Satan, opposes the light and thereby becomes the object of God's wrath. This fact makes it all the more remarkable that God "loved the *Love* world" (3:16). His *love* came through Jesus Christ and continues to manifest itself through the love of Jesus' disciples for one another. To demonstrate God's love, Jesus descended from the Father and *The Hour* worked toward his *"hour,"* the time of his suffering and death on be-*Glory* half of the world. For revealing the Father's *glory* in this way, the Father in turn glorified the Son with heavenly exaltation. By God's *Election / Believing* *election* and their own *believing* (John lets stand the antinomy be-*Regeneration* tween divine and human choices) some people experience *rebirth* by *Knowledge* the Holy Spirit, so that they come to *know* God through Christ. But

though election and believing characterize only some, *universality* *Universality*
characterizes the invitation. Those who do accept the invitation re-
ceive *eternal life* (not only quantitatively everlasting but also qualita- *Eternal Life*
tively divine), an *abiding* place in Christ, and the *Paraclete*, or Holy *Abiding / The Paraclete*
Spirit in his roles as Comforter, Counselor, and Advocate. To men-
tion these themes is but to skim the surface of Johannine theology;
each one has nuances that deserve a full elaboration.

Preeminently, however, John writes a gospel of *believing*: *Believing in Jesus*

> Many other signs therefore Jesus also performed in the pres-
> ence of his disciples, which are not written in this book; but
> these have been written that you may *believe that Jesus is the
> Christ, the Son of God*; and that believing you may have life in
> his name (20:30–31).

Christological in content, this believing highlights the *deity* of Jesus *Jesus' Deity*
as the unique and preexistent Son of God who in obedience to his
Father became a *real human being* to die sacrificially for the salvation *Jesus' Humanity*
of other human beings. Such an emphasis went against the denial of
his humanity and death by Gnostics, early Christian heretics who
thought anything material or physical to be inherently evil.[9] Thus,
not only does the deity of Jesus receive emphasis (beginning with
"the Word was God" [1:1] and many times throughout the gospel);
so also his humanity: "the Word became flesh" (1:14), grew tired
and thirsty (4:6–7; 19:28), wept (11:35), and physically died and
rose again (19:30–42; 20:12, 17, 20, 27–28). Jesus himself demands
this Christological belief by making a series of "I am . . ." claims in *"I am . . ."*
the fourth gospel:

> "I am the bread of life" (6:35, 48; compare 6:41, 51);
> "I am the light of the world" (8:12);
> "I am the door" (10:7, 9);
> "I am the good shepherd" (10:11, 14);
> "I am the resurrection and the life" (11:25);
> "I am the way and the truth and the life" (14:6);
> "I am the true vine" (15:1, 5).

In addition, there are "I am" statements not followed by a complement. These suggest the claim to be the I AM-YAHWEH of the
Old Testament (4:25–26; 8:24, 28, 58; 13:19; compare 6:20; 7:34,
36; 14:3; 17:24; Ex. 3:14).

---

9. *See pages 60–61.*

Realized Eschatology   When people believe, they receive eternal life immediately—hence C. H. Dodd's phrase: "realized eschatology."[10] Full enjoyment awaits in the future, but every believer savors a foretaste in the present. (Perhaps some Christians were perturbed and some non-Christians incredulous over the delay in Jesus' return; thus the Johannine emphasis on salvation now.) With this emphasis John seeks to evangelize unbelievers with the gospel or to establish Christians in their faith. (It is difficult to decide whether he wrote for unbelievers, for believers, or for both.)

Anti-Baptist Polemic   The correction of a cult that had grown up around the figure of John the Baptist provides a possible subsidiary purpose behind the writing of the fourth gospel. Acts 19:1–7 reveals the presence of Baptists in Ephesus some decades earlier, during the time of Paul; and according to early tradition, John the apostle wrote his gospel in Ephesus. Moreover, John takes great pains to show that Jesus surpassed the Baptist, that the Baptist had to decrease and Jesus increase, that through his disciples Jesus baptized more followers than the Baptist did, and that Jesus had testimony even greater than what the Baptist gave him (1:15–37; 3:25–30; 4:1–2; 5:33–40). The matter hangs in doubt, however, because these phenomena may instead reflect the apostle John's own experience of conversion from the Baptist to Jesus.

Anti-Jewish Polemic?   It is unlikely that John wrote his gospel as a polemic against Judaism; for although "the Jews" appear in a bad light because of their unbelief, "the world" does, too (for example, see 15:18–19). Toward the end of the first century, Jews incorporated into the liturgy of their synagogue services the Benediction against Heretics to root out all Jewish Christians who might still be participating in those services.[11] Some have thought that this benediction provided the occasion for the fourth gospel as an encouragement to Jewish Christians to endure ostracism from the synagogue without recanting their Christian profession. But though the Benediction against Heretics may have given special point to the references in 9:22 and 16:2, which mention the putting of Jesus' disciples out of syna-

---

10. *But against a thoroughgoing realized eschatology in which nothing remains for the future, see the references to final resurrection and judgment in 5:25–29. The phrase "inaugurated (or proleptic) eschatology" serves better.*

11. *"For the excommunicated let there be no hope, and quickly root out the kingdom of pride in our days, and let the Christians and the heretics perish as in a moment. Let them be blotted out of the book of life, and with the righteous let them not be written. Blessed are you, O Lord, who subdue the proud."*

gogues, the fourth gospel (in contrast with Matthew, Hebrews, and James) does not give the impression of having been written to an audience so narrow as to include only Jewish Christians. Jewish features do not predominate, and those that appear reflect the Jewish milieu of Jesus' life rather than arising by way of John's accent.

On the other hand, there is no suppression of Jesus' Jewishness. We must therefore reject the hypothesis that the fourth gospel represents a Hellenistic portrait of Jesus in which he is played up as a divine man in contrast with a historically realistic portrayal of him as an eschatological prophet. As a matter of fact, Jesus' deity appears clearly and early already in the synoptics, and even earlier in the epistles. Furthermore, the Dead Sea Scrolls have shown that the religious vocabulary of John's gospel is characteristic of first-century Judaism; hence, no need exists to search for Hellenistic models further afield. *Jewish vs. Hellenistic Traits*

Theories of literary sources behind the fourth gospel stumble against the unity of style which pervades the entire book. Theories of disarrangement in the original text solve some problems of interpretation only to create others; and with one minor exception they lack manuscript evidence. *Sources and Disarrangement?*

In several respects John 1:11–12 presents a summary of the kinds of material included in the fourth gospel: (1) "Those who were his own did not receive him"—the somber backdrop of the gospel consists in repeated rejections of Jesus by the Jews. (2) "But as many as received him"—in contrast with the general rejections, a number of individuals did receive Jesus through personal encounter with him. (3) "To them he gave authority to become children of God"—John details a number of miracles performed by Jesus, but calls them "signs" and "works" because of their value in symbolizing the transformation that takes place in those who receive Jesus. All three lines converge in the story of his death and resurrection: "Those who were his own did not receive him"—crucifixion at the hands of the Jews; "but as many as received him"—the three Marys and the beloved disciple standing beside the cross; "to them he gave authority to become children of God"—transformation through the power of Christ's resurrection. *Contents*

Signs, Works

An Outline of John

Prologue: Jesus Christ the revelatory Word [Logos] of God (1:1–18)

I. The Faith-Producing Impact of Jesus' Initial Ministry (1:19–4:42)
   A. Narrative (1:19–2:25)
      1. The testimony of John the Baptist and the making of the first disciples (1:19–51)
      2. The turning of water to wine at a wedding in Cana (2:1–12)
      3. The cleansing of the temple and the performing of signs in Jerusalem (2:13–25)
   B. Discourse[12] (3:1–4:42)
      1. The new birth, in conversation with Nicodemus (3:1–21)
      2. The superiority of Jesus, as testified by John the Baptist during their concurrent ministries of baptism (3:22–36)
      3. The water of life, in conversation with the Samaritan woman, plus her conversion and that of her fellow townspeople (4:1–42)

II. The Authority of Jesus' Life-Giving Words (4:43–5:47)
   A. Narrative (4:43–5:8)
      1. The healing of an official's son (4:43–54)
      2. The healing on a Sabbath of the invalid by a pool in Jerusalem (5:1–9a)
   B. Discourse: the authority of Jesus' words (5:9b–47)

III. The Giving of Jesus' Flesh and Blood for the Life of the World (6:1–71)
   A. Narrative: the feeding of the five thousand and the walking on the water (6:1–21)
   B. Discourse: the bread of life (6:22–71)

IV. The Illumination of People by Jesus, with Their Resultant Division into Unbelievers, Destined for Judgment, and Believers, Destined for Eternal Life (7:1–8:59)
   A. Narrative: the attendance of Jesus at the Festival of Tabernacles and a division of opinion about him (7:1–52)
   B. Discourse: the light of the world and the true children of Abraham (8:12–59)

V. The Tender Concern of Jesus in Contrast with the Cruelty of the Jewish Religious Authorities (9:1–10:39)

---

12. "Discourse" often includes a measure of dialogue.

A. Narrative: the healing of a blind man and his excommunication from the synagogue (9:1–41)

B. Discourse: the Good Shepherd, hirelings, thieves, and robbers (10:1–39)

VI. The Gift of Life Through Jesus' Death (10:40–12:50)

A. Narrative (10:40–12:19)

1. The raising of Lazarus, with the Sanhedrin's consequent plot to kill Jesus (10:40–11:57)

2. The anointing of Jesus by Mary of Bethany and the Sanhedrin's plot to kill Lazarus (12:1–11)

3. The Triumphal Entry (12:12–19)

B. Discourse: the grain of wheat that dies and springs to fruitful life (12:20–50)

VII. The Departure and Return of Jesus (13:1–20:29)

A. Discourse (13:1–17:26)

1. The cleansing of the disciples and their menial service to one another, as signified by Jesus' washing their feet (13:1–20)

2. The announcement of betrayal and the dismissal of Judas Iscariot (13:21–30)

3. The advantages to the disciples of Jesus' departure and of the Paraclete's coming (13:31–16:33)

4. The prayer of Jesus for his disciples (17:1–26)

B. Narrative (18:1–20:29)

1. The arrest (18:1–11)

2. The hearings before Annas and Caiaphas, with Peter's denials (18:12–27)

3. The hearing before Pilate (18:28–19:16)

4. The crucifixion and burial (19:17–42)

5. The empty tomb and resurrection appearances to Mary Magdalene and the disciples (20:1–29)

Conclusion: the purpose of the fourth gospel to evoke life-bringing faith in Jesus as the Christ, the Son of God (20:30–31)

Epilogue (21:1–25)

A. Narrative: another resurrection appearance to the disciples, with a miraculous catch of fish, and breakfast on the shore of the Sea of Tiberias [Galilee] (21:1–14)

B. Discourse: the recommission of Peter (21:15–23)

Final Authentication (21:24–25)

Prologue   The fourth gospel opens with a prologue. *Read John 1:1–18.* Some scholars think that in this prologue the evangelist works over an earlier existing hymn, others that he composes on his own against the background of the Old Testament stories of creation and the giving of the law on Mount Sinai. "In the beginning" recalls

Word (Logos)   Genesis 1:1. "Was the Word [Greek: *Logos*]" recalls God's speaking the various elements of chaos into their created order (for example: "and God said, 'Let there be light,' and there was light"), only this speaking has turned into a personal being who preexisted with God, shared God's own identity, acted as God's agent in the Creation,

Incarnation   and in Jesus Christ became incarnate ("enfleshed")—that is, became a human being complete with a physical body ("flesh")—so as to communicate to the human race the glory of God, not in a show of lightning and thunder, as at Mount Sinai, but in a revelation of God's grace and truth, which have replaced the Mosaic law given at Sinai. Inasmuch as the verb for the Word's dwelling among us means to live in a tabernacle, a tent (1:14), this glory of God's grace and truth likewise replaces the divine glory which settled on the tabernacle, or tent-sanctuary, when Moses had completed its construction according to the blueprint given him on Mount Sinai. As God's visible speech, the Word contrasts with the Hellenistic divine title "Silence" and equates with the light of the knowledge of God, which in turn contrasts with the darkness of ignorance of God. This knowledge brings life to those who receive the Word, that is, believe in his name, believe him to be the one who his name says he is, the divine Word. Unlike the world (the society of unbelievers), believers have gained this life not by way of human procreation ("born not of blood or of the will of flesh or of the will of a male") but by way of divine (re)generation ("born . . . of God"; compare 3:3–8) and thus become God's children regardless of ancestry. By and large, not even the Word's own people, with whom he shared Jewish ancestry, received him so as to become the children of God. But they did not fail to receive him through any lack of testimony, for John the Baptist bore witness to him even to the extent of declaring him prior in rank because of his priority in time.

Though "in the beginning" relates the Word immediately to Genesis 1:1, other uses may also have influenced the evangelist's application of the term to Jesus Christ: (1) the use of "the word of the LORD" in the Old Testament; (2) the use of "the Word of the LORD" or "the Word of God" as a surrogate for God in the Old Testament

Targums; (3) the description in the Old Testament and intertestamental Jewish literature of personified wisdom in terms very like the fourth evangelist's description of the Word; (4) the New Testament use of "the word" for the gospel; and (5) the use of Logos by philosophers such as the Stoics and the first-century Alexandrian Jew, Philo, for the rational principle (Reason), which they thought governs the universe. Against influence from this philosophical use, the fourth evangelist writes of divine communication, not of divine thought; and differently from all possible influences, he identifies the Logos with a human being of recent history.

The uniqueness of this Logos or Word comes out in the adjective "only," traditionally translated "only begotten." There is a text critical question whether 1:18 should read "(the) only God," looking back to the equation of the Word with God in 1:1c and requiring in the following phrase of 1:18 a switch from "God" to "the Father," or "the only Son," looking forward to "the Father" in the following phrase and to the emphasis on Jesus' divine sonship throughout the remainder of the gospel. The earliest and best manuscripts read "God" instead of "Son." The fourth evangelist's identification of the creative Word with the only God seems to strike against the Gnostic teaching of Cerinthus that the Creator differs from the supreme God. Similarly, the incarnation of God the Word in the one human being Jesus Christ seems to strike against the Gnostic teaching of Cerinthus that distinguishes between a divine spirit, Christ, and a fleshly human being, Jesus, and makes Christ leave Jesus before the Passion even though Christ descended on Jesus at Jesus' baptism.[13]

The Baptist's Witness

The fourth evangelist now spells out the witness of John the Baptist to Jesus. Clearing the ground for this witness is John's denial to "the Jews" (not the whole people, but their leaders living in Jerusalem, Judea) that he himself is the Christ, or Elijah come back to earth, or the prophet whom many Jews expected to appear in the end-time. Also clearing the ground is John's self-identification with a mere voice. The witness itself identifies Jesus as the one whom John's Jewish questioners do not know (compare 1:10–11), the one whose sandal thong John is unworthy to loosen, the sacrificial lamb

Lamb of God

who not only is provided by God but who as God (1:1c) takes away the world's sin, the one who outranks John inasmuch as he existed before John, the one on whom John saw the Holy Spirit descend and stay in order that he might baptize people in the Holy Spirit

---

13. Irenaeus, *Against Heresies 1.26.1; 3.11.1, 3.*

rather than in mere water, and the one who is God's Son. Thus John's preaching of repentance turns into a testimony to Jesus, and John's baptism into an occasion for the manifestation of Jesus to Israel. *Read John 1:19–34.*

First Disciples   A repetition of John's witness leads two of his disciples, Andrew and an unnamed one (probably John the apostle and fourth evangelist), to follow Jesus and abide with him. Thus spatial abiding seems to symbolize the spiritual abiding in Christ spoken of later (15:1–7). The two disciples have addressed Jesus as a rabbi, or teacher; but in speaking to his brother Simon, Andrew identifies Jesus as the Messiah, or Christ. On seeing Simon, Jesus displays omniscience of Simon's present name, the name of Simon's father, and Simon's future name Cephas (Aramaic for the Greek name Peter, both meaning "stone" or, more traditionally but less accurately, "rock"). *Read John 1:35–42.* Counted from sunrise, "the tenth hour" would be 4:00 P.M.; but then so little of the day remains that the statement, "They abode with him that day," turns vapid. Better then to count from midnight for an abiding with Jesus from 10:00 A.M. onward.

Read John 1:43–51. Jesus takes the initiative in calling Philip. The description of Philip as "from Bethsaida" sets the stage for a description of Jesus as "from Nazareth," which in turn sets the stage for Nathanael's question whether anything good can come from Nazareth. This question and the additional description of Jesus as "son of Joseph" are ironic, for John the evangelist has located Jesus' origin "in the bosom of the Father" (1:18) and John the Baptist has described Jesus as "the Son of God" (1:34). But Philip's description of Jesus as the one about whom Moses and the prophets wrote rings true. Again Jesus displays omniscience, this time of Nathanael's character and activity. And this time "Rabbi" escalates to "the Son of God," which corrects "son of Joseph," and "King of Israel," which suits Nathanael's being "truly an Israelite." Correcting Philip's description of Jesus as "from Nazareth" is Jesus' describing himself, "the Son of man," as a ladder, like Jacob's (Gen. 28:12), connecting earth with heaven and enabling angels to climb down with messages from God and climb back up for more. Deity is many-named, and Jesus is deity—therefore the piling up of names for him throughout this chapter.

Water to   *Read John 2:1–12.* Identification of the day on which Jesus per-
Wine at Cana   formed his first sign as "the third day" may anticipate the climactic

sign of his resurrection on the third day (compare 2:19). A wedding suggests the festivity of salvation (compare Rev. 19:6–9; Matt. 22:1–14; 25:1–13). Jesus' changing water to wine symbolizes the replacement of Judaism with the gospel; for John describes the water in terms of Jewish rites of purification, and the keeping of the good wine until last can hardly fail to recall John's earlier statement that "the law was given through Moses, but grace and truth came through Jesus Christ" (1:17). Jesus' declaration of independence from his mother implies that he will act only in accord with the timetable of God his Father. This timetable will lead up to the hour of Jesus, that is, the climactic week of his death and resurrection (7:30; 8:20; 12:23, 27; 13:1; 17:1). The imperviousness of stone keeps the water inside from ritual defilement. The huge capacity of the stone pots, twenty or thirty gallons each, magnifies the coming sign. So also does the filling of the pots up to their brims. The steward's remark rests on an effect of drunkenness, namely, the inability to distinguish between good wine and inferior wine. "This beginning of the signs" implies more signs to come, and the use of "signs" rather than "miracles" (which means "acts of power") shows that John is directing his audience's attention to the symbolic significance of Jesus' actions, not to their physical effect.

John mentions Jesus' cleansing of the temple early, the synoptists not until Passion Week. Some think Jesus cleansed the temple twice to open and close his public ministry, others that the synoptists delay the cleansing through omission of all his visits to Jerusalem except the last one, and yet others that in line with a habit of anticipating the future John advances the cleansing to link it closely with the Baptist's identification of Jesus as the Lamb of God (1:29, 36) and to make room for Jesus' raising of Lazarus instead of the temple-cleansing as the event which triggers a plot by the Sanhedrin to kill Jesus (compare John 11:1–57; 12:9–19 with Mark 11:15–19). As is fitting for the one whom John has identified as God, Jesus takes initiative. His finding sellers in the temple, his making a whip, his driving out the cattle and sheep, his pouring out the coins of the money-changers, his telling the sellers of doves to take them away and stop making his Father's house a market place—none of these actions are mentioned in the synoptics, and they all represent the divine initiative of Jesus, which also gets emphasis from an Old Testament reference to zeal for God's house (Ps. 69:9). The driving out of animals being sold for sacrifice and the sending out of

Cleansing the Temple

The Temple Mount today, looking south.

sacrificial doves symbolize the outmodedness of these sacrifices now that the Lamb of God has appeared on the scene. In a cryptic reference to his own body, Jesus' ironic calling on the Jews to destroy "this temple" alludes to his sacrificial death at their hands (see 19:16–18); and his prediction that he will raise the temple in three days alludes to his raising that body from the dead by his own divine power (compare 10:17–18). Since by definition a temple is the dwelling place of deity, Jesus' being God (1:1–18) makes his body a new temple replacing the old one in Jerusalem. *Read John 2:13–22.* The forty-six years of building the old temple refers to a refurbishing initiated by Herod the Great.

Nicodemus and Rebirth

Read John 2:23–3:21. The story of Jesus and Nicodemus, a member of the Sanhedrin, illustrates Jesus' omniscience of the interior state of human beings. Nicodemus examples those who believe in the name of Jesus solely because of the signs he performs (compare 2:23 with 3:1–2) but whom Jesus knows to be still in need of a renewal so radical as to constitute a new birth, one that originates in heaven above (compare 2:24–25 with 3:3–8) and happens through belief in Jesus as God's unique Son who descended from heaven and ascended back to heaven by way of being lifted up on the cross (3:11–21). Coming at night to Jesus, the true light, symbolizes exit from the darkness of ignorance, evil, and death and entrance into the light of knowledge, truth, and life. Water and wind are figures of speech for the Holy Spirit, the agent of rebirth from above (compare 7:37–39; Ezek. 36:25–27; Titus 3:5). One Greek adverb means both "again, anew" and "from above." Likewise, one Greek noun means both "wind" and "Spirit." The blowing of the wind "where it wishes" stands for the sovereignty of the Holy Spirit in causing rebirth to occur (compare 6:44). The inadequacy of fleshly birth means the inadequacy of Jewish ancestry. Hearing the sound of the wind without knowing its origin and destination represents hearing the voice of the Spirit without understanding the mystery of the Spirit's movement (compare 10:16, 27; Rev. 2:7, 11, 17, 29 and so on). "Earthly things" means the metaphors of water and wind, "heavenly things" the realities of new birth from above by the Spirit's movement. For Moses' lifting up a bronze serpent for the salvation of Israel, see Numbers 21:8–9. Jesus' being lifted up is for everyone in the world. God's lifting him up by way of the cross defines the way God loved the world. Just as believers enjoy eternal life in advance of the age to come, so unbelievers stand under the sentence of condemnation in advance of the Last Judgment. But judgment not only means condemnation; it also means discrimination, here between evil-doers and those who practice the truth, that is, the truth of God in Jesus Christ.

Baptism The way back to Galilee leads first through the countryside of Judea along the Jordan River, where Jesus spends some time with his disciples. A reference to their baptizing people prepares for 4:1–2, but more immediately calls attention to Jesus' achievement of a success greater than John the Baptist's and gives occasion for a renewal of the Baptist's testimony to Jesus' superiority. Does all this emphasis on the Baptist's testimony to Jesus' superiority take aim at diehard followers of the Baptist in Ephesus, where John the apostle is reputed to be writing the fourth gospel (compare Acts 18:24–19:7)? *Read John 3:22–4:42.*

The Woman of Samaria   God's love for the world, not only for the Jews, shows itself in the necessity that Jesus go through Samaria for the salvation of people there, hated though they are by the Jews. Out of this necessity he takes the initiative in striking up a conversation with the Samaritan woman at Jacob's well. Counting from sunrise, the sixth hour would be noon, but the disciples' having gone into Sychar to buy food combines with the Jewish practice of eating two meals a day, one in the morning and another in late afternoon, to favor the sixth hour from noon (compare the comments on 1:39). Superficially, "living water" means flowing water, always fresh. But such water symbolizes the life-giving Spirit (compare 7:37–39). Like the water of purification in stone pots (2:6), the water in Jacob's well stands for Judaism, now to be replaced with water that brings eternal life. ("Will never thirst" refers, not to psychological satisfaction, but to everlasting salvation.) Do the woman's five husbands stand for the five books of Moses, the Pentateuch shared by Samaritans and Jews as the basis for their beliefs and practices, and the woman's present paramour for Samaritan apostasy from Judaism? "This mountain" is nearby Gerizim, where the Samaritan temple lies in ruins. We should not think of the human spirit and sincerity as the spirit and truth in which true worship of God the Father takes place; rather, of the Holy Spirit (3:5–8 and again 7:37–39) and Jesus the Truth (1:14, 17; 14:6). They provide the new locale of true worship. The harvest of which Jesus speaks to his returned disciples is eternal life for the Samaritans who come out to hear him and believe in him. He sows, he starts the process. The disciples will reap, will finish it in their work of evangelism.

Healing an Offical's Son   Jesus did not find trustworthy faith in Judea, called his "own country" because he should have found such faith there at the center of Judaism (see 2:23–25); so he proceeds onward to Galilee, where the Galileans receive him (compare 1:11–13). *Read John 4:43–54.* The emphasis on a nearness to death so great that the healing means living makes this second sign of Jesus symbolize salvation from eternal death to eternal life through believing his word. If counted from noon, "the seventh hour" (7:00 P.M.) allows for a day's journey of twenty miles (from Capernaum to Cana) by the royal official.

Healing a Lame Man on the Sabbath   As earlier, Jesus now goes to Jerusalem for a religious festival, this one unnamed, and there heals a sick man unable to walk. *Read John 5:1–47.* Like earlier mentions of Jewish water of purification, the water of Jacob's well, and the Samaritan woman's five husbands,

The summit of Mount Gerizim, showing remnants of a Samaritan shrine.

the mention of five porticoes enclosing the water at the Pool of
Bethzatha (or Bethesda or Bethsaida) combines with the issue of the
Sabbath to suggest a symbolic allusion to the five books of Moses,
the law, which is unable to give salvation, whereas Jesus is able to do
so—and does (again compare 1:17). (Modern archaeologists appear
to have discovered the five porticoes, so that John would not be
dealing in symbolism alone.) It may even be that the thirty-eight
years of sickness symbolically allude to Israel's thirty-eight years of
wandering in the wilderness (Deut. 2:14). In any case, Jesus' giving
the man strength in place of weakness (the Greek word for "sickness" in 5:5 means "weakness") symbolizes the life-giving power of
Jesus. The man's rising, picking up his mat, and walking when he
hears Jesus' word symbolizes the passing from death to eternal life
both presently, at conversion, and in the future, at the resurrection,
about which Jesus goes on to speak. Rabbinic law allows a physician
to treat sickness on the Sabbath only if the patient's life is in danger;

Pool of Bethzatha.

so Jesus' healing of this sickness, hardly a life-threatening emergency, as well as the carrying of a mat by the healed man breaches rabbinic law and brings persecution. Jesus equates his own work of healing on the Sabbath with the work of God his Father up to and including the present moment, Sabbath though it is. In such an equation, the calling of God his Father amounts to a claim of equal-

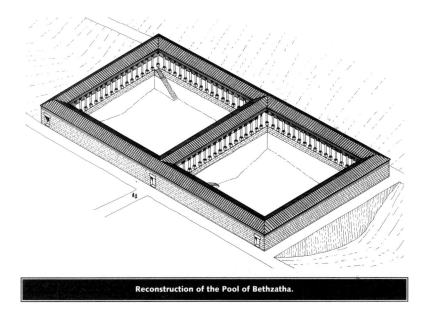

Reconstruction of the Pool of Bethzatha.

ity with God. But sonship to God also implies watching and doing what the Father does, just as an ordinary son, learning a trade, watches and does what his father does. The witness of Jesus on his own behalf is inadmissible, because Jewish courts treated people's testimony on their own behalf as possibly corrupted by self-interest; so Jesus appeals to the testimonies of John the Baptist, of the works that the Father has given Jesus to do, such as the preceding work of healing on the Sabbath, and of the Father himself in the form of his word (the Mosaic Scriptures and/or Jesus the Logos) abiding in believers. Jesus is often thought to mean that Moses wrote about him in Deuteronomy 18:15, 18. But the allusion may refer at least as much to the Mosaic story of God's giving manna to feed the Israelites on their way from Egypt to Canaan, for in the next chapter (John 6) Jesus will compare himself as the bread of life to that manna.

Read John 6:1–71. John's linking the feeding of the five thousand to the Passover combines with Jesus' comments about eating his flesh and drinking his blood to make the bread with which he feeds the crowd symbolic of his sacrificial death as the true Passover lamb. The locale on a mountain reinforces the symbolism by recalling Moses on Mount Sinai. As God incarnate, Jesus takes the initiative and exhibits his omniscience. The specification of barley

Feeding of the Five Thousand

bread recalls attention to the Passover symbolism, for Passover coincides with the barley harvest. No groupings of the five thousand are mentioned, and the grass is described as "much"; so John appears to portray the crowd as the "one flock" of Jesus the Good Shepherd who leads out his sheep to feed in verdant pastures (10:1–16). He gives the bread and the fish just as he gives his flesh as the bread of life. "That nothing be lost" makes the gathering of leftovers symbolize Jesus' losing none of those people whom the Father has given him. The identification of Jesus with "the prophet who is coming into the world" probably alludes to the prophet like Moses in Deuteronomy 18:15 (though that text originally referred with a collective singular to a whole line of Moses-like prophets whom God would raise up). Jesus will not be made king by those who recognize no sign but only like the feeling of a full belly. Believing in him is the work that God requires in the sense that saving faith is active and persevering. Yet equal stress falls on the necessity of **Bread of Life** God's drawing people to Jesus. As the bread of life Jesus is both living and life-giving. The heavenly origin of manna represents the heavenly origin of Jesus, the Word who in the beginning was with God and was God (1:1). Jesus' comments on eating his flesh and drinking his blood come so close to the Words of Institution at the Last Supper that John will omit those words in his account of that supper. The thought of cannibalism repulses the Jews, and Leviticus 17:10–14 prohibits the drinking of blood. But Jesus uses eating and drinking as metaphors of believing, that is, believing in the benefit of his sacrificial death; for the separation of flesh and blood denotes the violence of such a death. The flesh that contrasts with the Spirit and profits nothing is not Jesus' sacrificial flesh, but the useless flesh of ordinary human beings, as in 3:6. The turning away of many of Jesus' disciples previews the apostasy of professing Christians like the Gnostics at the time of John's writing.

The Jewish authorities in Jerusalem, Judea, are still seeking to kill Jesus (compare 5:18); so for the time being he stays in Galilee. Not even the sarcastic urging of his unbelieving brothers induces **Festival of** him to go along with other pilgrims to the Festival of Tabernacles, **Tabernacles** though its being the most popular and therefore most heavily attended of the Jewish religious festivals would give him the best of opportunities to display his supernatural powers. *Read John 7:1–9.*

Jesus follows a different timetable from that of his brothers, whom the world cannot hate because they belong to the world, whereas the hatred of the world for Jesus because he exposes its evil deeds means that he must regulate his travels in a way that avoids a premature death.

Read John 7:10–52. The delay and the secrecy of Jesus' journey to the Festival of Tabernacles and his remaining incognito until the middle of the festival keep him from exposure to arrest. By the time he does make a public appearance, he has become so lively a topic of discussion that the marvelousness and boldness of his teaching dumbfound some of the multitude and even freeze into inaction the officers sent by the chief priests and Pharisees to arrest him. He makes his having learned from God his Father more than compensate for his lack of a rabbinic education. By contrast, the teachings of a rabbi come from himself, a transgressor of the Mosaic law. When Jesus asks the Jewish authorities why they are seeking to kill him, the multitude from Galilee scoff. They do not know of the authorities' seeking to kill him (though for fear of the authorities they did not speak openly about him). Since the desire to kill him goes back to his healing a sick man at the Pool of Bethzatha on a Sabbath (5:1–18), he defends that healing by noting that the Mosaic law makes circumcision, the mutilation of one part of the body, more important than the Sabbath: circumcision must be performed on the eighth day after birth even though that day is a Sabbath. How much more should the healing of a man's whole body override the Sabbath law, Jesus argues. Unlike the multitude from Galilee, some of the Jerusalemites know about the authorities' seeking to kill him, ask whether they do not kill him because they know him to be the Christ, and themselves deny his messiahship because they know he comes from Galilee, whereas they believe the origin of the Christ should be unknown. Jesus retorts with a claim to have come from God as well as from Galilee. Divinely invincible against arrest until "his hour" comes, he goes on to say that he will go away. The Jewish authorities think of a teaching mission to Gentiles ("Greeks") living outside Palestine ("the Dispersion"), but he means a return to his Father in heaven. During the first seven days of the Festival of Tabernacles, priests bring water in a gold vessel from the Pool of Siloam to the temple and ceremoniously pour it out. On the climactic eighth (or seventh) day of the festival, Jesus shouts that he is the source of the true water, the life-giving Spirit. But some of the multitude, thinking of him as only a Galilean, object that he cannot be the Christ because he comes from Galilee rather than from Bethlehem (see Mic. 5.2). Thus in this one passage are reflected the apparently contradictory views that the origin of the Christ will be unknown and that he will be known to have been born in Bethlehem.[14]

Light of the World

The dialogue continues. *Read John 8:1–59.* Through the week-long Festival of Tabernacles the Jews keep four huge candelabra burning in the temple area to commemorate the pillar of fire which led and guarded Israel in the wilderness. That custom forms the background for Jesus' claim to be the light of the world, which in the first instance means the sun but ultimately means the light of eternal life brought by him. (Because in those days people kept a fire burning to avoid the laborious task of rekindling it, light came to be associated with life, darkness with death; for the dying of a person meant the dying out of the fire that he or she had kept going.) But light brings judgment on darkness. So Jesus plays on several possible meanings of judgment: (1) formation of an opinion, here in a super-ficial way; (2) condemnation; and (3) discrimination. When the Pharisees ask, "Where is your Father?" they are not only challenging Jesus to produce his father as a witness. They are also insinuating that he was born out of wedlock. The claim of Jewish unbelievers to be free overlooks their political servitude to Rome and to preceding world powers. To their boast of descent from Abraham Jesus replies that moral descent outclasses physical descent. The Jews have sub-jected themselves to the slavery of sin; thus they are more like the

---

14. *The story of the woman taken in adultery (John 7:53–8:11) does not belong here or any-where else in the Bible. The earliest and best manuscripts, undiscovered when the King James Version was published in 1611, omit it entirely. Later, inferior manuscripts have it inserted at various locations, some here, others after John 7:36, or 21:24, or Luke 21:38. The very princi-ples of textual criticism which assure the reliability of the rest of the New Testament text rule out this passage. Conversely, to insist on the originality of this passage in the text of the New Testament is to undermine the bases of our assurance that we have a substantially accurate text elsewhere in the New Testament. The story itself may be historically true, however, having been preserved in Christian oral tradition before interpolation into the canonical text. In the story, Jesus' accusers try to put him on the horns of a dilemma. If he recommends the death penalty in accordance with the Mosaic law, they can accuse him of going against Roman authority, which forbids Jews to impose the death penalty. If he does not recommend the death penalty, they can destroy his reputation by telling the people that he does not hold to the Mosaic law. It is custom-ary for the eldest accuser to throw the first stone. The center of attention, therefore, shifts to the el-dest when Jesus challenges them, "Let him who is sinless among you throw a stone at her." Each accuser leaves as he becomes the eldest in the group through the exit of someone older. Various suggestions concerning what Jesus writes on the ground are inconclusive. The final "sin no more" keeps Jesus from teaching an easygoing attitude toward sexual immorality.*

slave-born Ishmael, who had to leave Abraham's household, than the free-born Isaac, who remained in it. The statement, "Before Abraham was, I am," presents a claim to be the eternal God of redemption, Yahweh, I AM WHO I AM (Ex. 3:14).

Some Jews thought that a man could commit sin in a previous existence or in his mother's womb and be punished for it in this life. Others thought that children suffer for the sins of their parents. The disciples consider these possibilities when they see a blind man whom Jesus proceeds to heal. *Read John 9:1–41.* This healing brings light to a blind man and thus carries on the theme of Jesus as the light of the world. That the man has been blind from birth makes his healing a kind of new birth (compare 3:3–8). Jesus makes clay with spittle and applies it to the blind man's eyes to elicit faith, because spittle is popularly thought to have curative power, and also to set the stage for washing, which symbolizes a moral cleansing by the Holy Spirit. The meaning of Siloam, "Sent," points to Jesus as the one whom God has sent to give the Spirit, represented by the water from Siloam in the background to 7:37–39. Once again Jesus breaks the rabbinic rule that cures are not to be performed on the Sabbath unless life is in danger. Additionally, the making of clay constitutes kneading and therefore work. The fear of the Jewish leaders (Pharisees) on the part of the former blind man's parents probably represents fear of Jewish persecution on the part of Christians in John's community. The casting out in 9:34 refers to excommunication of the former blind man from the synagogue and appears to represent the later excommunication of Jewish Christians from synagogues. Counteracting this move, Jesus pronounces judgment on the Pharisees by saying that if they were blind, they would realize their need, repent, believe, and have their sins removed. But since they see, they feel self-sufficient and therefore remain unrepentant and unforgiven.

Healing of a Man Born Blind

The allegory of the Good Shepherd comments on the blind man (a sheep), Jesus (the Good Shepherd), and the Pharisees (thieves and robbers). Shepherds leave their sheep overnight in a walled enclosure (fold) in charge of a porter. In the morning the shepherds come to the porter and call out their sheep, who recognize the shepherd's voice and their own names. In contrast, thieves and robbers climb over the wall of the sheepfold and thereby cause the sheep to panic. In other words, the shepherd is known by his gentleness and the favorable response of the sheep, as in the story of the

The Good Shepherd

Stone carving of a menorah, a candelabrum with seven branches, found in excavations of the Jewish Quarter, Jerusalem.

blind man and Jesus. Thieves and robbers are known by their savage treatment of the sheep and by the unfavorable response of the sheep, as in the altercation between the blind man and the Pharisees. *Read John 10:1–21.* When Jesus claims to be the door of the sheep, he changes the metaphor slightly, in accordance with the necessity that shepherds themselves guard the opening of the sheepfold with their sleeping bodies when a porter is unavailable. This exposure of a shepherd to danger develops into Jesus' reference to laying down his life for the sheep, but with emphasis on his authority not only to lay it down on his own initiative but also to take it up on his own initiative. His death and resurrection will not happen to him; as God incarnate and in obedience to his Father, he will make them happen. The "other sheep" that he must bring into the one flock, the undivided church of true believers (heretics like the Gnostics do not count), represent Gentiles.

The setting switches to the Festival of Dedication, also called Lights or Hanukkah and held in December to commemorate the rededication of the temple by Judas Maccabeus after Antiochus Epiphanes had desecrated it. There, in the dead of winter and in the shelter of Solomon's portico at the temple, are no crowds of Galilean pilgrims sympathic to Jesus. So when "the Jews," John's term for the authorities in Jerusalem, encircle Jesus they have him trapped for stoning or for arrest; and when he marches out from their hand, or grasp, he does so by the sheer force of his deity. *Read John 10:22–42.* According to Jesus, the unbelief of the Jewish authorities does not show him up as a false pretender; it shows them up as not belonging to the flock of his and God's people. When exception is taken to Jesus' claiming equality with God, Jesus argues that if the Jews' own Scripture uses "gods" for those to whom the word of God came (see Ps. 82:6), no one should object to the claim of Jesus, the very Word of God who in the beginning was with God and was God (1:1), to be the Son of God. His sanctification does not refer to a cleansing from sin, but to consecration for his task of doing the Father's works in the world.

In a reference to Lazarus, Mary, and Martha, the description of Mary as the one "who anointed the Lord with perfume and wiped [the perfume] off his feet with her hair" anticipates the story in 12:1–8 and makes Jesus' raising of Lazarus from the dead symbolize Jesus' raising himself from the dead, for the anointing will prepare Jesus for burial and the wiping of his feet will signify that because of resurrection the perfume will not be needed for long (compare also in both the story of Lazarus and that of Jesus the mention of a mourning woman, grave clothes with separate mention of a face-cloth, a stone closing the mouth of the tomb, and the doubt of Thomas). *Read John 11:1–44.* As himself in resurrection, Jesus not only raises Lazarus and will raise himself from the dead; he will also raise to eternal life believers in him who die before the Last Day. Believers who have not yet died by then will never die (compare 1 Thess. 4:16–18). Jesus' groaning with indignation and stirring himself up show him working up his divine power. His weeping for Lazarus shows love for the deceased and provides occasion for the onlookers' asking whether Jesus could not have kept Lazarus from dying. That question, in turn, makes Jesus' raising of Lazarus go one better than preservation from death. The raising of Lazarus proves all the more remarkable in that Jews believed a deceased person's spirit hovers over the corpse for three days and then leaves, despairing of a resuscitation, whereas Lazarus has been dead four days, one day beyond hope, as evident from the stench that has

Raising of Lazarus

Shepherds and their flock, roaming the open fields near Jerusalem.

developed. Notably, it is at the word of Jesus the Word that Lazarus comes out of his tomb (compare 5:25, 28–29).[15]

The Sanhedrin
The Sanhedrin gets scared that by reviving his popularity this latest of Jesus' signs may bring about a messianic revolt which would draw Roman reprisal. Caiaphas the high priest brushes aside the Sanhedrin's hesitancy by recommending the death penalty for Jesus, so that the death of one man may save the whole nation from destruction at the hands of Rome. His words carry a deeper meaning than he himself understands, however, for he is unconsciously predicting the death of Jesus to bring salvation from sin—and that not only for the Jewish nation, but also for all God's people, both Jews and Gentiles in the one church. *Read John 11:45–54.*

---

15. *With regard to Lazarus's graveclothes, Jewish custom was to lay a corpse on a sheet of linen twice as long as the corpse, its feet at one end of the sheet, to fold the remainder of the sheet over the head and cover the corpse with it, to tie the feet together and the arms to the body with strips of linen, and to tie another cloth over the face.*

Pilgrims are now arriving in Jerusalem from Galilee and elsewhere for the Passover festival. The Sanhedrin therefore issues a decree seeking information on Jesus' whereabouts in order that they might arrest and execute him. They also plot the death of Lazarus because of the convincing force of his being brought back to life by Jesus. *Read John 11:55–12:11.* Enhancing the dignity of Jesus as God incarnate are the large amount of the perfume used for ointment (a pound = half a pint), its exoticness (pure nard), its expensiveness (300 denarii come to nearly a full year's wages for a manual worker), and its application to Jesus' feet (which you would expect to be washed with water, not with even cheap perfume—compare 13:1–11). Since Mary has already expended the perfume on Jesus' feet, 12:7 should be translated, "Let her alone in that she has kept the perfume until the day of my burial-preparation." This day is that day; and Mary's keeping the perfume means that she has not sold it, as Judas suggested it should have been, to benefit the poor.

Mary's Anointing of Jesus

John's account of the Triumphal Entry repeatedly stresses the large size of the crowd that comes out from Jerusalem to greet and acclaim Jesus and escort him into their city as a visiting dignitary, the king of Israel, symbolized by palm branches such as were imprinted on Jewish coins of the period. To the exasperated Pharisees it looks as though the whole world has gone after him; and, indeed, the largeness of the crowd previews the coming success of the gospel throughout the world, Gentiles included, as confirmed by the immediate request of some Greeks to see Jesus. *Read John 12:12–50.* The Greeks are Gentile proselytes or God-fearers. As Greeks they direct their request to Philip, whose name is Greek; and Philip tells Andrew, whose name is likewise Greek. Jesus responds that his hour of suffering and exaltation has finally come; and he compares his death, burial, and resurrection, and the resultant eternal life for all who believe, to a grain of wheat that falls into the earth, germinates, and springs up into multiplied life. To this talk about dying the Jews object that he cannot then be the Christ. According to their view the Christ will not die. They therefore conclude that the dying Son of man of whom Jesus speaks must differ from the immortal Christ, and that Jesus must be claiming to be the Son of man rather than the Christ. On the other hand, Jesus portrays death and rising as a glorification of his Father's name (not a disgrace to it), as a judgment against the world (not its judgment against him), as an exorcism of Satan (not Satan's getting rid of Jesus; note that the

Triumphal Entry on Palm Sunday

Greeks

Grain of Wheat

fourth gospel relates no other exorcism by Jesus), and as an uplifting from the earth (not a stoning, as was earlier attempted in 8:59; 10:31-33; 11:8, but a crucifixion that becomes the first step in a return to heavenly exaltation with the Father). The unbelief of some is due to a prophecy in Isaiah 6:10, and the secrecy of others' belief draws criticism so as to warn John's community against failure of Christian witness through fear of persecution. The command of the Father which Jesus equates with eternal life consists of the Father's command that Jesus lay down his life that he might take it again (10:17–18), for eternal life is based on his death and resurrection.

Washing the Disciples' Feet   *Read John 13:1–20.* "Before the Passover" leaves Jesus' death to be itself the Passover (compare 1:29, 36; 18:28; and 19:33 with Ex. 12:43–46; Num. 9:12). His laying down his garments and taking them again symbolize his laying down his life and taking it again (see 10:17–18). His washing the disciples' feet symbolizes cleansing from sin by the Holy Spirit, represented by water (3:5; 7:37–39) and released to the disciples by Jesus' death and resurrection (19:30, 34; 20:22), but a cleansing that goes beyond the bath of regeneration, which takes place at conversion. His washing the disciples' feet also sets a pattern for humble service to one another in the church. Only slaves have to wash the feet of others. Among Jews, the pupils of a rabbi have to perform the duties of a slave for him except for washing his feet. Here, the rabbi (Jesus) does for his pupils (the disciples) what is considered too menial even for them to do for him.

The Betrayer   *Read John 13:21–30.* "On Jesus' breast" means that the beloved disciple (presumably John) is reclining on his left side with his back toward Jesus, so that to speak with Jesus privately he has only to lean backwards onto Jesus' chest. The sop or morsel that Jesus gives to Judas Iscariot is a piece of bread dipped in the common dish of broth and customarily presented to the honored guest. Taking the initiative as he usually does in John's gospel, Jesus commands Judas to do quickly what he is going to do. Not even under Satan's control, then, can Judas betray Jesus apart from Jesus' command. The "quickly" of that command and the "immediately" of Judas's exit ensure that the betrayal will take place on schedule. Jesus' hour has come and he will not let it pass without seeing to it that the Father's will is accomplished. The notation that it was night when Judas went out contrasts with the earlier notation of Nicodemus's having come to Jesus by night (3:2) and calls attention to the symbolism of

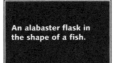

An alabaster flask in the shape of a fish.

entering the darkness of sin and judgment on leaving Jesus, the light of salvation.

After Judas's exit, Jesus speaks of his impending death and resur- *Upper Room* rection as a glorification of himself and of God. "Immediately" *Discourse* stresses the quickness with which the glorification in resurrection will occur. *Read John 13:31–38.* The disciples' loving one another is designed to help make up for Jesus' coming absence. The descrip- tion of the love-commandment as "new" relates to the earlier part of *Loving One* John's gospel, in which Jesus has given no commandments to his *Another* disciples. This new commandment rests on the commandment to love your neighbor as yourself (Lev. 19:18; compare Mark 12:31 parr.); but your neighbor has changed to your fellow believer in Jesus, and "as yourself" has changed to "as I [Jesus] have loved you," that is, to the extent of sacrificing your own life when necessary. The truth is just the reverse of Peter's statement, "I will lay down my life for you." Jesus will lay down his life for Peter (see 10:11).

Peter has asked where Jesus is going. Jesus now answers that question: he is going to the Father. *Read John 14:1–31.* Jesus' answer starts on two levels: his Father's house means both heaven and household; "many dwellings" means both places in heaven and places in the very persons of Jesus and the Father (compare the later theme of abiding in Jesus the vine, 15:1–8); the preparation means both Jesus' death and his resurrection-ascension; and his coming back to receive the disciples to himself means both his re- union with them after the Resurrection and his second coming. The disciples know the way to the Father because they know Jesus, who is that way; and he is that way because he is also the truth, the very manifestation of God in human flesh (1:14); and as the truth of God incarnate he is the life, for in him believers find the eternal life of God himself. The works they do will not be greater than those of Jesus in the sense of exhibiting more power (John never uses the term "miracles," which means "acts of power"), but greater in the sense of extending throughout the world. Jesus has confined himself to Palestine; his disciples will carry the gospel far and wide. Asking in his name means appealing to his authority. Asking *him* in his own name (14:14) implies his oneness with the Father, since prayers are normally directed to the Father (15:16; 16:23). A Greek word *The Paraclete* transliterated as "Paraclete" stands behind various English translations, such as "Comforter," "Counselor," "Helper," and "Advocate," and refers to the Holy Spirit, though "another Paraclete" implies that Jesus, too, is a paraclete. Just as in these roles Jesus has represented the Father to the disciples, so from now on the Holy Spirit will represent him and the Father in these roles. Through the Spirit, in fact, Jesus and the Father will abide with believers just as they will abide in Jesus and the Father. The Spirit's teaching the disciples everything by reminding them of everything that Jesus has said gives the lie to revelations purporting to go beyond him, as in the case of Gnostic revelations. As God incarnate, Jesus provides the complete revelation of God. The Spirit can only expound that revelation. More immediately, the ruler of the world (Satan) is coming in the person of Judas Iscariot, whom he has entered (13:27) and who is making his way to the Garden of Gethsemane. So Jesus' saying, "Get up, let's go from here," shows him determined to be there for his arrest. He will not miss his hour.

Allegory In the Old Testament a vine symbolized Israel (Ps. 80:8–18; Isa. *of the Vine* 5:1–7; Jer. 2:21; Ezek. 19:10–14; Hos. 10:1). Now that Israel has been set aside because of her rejection of Jesus, he and those united to him by faith become the new and true vine of God's planting. Jesus is the whole vine, not just the stem, so that as branches those who believe in him are not merely connected to him; they are absorbed by him. The fruitbearing of branches represents obedience to Jesus' commands, most especially the one that believers should love one another. The removal and burning of branches that do not bear fruit represents the doom of false believers. The pruning of branches that do bear fruit represents the cleansing of true believers, more particularly, ongoing cleansing after an initial cleansing at conversion, just as did Jesus' washing of the disciples' feet in relation to the disciples' having been bathed already (13:10). By way of contrast with Gnostic secessionists who despise the human Jesus, deny the Incarnation, and consequently fall into disobedience to Jesus' commandments (most especially the disobedience of haughtily failing to love true believers), abiding in the vine represents abiding in Jesus by adherence to orthodox Christian belief. *Read John 15:1–27*. The figure changes from that of a vine with branches to that of friends. Though in other respects the relation of Jesus' disciples to him is one of slavery, his revelation of the Father to them has resembled the free and open communication of friend to friend. And now, despite incurring the world's hatred, disciples are to join the Paraclete, the Spirit of truth, in bearing witness to this revelation.

Read John 16:1–33. "Their hour" (16:4) is the time of Jesus' physical absence and of his enemies' persecution of the disciples. Since Peter has asked Jesus where he is going (13:36; compare 14:5), Jesus' statement, ". . . none of you is asking me, 'Where are you going?'" implies that he should be asked again. Instead, sorrow over their coming persecution has crowded out curiosity about his destination. But the coming of the Paraclete more than makes up for Jesus' departure and the consequent persecution of those who truly believe in him. For the Paraclete will bring to light the sin of the world's unbelief in Jesus, the righteousness of Jesus to be seen in his return to the Father, so that not even the disciples can see him, and the judgment inflicted on Satan at the Cross. The Paraclete's disclosure to the disciples of coming events (16:13) will still center on Jesus (compare the book of Revelation). The "little while" of Jesus' absence will be the interval of the disciples' sorrow between his death and resurrection, a sorrow like the pain of childbirth both in its intensity and in its replacement by joy, here the joy of Easter, a joy so secure as to overcome the trauma of persecution. And the joy of Easter is made full by the joy of receiving answers to prayer offered in Jesus' name, for those answers provide continuing, repeated proof that he is risen indeed.

Now Jesus directs his words away from the disciples to his Father in heaven and first takes up the subject of his and the Father's glorification, already broached in 13:31–32, and then the safekeeping, sanctification, and unity of believers, that is, their being kept from apostasy and its results: worldliness and division in the church. *Read John 17:1–26*. Jesus prays for his disciples, but not for the world, because the disciples belong to the Father but the world does not, because they belong to Jesus but the world does not, and because Jesus has been glorified in them but not in the world. His going out of the world to the Father leaves them exposed to Satanic danger— hence his prayer for their protection. Sanctification means a setting

Prayer for the Disciples

apart from the world. "The son of perdition" (17:12) refers to Judas Iscariot and describes him as destined to be lost. Jesus' prayer for the disciples culminates in a request that they may join him in his heavenly glory.

Arrest   Though Jesus told the disciples to get up and go with him as far back as 14:31b, only now do he and they leave supper and go across the Kidron Valley, immediately east of Jerusalem and the temple, to Gethsemane, which John calls a garden to match the garden where Jesus will lay down his life and take it again (see 19:41; 20:15). His gathering the disciples in this garden therefore symbolizes the larger gathering of God's children on the basis of Jesus' death and resurrection (the Greek verb for gathering occurs in both 18:2b and 11:52). He has already prayed, at length; so the narrative moves right to his arrest. Indeed, he goes to the garden to get arrested. When his arresters fall back on the ground at his self-identification, "I am [Jesus the Nazarene]," which carries connotations of the divine title "I AM" (compare 8:58; Ex. 3:14), he insists on getting arrested, but under the condition that his disciples be let free as a symbol of their salvation through his suffering. He is laying down his life on his own initiative (10:17–18). Peter's swordplay in defense of Jesus provides a foil against which Jesus' will to die stands out. *Read John 18:1–11.*

Before Annas   Though Caiaphas is high priest during the year of Jesus' death, Jesus is taken first to Caiaphas's father-in-law Annas, formerly the high priest, still called such, and still the dominant political force in Jewish hierarchy. *Read John 18:12–27.* Since Jesus has insisted on his own arrest, the binding of him produces irony. The disciple known to the high priest Annas and following Jesus, as Peter follows him, is probably the beloved disciple (John the apostle). So when Annas questions Jesus about his disciples and his teaching, he is questioning Jesus about Peter and the disciple with whom Annas is acquainted and about what Jesus has taught them. Not at all silent, Jesus the *Before Caiaphas*   Word answers so vociferously that Annas can only send him to Caiaphas. The "also" in the first two questions to Peter alludes to the *Peter's Denials*   presence of the disciple known to Annas. Peter's denials of Jesus offer a dramatic foil to Jesus' unapologetic outspokenness.

Before Pilate   Irony appears again in the Jewish leaders' staying outside the Praetorium, or palace of the pagan governor, to avoid a defilement that would keep them from eating the Passover. But by engineering the death of Jesus they become instruments in the offering of Jesus and miss this true Passover. In particular, Caiaphas becomes a tool in the fulfillment of his own unconscious prophecy at 11:49–52. *Read John 18:28–40.* Jewish custom would have dictated death by stoning. The reservation of capital punishment to Roman authority (in fact, Annas had lost the high priesthood for violating this reservation) ensures Jesus' death by crucifixion, a lifting up by means of a cross rather than a knocking down by means of stones, and thus in a divine reversal an exaltation, as befits God incarnate, rather than a humbling. Jesus' statement, "Everyone who is of the truth hears my voice," assumes the Greek principle of knowledge that like understands like (compare the modern American saying, "It takes one to know one"). Pilate's question, "What is truth?" strikes another ironic note, since he who is the Truth is standing right in front of Pilate. Pilate's verdict, "I find nothing to accuse him of," indicates Jesus' qualification to die as the Lamb of God who takes away the sins of others, of the world (1:29).

Read John 19:1–16. Twice more Pilate affirms Jesus' innocence, and tries to satisfy Jesus' enemies by having him flogged and mocked. When they let slip that Jesus has claimed to be the Son of God, Pilate, whose pagan mythology included stories of gods' becoming angry with human beings for not recognizing them when they masqueraded among them, interrogates Jesus further out of fear that Jesus may be a god masquerading as a human being. But Jesus refuses to answer a question about his origin lest the answer, "From heaven," scare Pilate from letting Jesus be crucified. Jesus wills his crucifixion. Pilate succumbs to a threat of blackmail contained in the Jewish leaders' statement that as a king Jesus rivals Caesar (the implication: they will tattle on Pilate if he releases Jesus, and Caesar will get rid of Pilate). Counting from sunrise, the sixth hour of Pilate's delivering Jesus to the Jewish leaders for crucifixion *Crucifixion* would be noon. But as earlier in John, counting from midnight produces a better hour, 6:00 A.M.; for Roman governors held court very early in the morning (compare the comments on 1:39; 4:6, 52; also 20:19, where John's description of the first Easter Sunday evening as the evening of "the first day of the week" most certainly represents a counting from midnight and noon, for a counting from sunset and sunrise would make that evening the evening of the second day of the week). "Preparation of the Passover" means the Friday when the Passover was sacrificed and roasted for eating in the evening. As

The Mount of Olives.

the true Passover sacrifice, then, Jesus the Lamb of God will die at just the right time.

It is "the Jews," the very leaders to whom Jesus said, "Destroy this temple [his body] . . . (2:19)," who take and crucify Jesus; but true to no one's taking his life from him and his laying it down on his own initiative (10:17–18), he carries his cross by himself. The omission of Simon of Cyrene also keeps anyone from thinking, as some Gnostics did, that Simon rather than Jesus died on the cross. Since Pilate has repeatedly declared Jesus guiltless, the inscription that Pilate writes and puts on the cross presents in this context an affirmation of Jesus' kingship over the Jews, not an accusation of insurrection against Caesar. Pilate's refusal to alter the inscription underlines the affirmation. John's listing the three languages of the inscription—Hebrew, Latin, and Greek—alludes to the universality of this Jewish king's death as the Lamb of God to take away the sin of the world, not just of the Jews (1:29). *Read John 19:17–22.*

Through association with the four corners of the earth (compare Rev. 7:1), the division of Jesus' outer clothes into four portions may likewise allude to the universal benefit of the Crucifixion as well as fulfill Psalm 22:18. The seamlessness of Jesus' tunic, or undergarment, can hardly allude to the seamless robe worn by Jewish high priests; for that was an outer garment. Rather, seamlessness provides the reason for lot-casting (in avoidance of spoiling such a fine tunic by tearing it up), which helps fulfill Psalm 22:18 exactly. Ever in control, even on the cross, the Word who is God calmly commits the beloved disciple to his (Jesus') mother, and her to the beloved disciple, and by so making this disciple his adoptive brother enhances the testimony of the beloved disciple, author of the fourth gospel (19:35; 21:24). *Read John 19:23–27.*

Blood and Water

Still in full possession of his divine powers, Jesus orchestrates the manner of his death to fulfill Scripture. *Read John 19:28–37.* Not only does "I am thirsty" recall Psalm 22:15; 69:21. It also recalls Jesus' thirst at 4:6, which issues in his offering to give the living

Olive trees in the Garden of Gethsemane.

water of the Holy Spirit (compare 4:10, 13–14 with 7:37–39) just as here water flows from Jesus' pierced side. Therefore he breathes the Holy Spirit on the disciples as soon as he sees them after the Resurrection (compare 19:34 with 20:22). Hyssop has association with the blood of the Passover sacrifice (Ex. 12:22), and the outflow of Jesus' blood makes him just such a sacrifice. It is the work of salvation given him by his Father that Jesus pronounces finished (compare 19:30 with 4:34; 17:4; 19:28). "He bowed his head" shows him laying down his life by his own initiative: God incarnate dies with all deliberation. "He gave over his spirit" carries the double meaning of expiration and the coming gift of the Spirit to Jesus' disciples.

Burial   *Read John 19:38–42.* The notation that Joseph of Arimathea was a secret disciple because he feared the Jews may criticize disciples who are secret for the same reason in the circumstances within which John writes his gospel. On the other hand, Joseph's burial of Jesus may provide the good example of a secret disciple's coming out of the closet, as did Nicodemus in 7:50–51. Supporting this view are their present pairing and the reminder that at first Nicodemus came to Jesus at night, though now he comes by day carrying a load of spices weighing about 100 litras (about 75 pounds, since one litra equals 12 ounces). The hugeness of this amount befits the burial of God incarnate and forestalls any stench of decay such as characterized the corpse of Lazarus (11:39). Thus, Jesus' burial adds to his glorification rather than robbing him of it.

Resurrection   *Read John 20:1–31.* The coming of Mary Magdalene to Jesus' tomb so early that it is still dark makes his subsequent appearance to her a reshining of him as the light of the world (compare 8:12). The beloved disciple's not entering the empty tomb though he arrives before Peter favors historicity, because bias for the beloved disciple would surely have led to fictionalizing his entrance first. Again historically, thieves would hardly have unwrapped Jesus' corpse before carrying it away, or have rolled up his face-cloth and placed it aside. Theologically, the lying there of the linen wrappings and of the face-cloth shows that Jesus has taken up his life by his own initiative, under his own divine power: nobody has had to unwrap him as Lazarus had to be unwrapped (11:44; compare 2:19; 10:18). The seeing and believing of the beloved disciple encourages belief on the part of those who have not seen but hear his gospel read to them (compare 20:8 with 20:29). And it was seeing, not scriptural expectation, which led to believing; for the disciples did not yet understand the Old Testament to have taught the resurrection of the Christ.

As often in John, ironies abound. Several of them: Mary thinks Jesus' corpse has been transferred elsewhere; she fails to recognize him when he appears to her; she thinks him to be the gardener, calls him "Lord" in the sense of "Sir" though he is "Lord" in the sense of "God" (compare 20:28), supposes that as the gardener he has carried Jesus off and laid him somewhere, and says that she will take him up, whereas Jesus has taken himself up and left the tomb. As the Good Shepherd, he calls her by name: "Mary." As one of his sheep, she then recognizes his voice (compare 10:3–4, 14, 16, 27). "Stop clutching me" implies that Mary has grabbed Jesus and means that she must now release him for his ascension, for only after the Ascension has completed his glorification can he give the Holy Spirit to his disciples, as he does on the evening of this first Easter Sunday. The "therefore" in 20:19 indicates that the Ascension has taken place by evening (compare 7:39 with 20:17, 19–22). Against Gnostic denials of the divine Word's physical death and resurrection, John mentions the risen Jesus' exhibition of his hands and side, scarred by crucifixion, and stresses the disciples' recognition of Jesus as the Lord. Especially prominent is the exclamation of doubting Thomas, "My Lord and my God." Jesus' pronouncing peace on disciples who equate the Crucified One with the risen Lord God and commissioning them with the gift of the Holy Spirit and with the authority to forgive and retain sins leaves Gnostic deniers out in the cold. Forgiving and retaining sins means declaring sins forgiven or unforgiven according to belief and unbelief in the orthodox gospel (that is, the only gospel). John even uses Thomas, a Gnostic hero (compare the Gnostic so-called Gospel of Thomas), against the Gnostics: though at first sceptical of Jesus as the physically risen Lord and God, Thomas comes round to this orthodox belief. Thus, like other signs performed by Jesus in such abundance that John's gospel cannot include them all, the Resurrection is a sign performed by Jesus and written up by John to induce people to equate the human Jesus with the divine Christ and by this kind of believing to have life in his name, that is, eternal life through believing that Jesus is who his name "the Christ, the Son of God" (for John they are one and the same name) says he is (compare 1:12).

Because 20:30–31 contains a statement of purpose for "this book," 21:1–25 looks like an epilogue added by the author of the

Epilogue

289

Fisherman with nets.

book, who at the very end finally switches from speaking *of* himself as the beloved disciple to speaking *as* himself, "I." The epilogue subdivides into a third appearance of the risen Jesus to his disciples, a conversation between him and Peter, and a conclusion similar to the one in 20:30–31. *Read John 21:1–25.*

Fishing   Night and darkness go together with Jesus' absence and the disciples' failure to catch any fish. His standing on the beach as the light of the world goes together with daybreak and overwhelming success in catching fish. The catching of fish stands for evangelism, and the putting together of fish caught by the disciples with fish that Jesus already has on a charcoal fire stands for the one church or, to repeat an earlier metaphor, the one flock (10:16; 11:51–52). The charcoal fire prepares for Peter's compensating for three denials of Jesus with three affirmations of love for him, for it was over a charcoal fire that Peter denied Jesus (18:17–18, 25–27). The comment that the net did not tear combines with a notation of the large number of fish caught (153) to symbolize Jesus' not losing any of those whom the

Father has given him (compare 6:12, 39; 10:28–30; 17:11–15; 18:8–9). The mention of bread as well as fish recalls the feeding of the five thousand, and Jesus' giving the disciples bread represents his giving them himself, his sacrificial flesh, as the bread of life (6:1–50).

The distinction in meaning that is often seen between two Greek verbs used for "love" in Jesus' conversation with Peter does not survive scrutiny. The verb usually considered inferior (*philein*) occurs elsewhere in John for the Father's loving the Son and the disciples (5:20; 16:27) and for Jesus' loving Lazarus (11:3, 36) and the beloved disciple (20:2), as well as for destructive self-love (12:25) and worldly love (15:19); and the verb usually considered superior (*agapan*) occurs elsewhere in John for people's loving darkness rather than light (3:19) and for their loving human glory (12:43) as well as for the Father's loving the Son (3:35; 10:17; 15:9; 17:23, 24, 26) and the disciples (14:21, 23; 17:23), for God's loving the world (3:16), and for Jesus' loving the Father (14:31), the disciples (13:1; 15:9, 12), Martha, Mary, and Lazarus (11:5), and the beloved disciple (13:23; 19:26; 21:7). John is fond of using pairs of words as synonyms, as in this very same passage for shepherding and sheep (see the Greek text). "More than these" means "more than the other disciples on hand [see 21:2] love me [Jesus]." As catching fish represented evangelism, shepherding sheep represents pastoral care of the converted. Jesus predicts for Peter a death by crucifixion in old age (hands stretched out to carry his cross while being led to the unwanted site of crucifixion),[16] as has almost certainly happened by the time John writes. But against a popular misunderstanding, Jesus does not say that the beloved disciple will survive until the Second Coming. The denial that Jesus said so does not imply the beloved disciple's death by the time the fourth gospel is written, for that disciple "is testifying" (present tense) at the time of writing. Only his old age and possibly the imminence of his death are implied. Though many regard at least 21:24 (if not more or the whole of chap. 21) as added by the Christian community centered around the beloved disciple John, the "we" who bear witness to the truth of the beloved disciple's testimony may include that disciple himself, just as earlier in this gospel Jesus joined others in bearing witness to himself (5:31–47; 8:12–20).

Peter's Restoration

---

16. *Nothing hints at crucifixion upside down. The first mention of this probably legendary detail concerning Peter's martyrdom comes in the apocryphal Acts of Peter 33–41, late in the second century.*

Besides what is mentioned above, what other symbolism might be legitimately found in the fourth gospel?

Is this gospel simple or complex? Give evidence supporting your answer.

Does John write to convince unbelievers to believe in Jesus, or to convince believers to abide in Christian faith?

Barrett, C. K. *The Gospel According to St. John.* 2d ed. Philadelphia: Westminster, 1978. Advanced.

Beasley-Murray, G. R. *John.* Dallas: Word, 1987. Advanced.

Brown, R. E. *The Gospel According to John.* 2 vols. Garden City, N.Y.: Doubleday, 1966, 1970. Advanced.

Carson, D. A. *The Gospel According to John.* Grand Rapids: Eerdmans, 1990.

Lindars, B. *The Gospel of John.* London: Oliphants, 1972.

Michaels, J. R. *John.* Peabody, Mass.: Hendrickson, 1989.

Morris, L. *The Gospel According to John.* Grand Rapids: Eerdmans, 1971.

Schnackenburg, R. *The Gospel According to St. John.* Vol. 1: New York: Herder & Herder, 1968. Vol. 2: New York: Seabury, 1980. Vol. 3: New York: Crossroad, 1982. Advanced.

Talbert, C. H. *Reading John.* New York: Crossroad, 1992.

A COMPARATIVE CHART OF THE FOUR GOSPELS

The Gospels	Mark	Matthew	Luke	John
Probable date of writing	50s	50s or 60s	60s	80s or 90s
Probable place of writing	Rome	Antioch, Syria	Rome	Ephesus
Intended audience	Nonchristian Gentiles	Mixed church under persecution	Gentile inquirers	Those threatened by Gnostic heresy
Thematic emphasis	Jesus' power as counteracting the shame of his crucifixion	Jesus as builder of the church	Historical reliability of the gospel	Believing in Jesus as the Christ, God's Son, for eternal life

What are the advantages and disadvantages of having a fourfold, as op-posed to a single, portrait of Jesus in the New Testament?

FOR
FURTHER
DISCUSSION

Which of the gospels is best suited to the following modern audiences, and why?

    (a) White middle-class Americans

    (b) People of color

    (c) Intellectuals

    (d) Children

    (e) Young people

    (f) Elderly people

    (g) Those who have never heard the gospel

Do the gospels differ among themselves in the clarity and earliness with which Jesus' messiahship comes in view? If so, how is the difference to be explained?

How much editing of Jesus' deeds and words by the evangelists is con-sonant with an accurate account?

To what extent is Christian faith dependent on history and historical re-search? Compare the Lucan perspective on Jesus' life.

(The literature on higher criticism of the gospels is so extensive that it is best to give only several general treatments, which will in turn refer interested readers to many specialized discussions.)

FOR
FURTHER
INVESTIGATION

Carson, D. A., D. J. Moo, and L. Morris. *An Introduction to the New Testament.* Grand Rapids: Zondervan, 1992.

Collins, R. F. *Introduction to the New Testament.* Garden City, N.Y.: Doubleday, 1983.

Guthrie, D. *New Testament Introduction.* 2d ed. Downers Grove, Ill.: InterVarsity, 1990.

Kümmel, W. G. *Introduction to the New Testament.* 2d ed. Nashville: Abingdon, 1975.

Wikenhauser, A. *New Testament Introduction.* New York: Herder and Herder, 1958.

See also Moule, C. F. D. *The Birth of the New Testament.* 3d ed. New York: Harper & Row, 1982.

The Cilician Gates, a main mountain pass through the Taurus range in Asia Minor. Through this corridor Alexander the Great and his army passed eastward for conquest, and later Paul and his companions passed westward to begin his second missionary journey.

11

Acts: A Promotion of Christianity in the Greco-Roman World at Large

(Continued from the Gospel of Luke)

❖ *What is the relation of Acts to the gospel of Luke as to authorship, style, date, and purpose of writing?*

❖ *Where did Luke get the information he recorded in Acts, and of what historical value is it?*

❖ *Why does Acts end very abruptly?*

❖ *In what geographical and theological directions did Christianity develop—in relation to the Roman Empire, Judaism, and pagan religions—and under what leaders?*

❖ *How and why did Christianity separate from Judaism?*

❖ *What was the legal status of Christianity and from what source or sources did the first persecutions come?*

❖ *How and why was Paul very important to the history of the early church?*

According to early church tradition, Luke wrote the book of Acts. If he did, the book is a sequel to the gospel of Luke. Evidence within Acts supports authorship by Luke. Just as his gospel opens with a dedication to Theophilus, so also does Acts. Vocabulary and style are very similar in the two books. Though it does not prove that he wrote Luke-Acts, frequent use of medical terms agrees with Luke's being a physician (Col. 4:14). By his use of "we" in narrating parts of Paul's journeys, the author of Acts implies that he was a traveling companion of Paul. Other traveling companions do not fit the data of the text. For example, Timothy and

Authorship by Luke

several others are mentioned apart from the "we" and "us" of Acts 20:4–6. According to Paul's epistles, neither Titus nor Silas accompanied him to Rome or stayed with him there. Yet the narrative of his voyage to Rome makes up one of the "we"-sections. By such processes of elimination Luke remains the only likely candidate for the authorship of Acts.

Literary Technique Together with the gospel of Luke and the epistle to the Hebrews, the book of Acts contains some of the most cultured Greek writing in the New Testament. On the other hand, roughness of Greek style turns up where Luke appears to be following Semitic sources or imitating the Septuagint (as a few Christians still imitate in their prayers the English style of the King James Version of the Bible, particularly its thee's and thou's and corresponding verbal forms). Some scholars regard the speeches and sermons in Acts as literary devices improvised by Luke himself to fill out his stories. That some ancient historians followed such a practice is true, but not to the extent that has sometimes been claimed. And though Luke need not have given verbatim reports of speeches and sermons, it does seem that he accurately gives the gist of what was said. Support for such accuracy comes from striking parallels of expression between Peter's sermons in Acts and 1 Peter, and between Paul's sermons in Acts and his epistles. These parallels can hardly have arisen by chance; and no other evidence exists to indicate that Luke imitated or used in any other way the epistles, or that Peter and Paul imitated Acts when writing their epistles. The only adequate explanation: Luke did not make up the speeches and sermons, but summarized their contents so accurately that the characteristic phraseology of Peter and Paul is evident in Luke's reporting, as well as in their epistles.

Sources For the material in Acts, Luke drew on his own recollections where possible. He may have put some of these in a diary at the time of the events. Doubtless, additional information came to him from Paul, from Christians in Jerusalem, Syrian Antioch, and other places that he visited with and without Paul, from other traveling companions of Paul, such as Silas and Timothy, and from Philip the deacon and evangelist and an early disciple named Mnason, in whose homes he stayed (Acts 21:8, 16). Also available were written sources, such as the decree of the Jerusalem Council (Acts 15:23–29) and perhaps Aramaic or Hebrew documents relating the early events of Christianity in and around Jerusalem.

To a large degree, archaeological discoveries have supported Luke's historical accuracy. For example, we now know that his use of titles for various kinds of local and provincial governmental officials—procurators, consuls, praetors, politarchs, Asiarchs, and others—was exactly correct for the times and localities about which he was writing. This accuracy is doubly remarkable in that the usage of these terms was in a constant state of flux because the political status of various communities was constantly changing.[1]

Historical Accuracy

The book of Acts ends very abruptly. Luke brings the story of Paul to the point where Paul, imprisoned in Rome, has been waiting for two years to be tried before Caesar. But we read no more. What happened to Paul? Did he ever appear before Caesar? If so, was he condemned? Martyred? Acquitted? Released? Luke does not tell. Many suggestions are offered to explain the abruptness of this ending. Perhaps Luke intended a third volume that would answer the lingering questions. But his first volume, the gospel of Luke, closes with a sense of completeness even though he probably intended already to write Acts. Or maybe he came to the end of his papyrus scroll. But presumably he would have seen that space was running out and formed an appropriate conclusion. Personal catastrophe may have prevented him from finishing the book. But it is already long enough to fill a lengthy papyrus scroll. Perhaps Acts 20:22–25; 21:4, 10–14 imply well enough that Paul was martyred in Rome. But those passages set out the possibility of martyrdom at the hands of hostile Jews in Jerusalem, not at the hands of Caesar in Rome; and the remainder of Acts tells of Paul's escaping martyrdom at the hands of such Jews and of his exoneration by Roman officialdom. Perhaps Luke accomplished a purpose of showing the progress of Christianity from Jerusalem, the place of origin, to Rome, capital of the empire. But Paul's prison ministry in Rome makes a disappointing climax; a Christian community already existed there; and the problem remains why Luke did not tell what happened to Paul, the dominant character in Acts 13–28.

Ending and Date

The best solution is to say that Luke wrote up to the events so far as they had happened; that is, at the time of writing Paul was still

---

1. *Confirmation of the historical accuracy of Acts has outmoded the "Tübingen Hypothesis" of the nineteenth century that a second-century author wrote Acts to reconcile the supposedly conflicting standpoints of Petrine and Pauline Christianity. Evidence is lacking for such a division, and a late author could hardly have written so accurately as Luke does about first-century conditions. F. C. Baur of the University of Tübingen, Germany, led the Tübingen school of thought. According to his hypothesis, Petrine Christianity was legalistic, Pauline Christianity antilegalistic.*

awaiting trial before the Caesar, Nero. Surely it would have been irrelevant for Luke to prove the political innocence of Christianity, as he does throughout the book, if he were writing after Nero had turned against Christians (A.D. 64). Too late then to appeal to the favorable decisions of lesser officials! Luke wrote Acts, therefore, when Paul had been in Rome for two years (c. A.D. 63).[2] Theologically, the very abruptness with which Acts ends suggests the unfinished task of worldwide evangelism. What the early church began, the later church is to finish.

Purpose   As in his gospel, Luke slants the book of Acts toward Gentiles, especially those with open-minded interest in the historical origins of Christianity. In so doing, he continues to emphasize the religious piety, moral purity, and political innocence of believers in Jesus, and to portray Christianity as universal, a traditional religion rooted in Judaism but open to all. As in Luke the narrative progressed to Jerusalem, the center of Judaism, so in Acts the narrative progresses to Rome, center of the world. The power of the Holy Spirit makes possible this progress. Luke does not write about the spread of Christianity to Egypt or to the East, but we do read recurring statements which summarize the success of the gospel wherever Christians proclaimed it: "and the word of God kept growing, and the number of the disciples kept multiplying greatly . . ." (Acts 6:7; see also 9:31; 12:24; 16:5; 19:20; 28:30–31).

Special attention goes to showing that Christianity deserves continued freedom because it derives from Judaism, which has legal standing, and because it does not pose any threat to the Roman government. Repeatedly, Luke describes Christianity as a kind of fulfilled Judaism and cites favorable judgments concerning Christianity and its proponents by various kinds of local and provincial officials. Such an apology was needed because Christianity had started with the handicap that its founder had died by crucifixion, the Roman means of executing criminals, and because disturbance arose wherever Christianity spread. Already in his gospel, Luke has shown that both Pilate and Herod Antipas pronounced Jesus innocent and that mob pressure led to a miscarriage of justice. In Acts, too, Luke shows that disturbances over Christianity arose from the

---

2. *Also favoring an early date is the lack of allusions to the persecution under Nero in the 60s, to the martyrdom of James the Lord's brother in the 60s, and to the destruction of Jerusalem in A.D. 70. Relatively undeveloped theology and controversy over the status of Gentile Christians possibly point in the same direction, but may instead reflect Luke's accuracy in describing the primitive church, without implications for the date of writing.*

violence of mobs and from false accusations, often by unbelieving Jews, not through any misdeeds of the Christians themselves. In this way Luke hopes to dispel prejudice against Christianity and to win sympathy from the likes of Theophilus, whose designation "most excellent" in Luke 1:3 may indicate influential political position as well as aristocratic, or at least middle class, social standing.[3]

An Outline of Acts

I. THE ACTS OF THE SPIRIT OF CHRIST IN AND OUT FROM JERUSALEM (1:1–12:25)

A. In Jerusalem (1:1–8:3)

1. The post-resurrection ministry and ascension of Jesus (1:1–11)
2. The replacement of Judas Iscariot with Matthias (1:12–26)
3. The Day of Pentecost: an outpouring of the Holy Spirit, speaking in tongues, Peter's sermon, mass conversion, and Christian community (2:1–47)
4. The healing of a lame man and Peter's sermon (3:1–26)
5. The imprisonment and release of Peter and John (4:1–31)
6. The community of goods in the Jerusalem church and the death of Ananias and Sapphira (4:32–5:11)
7. Miracles, conversions, imprisonment of the apostles, and release (5:12–42)
8. A dispute over food rations and the choice of seven "deacons" (6:1–7)
9. The sermon and martyrdom of Stephen and a general persecution following (6:8–8:3)

B. Out from Jerusalem (8:4–12:25)

1. Philip's evangelization of Samaria, the Samaritan reception of the Spirit, and the story of Simon the magician (8:4–25)
2. Philip's conversion of the Ethiopian eunuch (8:26–40)
3. The conversion of Saul (Paul), his preaching in and escape from Damascus, return to Jerusalem, and flight to Tarsus (9:1–31)
4. Peter's healing of Aeneas and raising of Tabitha (9:32–43)

---

3. Compare the address, "most excellent Festus," to a Roman governor in Acts 26:25.

5. The salvation of Cornelius and his Gentile household, including Peter's vision of a sheet, a sermon by him, and Gentile reception of the Spirit (10:1–11:18)
6. The spread of the gospel to Antioch in Syria (11:19–26)
7. The bringing of famine relief from Antioch to Jerusalem by Barnabas and Saul (Paul) (11:27–30)
8. Herod Agrippa I's execution of James the apostle and imprisonment of Peter, Peter's miraculous release, and Herod's horrible death (12:1–25)

II. THE ACTS OF THE SPIRIT OF CHRIST FAR AND WIDE THROUGH THE APOSTLE PAUL (13:1–28:31)
   A. Paul's first missionary journey (13:1–14:28)
      1. The sending from Antioch, Syria (13:1–3)
      2. Cyprus: the blinding of Elymas and conversion of Sergius Paulus (13:4–12)
      3. Perga: the departure of John Mark (13:13)
      4. Antioch of Pisidia: Paul's sermon in the synagogue (13:14–52)
      5. Iconium, Lystra, and Derbe: the healing of a cripple, worship of Barnabas and Paul as Zeus and Hermes, and stoning of Paul at Lystra (14:1–18)
      6. The return to Antioch, Syria, with preaching in Perga (14:19–28)
   B. The Judaizing controversy (15:1–35)
      1. Debate in Antioch, Syria (15:1–2)
      2. The Jerusalem Council: a decision for Gentile freedom from the Mosaic law and considerateness toward Jewish Christians (15:3–35)
   C. Paul's second missionary journey (15:36–18:21)
      1. A dispute with Barnabas over John Mark and the departure from Antioch, Syria, with Silas (15:36–41)
      2. A journey through South Galatia and the selection of Timothy (16:1-5)
      3. Troas: a vision of the man of Macedonia (16:6–10)
      4. Philippi: the conversion of Lydia, deliverance of a demon-possessed girl, jailing of Paul and Silas, earthquake, and conversion of the jailer and his household (16:11–40)
      5. Thessalonica: a Jewish assault on the house of Jason, Paul's host (17:1–9)

6. Berea: the verifying of Paul's message with the Old
Testament (17:10–15)

7. Athens: Paul's sermon on Mars' Hill (17:16–34)

8. Corinth: Paul's tentmaking with Aquila and Priscilla, a favorable decision by the Roman proconsul Gallio, and general success (18:1–17)

9. The return to Antioch, Syria, via Cenchrea (18:18–21)

D. Paul's third missionary journey (18:22–21:16)

1. A journey through Galatia and Phrygia (18:22–23)

2. The preparatory ministry of Apollos in Ephesus
(18:24–28)

3. Ephesus: the Christian baptism of disciples of John the
Baptist, successful evangelism, and a riot led by
Demetrius (19:1–41)

4. A journey through Macedonia to Greece and back
through Macedonia (20:1–5)

5. Troas: Eutychus's fall from a window during Paul's sermon (20:6–12)

6. A journey to Miletus and Paul's farewell speech to the
Ephesian elders (20:13–38)

7. A voyage to Caesarea and predictions of misfortune for
Paul in Jerusalem (21:1–14)

8. A journey to Jerusalem (21:15–16)

E. Events in Jerusalem (21:17–23:35)

1. Paul's involvement in a Jewish vow (21:17–26)

2. A riot in the temple area, Paul's arrest, defense before a
mob, and conversation with Claudius Lysias
(21:27–22:29)

3. Paul's defense before the Sanhedrin (22:30–23:11)

4. A Jewish plot against Paul and his transfer to Caesarea
(23:12–35)

F. Events in Caesarea (24:1–26:32)

1. Paul's trial before Felix (24:1–23)

2. Paul's private hearing before Felix and Drusilla
(24:24–27)

3. Paul's trial before Festus and appeal to Caesar (25:1–12)

4. Paul's hearing before Festus and Herod Agrippa II
(25:13–26:32)

G. Paul's voyage to Rome, including a shipwreck on Malta
(27:1–28:16)

H. The preaching of Paul to Jews and Gentiles in his Roman
house-prison (28:17–31)

Awaiting
the Spirit
Read Acts 1:1–26. "The first treatise" is the gospel of Luke.
Emphasis falls on Jesus' choice and instruction of the apostles as the
link between him in the past and Christians in the present, and on
the persuasive force of his resurrection appearances. "Not many
days from now" looks forward to the outpouring of the Holy Spirit
on the Day of Pentecost (2:1–4). The apostles then wonder whether
Jesus will now restore the kingdom to Israel, that is, whether he will
immediately establish the messianic kingdom on earth with Israel
occupying the most favored, central position. They think of this
possibility because the Old Testament associates the outpouring of
God's Spirit with the messianic age (Isa. 44:3; Ezek. 36:24–27;
39:29; Joel 2:28–29). In effect, Jesus' answer turns their attention
from messianic chronology, dealing with the nation of Israel, to uni-
The Great
Commission
versal evangelism, dealing with all nations. Harmoniously with 1:8,
then, the gospel will spread throughout Jerusalem and Judea in
chapters 1–7, to Samaria and other outlying regions in chapters
8–12, and to distant parts in chapters 13–28. And as Peter will be
the leading figure in evangelizing Jews for the most part in chapters
1–12, so Paul will be the leading figure in evangelizing Gentiles for
The Ascension the most part in chapters 13–28. The two men at Jesus' ascension
recall the two at his transfiguration and resurrection (Luke 9:30–31
[Moses and Elijah]; 24:4–7). The cloud into which he ascends represents the presence of God the Father, as at Jesus' baptism, transfiguration, and second coming. "A sabbath day's journey" amounted
to three-fifths of a mile.[4] By implication, Jesus and the disciples
have not traveled farther away from their residence than allowed on
the Sabbath: they are law-keepers rather than law-breakers. And
they are pious, too, devoting themselves constantly to prayer—but
not in exclusion of others; for women, including the mother of
Jesus, and his brothers belong to the same company, an ideal reli-
The Choice of gious community. Not even the betrayal of Jesus by Judas Iscariot
Matthias can spoil this community; for that betrayal fulfilled a Spirit-inspired
Scripture, received its just and well-publicized punishment, and left
a vacancy soon filled with an equally qualified replacement. As did
all the apostles, Matthias followed Jesus from the time of John the

---

4. See page 74.

Baptist's ministry to the Ascension; and the falling of the lot on Matthias indicates that as the exalted Lord, Jesus chooses him for apostleship just as he chose Judas and the rest for it.

The Day of Pentecost[5] brings the promised baptism in the Spirit, here called a filling and an outpouring. All these figures stress abundance. The accompanying noise, like that of a violently blowing wind, stresses power and plays on the use of cognate Greek words for "wind" and "Spirit." The appearance on each disciple of a tongue-shaped flame of fire represents the ability to speak in tongues, that is, in foreign languages—a sign of the universality of the gospel. Non-Palestinian pilgrims attending the festival, both Jews of the Diaspora and Gentile proselytes, are amazed to recognize the languages of their homelands being spoken by Palestinians who have never learned those languages. But the Palestinians in the audience do not understand them and so make a false and foolish charge of drunken babbling. *Read Acts 2:1–47.*

Pentecost

Quick distinction, but could be argued

Peter equates what has happened with a prophecy in Joel 2:28–32. Though the predicted celestial signs await fulfillment at the Second Coming, he carries on his quotation to include the universalistic statement that everyone who calls on the name of the Lord will be saved. For Peter, Jesus is the Lord whose name spells salvation. Peter's sermon goes on to stress God's attestation of Jesus with miracles, God's plan and the Jews' guilt in Jesus' death, God's raising Jesus from death in fulfillment of Scripture, and the heavenly and therefore politically unthreatening character of Jesus' kingship. Baptism signals repentance, and the gift of the Spirit signals forgiveness. "For all who are far away" stresses God's calling of Gentiles as well as Jews. Numerous conversions enlarge the Christian community, so that its piety and power, its unselfishness and harmony, become so conspicuous as to earn both universal admiration and universal awe.

Peter's Sermon

Read Acts 3:1–4:31. Peter's and John's going to the temple at the hour of prayer, the ninth hour (3:00 P.M.), shows them living out their Christianity within Judaism. The miracle of healing which they perform produces praise of God, and with true piety Peter takes no credit. Instead, he describes Jesus as the holy, righteous, and resurrected one to whom all credit is due. Another emphasis on Jewish guilt in Jesus' death is balanced by Peter's magnanimity ("I

Healing of a Cripple

---

5. See page 69.

Panoramic view of Jerusalem from south to north showing the remains of the City of David and the village of Silwan (foreground), the Old City (center), and the modern city outside the walls.

know that you acted in ignorance, as did also your rulers") and God's plan ("In this way God fulfilled what he had foretold through the mouth of all the prophets"). An emphasis on repentance makes Christianity a movement of moral reform. "The restoration of all things" makes it universal, as does also the quotation of God's promise that in Abraham's descendants all the families of the earth will be blessed. And so despite an arrest by the Sadducees, who believe in no resurrection at all, much less in Jesus' resurrection, believers multiply by the thousands, the Holy Spirit fills Peter, and he calls the miracle of healing for what it is, "a good deed" such as the Hellenistic world admires. His declaration that there is salvation in no one besides Jesus puts forward a gospel for all as much as it excludes any other way of salvation. And the bravery and boldness of

Peter, John, and the whole Christian community exhibit their devotion to God, loyalty to truth, and empowerment by the Holy Spirit.

Once again the sharing of goods comes into Luke's description of this ideal community (compare 2:44–45); and just as the betrayal of Jesus by Judas received a just and swift punishment in 1:15–20, so also the dishonesty and incomplete charity of Ananias and Sapphira contrast with the unstinting charity of Barnabas and receive a just and swift punishment. The ideal is thus maintained (compare the disciplinary deaths of Nadab and Abihu in Lev. 10:1–11). *Read Acts 4:32–5:11.* *Communal Living*

Signs, wonders, and conversions increase. The converted include women as well as men. Unity reigns. Solomon's portico locates believers at the cultic center of Judaism, the temple. Admiration and awe of them continue. *Read Acts 5:12–42.* Opposition arises out of envy, not out of any legitimate complaint. Angelic intervention and popular favor frustrate the Sanhedrin; and right within the Sanhedrin a voice of reason prevails, that of the universally respected teacher of the law, Gamaliel. *Signs and Wonders*

When Hellenistic believers complain that their widows are being neglected in the doling out of food rations, Hebraistic believers graciously choose to supervise the dole seven Hellenistic men, as shown by these men's Greek rather than Hebrew or Aramaic names. Perhaps the later church office of deacon ("servant, helper"), having to do with mundane matters of church life and especially with the dispensing of charity, developed out of this incident. *Read Acts 6:1–8:1a.* The conversion of many priests strengthens the ties of Christianity to Judaism. Stephen, one of the seven, not only waits on tables. He also performs wonders and signs and preaches. It takes the action of a lynch mob and the testimony of false witnesses to bring about his martyrdom.[6] The angelic look of his face, his vision of God's glory and of Jesus standing at the right hand of God, and his prayers of trust and forgiveness exonerate him, whereas the rage, teeth-gnashing, and impulsiveness of the Sanhedrin condemn their stoning of him. Saul, at whose feet they lay their robes for ease of throwing stones, will become the apostle Paul, as he is better known. (But the man's two names do not represent the unbelieving and believing phases of his life, respectively; for Saul is simply his *Widows*

Stephen

---

6. *The Romans reserved almost entirely to themselves the right to impose capital punishment, but the stoning of Stephen starts and proceeds as a lynching. Even the Sanhedrin turn into a lynch mob. They do not so much as bother to reach a verdict.*

Hebrew name, and Paul his similar-sounding and common Greco-Roman cognomen, or family name.) Stephen's sermon exposes the falsity of the charge that he blasphemed Moses and God, the law and the temple. Rather, it is his accusers who committed such blasphemy by following the example of their ancestors' rejection of God's messengers, including Moses, in their own murder of Jesus. As for the temple, they have corrupted its legitimacy by failure to recognize that God dwells in the universe of his own making, not in the humanly made temple, just as their own prophet Isaiah said (Isa. 66:1–2).

Saul

The stoning of Stephen triggers a persecution in Jerusalem of believing Jews by unbelieving ones, led by Saul. The resultant scattering of believers leads to the evangelization of Judea and Samaria,

Philip

as in the stories of Philip's preaching in Samaria and elsewhere. *Read Acts 8:1b–40.* The baptism of Samaritans, women as well as men, broadens the inclusiveness of the church. The belief and bap-

Simon the Magician

tism of Samaritans who have previously adulated Simon for his practice of magic show the superiority of Philip's signs and miracles. So also do the belief, baptism, and amazement of Simon himself.

Samaritan Reception of the Spirit

The Holy Spirit does not come on the Samaritan believers until Peter and John come, pray, and lay their hands on them as a sign of solidarity between Jewish and Samaritan believers. This delay enables apostolic representatives of Jewish believers to see for themselves that God has equally accepted Samaritan believers, as shown by their receiving the Spirit in the apostles' presence. The apostles' horrified refusal to sell Simon authority for bestowing the Spirit exhibits their pecuniary purity; and his request that they pray for him exalts their superiority over this magician, and therefore their

The Ethiopian Eunuch

gospel over his magic.[7] The baptism of an Ethiopian eunuch, a high governmental official no less, broadens the inclusiveness of the church yet further.[8] Luke is appealing to the cosmopolitanism of his

---

7. The attempt by Simon Magus (Simon the Magician) to buy authority for bestowing the Spirit has turned his name into the nouns simony and simonism, the crime of buying or selling ecclesiastical preferment. Early Christian tradition traces the heretical movement of Gnosticism to Simon.

8. The story of an Ethiopian eunuch foreshadows the Gentile missions of Paul. The eunuch has been attending a Jewish religious festival in Jerusalem. He is therefore at least a God-fearer, perhaps a full proselyte. Eunuchs lack religious privileges in Judaism according to Deuteronomy 23:1, but the law may have been relaxed (compare Isa. 56:3ff.); or in Acts "eunuch" may be an official title, not a physical description. It was customary for lone travelers like Philip to attach themselves to caravans like the eunuch's. Reading aloud, as the eunuch was doing, was customary in ancient times, even for private study.

Hellenistically minded audience. And Philip's interpreting Isaiah 53:7–8 as a reference to Jesus roots the gospel in ancient tradition. Christianity is no "Johnny-come-lately."

Luke comes back to Saul's persecution of "the Way" (the first name used for Christianity, though we do not know why: as a reference to the way of the Lord prepared by John the Baptist in accordance with Isaiah 40:3? as a reference to the way of the Cross? as a reference to the way of righteousness? as a reference to Jesus, the way of salvation?). But on the road to Damascus, Syria, Saul the persecutor of Jesus turns into Saul the preacher of Jesus. *Read Acts 9:1–31.* Saul's persecution of Jesus in the persecution of Jesus' disciples implies a union of them on earth with him in heaven, a theme to become prominent in Pauline theology, where "in Christ" and "with Christ" occur over and over again for this union. According to 9:7, Paul's companions hear Jesus' voice; according to a parallel account in 22:9 they do not hear his voice. But the underlying Greek constructions differ in such a way as to suggest that in 9:7 the companions hear his voice as a sound, and that in 22:9 they do not hear it as meaningful words. Saul's conversion makes him pray, see a vision, enjoy acceptance as a brother in the community of Jesus' disciples, receive the Holy Spirit, proclaim Jesus to be God's Son and the Christ, and suffer the kind of persecution that he once perpetrated.

"The Way"

Conversion of Saul

Excursus on Saul-Paul

Saul was born a Roman citizen in Tarsus, a city of southeastern Asia Minor (see the map on page 311), and therefore must have had a *praenomen* and a *nomen gentile* as well as his *cognomen* Paul, but the former have not survived. How his father had obtained Roman citizenship—whether through purchase, service to the state, or some other means—we do not know. But Roman citizenship gave legal privileges and protection that served Saul well in his later endeavors as a Christian missionary. He, his father, and at least his grandfather, too, were Pharisees (note the plural "fathers" in Acts 23:6) and, resisting Hellenism as much as possible, lived Hebraistically (Phil. 3:5–6). Most of his young manhood Saul spent in Jerusalem, where he studied under the famous rabbi Gamaliel (Acts 22:3). We do not know whether Saul ever saw Jesus in person or whether he ever married. He does not mention a wife in his epistles, but since bachelorhood was rare among Jews, some have surmised that he lived as a widower.

Peter's Miracles and Visions

Read Acts 9:32–11:18. Peter's miraculous healing of Aeneas and raising of Tabitha (or Dorcas), whose many charitable deeds typify the behavior of believers, demonstrate an enjoyment of the presence and power of God during the very period that Peter preaches to Gentiles and accepts them into the church, actions for which narrow-minded Jewish Christians later censure him. The fact that he is lodging with a tanner named Simon shows that he has already shed some of his Judaistic scruples, for tanners are ritually unclean through ongoing contact with dead animals and are therefore to be avoided. It takes a threefold vision to convince Peter, a threefold denier of Jesus, that contact with Gentiles is permissible. He sees a sheet, perhaps suggested by an awning under which he may have been taking a midday nap on the rooftop. The sheet is full of ritually impure creatures. God's command to kill and eat indicates that the Mosaic dietary restrictions, and indeed all other ritual restrictions, are now lifted. Finally persuaded, Peter goes on a preaching mission

Salvation of Gentiles in Cornelius's House

to Gentiles in the house of Cornelius, a Roman centurion, God-fearer, almsgiver to the Jews, man of perpetual prayer, and most recently a visionary. That such a man will believe the gospel recommends it. Peter's sermon to the household of Cornelius offers C. H. Dodd's prime example of the kerygma.[9] Appropriately to a Gentile audience, the sermon sounds a note of universality again and again: "in every nation . . . Lord of all . . . everyone who believes in him." The portrayal of Jesus as a doer of good appeals to high-minded Gentiles like Cornelius, himself a man of good deeds. A mention of the risen Jesus' eating and drinking with the disciples revives the picture of table fellowship dear to the hearts of Luke's Hellenistic audience. In contrast to what happened in Samaria, an apostle is already present as witness. Therefore God gives his Spirit to the Gentiles immediately on their exercise of faith, even before Peter finishes preaching and before baptism or the laying on of hands can be administered. In this way God dramatically demonstrates his accepting Gentile believers into the church on equal terms with Jewish and Samaritan believers. Peter is then able to use God's sudden action to defend himself against parochially minded Jewish believers in Jerusalem who criticize his going to the Gentiles. It takes much longer for these believers to understand the far-reaching implications that the Mosaic law is repealed in its entirety (though many of its moral precepts are repromulgated for

9. *See page 104.*

Gateway to Straight Street in Damascus, where Paul began his preaching mission after his conversion.

Christians), that the synagogues and the temple are no longer required places for worship, and that Gentile converts do not need circumcision.

With the further scattering of disciples as far as Antioch, Syria, comes a concerted and highly successful effort to evangelize Gentiles ("Greeks"[10]). Thus the episode of Gentile conversions in Cornelius's house turns into a wholesale program in the third largest city of the Roman Empire, which city is about to become the base of extensive Gentile evangelism throughout the empire. Luke's emphasis on inclusiveness is growing, and he shows how Saul comes to be linked with the church in Antioch and with Barnabas as a

Gentile Evangelism in Antioch

10. *Some of the earliest textual tradition reads "Hellenists," that is, Hellenistic Jews, instead of "Greeks" (11:20). But Hellenistic Jews would not make the needed contextual contrast with Jews (compare 14:1; 16:1; 17:4–5; 18:4; 19:10, 17; 20:21; 21:27–28), so that "Hellenists" looks like influence on a copyist from 6:1; 9:29, in the former of which Hellenistic Jews contrast with Hebraistic Jews, a contrast lacking in 11:20 because of the use of "Jews" rather than "Hebrews" in 11:19.*

traveling companion (compare 9:27). *Read Acts 11:19–30.* The concern of the church in Jerusalem for the religious well-being of Gentile believers in Antioch and the concern of the church in Antioch for the economic well-being of Jewish believers in Jerusalem and Judea illustrate the social benefit of Christianity: it heals divisions. The description of Barnabas as good and full of the Holy Spirit and of faith puts him forward as an example of the individual virtues characteristic of Christians. So Luke is able to offer *"Christians"* without embarrassment—on the contrary, with pride—the historical note that disciples were called Christians first in Antioch, though originally the designation may have carried a derisive connotation, as in "Christites" (compare "Reaganites," "Thatcherites," etc., always used sneeringly by opponents at the beginning).

Herod *Read Acts 12:1–25.* The Herod who figures in this passage is *Agrippa I* Herod Agrippa I, grandson of Herod the Great. Posing as a champion of Judaism, he martyrs James the apostle and brother of John and imprisons Peter. Luke describes these actions as mistreatment and the currying of political favor. God's estimate is seen in the contrast between the angel of the Lord's rescuing Peter from prison and that same angel's striking Herod with a disease that kills him. Luke's description of the disease makes one think of intestinal cancer.[11] The death of Herod occurred about A.D. 44, so that the whole account represents a chronological stepping back from the famine relief visit (11:27–30; about A.D. 47). Since James the apostle has died as a martyr, the James to whom Peter sends a report must be James the brother of Jesus.

Saul's first Now Luke starts to narrate the more extensive missionary en-*Missionary* deavors of Saul. As a skillful author Luke has prepared his audience *Journey* by describing the spread of the gospel through Stephen's preaching to Hellenistic Jews in Jerusalem, the scattering of Christians through persecution with resultant expansion of the Christian witness, Philip's evangelizing Samaria and converting the Ethiopian eunuch, Saul's preaching in Damascus and to Hellenists in Jerusalem, Peter's going to Lydda and Joppa and to Caesarea, where he converted a houseful of Gentiles, and the spread of Christianity to Antioch, Syria, where numerous Gentiles have become Christians. Furthermore, Barnabas and Saul have already appeared as partners, Barnabas having introduced Saul to the church in Jerusalem and both of them having ministered in Antioch and traveled together to

---

11. So also *Josephus*, Antiquities of the Jews *19.8.2 §§343–52.*

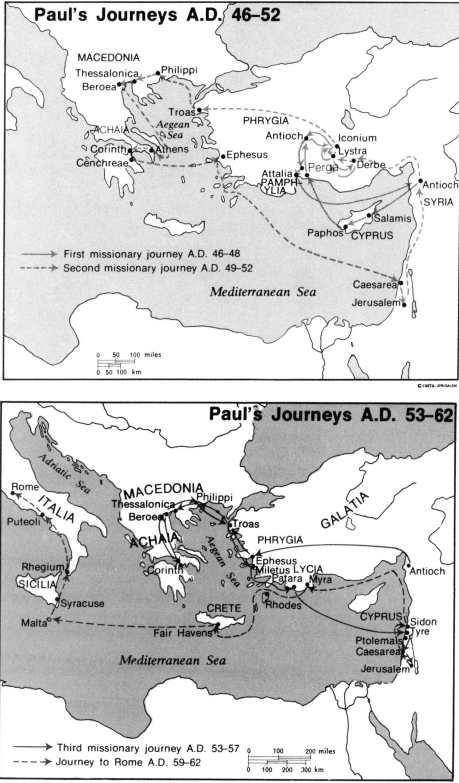

Paul's Journeys A.D. 46–52

MACEDONIA
Thessalonica
Beroea
Philippi

Troas
Aegean Sea
PHRYGIA

ACHAIA
Corinth
Athens
Cenchreae
Ephesus

Antioch
Iconium
Lystra
Derbe
Perga

Attalia
PAMPHYLIA

Antioch
SYRIA

Salamis
Paphos
CYPRUS

→ First missionary journey A.D. 46–48
--→ Second missionary journey A.D. 49–52

Mediterranean Sea

Caesarea
Jerusalem

0 50 100 miles
0 50 100 km

© carta, JERUSALEM

Paul's Journeys A.D. 53–62

Adriatic Sea

Rome
ITALIA
Puteoli

MACEDONIA
Thessalonica
Beroea
Philippi

GALATIA

Rhegium
SICILIA
Syracuse
Malta

ACHAIA
Corinth

Aegean Sea

Troas

PHRYGIA

Ephesus
Miletus LYCIA
Patara Myra

Antioch

Rhodes
CRETE
Fair Havens

CYPRUS
Sidon
Tyre
Ptolemais
Caesarea
Jerusalem

Mediterranean Sea

→ Third missionary journey A.D. 53–57
--→ Journey to Rome A.D. 59–62

0 100 200 miles
0 100 200 300 km

© carta, JERUSALEM

PAUL'S MISSIONARY JOURNEYS

A Summary of the Main Stopping Places and Events

A.D. 33		Jesus died and rose.
34		
		Paul was converted, preached in Damascus, and escaped a Jewish plot by being let down in a basket through an opening in the wall at Damascus.
		Barnabas introduced Paul to the church in Jerusalem.
		Paul returned to Tarsus.
		Barnabas brought Paul to Antioch in Syria.
47		Barnabas and Paul took famine relief to Jerusalem.

I. THE FIRST MISSIONARY JOURNEY

Antioch in Syria
Cyprus—Bar-Jesus (Elymas) was blinded and the proconsul
  Sergius Paulus converted.
Perga in Pamphylia—John Mark returned.
Antioch of Pisidia—Paul preached in the synagogue.
Iconium
Lystra—Paul healed a cripple, Barnabas and Paul were worshiped
  as Zeus and Hermes; Paul was stoned.
Derbe
Lystra
Iconium
Antioch of Pisidia
Perga in Pamphylia

49	GALATIANS	Antioch in Syria
	(under early date	
50–51	of South	The Jerusalem Council (Acts 15)
	Galatian theory)	

II. THE SECOND MISSIONARY JOURNEY
(Paul and Barnabas disagreed whether to take John Mark; Paul
  took Silas.)

Antioch in Syria
Derbe
Lystra—Paul took Timothy. ⎫
Iconium   ⎬ Phyrgia and South Galatia
Antioch of Pisidia   ⎭
Troas—Paul saw the man of Macedonia in a vision.
Philippi—Lydia was converted, a demon-possessed girl was deliv-
  ered; Paul and Silas were jailed; an earthquake occurred at
  midnight; the jailer was converted.
Thessalonica—a Jewish-inspired mob assaulted the house of
  Jason, where Paul was staying.
Berea—the Bereans "searched the [Old Testament] scriptures" to
  verify Paul's message.
Athens—Paul was alone; he preached his sermon on Mars' Hill;
  Timothy and Silas rejoined Paul, but Paul sent Timothy back
  to Thessalonica and Silas elsewhere.

1 and 2
THESSALONIANS

Corinth—Paul made tents with Priscilla and Aquila; Timothy and
  Silas rejoined Paul; Paul moved his preaching from the synagogue to the house of Titius Justus; Crispus the synagogue

With the Pauline Epistles Synchronized (All dates approximate)

A.D.		
		ruler was converted; in a vision Jesus told Paul to stay; the Roman proconsul Gallio refused to condemn Paul for preaching; Paul spent one and a half years in Corinth.
		Cenchrea—Paul shaved his head.
		Ephesus—Priscilla and Aquila accompanied Paul this far, but stayed in Ephesus.
		Caesarea
		Jerusalem
		Antioch in Syria

III. The Third Missionary Journey

		Antioch in Syria
		Galatia and Phyrgia
	1 Corinthians	Ephesus—disciples of John the Baptist received the Spirit; Paul preached in the school of Tyrannus; the seven sons of Sceva (unbelieving Jews) tried to use Jesus' name in exorcising demons; converts burned their books of magic; Demetrius led a riot in behalf of the goddess Artemis (Diana); Paul spent two years and three months in Ephesus.
	2 Corinthians Romans	Macedonia (Philippi, Thessalonica, Berea)
		Greece, or Achaia (Athens and Corinth)—Jews plotted to kill Paul on a voyage to Palestine.
		Macedonia
		Troas—Eutychus fell out of a window during Paul's sermon.
		Miletus—Paul bade farewell to the Ephesian elders.
		Tyre—Paul was warned not to go to Jerusalem.
		Caesarea—Paul stayed in the house of Philip; Agabus warned Paul with a symbolic girdle about what would happen in Jerusalem.
57		Jerusalem—Paul reported to the church; involved himself in a Jewish vow to show he was not against the Mosaic law; was seized in the temple; was rescued by Roman soldiers; spoke to the Jews from the castle stairway; spoke to the Sanhedrin; Jews plotted to ambush him; Claudius Lysias sent him to Felix in Caesarea.
		Caesarea—Paul stood trial before Felix, Festus, and Agrippa, and appealed his case to Caesar.

IV. The Journey to Rome

		Caesarea
		Crete—Paul's advice not to sail was rejected.
60		Storm on the Mediterranean Sea
		Malta (Melita)—shipwreck occurred; Paul shook a viper off his hand and suffered no ill effects.
	Philemon	
61	Colossians Ephesians Philippians	Rome—Paul rented a house-prison; preached to Jews and Gentiles; and for two years awaited trial before Nero.
63		Release from prison; further traveling.
	1 Timothy	
	Titus	Reimprisonment
65	2 Timothy	Martyrdom

Antioch, Syria.

take famine relief from the church there to the church in Jerusalem. Finally, the failure of Herod Agrippa I to stem the tide of Christianity has set up a foil for the wide-ranging evangelistic successes of Saul. *Read Acts 13:1–14:28 and follow Saul's journey on the map (page 311).*

Syrian Antioch

Luke attributes the sending of Barnabas and Saul both to the church at Antioch and to the Holy Spirit, who inspires the church to send them. The laying on of hands does not constitute a formal ordination into Christian ministry (Barnabas and Saul have been preaching for a long time), but indicates that the church is supporting this particular mission of Barnabas and Saul. It is natural for them to go first to the island of Cyprus, because Barnabas hails from there. Paul takes the initiative when a Jewish magician named Bar-Jesus, or Elymas, tries to dissuade the Roman proconsul Sergius Paulus from believing (doubtless because the magician can see that a converted Sergius Paulus will no longer seek his magical services). The description of Sergius Paulus as intelligent contrasts with the

Cyprus: Elymas and Sergius Paulus

description of the magician as "full of all deceit and of all fraud" and "an enemy of all righteousness." This contrast argues to Luke's Hellenistic audience that it is intelligent to believe the gospel, ignorant not to. From this point onward, Luke mentions Paul before Barnabas. The only exceptions appear at 14:12, where the mention of Barnabas before Paul will depend on the hierarchy of the Greek gods Zeus and Hermes with whom they are misidentified, and at 15:12, where in the setting of Jerusalem Luke will mention Barnabas before Paul because in the minds of Christians there Barnabas enjoys seniority over Paul. Luke switches from "Saul" to "Paul" for the first time in 13:9 and sticks with "Paul" for the rest of Acts. The mission to Gentiles makes this Greco-Roman name more appropriate than the Hebrew name "Saul." *From Paul to Saul*

At Perga in Pamphylia, John Mark, a cousin of Barnabas and helper to both Paul and Barnabas and later the author of a gospel, turns back. Luke does not say why. Suggestions range from homesickness to fear. Whatever the reason, Paul considers it invalid, Barnabas at least excusable (Acts 15:36–41). Paul now adopts the strategy of preaching in cities. From them the gospel can reverberate through the surrounding villages and countryside. Paul also adopts the strategy of preaching first in the local Jewish synagogue (if there is one). His epistles will display a deep concern for fellow Jews and a conviction that as the chosen people of God they should hear the gospel first (see, for example, Rom. 1:16; 9:1–5). And the synagogue provides a ready-made opportunity to preach, since it is customary for synagogues to offer qualified visitors like Paul a platform. Furthermore, audiences at synagogue include large numbers of Gentile proselytes and God-fearers as well as Jews. In fact, Paul usually enjoys his greatest success among these Gentiles, for their interest in Judaism has prepared them for his message. As a result, unbelieving Jews come to regard Paul as a poacher who seduces Gentiles from Judaism to Christianity by offering them salvation on easier terms than observance of the Mosaic law. For example, Paul's sermon in the synagogue at Antioch of Pisidia[12] reviews the history of Israel to proclaim that the messianic promise has found its fulfillment in Jesus Christ, but also strikes the note of justification from the sins from which the law of Moses cannot provide justifica- *Perga: John Mark*

Pisidian Antioch

---

12. This Antioch, smaller and less important than Antioch in Syria, is located near the border of Pisidia but not quite in Pisidia itself; hence, Pisidian Antioch or Antioch of Pisidia but not Antioch in Pisidia.

Remains of the theater at Perga.

Remains of a Roman-built aqueduct in Antioch of Pisidia which brought water to the city.

tion, a justification open to everyone who believes in Jesus. This will become a familiar theme in Paul's epistles. He also stresses the innocence of Jesus and the testimony of eyewitnesses to his appearances after resurrection. When the Jews come to their synagogue the next Sabbath, they find crowds of Gentiles occupying the pews and eagerly awaiting another sermon from Paul. Jealous, the Jews instigate persecution; and Paul and Barnabas leave after ministering briefly to the Gentiles. Thus a pattern develops: preaching in the synagogue—success especially among Gentile proselytes and God-fearers—Jewish hostility—withdrawal from the synagogue—further successful ministry among Gentiles—persecution—flight. Luke highlights the universality of the gospel by paying special attention to the large numbers of Gentiles converted, Paul's and Barnabas's turning from unbelieving Jews to the Gentiles, and the rejoicing of Gentiles because a door of faith has been opened to them.

As to persecution, Luke blames it on the jealousy of unbelieving Jews. Even when some Gentiles join in the persecution, it is jealous Jews who have stirred them up to do so. Persecution does not yet come from the Roman government, whose policy is one of granting freedom to traditional religions but banning new ones for fear of social disruption and consequent difficulties of administration. Only at a later date, when the Romans come to view Christianity as distinct from Judaism and socially disruptive will they begin to persecute Christians. Meanwhile, Luke emphasizes the linkage of Christianity with Judaism, portrays Christians as victims rather than culprits, and drums up admiration for the bravery of Paul and Barnabas in their persisting to evangelize Gentiles despite unbelieving Jews' persecuting them nearly to death.

The Legal Question

A legend that in the past an elderly couple in this region, Philemon (no relation to the Philemon who appears later in the New Testament) and Baucis, gave hospitality unawares to Zeus and Hermes, visiting incognito, probably leads the people of Lystra to misidentify Barnabas and Paul with these same two gods. Refusal to accept worship shows the genuineness of Paul's and Barnabas's piety. On the return trip from Derbe through Lystra, Iconium, and Pisidian Antioch, they avoid open preaching (they have just recently been driven out of those cities) and concentrate on strengthening believers and organizing churches by the appointment of elders to take charge. In this way and as another Lucan link between Christianity and Judaism, churches look like synagogues, each of

Lystra

which has a board of elders. Paul and Barnabas do preach openly on the way back through Perga, however; for apparently they passed through this city very quickly the first time.

The Judaizing Controversy   The report of Paul and Barnabas to their home church in Syrian Antioch emphasized the successful evangelization of Gentiles; so the stage is set for a dispute over the status of Gentile believers. Jewish believers come from Judea to Antioch and teach that Gentile believers must submit to circumcision, as prescribed by Moses, else they cannot be saved. In other words, Gentile believers must come into the church under the same terms that govern the entrance of Gentile proselytes into Judaism. Jewish believers and their Gentile followers who hold to such teaching are called Judaizers. The disagreement of Paul and Barnabas with the Judaizers leads the church in Antioch to refer this issue to the mother church in Jerusalem. Historically, the stakes can hardly be higher: set up the requirement of circumcision and Gentiles, for whom the rite mars the Greek ideal of beauty in the human body, will convert to Christianity in fewer and fewer numbers, so that it will turn into a small Jewish sect; or Gentiles will develop their own form of Christianity uninoculated against paganism and therefore degenerating into it. Theologically, too, the stakes can hardly be higher: set up the requirement of circumcision and the whole of the Mosaic law follows as a way of establishing one's own righteousness instead of trusting in Jesus alone for the righteousness of God. *Read Acts 15:1–35.*

Jerusalem Council   Luke paints a picture of Christian conciliation, a family of religious brothers who iron out their differences to the benefit of the Gentiles concerned. The report by Paul and Barnabas of Gentile conversions "brings great joy to all the brothers" in Phoenicia and Samaria. The church in Jerusalem, including the apostles and the elders, "welcomes" Paul and Barnabas. None less than Peter notes that God himself has not treated believing but uncircumcised Gentiles differently from circumcised Jews who believe, and even says that Jews, too, are saved by grace through faith rather than by the unbearable yoke of the Mosaic law. The whole multitude of Jewish believers listen in respectful silence as Barnabas and Paul speak of God's work among the Gentiles. James, a brother of Jesus, supports the freedom of Gentile believers from the law by citing Amos 9:11–12; Isaiah 45:21c. The restrictions that to avoid setting up barriers to social interchange with Jewish believers, Gentile believers should avoid eating meat that has been dedicated to an idol before sale, should avoid marrying close relatives (as Gentiles often did but Jews did not—compare Lev. 18:6–18, plus 1 Cor. 5:1, for the incestuous meaning of "fornication"), should avoid eating meat that comes from an animal which has been strangled, and should avoid eating meat that still contains the animal's blood—these restrictions do not burden Gentile believers so much as they enjoin reciprocal consideration on their part. Luke goes out of his way to emphasize that the apostles, elders, and church issue the Gentile believers a favorable decree unanimously, and lard it with a commendation of Barnabas and Paul, with an accompanying oral report by two of their own number, Judas (or Barsabbas) and Silas, so that no one will be able to think that Barnabas and Paul forged the decrees to their own advantage, and with an appeal to the Holy Spirit. Joy and encouragement all around. The ideal community stays intact.

After a while Paul's second missionary journey begins. Alas, a dispute over John Mark breaks up the partnership of Paul and Barnabas; but Luke makes the best of it by noting the justification of Paul's position in Mark's having deserted Paul and Barnabas, the replacement of Barnabas with Silas (who along with Paul will turn out to be a Roman citizen, 16:37), the commendation of Paul to the Lord's grace by the church in Syrian Antioch, and the replacement of Mark with Timothy on arrival in Lystra. A good report concerning Timothy contrasts with Mark's earlier desertion (though see Col. 4:10; 2 Tim. 4:11; Philem. 24 for Mark's restored companionship with Paul and a favorable comment about him by Paul himself). The circumcision of Timothy displays Paul's desire to avoid giving offense to the local Jews. Having won freedom from the law for Gentile believers, he regularizes the religious status of Timothy, half Jew and half Greek by birth, to that of a Jew so as to keep him from being regarded as an apostate Jew and therefore excluded from synagogues. *Read Acts 15:36–18:22 and follow Paul's journey on the map (page 311).*

Paul's Second Missionary Journey

Timothy

"Asia" means a Roman province in western Asia Minor, not the whole of Asia Minor, much less the continent of Asia. Some identify the man of Macedonia in Paul's vision with Luke. Against this identification, Luke writes "we" in narrating the departure from Troas for Macedonia; yet the man of Macedonia calls from the other side of the Dardanelles, "Come over . . . ." Philippi is a city of the first of the four administrative districts in Macedonia. Antony and Octavian (later known as Augustus) settled a number of Roman army veter-

The Man of Macedonia

Philippi

ans in Philippi and made the city a Roman colony after their victory in 42 B.C. over Brutus and Cassius, assassins of Julius Caesar. Octavian settled more colonists there after defeating Antony and Cleopatra at Actium (31 B.C.). Jews in the city pray beside a nearby river, apparently because their scant population does not provide the necessary ten adult men required for establishing a synagogue. Only

Lydia women are mentioned. Lydia's hospitality following baptism contributes to the communitarian ideal emphasized by Luke. On the one hand, the crying out of a spirit of divination gives supernatural attestation to Paul, his companions, and their message. On the other hand, Paul's patience in tolerating this annoyance day after day robs of any justification the arrest, disrobing, beating, and imprisonment of him and Silas for Paul's exorcism of the spirit. Similarly exposing the injustice are their accusers' pecuniary motive, appeal to anti-Jewish sentiment, and false charge that Paul and Silas are advocating anti-Roman customs, whereas it turns out that Paul and Silas are Romans being robbed of their rights as citizens. Their passing up an opportunity to escape demonstrates good citizenship, as does also

Philippian their influencing through prayers and hymns other prisoners not to
Jailer escape. The kindness and hospitality of the newly believing and

The traditional place in Philippi where Paul and Silas were imprisoned.

baptized jailer, who nearly commits suicide because he knows himself responsible on pain of death not to let any prisoners escape yet thinks that all of them have escaped, revives the communitarian ideal. So also does the baptism of all his household. Finally, a frightened plea by the city magistrates exonerates Paul and Silas. Since a "we"-section ends after the Philippi narrative and resumes with the return of Paul to Philippi at a later date, Luke must have stayed in Philippi, perhaps as a pastor and evangelist.

The jealousy of unbelieving Jews in Thessalonica and their en-   *Thessalonica*
gagement of ruffians from the market place, formation of a mob, and assault on the house of Jason, Paul's host, all expose the falsity of their charge that Paul and Silas are teaching insurrection against Caesar. By contrast, the numerousness of the Thessalonian God-fearers who believe, the leading positions of quite a few Thessalonian women who believe, the nobility and eagerness with which Berean Jews search the Old Testament to confirm Paul's and   *Berea*
Silas's message, the great number of conversions among the Berean Jews, and the high social standings of quite a few Berean Gentiles who believe all show the gospel's attractiveness to high-minded people. The same point is to be drawn from the conversion in Athens of Dionysius the Areopagite, that is, member of the   *Athens*
Athenian city council, and of the apparently prominent woman Damaris. The recording of Paul's attack on Athenian idolatry appeals to the high-mindedness of those Gentiles in Luke's audience who see through idolatry. The Athenians who hear Paul think that he is teaching Jesus and "resurrection" as two gods unfamiliar to them. (They may confuse "Jesus" with the similar-sounding Greek word for "healing" and thus misunderstand Paul to refer to related gods of healing and resurrection.) Either Paul has to present his teaching on Mars' Hill before the Areopagus, the city council, which   *Mars' Hill*
licenses teachers; or he preaches to a general audience who have withdrawn to Mars' Hill to escape the din of the market place. His portrayals of God as the universal Creator and Sustainer and the object of human groping, and of all humanity as having a single origin in God, appeal to the cosmopolitanism of Hellenistic culture represented in Luke's audience as well as Paul's. Underlining this appeal are quotations from two Greek poets, Epimenides and Aratus, called by Paul "some of your own poets." But despite mocking by most of the Athenians, neither Paul nor Luke will back down on the point of Jesus' bodily resurrection. The Greeks' best hope lay in immortality

A view of Mars'
Hill in Athens.

of the soul, but most of them remained sceptical even of that. We may question whether they would have so much as wanted to believe in bodily resurrection, for to them the body encumbers the soul.[13] Paul and Luke represent biblical anthropology, according to which God created the body as well as the soul, so that they belong together—hence the sacredness of the body and its resurrection.

13. See J. B. Skemp, The Greeks and the Gospel (London: Carey Kingsgate, 1964), 78–89, for a well-balanced discussion.

The Temple of Apollo at Corinth, built in the Doric style of architecture, dates from about the mid-fifth century B.C.

Earlier Corinth was noted for its debauchery: "to act like a Corinthian" meant to practice immorality, and "Corinthian girl" meant the same as "prostitute." Apparently short of funds on arrival in Corinth, Paul makes tents with his fellow Jews, Aquila and Aquila's wife Priscilla. Since Luke does not relate their conversion, they may have already become Christians. Around A.D. 49 or 50 the Emperor Claudius expelled them and other Jews from Rome because of rioting in the Jewish quarter over "Chrestus," probably intra-Jewish strife over the preaching of "Christus" (Latin for "Christ," but misspelled "Chrestus," a common slave's name because it rests on the Greek *chrêstos*, which means "useful," as slaves are).[14] Lukes' emphasis falls on the seriousness of Paul's attempt to convert the Corinthian Jews, on the blasphemy of those who refuse to believe, on Paul's turning to Gentiles, on the conversion of the synagogue leader Crispus and his household and the large number of

Corinth

Aquila and Priscilla

---

14. Suetonius (Claudius 25.4) seems to think that Chrestus himself instigated the rioting, but writing seventy years afterwards he probably mistakes preaching about Christ for preaching (or rabble-rousing) by Christ.

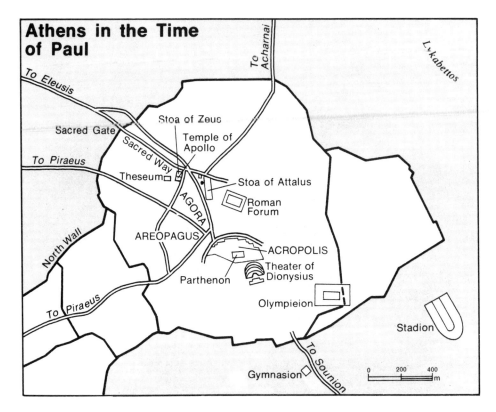

Athens in the Time of Paul

To Acharnai

Lykabettos

To Eleusis

Sacred Gate

Sacred Way

To Piraeus

Stoa of Zeus

Temple of Apollo

Theseum

AGORA

Stoa of Attalus

Roman Forum

North Wall

AREOPAGUS

ACROPOLIS

Theater of Dionysius

Parthenon

To Piraeus

Olympieion

To Sounion

Stadion

Gymnasion

0   200   400
m

Gallio resultant conversions, on the length of Paul's stay, on the Roman proconsul Gallio's dismissal of charges against Paul on the ground that they have to do with intra-Jewish disputes rather than with crimes against Roman law, and on Gallio's being so unimpressed with the Jewish charges against Paul that he does not stop the beating of a new synagogue leader named Sosthenes right in front of the judgment seat (an open air platform still visible in Corinth). Apparently it is others besides Paul's unbelieving Jewish accusers who take advantage of Gallio's snub to the Jews by beating up Sosthenes (though some think that unbelieving Jews beat up their own new leader for a lack of forcefulness in his pressing of charges against Paul, so that in accordance with 1 Cor. 1:1 Sosthenes becomes the second synagogue leader in a row to turn Christian). A Latin inscription found at Delphi, Greece, indicates that the proconsulship of Gallio lasted from about A.D. 51 to 53. The importance of his decision to allow Christian evangelism lies in the breadth of his jurisdiction (it covered the whole province of Achaia, or Greece) and in its setting a precedent to be followed in other provinces making up the Roman Empire. Paul's shaving his head in Cenchrea, a port town serving Corinth, points up his piety, for such a shave indicates the completion of a religious vow (but in this case not a Nazirite vow, for that kind cannot be observed or completed outside the land of Israel—compare Num. 6:1–21).

Paul's third missionary journey begins again in Antioch, Syria. As on the second journey, he first of all revisits the region of Galatia and Phrygia and thus the churches in Derbe, Lystra, Iconium, and Pisidian Antioch. Then he goes to Ephesus, where after a brief visit he left Priscilla and Aquila on his second journey. *Read Acts 18:23–19:41 and follow Paul's journey on the map (page 311).* *Paul's Third Missionary Journey*

By emphasizing Apollos's learning (or eloquence or culturedness) and powerful use of the Old Testament to refute unbelieving Jews in public, Luke furthers his portrayal of Christianity as fulfilled Judaism. The episode concerning Apollos also prepares for Paul's finding in Ephesus some disciples who know only John the Baptist's teaching about Jesus as the Coming One and John's baptism of repentance, both apparently passed on to them by Apollos before his fuller instruction by Priscilla and Aquila (Priscilla's name being mentioned first in the present Ephesian context probably because she took the instructional lead—contrast 18:2). Since these disciples received only the baptism of repentance despite Jesus' and then the Holy Spirit's having come in the meantime, Paul baptizes them in the name of Jesus and they receive the Holy Spirit, as demonstrated by their speaking in tongues and prophesying. (Had they received the baptism of repentance before the comings of Jesus and the Holy Spirit, by implication they would not need rebaptizing in Jesus' name.) Notably, each of the spectacular bestowals of the Holy Spirit in Acts has to do with the entrance of different groups into the church: the original Jewish believers (chap. 2), the Samaritans (chap. 8), the Gentiles (chap. 10), and followers of the Baptist (chap. 19). This special evidence of God's approval thus contributes to Luke's emphasis on universality. *Apollos* *Ephesus Baptists*

Inkresting!

For the rest of Paul's ministry in Ephesus, Luke emphasizes its boldness and persuasiveness (both admired in Hellenistic as well as Classical Greek culture); its extension in time (two years) and reach (echoing throughout the whole province of Asia); its accompaniment by extraordinary miracles (counteracting the influence of Ephesus as a center for the practice of magic and publication of magical formulas); the testimony of an evil spirit to Jesus and Paul

Demetrius

(causing fear and conversions); and the origination of social unrest, not in any actions of Paul and his missionary companions, but in the self-aggrandizing concerns of Demetrius and his fellow craftsmen and in the appearance of an unbelieving Jew, Alexander, as opposed to the friendship and friendly advice given Paul by some high officials called Asiarchs and to the townclerk's exoneration of Paul and his fellow missionaries as neither robbers of temples nor blasphemers of Artemis and his rebuke of Demetrius and company.

Sceva
and Sons

According to an early tradition, Paul uses the school of Tyrannus from 11:00 A.M. until 4:00 P.M. Paul may spend his mornings making tents, his afternoons teaching people interested enough in the gospel to forgo their midday siesta. The Jewish exorcist Sceva is a high priest only by his own claim. Jews were highly regarded as exorcists because it was thought they alone could pronounce the potent name "Yahweh" correctly, and success in casting out demons supposedly required a correct pronunciation of the proper formulas. Sceva's seven sons, apprentices in the exorcising trade, try to use the name "Jesus," but find the results disconcerting; for Christian exorcism does not depend on the recitation of magical names. When the

Book-Burning

converts in Ephesus burn their books of magical formulas, they also divulge those formulas to make them useless to the pagan onlookers, who believe secrecy as well as correct pronunciation to be necessary for success.[15]

Artemis

Artemis is a local fertility goddess identified with the Greek goddess Artemis (Roman name: Diana). Her image in the Ephesian temple apparently consisted of a meteorite thought by the Ephesians to resemble a many-breasted female. The temple itself, one of the seven wonders of the ancient world, had a floor area of

Riot

almost 10,000 square feet. When a rioting mob fills the amphitheater, which accommodated about 25,000 people, unbelieving Jews fear that they will suffer by association with the Christians because the Jews, too, preach against idolatry. So they put up Alexander to tell the mob that the Jews have nothing to do with the Christians, but his voice is no match for the uproar.

After two years and three months in Ephesus, Paul travels to Macedonia and Achaia and, as he himself says in Romans 15:25–27; 1 Corinthians 16:5; 2 Corinthians 8–9 (see also Acts 24:17), takes up an offering for the church in Jerusalem as he proceeds. He in-

---

15. *Compare C. K. Barrett, The New Testament Background: Selected Documents, 2d ed. (San Francisco: Harper & Row, 1989), 34–37.*

Statue of Artemis from Ephesus, second century A.D.

tends to go to Rome after delivering the offering to Jerusalem; and go to Rome he will, but under circumstances different from those presently envisioned. For he will go in chains as a prisoner. Meanwhile, his plan is to take a Jewish pilgrim ship from Greece to Palestine for the upcoming Passover. Unbelieving Jews plot to do away with him during the voyage, however; so changing plans, he goes back through Macedonia. Then on his way down the west coast of Asia Minor he bids farewell to the Ephesian elders, who meet him at Miletus. As his journey progresses toward Jerusalem, repeated warnings come that he will be arrested and persecuted there; but he presses on. *Read Acts 20:1–21:16 and follow Paul's journey on the map (p. 311).*

Ephesian Farewell

This section reads even more like a travelogue than preceding sections; in most of it Luke includes himself (thus "we," "our," and "us"). He is capitalizing on the popularity of travelogues in the Greco-Roman world. His communitarian emphasis resurfaces in the description of a meal at Troas, of Paul's extensive table talk afterwards, in the restoration of Eutychus, in the farewell scene with the Ephesian elders at Miletus, and in the Christian concern for Paul's welfare as expressed in Tyre and Caesarea—all of these in contrast with the foul plot that has changed his plans for travel. And proving that Paul is no charlatan, as are a good many of

To Jerusalem

327

Arcadian way of Ephesus led from the city to the harbor. The street was lined with columns, shops, and public buildings.

the numerous traveling teachers who criss-cross the Greco-Roman world, are his humility, tears, endurance of trials, refusal to pander, industriousness in private as well as public teaching and in supporting by manual labor his fellow missionaries as well as himself, concern for the well-being of his converts after his departure, and life-risking venture to Jerusalem. The notation that Philip has four virgin daughters who are prophetesses appeals to Hellenistic fascination with virgin prophetesses.

Paul's Arrest in Jerusalem According to rumor, Paul tells Jewish Christians of the Diaspora not to keep the Old Testament law. When he arrives in Jerusalem, four Jewish Christians have contracted ceremonial defilement during the period of a temporary Nazirite vow and are undergoing a seven-day period of purification. The law says that these men are required to shave their heads on the seventh day and bring offerings on the eighth before they can resume their vow (Num. 6:9–12).

Since the week of purification is soon to be completed, the elders of the church suggest that Paul join these men in the purificatory rites and pay the expenses of their offerings to demonstrate that he does not teach against the Mosaic law. He cooperates, but certain Jews from Asia Minor have previously seen that with him in Jerusalem is a Gentile companion named Trophimus, an Ephesian. They mistakenly suppose that Paul has brought him into the inner courts of the temple, where only Jews are allowed. On pain of death even for Roman citizens, Gentiles are forbidden to enter these courts. The outcry of the Jews causes a riot, from which the soldiers of the Roman tribune Claudius Lysias rescue Paul. The fortress of Antonia, into which Paul is taken, lies northwest of the temple precincts. Roman soldiers garrison the citadel, and a double flight of stairs connects it with the outer court of the temple. Three years before this incident an Egyptian Jew appeared in Jerusalem claiming to be a prophet. He led a large group to the Mount of Olives and told them to wait until the walls of Jerusalem fell at his command. Then they would march into the city and overthrow the Roman garrison. The governor Felix sent troops, killed several of the Jews, and imprisoned others. But the Egyptian Jew escaped. At first Claudius Lysias thinks Paul might be that same imposter, on whom the Jews are now trying to take revenge for his having duped them. *Read Acts 21:17–23:35.*

Luke's portrayal of Christianity as an ideal community revives in the gladness with which the Jewish Christians in Jerusalem welcome Paul and his fellow missionaries, in James's and the church elders' glorification of God for widespread salvation among the Gentiles, and in Paul's acceding to the request that he engage in and pay for the purificatory rites of Jewish Christians. The riot in the temple and attempt to kill Paul show unbelieving Jews, not believing ones, to be the cause of social unrest. Rescue by a cohort (one thousand strong) puts the Romans in a good light.

In his defense before the Jewish mob, Paul stresses what a zealous Jew he has been and what a devout Jew Ananias, the Christian who helped him in Damascus, was. He also emphasizes his miraculous vision of Christ on the road to Damascus and another vision at prayer in the temple. The unbelieving Jews listen until Paul says that God has told him to preach to the Gentiles. Unable to tolerate pro-Gentilism, the Jews cry out for Paul's blood just as they demanded the death of Jesus. This prejudice against Gentiles makes

Paul's Defense

One of the Greek tablets from Herod's temple forbidding Gentiles to enter the inner courts. Inscription reads: "No stranger is to enter within the balustrade round the temple and enclosure. Whoever is caught will be responsible to himself for his death which will ensue."

Roman theater at Ephesus where the riot recorded in Acts 20 occurred. Built in the first century, the theater seated 25,000 people.

Paul and his gospel look all the more attractive to Luke's Gentile audience. A subsequent conversation between Paul and Claudius Lysias reveals that Paul is a free-born Roman citizen, whereas Claudius Lysias had to purchase his citizenship "for a large sum," which may have constituted a bribe. Paul's citizenship by birth is superior in status. The names of citizens were registered in Rome and in places of residence. The citizens themselves possessed wax, wooden, or metal certificates inscribed with the names of witnesses as well as their own name. Execution was the penalty for a false claim to citizenship. If a citizen was not carrying his certificate or if his certificate was suspected of forgery, the authorities might ask for witnesses. Possibly for this reason Paul, who traveled far away from Tarsus (the location of his witnesses), did not appeal to his Roman citizenship very often. *Roman Citizenship*

To determine a reason for the riot, Claudius Lysias brings Paul before the Sanhedrin; but the session ends in confusion. When Paul's young nephew hears of a plot to ambush and kill Paul as Paul is being taken from place to place within Jerusalem, he informs Claudius Lysias. The tribune immediately sends Paul to Caesarea under cover of night and with a large contingent of soldiers for protection. According to his letter to Felix, the governor in Caesarea, Claudius Lysias rescued Paul on discovery that he was a Roman citizen. Actually, he did not discover Paul's Roman citizenship until Paul was about to be scourged[16] for the purpose of extracting information from him, an illegal procedure when directed against an uncondemned Roman citizen. In these episodes a number of items contribute to Luke's defense and promotion of Christianity: the good conscience of Paul right up to his present Christian moment; the unlawful mistreatment of him by the high priest; Paul's respectful apology for unknowingly rebuking the high priest; the division between Pharisees and Sadducees, which argues that since unbelieving Jews disagree among themselves, their disagreement with Christians does not rule Christians out of Judaism; the support of Paul by some of the Pharisaical scribes; the unbelieving Jews' verging on physical violence; the conspiracy to assassinate Paul, including an attempt to deceive the Roman tribune; and the tribune's finding Paul innocent of any crime deserving of death or even of imprisonment. *To Caesarea*

---

16. *To be scourged was to be beaten with a flagellum (Latin), which consisted of leather thongs attached to a wooden handle and weighted with sharp bits of bone and metal. Victims often died from the ordeal.*

Before Felix   A man named Tertullus acts as prosecutor for the Sanhedrin in
pressing charges against Paul in Caesarea. His flattery of Felix and
promise of brevity are traditional ways to begin speeches. The
charges against Paul are that he has disturbed the peace and tried to
desecrate the temple. Disturbing the peace was an elastically defined
crime which tyrannical emperors used as a weapon of political terror. Almost anything could be put in this category. By way of defense, Paul answers that he has nowhere agitated the people. In fact,
he came to Jerusalem, not in a spirit of contention, but for worship
in a state of ritual purity and with charity for the aid of Jews who re-
side in Jerusalem. He particularly notes that the Jews from Asia
who provoked a riot in the temple and originally accused him have
not appeared in court against him. As a Christian, he does not oppose Judaism, but serves the God of the Jewish patriarchs and believes everything written in the Old Testament law and prophets.
Before the Sanhedrin in Jerusalem his only "crime" was to declare a
belief in the resurrection, and even the Pharisaical faction of the
Sanhedrin supported his position (though of course they do not believe in the resurrection of Jesus, as Paul does). Putting off an immediate decision concerning Paul, Felix keeps him in custody but
Before Felix   hears him again in private audience with Drusilla. She is a girl bride
and Drusilla   not yet twenty years old. As a small child she was engaged to a
crown prince in Asia Minor; but the marriage did not take place, because the prince refused to embrace Judaism. Later, she married
the king of a petty state in Syria. When she was sixteen, Felix, with
the help of a magician from Cyprus, lured her from her husband to
become his third wife. Quite understandably, then, when Paul discusses righteousness, self-control, and the coming judgment, Felix
thinks the discussion uncomfortably pointed and personal, and dis-
misses Paul. *Read Acts 24:1–27.*

The fear of Felix at Paul's preaching combines with Felix's hoping for a bribe from Paul to explain why Felix keeps Paul in custody
for so long as two years. The length of time has nothing to do with
any suspicion that Paul is guilty. Otherwise Felix would not give
him some privileges, such as allowing friends of Paul to take care of
his needs. But hope for a bribe is not the only factor that prevents
Felix from releasing Paul. Though unmentioned by Luke, Felix's
offending the Jews on a number of previous occasions and a change
of administration in the central government at Rome have made his
political position precarious. Even on leaving the governorship he

This Roman-built aqueduct near Caesarea brought water into the city from the north.

dares not risk offending the Jews again and facing a complaint against him in Rome.

A man named Festus succeeds Felix in the governorship and im- *Before Festus* mediately visits Jerusalem to make acquaintance with the leading Jews, members of the Sanhedrin. They renew charges against Paul and ask Festus to bring Paul to Jerusalem for trial. They plan to assassinate Paul en route, as they plotted before. Since Festus does not intend to stay very long in Jerusalem, he tells them to send a delegation of accusers to Caesarea. They do, but Luke notes that they cannot prove their accusations, whereas Paul can say truthfully that he has done nothing against the Jewish law, the temple, or Caesar. It does not matter to Festus whether Paul's trial takes place in Caesarea or in Jerusalem, however, and friendly relations with the Sanhedrin would ease the governorship of Festus; so he suggests to Paul that the trial be held in Jerusalem. Paul may fear assassination en route; or perhaps he thinks that the Sanhedrin may convince Festus, a novice in Jewish affairs, that they should have jurisdiction over Paul. They could support such a claim by arguing that Paul is supposed to have committed a sacrilege against the temple, the kind of crime over which the Romans often gave jurisdiction to the Jews. Paul could easily guess the verdict should Festus turn him over to the Sanhedrin for trial. Whatever his reasoning, Paul exercises his right as a Roman citizen to appeal to the Caesar in Rome. *Read Acts 25:1–12.*

Before Festus and Herod Agrippa II   Herod Agrippa II is a great-grandson of Herod the Great, a brother of Drusilla (the wife of the ex-governor Felix), and the king of a small district near Lebanon. His younger sister Bernice is living with him at Caesarea Philippi during this time. While Agrippa is paying Festus an official visit of welcome to his new governorship, Festus decides to take advantage of the visit by having Agrippa, an expert in Jewish affairs, hear Paul and help draw up a list of charges against him; for Festus has discovered in Paul no capital crime, but only some theological differences with other Jews. The list of charges will accompany Paul when he goes to Rome for an appearance before Caesar. *Read Acts 25:13–27.*

To prove the reality of his vision on the Damascus road, Paul stresses his leading part in the persecution of Christians. He also underscores his strict upbringing as a Pharisee who believed in resurrection. Now he is preposterously being charged for preaching a fulfillment in Jesus Christ of the very doctrine he always believed as a Pharisee. And of all people, those accusing him are the Jews who, except for Sadducees, likewise believe in the resurrection. Festus, the host, rudely interrupts Paul's speech with the charge that he has gone insane through excessive study. But Paul appeals to Agrippa, the guest, by noting that the things about Jesus are matters of public knowledge and by asking Agrippa whether or not he believes in messianic prophecy. *Read Acts 26:1–32.* Paul's appeal embarrasses Agrippa, who can hardly say that he agrees with Paul right after Agrippa's host Festus has charged Paul with insanity. Neither can

Agrippa say that he does not believe in the prophets without damaging his reputation among the Jews. Wryly, then, he says that Paul is trying to make him act like a Christian. Luke's purpose in narrating this episode is to show that the expert Jewish opinion of Agrippa agrees with the Roman opinion of Felix and Festus that Paul has committed no real crime. In this respect, Paul represents Christianity as a whole.

Read Acts 27:1–28:31 and follow the journey of Paul from Caesarea to Rome on the map (page 311). Again Luke treats his Hellenistic audience to a travelogue, this time almost entirely a voyage. Despite being a prisoner, Paul gets good treatment, proves correct in his predictions, manages the salvation of all on board, suffers no ill from a snake bite, and performs miraculous healings. The hoisting up of a boat during the storm at sea refers to the hauling aboard of a small lifeboat, which in fair weather is towed behind the large ship. The sailors pass cables underneath and around the ship and tighten them to keep the timbers from breaking apart under the leverage of the mast. Lowering the gear means the dropping of a drift anchor or the taking down of top sails, which are used only in fair weather, though storm sails are still set. Next the cargo is jettisoned, and finally all the spare gear. Throughout eleven dreary days and nights the ship is doubtless leaking badly. The only hope lies in making for shore, but the sailors do not know in what direction to steer the ship. Storm clouds have blotted out the sun and stars, and compasses have yet to be invented. Despair grips those on board. Seasickness keeps them from eating. But in the end, God's purpose for Paul results in the safety of all. The hospitality of Christians in Puteoli and the welcoming party of Christians from Rome revive Luke's portrayal of the church as an ideal community.

To the Jewish leaders in Rome, Paul emphasizes that he is there purely in self-defense. He does not intend to accuse the Jewish nation or its leaders. The Roman Jews deny knowledge of Paul and any direct knowledge of Christianity, though they admit to having heard negative reports about it. Nevertheless, news of Paul may have already reached the Jews in Rome. And surely they have come into contact with Christians at Rome, for the church there is long and strongly established. Paul wrote an epistle to it, and even earlier the Emperor Claudius banished Jews from Rome, probably because of unrest among them over the preaching of Christ. It appears that the representatives of non-Christian Jews in Rome are feigning igno-

Paul's Voyage to Rome

Storm

Shipwreck

Rome

Roman Colosseum, exterior view.

The floor of the Colosseum seen from above, showing prisoners' cells.

rance. Later, on a prearranged day, a large number of these Jews hear Paul explain the gospel. Some believe, but most do not. As usual, then, Paul turns his attention to the evangelization of Gentiles.

The delay of at least two years in Paul's trial may be due to one or more of several factors: (1) the necessity for accusers to come from Palestine; (2) the loss in shipwreck of Festus's list of charges against Paul, with the consequent need for a duplicate to be sent from Caesarea; (3) the crowdedness of Nero's court calendar. During the period of delay Paul enjoys considerable freedom for a prisoner. Though chained to a Roman soldier and confined to the house he rents, he can receive visitors and any kind of attention from his friends. The reason for this laxity is that he is a Roman citizen against whom no charge has yet been proved. He takes advantage of this semifreedom by preaching. Luke wants his readers to note that even in Rome, capital of the empire, the gospel is not banned as illegal. Thus he has traced its spread from Jerusalem to Rome.

Compare the tensions and disagreements that arose in the early church with those in contemporary Christendom as to source, kind, and attempted solution. **FOR FURTHER DISCUSSION**

Identify similarities and differences between the structure of the early church and that of the modern church. What accounts for the differences?

Trace the development of the church from a Jewish to a transethnic and international body. Are today's churches truly transethnic in character? Is today's church truly international?

Do current methods of evangelism, missionary endeavor, and church-building follow Paul's methods or diverge from them, and in what ways?

Does the activity of the present-day church lack the visible evidence of the Holy Spirit that receives repeated mention in Acts?

Would the church in Acts be counted successful by contemporary standards?

Bruce, F. F. *The Acts of the Apostles.* 3d ed. Grand Rapids: Eerdmans, 1990. Advanced.

———. *The Book of Acts.* 2d ed. Grand Rapids: Eerdmans, 1988.

Haenchen, E. *The Acts of the Apostles.* Philadelphia: Westminster, 1976. Advanced. **FOR FURTHER INVESTIGATION**

Hemer, C. J. *The Book of Acts in the Setting of Hellenistic History*. Tübingen: Mohr, 1989. Advanced.

Longenecker, R. N. "The Acts of the Apostles." In *The Expositor's Bible Commentary*. Edited by Frank E. Gaebelein. Grand Rapids: Zondervan, 1981. Vol. 9, pp. 205–573.

Marshall, I. H. *The Acts of the Apostles*. Grand Rapids: Eerdmans, 1984.

Ramsay, Sir William M. *St. Paul the Traveller and the Roman Citizen*. 14th ed. London: Hodder & Stoughton, 1920.

———. *The Cities of St. Paul and Their Influence on His Life and Thought*. Grand Rapids: Baker, 1949.

Van Unnik, W. C. *Tarsus or Jerusalem, the City of Paul's Youth*. Naperville, Ill.: Allenson, 1962.

PART IV
The Epistles

12

The Early Epistles of Paul

❖ *What were the style, contents, and techniques used in the writing of letters in ancient times? How do Paul's epistles compare?*

❖ *Why is Galatians crucial in the history of Christianity?*

❖ *Who are the addressees, and what are the dates, occasions, purposes, and contents of Paul's earlier epistles?*

Paul's Epistles and Letter-Writing in the Greco-Roman World

In the Greco-Roman world private letters averaged close to 90 words in length. Literary letters, such as those written by the Roman orator and statesman Cicero and by Seneca the philosopher, averaged around 200 words. Since the usual papyrus sheet measured about 9 1/2 inches x 11 1/2 inches (approximately the size of modern notebook paper) and could accommodate 150–250 words, depending on the size of writing, most ancient letters occupied no more than one papyrus page. But the average length of Paul's epistles runs to about 1,300 words, ranging from 335 words in Philemon to 7,114 words in Romans. As can be seen, these epistles are several times longer than the average letter of ancient times, so that to a certain extent Paul invented a new literary form, the epistle—new in its prolongation as a letter, in the theological character of its contents, and usually in the communal nature of its address. From another standpoint, however, Paul's epistles count as true letters in that they have genuine and specific addresses, unlike ancient literary epistles,

Length, Contents, Address

Arch of Titus in Rome.

written for general publication in spite of their artificial addresses (compare modern "Letters to the Editor" intended for a broad readership rather than for an editor).

For long documents like Paul's epistles, single papyrus sheets were joined edge to edge and rolled to form a scroll. Since the coarse grain of papyrus made writing tedious, authors usually dictated their letters to a professional scribe, called an *amanuensis*, who used shorthand during rapid dictation. The ruggedness of Paul's literary style— seen, for example, in numerous incomplete sentences—suggests that at times he dictated too rapidly for close attention to careful sentence structure and that his amanuenses found it difficult to keep up. Sudden breaks in thought similarly suggest temporary suspension of dictation, perhaps overnight, or for shorter or longer periods. Sometimes an author simply left oral instructions, a rough draft, or notes for his amanuensis to follow. Under such circumstances the amanuensis himself molded the exact phraseology, a factor that may account for some of the stylistic differences among epistles by the same author. The author finally edited the letter. We know for certain of Paul's using amanuenses from the fact that one of them identified himself by name (Tertius, Rom. 16:22). Also, Paul's frequent statements that he is writing the final greeting with his own hand imply that the rest was written with the help of amanuenses (1 Cor. 16:21; Gal. 6:11; Col. 4:18; 2 Thess. 3:17; compare Philem. 19).

Amanuensis

Ancient letters opened with a greeting, which included the name of the sender and that of the recipient and usually wishes for good health and success and an assurance of the sender's prayers. The main body of the letter followed, and finally the farewell and sometimes a signature. Many times the farewell included greetings from others besides the author, and further good wishes. Through fear that documents were being or might be forged in his name, Paul adopted the practice of writing the farewell lines as well as a signature with his own hand to guarantee authenticity. Usually letters carried no date. The lack of public postal service made it necessary to send letters with travelers.

Format

Paul closes several of his epistles with a section containing ethical instructions. Such instructions appear scattered throughout his other epistles and epistles by other writers of the New Testament. Scholars have noted striking similarities to Jewish and Stoic ethical codes of the same historical period. Nevertheless, the New Testament writers root Christian conduct in the dynamics of faith in Jesus rather than throwing out a lofty but lifeless set of precepts

Parenesis

without power to effect their own fulfillment. The similarities of exhortations in the epistles suggests that the authors draw from a common stock of parenetic (hortatory, instructional) tradition in the church, originally designed for catechizing newly converted candidates for baptism. On the other hand, Paul may simply develop his own set of ethical instructions for converts and influence later writers, such as Peter, who read at least some of his epistles (2 Peter 3:15–16). One further element needs mention, a drawing on Jesus' ethical teaching, preserved in oral and written tradition and often reflected in the phraseology and concepts of the epistles.

Order   In our present New Testament, the order of Paul's epistles written to churches depends on length, beginning with the longest (Romans) and ending with the shortest (2 Thessalonians). The same principle of arrangement holds for his epistles written to individuals (1 and 2 Timothy, Titus, and Philemon). We will consider these epistles in the chronological order of their writing so far as that order can be determined with some probability.

Galatians: Against the Judaizers

The Crucial Issues   Paul's epistle to the Galatians has to do with the Judaizing controversy about which the Jerusalem Council met (Acts 15).[1] As with that council, so also with Galatians it is almost impossible to overestimate the historical cruciality of the theological issues at stake. Many of the first Christians, being Jewish, continued in large measure their Jewish mode of life, including attendance at the synagogue and temple, offering of sacrifices, observance of Mosaic rituals and dietary taboos, and social aloofness from Gentiles. Conversion of Gentiles forced the church to face several important questions: Should Gentile Christians be required to submit to circumcision and practice the Jewish way of life, as Gentile proselytes to Judaism were required to do? To those Gentile Christians unwilling to become wholly Jewish, should the church grant a second class citizenship, as for Gentile "God-fearers" in Judaism? And most importantly, what makes a person Christian—faith in Christ by itself, or faith in Christ plus adherence to the principles and practices of Judaism? See again the discussion of Acts 15.

Themes and Address   Galatians insists on Christian liberty from any doctrine of salvation that requires human effort in addition to divine grace, and on the unity and equality of all believers in Jesus Christ. Paul writes this

---

1. *Some scholars think that Paul's opponents in Galatia were semipagan (Gnostic), semi-Jewish syncretists.*

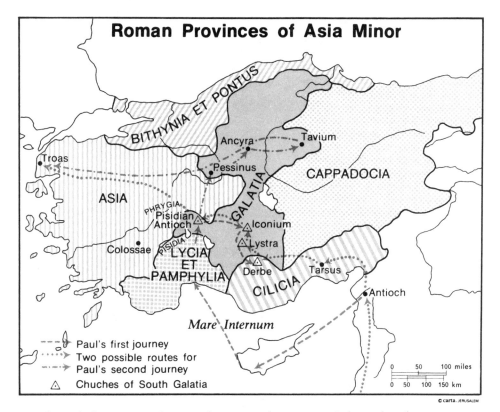

Roman Provinces of Asia Minor

BITHYNIA ET PONTUS

Troas

Ancyra • — → Tavium

Pessinus

CAPPADOCIA

ASIA

GALATIA

PHRYGIA

Pisidian Antioch △ — △ Iconium

Colossae • PISIDIA

LYCIA ET PAMPHYLIA △ Lystra

△ Derbe   Tarsus •

CILICIA

• Antioch

Mare Internum

- -○- → Paul's first journey
- ······→ Two possible routes for
- - - → Paul's second journey
- △ Chuches of South Galatia

0   50   100 miles
0   50 100 150 km

© Carta, JERUSALEM

epistle to believers residing in the region known as Galatia, but his use of the term Galatia has caused a debate that affects the date of the letter. In agreement with its original meaning, the term may refer exclusively to territory north of the cities of Pisidian Antioch, Iconium, and Lystra. Or it may also include those cities, for the Romans added southern districts when they made Galatia a province.

According to the North Galatian theory, Paul addresses the epistle to Christians in North Galatia, which he did not visit until his second journey on his way from Pisidian Antioch to Troas. Under this view the epistle could not have been written until some time after the beginning stage of the second journey and therefore after the Jerusalem Council of Acts 15, which preceded the second journey. Then the visit to Jerusalem which Paul describes in Galatians 2 probably refers to the Jerusalem Council, recently held. Perhaps the strongest arguments for the North Galatian theory, with its late dating, are the original restriction of the term Galatia to the northern territory and the similarity of the statements by Paul concerning

North Galatia

345

justification by faith to what he says in Romans, which he certainly wrote at a later date (see page 377–78).

NORTH GALATIAN THEORY	SOUTH GALATIAN THEORY
Paul's first missionary journey	Paul's first missionary journey
Jerusalem Council	Writing of Galatians
Paul's second missionary journey	Jerusalem Council
Writing of Galatians	Paul's second missionary journey

Against the North Galatian theory, Luke nowhere suggests that Paul evangelized North Galatia. It is even doubtful Paul visited that territory on his second journey, for "the region of Phrygia and Galatia" in Acts 16:6 most naturally refers to the southern territory. A traversing of North Galatia would have required an unlikely wide detour to the northeast. And elsewhere in his epistles Paul consistently uses geographical terms in an imperial sense, which would allow South Galatia in his epistle to the Galatians.

South Galatia   According to the usual form of the South Galatian theory, Paul addresses his first epistle to the churches of South Galatia just after the first missionary journey but before the Jerusalem Council. Then the visit to Jerusalem described in Galatians 2 cannot refer to the Jerusalem Council, but refers instead to the famine relief visit mentioned in Acts 11:27–30. An argument in favor of the South Galatian address and early date is that if Paul wrote the letter after the Jerusalem Council, he would probably have capitalized on that council's decree favoring Gentile Christian freedom from the Mosaic law, the main topic under discussion in Galatians. But he makes no mention of the decree. This unlikely omission implies that the epistle was written before the council met and therefore at a time when Paul had as yet visited only South Galatia. It is also doubtful that Peter would have vacillated, as he did according to Galatians 2:11ff., after the Jerusalem Council, where he strongly supported the position of freedom from the Mosaic law. By the time Paul went through North Galatia—if he did so at all on his second journey—Peter had declared that not even Jews were able to keep the law (Acts 15:10). It remains possible to adopt a South Galatian address and, despite Paul's failure to mention the decree of the Jerusalem Council, a late date (say, shortly before Romans). Such a hybrid view pays homage to the most likely route of Paul's travels and to the similarity of Galatians to Romans, though that similarity may depend on an identity of issue without requiring closeness in time.

An Outline of Galatians

INTRODUCTION: A GREETING TO THE GALATIANS AND AN ANATHEMA ON THE JUDAIZING PERVERTERS OF THE TRUE GOSPEL (1:1–10)

I. AN AUTOBIOGRAPHICAL ARGUMENT FOR THE GOSPEL OF GOD'S FREE GRACE (1:11–2:21)

A. The direct revelation of that gospel by Jesus to Paul (1:11–12)

B. The impossibility of its originating from Paul's own very Judaistic past (1:13)

C. The impossibility of Paul's having learned it from merely human sources, the apostles, whom Paul met not until three years after his conversion and then only for a brief time (1:14–24)

D. The later acknowledgment of Paul's gospel by the ecclesiastical leaders in Jerusalem (2:1–10)

E. Paul's apparently successful rebuke of Peter for his yielding to Judaizing pressure in Antioch, Syria (2:11–21)

II. A THEOLOGICAL ARGUMENT FOR THE GOSPEL OF GOD'S FREE GRACE (3:1–5:12)

A. The sufficiency of faith (3:1–5)

B. The example of Abraham (3:6–9)

C. The curse of the law (3:10–14)

D. The divine covenant of promise to Abraham and his offspring, or seed (Christ and those united to him by faith), prior to the law of works (3:15–18)

E. The purpose of the law, not to provide a way of salvation through human merit, but to demonstrate the necessity of divine grace through faith in Christ (3:19–4:7)

F. A plea to retain trust in God's grace alone, with an allegory on Christian freedom using Abraham and his two sons, slaveborn Ishmael and freeborn Isaac (4:8–5:12)

III. A WARNING AGAINST ANTINOMIANISM (5:13–6:10)

A. Christian liberty, living by the Spirit rather than according to the flesh (5:16–24)

B. Christian love (5:25–6:5)

C. Christian liberality (6:6–10)

CONCLUSION: A CONTRAST BETWEEN THE JUDAIZERS' FEAR OF PERSE-
CUTION AND THEIR BOASTFUL PRIDE, PAUL'S HUMILIATING PERSE-
CUTIONS, AND A BENEDICTION (6:11–18)

Introduction

The epistle opens with a greeting in which Paul stresses his apostleship, for he wishes to establish his authority against the Judaizers.
In place of the usual thanksgiving for his audience, Paul immediately
and violently introduces the reason for his writing. He is shocked
that the Galatian Christians are deserting to another gospel, which is
not really a gospel ("good news") at all. *Read Galatians 1:1–10.*

Autobiographical
Argument

Now Paul puts forward an autobiographical argument for the
gospel of God's grace over against the Judaizing message, which
requires adherence to the Mosaic law for salvation. He states that
this gospel came to him by direct revelation from Jesus Christ. It
certainly could not have come from his past, he argues, for before
his divine call he had been zealous for Judaism. Nor did he learn it
from the apostles in Jerusalem, for he did not even meet them until
three years after his conversion. And when he did visit Jerusalem, he
saw only Peter (whom Paul calls by the Aramaic equivalent and
original Cephas) and James (Jesus' brother), stayed only fifteen days,
and did not become acquainted with the Judean Christians at large.
Since the gospel of grace could not have come from his Jewish past
or from his Christian contacts in Jerusalem, it must have come from
God. When he visited Jerusalem again after fourteen years (figured
either from his call or from his first visit to Jerusalem), the leaders
there—James, Peter, and John—formally acknowledged the correct-
ness of the gospel of grace that he had been preaching to the
Gentiles. They did so by giving him the right hand of fellowship.
Furthermore, they did not require Titus, his Gentile companion, to
be circumcised.

Peter in
Syrian Antioch

On coming to Antioch, Syria, Peter at first ate with Gentile
Christians, but then yielded to pressure from the Judaizers. Paul
publicly rebuked him. Despite much present opinion to the contrary, the implication seems to be that Peter yielded to the rebuke. If
not, Paul would hardly have brought up the incident as an argument
in his favor. The fact that even Peter stood rebuked by Paul demonstrates the authority of Paul's gospel of grace. *Read Galatians*
1:11–2:21.

Paul's summary of his reprimand to Peter contains the germ of his theological argument to follow. The term "justify," which appears repeatedly, means "*regard* as righteous," not "*make* righteous." In Classical Greek it meant "deal with someone according to justice," almost the opposite from Paul's usage, which goes back to the Old Testament, especially Isaiah, where God graciously intervenes to set things right between himself and human beings. God's gracious intervention remains just, however; for Christ suffered the penalty for others' sins, a penalty necessitated by God's holiness, and the imputation of God's righteousness to the believer in Christ now makes it unjust for God to condemn that believer.

"Justify"

A paraphrase may aid the understanding of 2:17–21: "If we have to forsake the law to be justified by faith in Christ, does Christ encourage sin? No; rather, if I go back to the law, I imply that I was sinning in abandoning it. But I did not sin in so doing, for Christ died under the judgment of the law against sin. As a believer, I died with Christ in the sense that God looks at me as having done so. The law has no authority over a dead person, especially one who has died under its penalty; so I am no longer obligated to keep the law. But Christ rose and lives in me; thus, though I died in Christ when he died and thus became free from the law, I rose in Christ to a new life of righteousness. Therefore, if human beings could become righteous through keeping the law, Christ did not need to die."

Paul now develops his theological argument. If a person is justified by faith at the start, why not continue by faith rather than by the law? Abraham was justified long before the law was given; so even in the Old Testament righteousness came by faith, not by the law. The law can only curse or condemn, because no one obeys it entirely. Christ died to deliver us from the law and its inevitable curse. God's making a covenant with Abraham before giving the law through Moses indicates that the Abrahamic covenant is more basic than the law. The law, then, did not annul it. On God's side, the Abrahamic covenant consisted of a promise to bless Abraham's seed; on the side of human beings, an acceptance of God's promise by faith. Abraham's seed consists of Christ plus all those incorporated into him by following Abraham's example of faith.

Theological Argument

The law of Moses did have a purpose, but only a temporary one. It was to lead people to Christ as ancient slave-tutors led children to school. The law accomplished this purpose by making people keenly aware of their inability to make themselves righteous. Being under the law, therefore, was like being minors or slaves. But in Christ

349

people live as free adults, adopted into God's family as sons and heirs with grown-up privileges and responsibilities. Why revert to an inferior status?

Paul then recalls how the Galatians accepted his message at their conversion and pleads with them to accept his present message as they did his first. He further supports his argument in rabbinic style by allegorizing an Old Testament story. Hagar the slave woman stands for Mount Sinai, which in turn stands for the Mosaic law and its headquarters in Jerusalem, Palestine. Ishmael her slaveborn son stands for those who are enslaved to the law. Sarah stands for Christianity and its capital, the heavenly Jerusalem. Isaac her promised and freeborn son stands for all the spiritual children of Abraham, that is, those who follow Abraham's example of faith and are therefore freed in Christ from the law. *Read Galatians 3:1–5:12.*

Against Libertinism, Antinomianism   The last main section of the epistle warns against *libertinism*, or *antinomianism* (literally, "against-law-ism"), the attitude that freedom from the law means license to sin. Not so, writes Paul. Christians must conduct themselves according to the Holy Spirit rather than according to the flesh (the sinful urge). Moreover, they must lovingly help others, especially their fellow Christians, and give liberally to those who minister the gospel. *Read Galatians 5:13–6:10.*

The contradiction between 6:2, "Bear one another's burdens," and 6:5, "For each shall bear his or her own load," is only apparent. In the first, Paul means that Christians should help one another in their present difficulties; in the second, that at the future judgment each person will answer to God for his or her own conduct alone.

To his prolonged attack on the Judaizers' legalism, Paul appends numerous precepts governing Christian conduct. These show that legalism does not consist merely in having rules. The books of the New Testament contain many rules of behavior. Legalism is rather the imposition of wrong rules, and particularly more rules than a situation warrants, so that in a maze of minutiae people lose their ability to distinguish the more important from the less important, the principle from its application. Legalism also includes a feeling of merit in one's obedience, over against a recognition that obedience is nothing more than one's duty. The personal dimension of enjoying fellowship with God on the basis of his grace alone is consequently lost.

Paul adds a conclusion in his own handwriting. The "large letters" *Conclusion* which he uses may be for emphasis, though some think that poor eyesight necessitated them. He charges that the Judaizers are motivated by desire to avoid persecution from unbelieving Jews and by ambition to boast that they are able to steal converts from him. By way of contrast, he calls attention to the sufferings which he has gladly endured for his message and appeals to the Galatians that they themselves judge who has the purer motives, he or the Judaizers. *Read Galatians 6:11–18.*

What manifestations of legalism exist within contemporary Christendom? **FOR FURTHER DISCUSSION**

What modern forms does antinomianism take?

Compare Paul's concept of Christian freedom with current situational ethics, and the Christian ethic of love with the secular ethic of love.

How does Paul's emphasis on love tally with his anathema on the Judaizers?

How can Christian parents avoid both legalism and overpermissiveness in rearing their children? How can Christian educational institutions, churches, and missionary agencies avoid both legalism and libertinism?

Compare Paul's account of his visit to Jerusalem (Gal. 2:1–10) with Luke's account of the Jerusalem Council (Acts 15:1–29). How are they similar? How do they differ? Are they readily harmonized?

Betz, H. D. *Galatians*. Philadelphia: Fortress, 1979. Advanced. **FOR FURTHER INVESTIGATION**

Bruce, F. F. *The Epistle to the Galatians*. Grand Rapids: Eerdmans, 1982.

Bligh, J. *Galatians*. London: St. Paul Publications, 1969.

Bunyan, J. *Grace Abounding to the Chief of Sinners.*

Chafer, L. S. *Grace*. Grand Rapids: Zondervan, 1922.

Danby, H. *The Mishnah*. London: Oxford, 1933. Almost any part of this translation of the Mishnah will give the flavor of rabbinic legalism.

Genesis 15–17; 21:1–21. For Old Testament passages referred to by Paul.

Guthrie, D. *Galatians*. 2d ed. Grand Rapids: Eerdmans, 1981.

Longenecker, R. N. *Galatians*. Dallas: Word, 1990. Advanced.

Luther, M. "The Argument of St. Paul's Epistle to the Galatians." In *Luther's Works*. Vol. 26, *Lectures on Galatians 1535 Chapters 1–4*. Edited and translated by J. Pelikan. Associate editor, W. A. Hansen. St. Louis: Concordia, 1963. Pp. 4–12.

———. "The Freedom of a Christian." In *Luther's Works*. Vol. 31, *Career of the Reformer: I*. Translated by W. A. Lambert. Edited and revised by H. J. Grimm. General editor, H. T. Lehmann. Philadelphia: Muhlenberg, 1957. Pp. 328–77.

Arch of Galerius, located on the Egnatian Way in the heart of Salonika (modern Thessalonica).

First Thessalonians: Congratulations and Comfort

Paul's epistles to the church in Thessalonica are best known for *Themes* their teaching about the second coming of Jesus Christ and associated events. These two epistles, the Olivet Discourse of Jesus, and the Apocalypse of John (the book of Revelation) form the three main prophetic portions of the New Testament. In 1 Thessalonians this eschatological note belongs to the second of the two overall themes, (1) congratulations to the Thessalonian believers on their conversion and progress in the Christian faith and (2) exhortations toward further progress, with particular emphasis on comfort from and expectancy toward the Second Coming.

Thessalonica, the capital city of Macedonia, lay on the Via *Background* Egnatia, the main highway connecting Rome with the East. The city had its own government, led by politarchs, and a Jewish settlement. Paul evangelized the city on his second missionary journey. Some Jews and many Greeks and prominent women embraced the Christian faith. Paul's statement, "You turned to God from idols" (1 Thess. 1:9), implies that the majority of Christians there were Gentiles; for Jews of that era did not practice idolatry. (The Assyro-Babylonian exile had cured them of it.) Unbelieving Jews in Thessalonica violently opposed the gospel by assaulting the house of Jason, Paul's host, and later traveled to Berea to drive Paul out of that city, too.

According to Acts 17:2, Paul spent three Sabbaths preaching in the synagogue at Thessalonica. Luke's narrative seems to imply that the riot which forced Paul to leave occurred immediately following his ministry in the synagogue, and Acts 17:10 indicates that the Christians sent Paul away right after the riot. Some scholars have nevertheless put a gap between the ministry in the synagogue and the riot, because Paul mentions having worked for his own living in Thessalonica (1 Thess. 2:7–11) and having received one or two gifts from Philippi during his stay in Thessalonica (Phil. 4:16). But he may have begun working immediately on arrival in Thessalonica and continued for three or four weeks. Likewise, two offerings could have arrived from Philippi within one month.

Another argument for a longer stay in Thessalonica is that 1 and 2 Thessalonians presuppose more doctrinal teaching than Paul could have given in a month or so. But Paul probably taught his converts outside the synagogue on weekdays; and Timothy, who stayed longer in Thessalonica and after leaving returned again, must have

Occasion taught them yet more. Therefore we should probably limit Paul's ministry in Thessalonica to about a month.

Timothy rejoined Paul in Athens, went back to Thessalonica, and then rejoined Paul in Corinth. His report provided the occasion for Paul's writing of 1 Thessalonians (compare 1 Thess. 3:1–2 with Acts 18:5). We infer, then, that Paul wrote 1 Thessalonians from Corinth during his second journey, not very many weeks after evangelizing the addressees.

An Outline of First Thessalonians

INTRODUCTION: GREETING (1:1)

I. CONGRATULATIONS (1:2–3:13)
   A. Thanksgiving for the exemplary conversion of the Thessalonian believers (1:2–10)
   B. Paul's reminiscences concerning his ministry in Thessalonica (2:1–16)
   C. Timothy's glowing report about the progress of the Thessalonian Christians (2:17–3:10)
   D. A prayer for the Thessalonian believers (3:11–13)

II. EXHORTATIONS (4:1–5:22)
   A. To morality (4:1–8)
   B. To mutual love (4:9–12)
   C. To consolation over deceased fellow Christians because of their participation in the Parousia[2] (4:13–18)
   D. To expectant readiness for the Day of the Lord (5:1–11)
   E. Miscellaneous exhortations (5:12–22)

CONCLUSION: A BENEDICTION AND FINAL INSTRUCTIONS (5:23–28)

Congratulations The first main section of 1 Thessalonians consists of congratulations to the Thessalonian believers on their conversion and on their progress in the Christian life. Their fidelity even in the midst of persecution is providing a good example to other Christians in Macedonia and Greece (Achaia). Timothy's report about them has indeed been good. *Read 1 Thessalonians 1:1–3:13.*

As usual, Paul combines the typical Greek greeting in a transmuted Christian form, "grace," with the typical Semitic greeting, "peace." The form of the word "grace" which non-Christian Greeks used carries the simple meaning of "hello," but Paul changes the

---

2. *See page 196.*

term to carry overtones of divine favor bestowed through Jesus Christ on ill-deserving sinners. "Peace" means more than the absence of warfare; it also carries the positive connotation of prosperity and blessing. A well-known triad of Christian virtues appears in 1:3: faith, love, and hope. Faith produces good works. Love results in labor, which means deeds of kindness and mercy. And hope, an eschatological term referring to confident expectation of Jesus' return, generates steadfastness under trial and persecution. In the middle of this congratulatory section Paul reminds the Thessalonians of his loving, self-sacrificial ministry among them. Some have thought that he defends himself here against slander intended to destroy his influence. More probably, he stresses that in view of his laboring fervently among the Thessalonians it gratifies him that they have responded well to the gospel.

Read 1 Thessalonians 4:1–5:28. Paul expertly passes from congratulation to exhortation by telling the Thessalonian Christians to continue their progress. The commands to live quietly and keep working may rebuke those who believe so strongly in the immediacy of Jesus' return that they are leaving their jobs. Paul's unblushing advocacy of manual labor contrasts with the view typical of Greeks, who held that sort of work in contempt.

Exhortations

Rapture is the term commonly used to designate the catching up of Christians at the Second Coming, as described in 4:16–17. *Translation* designates the immortalizing and glorifying of the bodies of Christians alive on earth when Jesus returns. Lack of need for a resurrection will necessitate such a change in their still-living but mortal bodies. The Thessalonian Christians have been sorrowing over the decease of fellow Christians, apparently because they do not realize that these fellow Christians will share in the joy of Jesus' return. Perhaps they think of death before the Parousia as chastisement for sin, or even as an indication of lost salvation. Paul reassures his audience by explaining that deceased Christians will be resurrected just before the Rapture in order that they may be taken up along with Christians who are still alive on earth.

Then Paul shifts from comfort to warning. Christians must watch for the Day of the Lord (the Second Coming and following events) lest they be taken by surprise. Failure to watch is to put oneself in the category of the wicked, who will be caught unexpectedly. On the other hand, preparedness for the Day of the Lord consists of more than mental awareness. It includes also a mode of conduct characterized by obedience to commands such as those with which the epistle closes.

Second Thessalonians: Correction on the Second Coming

Occasion and Theme   Paul writes 2 Thessalonians from Corinth on his second missionary journey, shortly after writing 1 Thessalonians.[3] During the interval between writings, fanaticism increased in the church at Thessalonica. The fanaticism arose out of a belief in the immediacy of Jesus' return. Apparently that belief arose in turn out of a desire for deliverance from persecution. (The wish was the father of the thought.) Paul therefore writes this second epistle to the Thessalonians to quiet the fanaticism by correcting the eschatology that gave rise to it.

An Outline of Second Thessalonians

INTRODUCTION: GREETING (1:1–2)

I. PERSECUTION (1:3–12)
   A. Thanksgiving for the Thessalonian believers' progress in the midst of persecution (1:3–4)
   B. Assurance of deliverance from persecution and of divine judgment on persecutors at the Parousia (1:5–10)
   C. Prayer for the Thessalonian believers (1:11–12)

II. THE PAROUSIA, RAPTURE, AND DAY OF THE LORD (2:1–17)
   A. Denial that the Day of the Lord has arrived (2:1–2)
   B. Affirmation of necessary precedents (2:3–15)
      1. The rebellion (2:3a)
      2. The man of lawlessness (2:3b–15)
         a. His divine claim (2:3b–5)
         b. The present restraint of his appearance (2:6–7)
         c. His doom (2:8)
         d. His deceitfulness (2:9–12)
         e. The protection of Thessalonian Christians from his deceitfulness and doom (2:13–15)
   C. Benediction (2:16–17)

III. EXHORTATIONS (3:1–15)

---

3. Some scholars reverse the order of 1 and 2 Thessalonians; but that view lacks support in ancient manuscripts and, among other considerations, 2 Thessalonians 2:15 ("you were taught through our letter") seems to presuppose 1 Thessalonians.

A. To prayer, love, and stability (3:1–5)

B. To industrious labor (3:6–13)

C. To disciplinary ostracism of disobedient church members (3:14–15)

CONCLUSION: A FURTHER BENEDICTION AND A FINAL GREETING, WITH EMPHASIS ON PAUL'S OWN HANDWRITING IN THE LAST FEW LINES TO GUARANTEE THE AUTHENTICITY OF THIS EPISTLE (3:16–18)

After an initial greeting, Paul again thanks God for the progress of the Thessalonian believers in their Christian life and for their patient endurance of persecution; but the commendation is much shorter than in 1 Thessalonians. Passing quickly to the subject of eschatology, Paul vividly describes the Second Coming, when persecutors will be judged and the persecuted relieved of their sufferings. His purpose is to encourage the Thessalonians to continued endurance by pointing forward to the turning of the tables when Christ comes back. Then Paul begins to deal with their misunderstanding of the Parousia by saying that it is not immediate. Therefore, they should return to their jobs and businesses. Looking for Christ's return does not mean cessation of normal living. He may not return for some length of time. *Read 2 Thessalonians 1:1–3:18.*

Encouragement

Paul's warning not to be deceived by a false prophecy or by an oral or written report forged in his name suggests that the leaders of the fanaticism in Thessalonica claimed his support. The phrase "man of lawlessness" (2:3) refers to the Antichrist, a world leader of wickedness and persecution in the last days. This evil figure will demand worship of himself in the temple of God; that is, he will try to force the Jewish people to worship his image, which he will place in the temple at Jerusalem (compare Mark 13:14; Matt. 24:15; Rev. 13:1–18). The suggestion that this concept of an Antichrist originates in the Nero-*redivivus* myth, according to which Nero will return from the dead, stumbles against the pre-Neronian date of the concept or would require us to reject without sufficient reason the authenticity of 2 Thessalonians by dating the epistle after Paul's martyrdom and after Nero's death. It is also suggested that Paul has in mind the unfulfilled order of Emperor Caligula in A.D. 40 that a statue of himself be erected for worship in the temple at Jerusalem. Perhaps so, but Daniel's prophecy concerning the abomination of desolation (9:27; 11:31; 12:11), the desecration of the temple by Antiochus Epiphanes in 168 B.C., and Jesus' allusion to a still future abomination of desolation (see the references above) provide the primary background for Paul's statements.

Correction

357

The Restraint or Restrainer Paul feels it unnecessary to identify what or who restrains the Antichrist from appearing until the proper time, for the Thessalonians already know from his oral teaching. According to the two most probable suggestions, the restraint consists (1) in the institution of human government, personified in rulers such as the Roman emperor and his underlings and ordained by God for the protection of law and order (the Antichrist will be "lawless") or (2) in the activity of the Holy Spirit, keeping back the Antichrist either directly or through the medium of the church. Others think that Paul refers to missionary preaching as the restraint and to himself, the leading missionary, as the restrainer; but it is difficult to think that he anticipated his own special removal as a condition of the Antichrist's appearance, for elsewhere he looks for the Parousia just as other Christians do. Finally, the emphasis on Paul's own handwriting as an indication of the genuineness of this epistle may imply that an epistle has been forged in Paul's name to support the fanaticism at Thessalonica.

FOR FURTHER DISCUSSION *What doctrines and how much insight from Paul's previous oral ministry do the Thessalonian epistles presuppose? Compare these doctrines with the level of evangelistic preaching today.*

From the Thessalonian epistles construct an outline of future eschatological events. Why is it sketchy? Attempt to fit it with Jesus' Olivet Discourse (Mark 13; Matthew 24–25; Luke 21) and the book of Revelation.

Infer the Thessalonians' reaction to 1 Thessalonians from what Paul writes in 2 Thessalonians. Then imagine what their response to 2 Thessalonians might have been.

FOR FURTHER INVESTIGATION Best, E. *The First & Second Epistles to the Thessalonians.* Peabody, Mass.: Hendrickson, 1987.

Bruce, F. F. *Thessalonians One & Two.* Dallas: Word, 1982. Advanced.

Ladd, G. E. *The Blessed Hope.* Grand Rapids: Eerdmans, 1956. For the view that the rapture of the church will not occur until after the Tribulation; also R. H. Gundry, *The Church and the Tribulation.* Grand Rapids: Zondervan, 1973.

Marshall, I. H. *1 and 2 Thessalonians.* Grand Rapids: Eerdmans, 1983.

Morris, L. *The First and Second Epistles to the Thessalonians.* 2d ed. Grand Rapids: Eerdmans, 1991. Advanced.

Walvoord, J. F. *The Rapture Question.* Revised and enlarged ed. Grand Rapids: Zondervan, 1979. For the view that the rapture of the church will occur before the Tribulation.

Wanamaker, C. A. *Commentary on 1 and 2 Thessalonians.* Grand Rapids: Eerdmans, 1991.

13

The Major Epistles of Paul

First Corinthians: Church Problems

❖ What were Paul's connections and communications with the Corinthian church prior to the writing of 1 Corinthians?

❖ How and why did the church in Corinth sink into

the deplorable condition reflected in 1 Corinthians?

❖ What were the specific problems in the church at Corinth and Paul's remedies for them?

The first epistle of Paul to the Corinthians demonstrates that lamentable conditions in the church do not characterize the postapostolic church alone. Aberrant beliefs and practices of astonishing variety and vulgarism flourished in the Corinthian church. It is to solve those problems that Paul writes this epistle.

Theme

Short of money on first arriving in Corinth, Paul made tents with Aquila and Priscilla. On Sabbath days he preached in the synagogue. After Silas and Timothy rejoined him, he wrote 1 and 2 Thessalonians; moved his preaching activity next door to the house of Titius Justus; converted Crispus, ruler of the synagogue; received from the Roman proconsul Gallio a dismissal of Jewish accusations against him; and ministered altogether one and a half years in the city.

Previous Ministry in Corinth

The statement in 1 Corinthians 5:9, "I wrote to you in my letter not to associate with immoral people," implies that Paul wrote to

A Lost Previous Epistle

359

the church in Corinth an earlier epistle, which has since been lost. The Corinthians misunderstood that epistle to mean that they were to dissociate themselves from *all* immoral people. Now Paul explains that he had in mind dissociation only from *professing Christians* who live in open and flagrant sin.

Time and Place of Writing First Corinthians, then, is really the second epistle written by Paul to the church in Corinth. He writes it from the city of Ephesus during his third missionary journey. The end of his stay there has nearly come, for he is already planning to leave (16:5–8). Some have thought from 16:10, "*when* Timothy comes" (RSV), that Timothy will carry the epistle to Corinth. But Acts 19:22[1] suggests that Timothy has gone to Macedonia by this time. The NRSV, NIV, and NASB give the better translation of 1 Corinthians 16:10: "*if* Timothy comes [from Macedonia to you in Corinth]." Were Timothy carrying the epistle, Paul would hardly write "if." Paul tried to induce Apollos, a very important figure, to visit Corinth and probably intended to send 1 Corinthians with him. But Apollos refused (16:12), so that the carrier remains unknown.

Occasion Two events prompted the writing of 1 Corinthians: (1) the bringing of oral reports by the household of Chloe regarding contentions in the Corinthian church (1:11); (2) the coming of a delegation from the Corinthian church—Stephanas, Fortunatus, and Achaicus—both with an offering (16:17) and with a letter asking the judgment of Paul on various problems, which he takes up successively with the introductory phrase, "Now concerning . . . ," or simply, "Now . . ." (7:1, 25; 8:1; 11:2; 12:1; 15:1; 16:1). At least this understanding seems to follow from 16:17 ("these [men] have supplied what was lacking on your part") and 7:1 ("now concerning the things that you wrote about"); otherwise, Stephanus, Fortunatus, and Achaicus merely assuaged Paul's desire to see all the Corinthian Christians in person and the letter from Corinth arrived through other hands. Chloe is a feminine name. The members of her household were probably slaves. It remains uncertain whether they visited Paul in Ephesus, having come from Corinth, or visited Corinth from Ephesus and reported back to Paul.

City Background The city of Corinth was located on a narrow isthmus between the Aegean Sea and the Adriatic Sea. The voyage around the southern tip of Greece was dangerous. Many ships were therefore carried or

---

1. Acts 19:22: "*And having sent into Macedonia . . . Timothy . . . he himself [Paul] stayed in Asia [the province in which Ephesus was located] for a while.*"

dragged on rollers across the isthmus and put to sea again. For various reasons several attempts to dig a canal were abandoned. As a juncture for commerce and travel, Corinth was quite cosmopolitan. The athletic games held there ranked second only to the Olympics. The outdoor theater accommodated twenty thousand people, the roofed theater three thousand. Temples, shrines, and altars dotted the city. Many so-called sacred prostitutes made themselves available at the temple of Aphrodite, the Greek goddess of love. The south side of the market place was lined with taverns equipped with underground cisterns for cooling the drinks. Archaeologists have discovered numerous drinking vessels in these liquor lockers; some bear inscriptions, such as "Health," "Security," "Love," and the names of gods. It is natural that a church set in such extreme paganism should bristle with problems. Consequently, 1 Corinthians deals with them almost entirely.

Church Problems

An Outline of First Corinthians

INTRODUCTION: GREETING TO AND THANKSGIVING FOR THE
    CORINTHIAN CHURCH (1:1–9)

  I. REPROOFS IN RESPONSE TO REPORTS BY THE HOUSEHOLD OF
     CHLOE (1:10–6:20)
    A. Divisions and the necessity of their healing by recognition of
      the weak humanity of Christian leaders and their followers
      over against the power of God in the gospel of the Cross
      (1:10–4:21)
    B. The case of a man cohabiting with his stepmother and the
      necessity of disciplining the offender by ostracism from
      Christian fellowship (5:1–13)
    C. Lawsuits between Christians and the necessity of their settlement by the church outside secular courts (6:1–8)
    D. Immorality in general and the necessity that Christians live
      virtuously by the indwelling Holy Spirit (6:9–20)

 II. REPLIES TO QUESTIONS RAISED IN A LETTER FROM THE
    CORINTHIANS (7:1–16:9)
    A. Marriage, its essential goodness, but the advantage to some
      of an unmarried state; restriction of divorce; and exhortation
      to reconciliation (7:1–40)
    B. Food, especially meat, offered to idols and its allowance for
      Christians provided they neither abuse their freedom by

injuring the consciences of the theologically uneducated nor join in idolatrous banquets (8:1–11:1)

    C. Order of public worship (11:2–14:40)

        1. The requirement of a head-covering for women who pray and prophesy in church services (11:2–16)

        2. The Lord's Supper, its desecration in the Corinthian church by disunity and overindulgence, and the requirements of reverence and discontinuance of love feasts (11:17–34)

        3. Spiritual gifts (12:1–14:40)

            a. Diversity of function within the unity of the church as the body of Christ (12:1–31)

            b. The supremacy of love (13:1–13)

            c. The superiority of prophesying and inferiority of speaking in tongues, with rules for orderliness (14:1–40)

    D. The resurrection, from Christ's in the past to believers' in the future (15:1–58)

    E. The collection for the church in Jerusalem, its manner of gathering and delivery (16:1–9)

CONCLUSION: TIMOTHY'S COMING VISIT TO CORINTH, APOLLOS'S FAILURE TO VISIT, MISCELLANEOUS EXHORTATIONS, FINAL GREETINGS, AND A BENEDICTION (16:10–24)

Disunity   *Read 1 Corinthians 1:1–4:21.* Corinthian factionalism has derived from hero worship. The admirers of Paul are loyal to him because he founded the church in Corinth, but he does not side even with his own admirers. The admirers of Apollos are apparently spellbound by his learning and eloquence. The followers of Cephas (Peter) may be a Jewish segment of the church or traditionalists who rest on the authority of the foremost original apostle. The admirers of Christ are sometimes regarded as those who want to avoid squabbles and therefore adopt an attitude of withdrawal and superior spirituality. More probably, "I belong to Christ" represents Paul's own position in condemnation of those who admire merely human leaders (see 3:21–23). Doctrinal differences seem not to underlie the personality cults. At least the factions are still meeting together, for Paul addresses a single letter to them.

In writing that he is glad for not having baptized very many of the Corinthians, Paul is not denying the validity of baptism (he admits to the baptism of some) but is strongly denying that he or any other

Christian evangelist should baptize converts to gain a personal following. On the contrary, the proper task of Christian evangelists is hardly popular, for the preaching of a Savior who died as a criminal—that is, by crucifixion—offends human pride and worldly wisdom. Consequently, most believers come from the lower strata of society. But what they lack by way of background and attainment Christ more than makes up: he is their wisdom, righteousness, sanctification, and redemption.

Paul recalls that on coming to Corinth from Athens, where the worldly wise philosophers had rejected him, he preached the cross of Christ in weakness and trembling, not with the rhetorical methods of sophistic philosophers. Alternatively, he did not preach that salvation comes through embracing wisdom, religiously and philosophically conceived and limited to the spiritually elite. Nevertheless, he claims to teach genuine wisdom, that which comes from the Holy Spirit, who alone knows the mind of God.

Because of the factionalism in Corinth, Paul charges the Christians there with carnality, or fleshliness in the sense of sinfulness. Boasting in human leaders is wrong, he says, because they are only human beings. Furthermore, they are fellow workers, not rivals. The section closes with an admonition to unity. By implication, Christians can achieve unity if they want it and work for it.

Read 1 Corinthians 5:1–7:40. Paul brings up the case of a man living immorally with his father's wife. Presumably she is his stepmother, since Paul does not identify her as the man's own mother. And apparently she is a non-Christian and therefore outside the jurisdiction of the church, since Paul does not prescribe punishment for her. He rebukes the Corinthians for their arrogant pride in condoning such flagrant sin within their number and commands discipline in the form of dismissal from the fellowship of the church, that is, social ostracism and exclusion from the Lord's Supper. The problem of Christians' going to court against one another may have some connection with the case of immorality, for the discussion of this problem occurs in the middle of Paul's reproof concerning immorality. He cautions that ceremonial freedom does not imply moral freedom and stresses that as a temple of the Holy Spirit the body is sacred. *Immorality*

Voluntary celibacy is good, writes Paul, but because of sexual desire God has provided marriage for the avoidance of illicit relationships. Within marriage, then, spouses should give themselves *Celibacy* sexually to each other. Paul wishes that all might be free from marital responsibilities, as he is, not because of any spiritual superiority in celibacy, but because of the single person's ability to devote full energy to preaching the gospel. Nevertheless, Paul concedes that in this respect God's will varies for different Christians.

Marriage and Divorce

On the question of divorce, Paul does not show so much flexibility. Divorce reached epidemic proportions in some classes of Greco-Roman society. Paul repeats Jesus' teaching against divorce so far as Christian couples are concerned and at most allows them separation with the possibility of reconciliation. But Jesus' words do not cover the case of husbands or wives who have converted after marriage but whose spouses have not. Therefore Paul advises the Christian spouse to stay with the non-Christian spouse, if at all possible, at least partly because the non-Christian and any children in the family are consecrated by the close range of Christian witness in the home. If the non-Christian insists on breaking up a marriage, however, the Christian is "not under bondage." It is debatable whether this phrase means that the Christian is not obligated to seek reconciliation or that the Christian is free to remarry within the Christian fellowship. Paul's indication that these instructions are his own rather than the Lord's does not imply that they lack authority, but only that Jesus said nothing on these points, and therefore Paul must give his own teaching as one who is "trustworthy" and possesses the Spirit.

The last part of chapter 7, especially verses 36ff., poses difficult problems of interpretation. Is Paul referring to spiritual marriages, never physically consummated? To engaged couples? To unengaged sweethearts? Or to a Christian father, his daughter, and her suitor? The main lessons, however, are clear. On the one hand, marriage is not to be condemned on the basis of asceticism. On the other hand, marriage is not to be contracted out of social pressure. Single Christians can often lead fuller, richer, and more productive lives than married Christians. Throughout, Paul stresses the critical nature of the period in which Christians are living. He probably has in mind the possibility of the Lord's return, a possibility that should lend a sense of urgency to Christian work and witness.

Food Dedicated to Idols

It is important to understand the background of Paul's discussion concerning food associated with the worship of idols. In the ancient world pagan shrines were the main suppliers of meat for human consumption. Thus, most of the meat in butcher shops had come from animals sacrificed to idols. The gods received a token portion—usually not a choice cut—burned on the altar. After priests and priestesses took their portions and the worshiper and family consumed further portions, the remainder of meat went up for sale to the general public. But Jews purchased their meat in Jewish shops, where they could be sure that it had not come from an animal sacrificed to a pagan god. Should Christians be as scrupulous as the Jews? *Read 1 Corinthians 8:1–11:1.*

Paul advocates freedom to eat, but cautions his audience lest their exercise of that freedom inflict spiritual damage on people with uninformed consciences. In other words, Christians who understand that an idol has no real divine existence may eat meat dedicated to the idol without damage to their conscience. But if people who mistakenly think that idols have real divine existence happen to be observing, better-informed Christians should then refrain from eating such meat, lest they damage the Christian life of uninformed, recently converted Christians and lest they mar their witness to uninformed, idolatrous non-Christians.

Christian Freedom and the "Law of Love"

It is to be noted that the balance between freedom and the "law of love" covers only ritual and other questions that are inherently neutral from the standpoint of morality. Paul warns that though he allows the judicious eating of meat dedicated to idols, by no means does he allow participation in idolatrous feasts associated with pagan worship. It would be blatant inconsistency for a Christian to partake both of the Lord's Supper and of suppers demonically designed to foster the worship of false gods. Paul notes that when in Old Testament times the people of Israel joined in pagan feasts, they also fell into forms of pagan worship which led to immoralities.

Paul's instructions on the head-covering of women are traditionally understood in terms of veiling (though not with the kind of veil that covers the face as well as the head). On the other hand, he never uses the specific Greek word for a veil; and he says that a woman's long hair is given her for a covering. In either case, his concern is to maintain a visible distinction between women and men with respect to long and short hair. *Read 1 Corinthians 11:2–16.*

Head-Covering

Read 1 Corinthians 11:17–34. Paul states that factionalism among the Corinthians makes mockery of their communion services, which are to be times of Christian fellowship. The Corinthians are celebrating the Lord's Supper in conjunction with a love feast, a kind of church potluck corresponding in a way to the Passover meal, during

The Lord's Supper and Love Feasts

which Jesus instituted the Lord's Supper. Some of them are coming early to the place of meeting, eating their meal, and taking communion before the arrival of others who have longer working hours. Some are even getting drunk. Maybe they take so sacramental a view of the Lord's Supper that they think the more bread and more wine, the more divine grace. So Paul commands discontinuance of the love feasts, delay of the Lord's Supper until the arrival of late-comers, introspection, and reverence. His rehearsal of the institution of the Lord's Supper comes from pre-synoptic tradition, which originated in the action of the Lord Jesus himself. "I received . . ." (11:23) is technical for the reception of tradition that has been handed down.

Speaking in Tongues   *Charismata* (gifts) and *glossolalia* (speaking in tongues) make up the subject matter of chapters 12–14. Many hold that the speaking in tongues discussed here by Paul consists of ecstatic speaking, not a speaking in bona fide human languages. He does indeed state that apart from the gift of interpretation not even a speaker in tongues knows what he or she is saying. But "interpretation" usually means *translation*. It would therefore seem that in Paul's usage, tongues-speaking consists in the miraculous speaking of unlearned human languages. The tongues are sometimes unintelligible, then, not because they are ecstatic non-languages, but because on some occasions neither the speaker nor anyone else present in the audience happens to possess the equally miraculous gift of translation.[2]

Through valuing tongues-speaking too highly the Corinthians have been overusing the gift. Paul devalues it and insists that its use be orderly and limited. At the expense of tongues-speaking he magnifies superior gifts, in particular, prophecy, which communicates direct revelation from God, needed especially though not necessarily exclusively in the early church in lieu of the New Testament

Love and Spiritual Gifts   Scriptures. Above all, Paul celebrates the Christian ethic of love in the prose poem of the famous thirteenth chapter. There is no proper exercise of the spiritual gifts apart from love; there is no love in the church apart from the exercise of spiritual gifts. *Read 1 Corinthians 12:1–14:40.*

Paul's concept of the church as the body of Christ stands out prominently in chapter 12 and emphasizes respect for the variety of spiritual gifts. The prohibition against women's speaking in church

---

2. See further R. H. Gundry, "'Ecstatic Utterance' (N.E.B.)?" Journal of Theological Studies, n.s. 17 (1966): 299–307.

(14:34–35) can hardly be absolute, for Paul has just given instructions in chapter 11 for the head-covering of women so that they may pray and prophesy in public worship. "If they want to learn anything, let them ask their own husbands at home" suggests that he is prohibiting the interruption of church services by women with outspoken questions and—if women sat separately from men, as in synagogues—perhaps also by disruptive conversation among women.

Paul now takes up the topic of bodily resurrection, a concept foreign to Greek thought. Some Athenians, entirely sceptical or hoping at best for immortality of the soul, mocked Paul when he spoke of bodily resurrection.[3] This scepticism may also be causing some Christians in Corinth to doubt and deny a future resurrection. But they are not denying the past resurrection of Christ, as would be expected of scepticism. So they may be denying a future resurrection under the view that Christ's is the only resurrection. Paul then argues from the common ground of belief in Christ's past resurrection to the disputed belief in a future resurrection of others: Christ is the first fruits of resurrection, not the whole harvest. *Resurrection*

The great chapter on resurrection opens with a summary of the gospel and a list of those to whom the risen Christ appeared, a list which Paul would not have dared to include with such reckless confidence unless the eyewitnesses were in fact available. "I received" indicates that he is quoting a confessional statement from Christian tradition even more ancient than the date of his writing. He continues with a description of the resurrected body and an analogy between death in Adam and life in Christ. Some rabbis taught that the resurrected body will be exactly the same as the present body. No, says Paul; the resurrected body will have continuity with the present body but be suited to the conditions of eternal life. The chapter comes to climax in a burst of triumphant praise. *Read 1 Corinthians 15:1–58.*

Various explanations have been devised for the reference in 15:29 to baptism for the dead. Perhaps Paul refers merely to those who have been converted and baptized out of a desire to be reunited with their Christian loved ones and friends at the resurrection. More likely he is referring to vicarious baptism in the full sense, but using it as a point of argument without supporting the practice ("What will *they* do . . . ?" and "Why are *they* getting baptized for them?" as *Baptism for the Dead*

---

3. See Acts 17:32 and pages 321–22.

opposed to "we" in the next verse). In other words, he is pointing out the inconsistency of those who undergo baptism for the very dead people whose future resurrection they deny. Just as an overly sacramental view of the bread and wine of the Lord's Supper may have contributed to eating and drinking too much, so an overly sacramental view of baptismal water may be contributing to baptism for dead people as well as for themselves. The fighting "with wild beasts" in 15:32 is probably metaphorical.[4] A "spiritual body" is not a nonphysical body, but a body made alive by the Spirit of Christ. Nor does the inability of flesh and blood to inherit the kingdom of God deny the physicality of resurrected bodies; it denies only their perishability, their mortality.

The Offering and Miscellany Paul's concluding chapter contains various exhortations, such as the one to lay aside money for the offering that he will collect on his arrival and take to Jerusalem with accredited companions. Appearing in 16:22 is the important Aramaic phrase, "Maranatha," which means "O [our] Lord, come!" (compare Rev. 22:20). It shows that the designation of Jesus as Lord dates from early times in Aramaic-speaking circles and is therefore not to be attributed to later, Greek-speaking Christianity—against the claim of some modern scholars that the view of Jesus as a divine figure was a rather tardy development, original neither to Jesus nor to the earliest church. *Read 1 Corinthians 16:1–24.*

FOR FURTHER DISCUSSION *How is it possible to strike the proper balance between the unity and the purity of the church without making one cancel the other?*

How are we to evaluate the modern ecumenical movement toward church unity?

How do Paul's strictures against immorality and emphasis on love compare with "the new morality"?

How is church discipline of erring members possible when today a Christian excluded from one church can easily gain admittance to another? How "serious" a sin requires discipline?

What current questions of Christian conduct validly fall within the area of private freedom and public responsibility?

---

4. Compare *the* Epistle of Ignatius *to the* Romans *5:1.*

Why do most churches not require women speaking in public services to wear a head-covering?

Does the Holy Spirit still grant the gifts of prophecy and tongues? If so, do their recipients exercise them in the manner prescribed by Paul?

From the standpoint of modern science, how could there be a continuity between the mortal body and the resurrected body?

Barrett, C. K. *A Commentary on the First Epistle to the Corinthians*. Peabody, Mass.: Hendrickson, 1987.

Bruce, F. F. *A Commentary on 1 and 2 Corinthians*. Grand Rapids: Eerdmans, 1980.

Conzelmann, H. *1 Corinthians*. Philadelphia: Fortress, 1975. Advanced.

Fee, G. D. *The First Epistle to the Corinthians*. Grand Rapids: Eerdmans, 1987.

Morris, L. *First Corinthians*. 2d ed. Grand Rapids: Eerdmans, 1988.

FOR FURTHER INVESTIGATION

Second Corinthians: Paul's Conception of His Own Ministry

❖ *After the writing of 1 Corinthians, what dealings between Paul and the church in Corinth led to the writing of 2 Corinthians?*

❖ *What was the mood of the Corinthian church and that of Paul at the time he wrote 2 Corinthians?*

❖ *What does the apology of Paul in 2 Corinthians imply about his apostolic self-image?*

More than any other epistle of Paul, 2 Corinthians allows us a glimpse into his inner feelings about himself, about his apostolic ministry, and about his relation to the churches which he founded and nurtured. This epistle is autobiographical in tone, then, though not in framework or substance.

After writing 1 Corinthians from Ephesus, Paul found it necessary to make a "painful visit" to Corinth and back—painful because of the strained relation between him and the Corinthians at the time. Luke does not record this visit in Acts. It is to be inferred, however, from 2 Corinthians 12:14; 13:1–2, where Paul describes his coming visit as the "third." Apart from the inferred painful visit, he has visited Corinth only once before. The statement in 2 Corinthians 2:1, "For I made up my mind not to make you another painful visit"

Theme

The Painful Visit

(RSV), implies a past painful visit which can hardly be identified with his first coming to give them the joyful tidings of salvation through Jesus Christ.

The Lost "Sorrowful Letter"

Whatever the reason for Paul's making the short, painful visit, he was unsuccessful in bringing the church into line. On returning to Ephesus, therefore, he wrote a now lost "sorrowful letter" to Corinth, which at first he regretted having sent (2 Cor. 2:4; 7:8). Despite frequent attempts at identification, his descriptions of the sorrowful letter do not fit 1 Corinthians very well. So the sorrowful letter is his second lost one to Corinth. It commanded the church to discipline an obstreperous individual who was leading the opposition against Paul (2 Cor. 2:5–10). Titus carried the letter to Corinth. Meanwhile, knowing that Titus would return via Macedonia and Troas and being anxious to hear from Titus the reaction of the Corinthians, Paul left Ephesus and waited in Troas. When Titus failed to arrive quickly, Paul went on to Macedonia, where Titus finally met him and reported the good news that the majority in the church had repented from their rebellion against Paul and disciplined the leader of opposition to him (2 Cor. 2:12–13; 7:4–16).

Occasion

Paul wrote 2 Corinthians from Macedonia on his third journey, then, (1) to express relief and joy at the favorable response of the majority of Corinthian Christians, and in so doing describes his ministry in vividly personal terms (chaps. 1–7); (2) to stress the collection that he wants to gather from the church for the Christians in Jerusalem (chaps. 8–9); and (3) to defend his apostolic authority to the still recalcitrant minority (chaps. 10–13).

A Summary of Paul's Relationships with the Corinthian Church

- Paul evangelizes Corinth during his second journey.
- Paul writes a lost letter in which he commands the Corinthian church to dissociate from professing Christians who live immorally.
- Paul writes 1 Corinthians from Ephesus during his third journey to deal with a variety of problems in the church.
- Paul makes a quick, "painful" visit from Ephesus to Corinth and back to straighten out the problems at Corinth, but fails to accomplish his purpose.

The ruins of Corinth.

- Paul sends another lost letter, called the "sorrowful letter," in which he commands the Corinthians to discipline his leading opponent in the church.
- Paul leaves Ephesus and anxiously waits for Titus, first at Troas and then in Macedonia.
- Titus finally arrives with good news that the church has disciplined Paul's opponent and that most of the Corinthians have submitted to Paul's authority.
- Paul writes 2 Corinthians from Macedonia (still on the third journey) in response to Titus's favorable report.

It has been argued that 2 Corinthians 10–13 is at least part of the otherwise-lost sorrowful letter, because Paul changes from a tone of happiness in chapters 1–9 to one of self-defense in chapters 10–13. But the distinction does not entirely hold true, for self-defense crops up also in chapters 1–9 (see 1:17ff.; 2:6, 17; 4:2–5; 5:12–13). The difference in emphasis may be due to Paul's addressing primarily the repentant majority in chapters 1–9, primarily the still-recalcitrant minority in chapters 10–13. Or fresh news of revived opposition may force him to change his tone from the tenth chapter onward. A number of considerations militate against dividing 2 Corinthians into two originally separate epistles: (1) if written earlier as the sor-

Integrity of 2 Corinthians

rowful letter, chapters 10–13 would likely precede chapters 1–9; (2) though firm in tone, chapters 10–13 hardly exhibit sorrow; (3) chapters 10–13 contain nothing about insulting behavior by the leader of Paul's opposition, yet that was the subject matter of the sorrowful letter according to 2:1ff.; (4) 12:18 mentions a *previous* visit of Titus, which must have been for delivering the sorrowful letter; but according to the theory of partition, 12:18 is itself part of the sorrowful letter!

An Outline of Second Corinthians

INTRODUCTION: GREETING (1:1–2)

I. THE RELATIONSHIP BETWEEN PAUL AND THE CORINTHIAN CHURCH WITH SPECIAL REFERENCE TO THE NOW-AGREEABLE MAJORITY (1:3–7:16)

A. Thanksgiving for divine comfort and protection (1:3–11)

B. Explanation of Paul's failure to visit Corinth again, not fearful vacillation but desire to avoid another painful visit (1:12–2:4)

C. Instruction to restore the disciplined, penitent leader of opposition to Paul, with a statement of forgiveness by Paul (2:5–11)

D. Inner description of Paul's ministry (2:12–6:10)

1. Anxiety over Titus's failure to come to Troas (2:12–13)

2. Thanksgiving for triumphant confidence in Christ (2:14–17)

3. The living recommendation of Paul's ministry in the Corinthian converts themselves (3:1–3)

4. The superiority of the new covenant over the old (3:4–18)

5. The determination of Paul to carry out his ministry (4:1–6:10)

E. Plea for mutual affection and separation from unbelievers (6:11–7:4)

F. Joy over Titus's report in Macedonia that the majority of Corinthian Christians have repented of their opposition to Paul (7:5–16)

II. EXHORTATION TO CONTRIBUTE TO THE COLLECTION FOR THE CHURCH IN JERUSALEM (8:1–9:15)

A. The example of Christians in Macedonia (8:1–7)

B. The example of Jesus (8:8–9)

C. The ideal of equality (8:10–15)

D. The coming of Titus and others to receive the collection (8:16–9:5)

E. The divine reward for liberality (9:6–15)

III. THE RELATIONSHIP BETWEEN PAUL AND THE CORINTHIAN CHURCH WITH SPECIAL REFERENCE TO A STILL-RECALCITRANT MINORITY (10:1–13:10)

A. The defense of Paul against charges of weakness and cowardice (10:1–11)

B. The rightful claim of Paul over the Corinthians as his converts (10:12–18)

C. Paul's concern over the danger of false teachers at Corinth (11:1–6)

D. Paul's refusal to take financial support from the Corinthians (11:7–15)

E. Paul's pedigrees of Jewish ancestry and Christian service, including the suffering of persecution (11:16–33)

F. Paul's visions and thorn in the flesh (12:1–10)

G. The apostolic miracles of Paul (12:11–13)

H. The coming visit of Paul to Corinth, with a threat of harshness and an appeal for repentance (12:14–13:10)

CONCLUSION: FAREWELL EXHORTATIONS AND GREETING, AND A BENEDICTION (13:11–14)

Review of Past and Present Relationships

The epistle opens with a greeting and thanksgiving for comfort from God in persecutions and hardships. Paul then begins to describe his ministry as sincere and holy and defends himself against the charge of vacillation—failure to carry out a threatened further visit—by claiming that his words are just as affirmative as the promises of God in Christ and by explaining that he has delayed his visit to give the Corinthians time for repentance. Their repentance would make for an arrival under happier circumstances than otherwise. Pleased that the Corinthian church has disciplined his leading opponent, Paul advises restoration of the man into churchly fellowship. This would be shown especially by allowing him to participate again in the Lord's Supper. The section closes with a metaphor of Christ as a victorious general entering Rome in triumphal procession, and another metaphor in which the Corinthian Christians, as Paul's converts, are a letter of recommendation for Paul written by Christ himself. *Read 2 Corinthians 1:1–3:3.*

Ministry of the Gospel Paul now describes the superiority of his gospel over the Mosaic law. The fading of God's glory from the face of Moses when he descended from Mount Sinai represents the temporariness of the Mosaic covenant. Christians are now free from the law and its condemnation. But just as Moses reflected the fading glory of the old covenant, Christians should reflect the permanent, greater, and increasing glory of the new covenant. How amazing that God should entrust the preaching of this glorious gospel of the new covenant to poor, weak human beings! But although we feel our inadequacy, writes Paul, we do not despair. The hope of resurrection makes us overlook our present physical dangers in preaching the gospel. With awareness of tremendous privilege and responsibility as a minister of the new covenant, Paul claims conscientiousness and integrity no matter how adverse or favorable the conditions of his ministry. *Read 2 Corinthians 3:4–7:16.*

Separation In the digression of 6:11–7:1 Paul portrays the life of separation from sin as an enlarging rather than confining experience. Some have thought that this digression formed part of his first lost epistle to Corinth, referred to in 1 Corinthians 5:9: "I wrote to you in my epistle not to associate with immoral people." But why an excerpt from that epistle should have been inserted here is difficult to say; and manuscript evidence is lacking to indicate that 6:11–7:1 did not originally belong to 2 Corinthians—a fact which also militates against the theory that 6:14–7:1 has been interpolated from a non-Pauline source.

The Offering Pleading for a generous offering to the church in Jerusalem, Paul presents the liberality of Macedonian Christians as worthy of Corinthian imitation; and even more so is the self-sacrifice of Christ. Sometime *you* may need help, Paul argues. Furthermore, you eagerly seized on the idea of such an offering when I first mentioned it some time ago. Do not prove that my bragging to the Macedonians about your zeal was unfounded. *Read 2 Corinthians 8:1–9:15.*

Apologia The opponents of Paul have accused him of boldness when absent, cowardice when present. He therefore reminds the Corinthians that meekness is a virtue of Christ; but like Christ he can be bold in their presence if he wants, and will be if necessary, though in the Lord, not in himself. *Read 2 Corinthians 10:1–13:13.* In these chapters Paul presents the credentials of his apostolic ministry: his sincerity as a preacher (he did not even accept wages from the Corinthians), his extensive sufferings, special revelations from God, and miracle-working powers. But Paul carefully guards against boastful pride by repeatedly insisting that the recalcitrants are forcing him to write in this vein and also by mentioning his weakness, particularly his "thorn in the flesh" (12:7–10). Among the suggested identifications of this thorn in the flesh are epilepsy, eye disease, malaria, leprosy, migraine headaches, depression, stammering, and false teachers. The epistle closes with an appeal that Paul's next visit may not have to be an occasion for rebuking the Corinthians again.[5]

For what historical and theological reasons might two of Paul's letters to the Corinthian church have been lost? Is it likely that had they been preserved, the church would have accepted them into the canon? How should they now be received if somehow discovered?

How do Paul's remarks about Christian stewardship of money compare with the Old Testament law of tithing?

Why did Paul not "turn the other cheek" rather than defend himself from personal attack?

Construct a profile of Paul's personality from this most self-revealing of his epistles.

FOR FURTHER DISCUSSION

Barrett, C. K. *A Commentary on the Second Epistle to the Corinthians*. Peabody, Mass.: Hendrickson, 1987.

Bruce, F. F. *A Commentary on 1 and 2 Corinthians*. Grand Rapids: Eerdmans, 1980.

Furnish, V. P. *II Corinthians*. Garden City, N.Y.: Doubleday, 1984. Advanced.

Martin, R. P. *Second Corinthians*. Dallas: Word, 1988. Advanced.

FOR FURTHER INVESTIGATION

Romans: The Gift of God's Righteousness Through Faith in Christ

❖ *What was the origin and composition of the churches in Rome?*

❖ *What leads Paul to write to the churches in Rome though*

he has never visited there?

❖ *What is the step-by-step progression in this most systematic of Paul's explanations of the gospel?*

The great theme of Romans is justification by God's grace through faith in Jesus Christ. Jesus himself implied this doctrine in

Theme

---

5. *Some scholars identify the Corinthian opponents of Paul at least partly with Gnostics, because he counteremphasizes true spiritual knowledge. But the setting of his Jewishness over against theirs (11:22) suggests an identification of them with Judaizers, who also would claim to possess the truth.*

his parables of the Prodigal Son, the Pharisee and the Publican, the Laborers in the Vineyard, and the Great Supper. The same implication lies behind his statement, "I came not to call the righteous, but sinners to repentance" (Mark 2:17), and behind his dealings with Zacchaeus (Luke 19:1–10). Thus, Paul did not invent the doctrine of free forgiveness; rather, he developed it in his own distinctive way. The doctrine receives its most systematic treatment in his epistle to the churches at Rome (see 16:5, 14, 15 for the presence of more than one church there).

Founding of the Churches in Rome

Toward the end of the first century, Clement of Rome suggested that Paul and Peter were martyred in his city. By the time of Tertullian (early third century) the church at large had generally accepted this tradition. The churches in Rome, however, were probably not founded by an apostle, certainly not by Paul and almost certainly not by Peter. As noted before, the Roman historian Suetonius wrote that the emperor Claudius banished Jews from Rome in A.D. 49 or 50 because of rioting at the instigation of one called "Chrestus," probably a misspelling of "Christus" (Latin for Christ), accompanied by a misunderstanding of preaching about Christ as preaching by him.[6] If so, Christianity had already gone to Rome. But Peter was still in Jerusalem at the Jerusalem Council, about A.D. 49. In Romans, moreover, Paul makes no reference and sends no greeting to the apostle Peter. Perhaps then some of the Jews and proselytes from Rome who were visiting Jerusalem on the Day of Pentecost converted to Christ and carried the gospel back to Rome at the very dawn of church history (Acts 2:10).

Jewish or Gentile?

Some scholars maintain that the Roman churches consisted mainly of Jewish Christians. They argue that emphasis on the Jewish nation in chapters 9–11, appeal to the example of Abraham, quotations of the Old Testament, and passages in which Paul appears to be arguing against Jewish objections (2:17–3:8; 3:21–31; 6:1–7:6; 14:1–15:3) imply predominantly Jewish churches. But according to chapters 9–11, God has temporarily turned his attention from the Jewish nation to the Gentiles; so these chapters may rather indicate that the original audience of the epistle consisted mainly of Gentile Christians. The appeals of Paul to Abraham and to the Old Testament may reflect his own Jewish background, not the background of his audience. And his answering typically Jewish objections may stem from his frequent debates with unbelieving Jews

---

6. *See pages 30, 323.*

Synagogue ruins believed to date back to the first century were uncovered at Ostia, an old Roman port city southwest of Rome.

and with Judaizers rather than from a Jewish Christian address for the epistle.

A number of passages demonstrate the predominantly Gentile composition of the Roman churches. Paul writes in 1:5–6, "among all the Gentiles . . . including yourselves." In 1:13 he writes, "among you just as also among the *rest* of the Gentiles." His statement, "I am speaking to you Gentiles" (11:13), characterizes the Roman churches as a whole, not a minority within them; for in 11:28–31 the audience is said to have obtained mercy because of Jewish unbelief. In 15:15–16 he speaks of his writing to them in conjunction with his ministry "to the Gentiles."

Paul has just completed collecting an offering for Christians in Jerusalem during his third missionary journey (15:25–26). He writes from Corinth, for Gaius the Corinthian is hosting him at the time (16:23; 1 Cor. 1:14). The mention of Erastus, a city treasurer (16:23), supports Corinth as the place of writing, for an inscription

Time and Place of Writing

377

discovered in Corinth and dating from the first century reads, "Erastus, the commissioner of public works, laid this pavement at his own expense." Strictly, "commissioner of public works" represents a lower office than that of "city treasurer"; but it is natural to think either that Erastus advanced from commissioner to treasurer or that he was demoted from treasurer to commissioner. It also remains possible that the two titles are roughly synonymous. Further support for Paul's writing from Corinth is found in the commendation of Phoebe, who belongs to the church at Cenchrea right by Corinth. This commendation probably indicates that she will carry the letter from Corinth to Rome (16:1–2).

Purpose   Paul writes Romans to prepare believers living in Rome for his first visit to their city. For a long time he has been intending to visit, but has been prevented (1:13; 15:22–24a). He purposes to strengthen the Roman Christians in their faith (1:11, 15) and to win their financial support for his projected mission to Spain after visiting Rome (15:24, 28). For the most part, what he writes seems to be what he has on his mind to tell Jewish Christians in Jerusalem when he arrives there with the offering which he has been collecting for them. He fears that the tension between Jewish and Gentile Christians in the East may have reached such proportions that the Jewish Christians in Jerusalem will refuse the offering because of its having been collected largely from Gentile Christians in Macedonia and Achaia and delivered personally by himself as the apostle to Gentiles (15:30–31). He also knows enough about the churches in Rome to warn Gentile Christians against boasting of superiority over Jewish Christians (11:17–32) and against despising them for their ritual observances (14:1–23). Claudius's banishment from Rome of Jews, including Jewish Christians, must have left the churches there in the charge of Gentile Christians who very likely are trying to maintain control even now that Jewish Christians are returning to Rome along with other Jews after the death of Claudius. Paul's warnings signal the fear of a full-scale rupture between Jewish and Gentile Christians in Rome as well as in the East. So he presents in Romans what he will present in Jerusalem, the gospel of justification by faith for Jews and Gentiles alike as the basis of Christian unity— and unity not for its own sake, but for the sake of further evangelism such as he plans to pursue in Spain. A rupture in Rome would spoil his chances of getting much support for the Spanish mission.

Because Paul knows only certain of the Christians in Rome, those who have moved there since he became acquainted with them elsewhere, Romans is more formal than any of Paul's other epistles. Nevertheless, chapter 16 contains many personal greetings; and he sends them even though he has never visited Rome. Some scholars have thought that the chapter originally belonged to an epistle sent to Ephesus, where Paul had certainly become acquainted with many people. But the chapter does not make up a whole epistle (it consists almost entirely of greetings); and there is no manuscript evidence that it ever circulated independently, either as a whole epistle or as part of one. The only other long series of greetings in Paul's epistles appears in Colossians, sent to another city that he had never visited. Probably, then, to establish friendly relations with churches he has never visited, Paul emphasizes his previous acquaintance with Christians who have moved to such churches, and to avoid favoritism he omits individual greetings in epistles to churches he has founded (Ephesians offering the special case of a circular letter to churches that he has neither founded nor visited).

Personal Greetings

Ancient manuscripts vary widely on the position of the doxology at 16:25–27 in English Bibles and on the position of the benediction in 16:20. The confusion may derive from Marcion, a Gnostic who possibly omitted chapters 15–16 because they contain Old Testament and Jewish references disagreeable to his anti-Judaistic way of thinking. The confusion may be compounded by a truncated form of the epistle lacking chapter 16, for which there is ancient textual evidence. Because of the personal greetings in that chapter, some editions probably omitted it to adapt the epistle for circulation throughout the Christian world.

Textual Confusion

The Development of Thought in Romans

In the opening part of this epistle Paul greets his audience and mentions his hope of visiting them in order that he may preach the gospel in Rome as elsewhere (1:1–15). He then states his theme in 1:16–17: The good news of deliverance from sin by the giving of God's righteousness to everyone who believes in Jesus Christ.

Introduction and Theme

The first main section delineates the need for justification because of human sinfulness (1:18–3:20). The latter half of chapter 1 describes the wickedness of the Gentile world, chapter 2 the self-righteousness and sin of the Jewish world, and the first half of chapter 3 summarizes the guilt of all humanity. It should be noted that

The Need: Sinfulness

for Paul sins in the plural symptomize the root problem of sin in the singular as a dominating principle of non-Christian existence.

The Remedy: Justification

Justification is God's remedy according to the second main section (3:21–5:21). The latter half of chapter 3 presents the sacrificial death of Christ as the basis of justification, and faith as the means of appropriating the benefits of his death. Chapter 4 portrays Abraham as the great example of faith, against the rabbinic doctrine of Abraham's store of merit so excessive that other Jews can draw on it. Chapter 5 lists the manifold blessings of justification—peace, joy, hope, the gift of the Holy Spirit, and others—and contrasts the unbeliever's position in Adam, where sin and death take effect, and the believer's position in Christ, where righteousness and life eternal take effect.

The Outcome: Sanctification

In the third main section the discussion progresses to the topic of sanctification, or holy living (chaps. 6–8). Should believers sin in order that God may exercise his grace all the more and thus gain more praise for himself? No! Baptism illustrates death to sin and coming alive to righteousness (chap. 6). This kind of sanctification does not consist in self-generated attempts to keep the Old Testament law, which can give only a sense of defeat, or in any human ability to surmount the demonic control of sin over human conduct (chap. 7). Rather, the Spirit of Christ gives overcoming power. Thus, chapter 8 climaxes in a burst of praise: "Who shall separate us from the love of Christ?" Paul lists the possibilities and denies them all.

The Problem: Israel's Unbelief

But despite divine covenants and other privileges, Israel appears to be separated from the love of Christ. So Paul's discussion turns to the problem of Israel in the fourth main section (chaps. 9–11). Because of his own Jewishness he is keenly concerned about the fate of his fellow Jews. All along he has been claiming that the gospel is no innovation, but a derivative from the Old Testament and a fulfillment of all that Abraham, David, and the prophets stood for. But if so, why have Jews by and large failed to accept the truth of this claim? Does rejection of the gospel by a Jewish majority imply a flaw in Paul's claim? By way of answer, chapter 9 stresses the doctrine of election, God's right to choose whomever he wishes. It is perfectly legitimate, argues Paul, for the sovereign God to do with Israel and the Gentiles what he wants to do. And it is as much God's prerogative to choose the Gentiles now as it was for him to choose the Jews earlier. But his current turn from Israel is not capricious, for Israel deserves it on account of her self-righteousness and refusal to believe what she has both heard and understood in the gospel (chap. 10). Furthermore, God's turning from Israel is only temporary and partial. By believing in Christ, a Jew may gain salvation as easily as a Gentile does; and in the future God will restore the whole nation to his favor. Meanwhile, Gentiles enjoy equality with Jews (chap. 11).

The fifth main section contains practical exhortations for Christian living, including commands to obey governmental authorities and to allow freedom on ritual issues (chaps. 12–14). Paul concludes the epistle by stating his plans and sending greetings (chaps. 15–16).

The Obligation: Christian Precepts

Conclusion

An Outline of Romans

INTRODUCTION (1:1–17)
    A. Greeting (1:1–7)
    B. Paul's plan to visit Rome (1:8–15)
    C. Statement of theme (1:16–17)

  I. THE SINFULNESS OF ALL HUMAN BEINGS (1:18–3:20)
    A. The sinfulness of Gentiles (1:18–32)
    B. The sinfulness of Jews (2:1–3:8)
    C. The sinfulness of Jews and Gentiles together (3:9–20)

 II. THE JUSTIFICATION OF SINNERS WHO BELIEVE IN JESUS CHRIST (3:21–5:21)
    A. The basis of justification in the propitiatory death of Jesus (3:21–26)
    B. Faith as the means of obtaining justification (3:27–4:25)
      1. Its exclusion of boasting in one's work (3:27–31)
      2. Its Old Testament examples in Abraham (especially) and David (4:1–25)
    C. The many blessings of justification (5:1–11)
    D. A contrast between Adam, in whom there is sin and death, and Christ, in whom there is righteousness and life (5:12–21)

III. THE SANCTIFICATION OF SINNERS JUSTIFIED BY FAITH IN JESUS CHRIST (6:1–8:39)
    A. Baptism as a representation of believers' union with Christ in his death with reference to sin and in his coming alive with reference to righteousness (6:1–14)

B. Slavery to sin and freedom from righteousness versus slavery to righteousness and freedom from sin (6:15–23)

C. Death to the law through union with Christ in his death, as illustrated by the cancellation of marriage through the death of one's spouse (7:1–6)

D. The failure of the law to produce righteousness as due to the inability of human beings to overcome their own sinful bent (7:7–25)

E. Righteous living through the Spirit by those who are justified through faith in Jesus Christ (8:1–27)

F. A statement of confidence and triumph (8:28–39)

IV. THE UNBELIEF OF ISRAEL (9:1–11:36)

A. The concern of Paul for Israel (9:1–5)

B. The unbelief of Israel as a matter of God's predetermined plan (9:6–33)

C. The unbelief of Israel as a matter of her own self-righteousness (10:1–21)

D. The present remnant of believers in Israel (11:1–10)

E. The future restoration and salvation of Israel (11:11–32)

F. A doxology to God for his ways of wisdom (11:33–36)

V. PRACTICAL EXHORTATIONS (12:1–15:13)

A. Consecration to God (12:1–2)

B. Ministries in the church (12:3–8)

C. Love in the Christian community, with attendant virtues (12:9–13)

D. Relations with unbelievers (12:14–21)

E. Obedience to the government (13:1–7)

F. Love (13:8–10)

G. Eschatological watchfulness (13:11–14)

H. Freedom and avoidance of offense on ritual questions, such as the eating of certain food and the observance of sacred days (14:1–15:13)

CONCLUSION (15:14–16:27)

A. Paul's plan to visit Rome after taking a gift of money to the Christians in Jerusalem (15:14–33)

B. Commendation of Phoebe (16:1–2)

C. Greetings (16:3–16)

D. Warning against false teachers (16:17–20a)

E. Benediction (16:20b)
F. Further greetings (16:21–24)
G. Doxology (16:25–27)

The Main Doctrines in Romans

Read Romans 1:1–3:20. By his quotation of Habakkuk 2:4 Paul highlights Old Testament support for the fundamental truth that righteousness comes through faith (1:17). Since the traditional translation, "The righteous will live by faith," sounds as though Paul is using this text with regard to the exercise of faith in daily life, we should prefer the translation, "The person who is righteous by faith will live," and understand Paul to be using the text with regard to eternal life. He also states that nature itself reveals the power and deity of God; therefore, pagans have no excuse (1:19–20). The rest of chapter 1 describes the retrograde nature of sin. Three times throughout the passage the statement, "God gave them up," tolls like a death knell (1:24, 26, 28).

Righteousness by Faith

In chapter 2, Paul describes self-righteous Jews, who delight in pointing out the sins of pagans but are just as guilty in their own proud way. Furthermore, he argues, genuine Jewishness does not consist in physical ancestry or in the rite of circumcision, but in a proper spiritual relation to God. In fact, Gentiles who follow God's law written in their consciences demonstrate a right relation to him that many Jews lack. The word "Jew" means "praise." Therefore, the true Jew is the one whose life is praiseworthy by divine criteria (2:17).

Human Guilt

In 3:1, Paul anticipates a Jewish objection: If Jews are no better than Gentiles, why did God choose the Jewish nation? Does not the whole Old Testament imply that God has specially favored the Jews? Yet you, Paul, are saying that God treats Jews and Gentiles in the same way! Paul freely admits that Jews do have the advantage of standing closest to divine revelation in the Scriptures. But higher privilege does not imply less sinfulness. With a string of Old Testament quotations Paul concludes the section by charging the entire human race with guilt before God.

The next paragraph forms the core of this epistle. "The law and the prophets" refers to the Old Testament. Paul emphasizes that though righteousness comes through faith in Jesus Christ rather than through keeping the law, yet the law and the rest of the Old Testament do attest righteousness by faith. "The glory of God,"

Propitiation

which human beings lack (3:23), is the splendor of God's character. The term "propitiation" (3:25) describes Jesus' death as a sacrifice which appeased the anger of God against human wickedness. The alternative translation "expiation" fails to imply that anger, though Paul has emphasized it (1:18). The term may also refer to the mercy seat, a gold lid over the ark of the covenant. On this lid the Jewish high priest sprinkled sacrificial blood once a year to atone for the sins of Israel. Paul indicates that God forgave sins during the Old Testament period only in anticipation of Christ's death. When he states that God is both "just and the justifier of the one who has faith in Jesus," he means that God's anger has been satisfied in that Jesus paid the penalty for human guilt, and that God's love has likewise been satisfied in that Jesus' death provided a way by which the guilty may be forgiven. Divine righteousness is inflexible enough to demand the imposition of a penalty for the upholding of justice, but flexible enough to allow the righteous to act on behalf of the unrighteous for the exercise of mercy. *Read Romans 3:21–31.*

Faith   Again Paul anticipates a Jewish objection: if a person gains righteousness merely by faith in Christ, there is no advantage in being a Jew or in keeping the law as a Jew. Essentially, Paul agrees with this conclusion; but he argues that the Old Testament itself indicates that righteousness comes by faith, not by works, as in the examples of Abraham and David. *Read Romans 4:1–5:21.*

Blessings   In the first verses of chapter 5 Paul lists the blessings that accompany justification: peace with God through Jesus Christ; introduction into the sphere of God's grace; joy in the hope of God's glory ("hope" meaning confident expectation that Jesus will return, and "the glory of God" here meaning the divine splendor that Christians will enter at the Second Coming); joy in present persecution; perseverance; proved character; hope (again); and an interior experience of God's love as ministered by the Holy Spirit. The terms "reconcile" and "reconciliation" in verses 10 and 11 refer to the turning of the sinner from hatred against God to love for God.

Original Sin   In 5:12–14 Paul argues that the reign of death before God gave the law through Moses proves that the whole human race was implicated in Adam's original sin; for before Moses' time there was no written law to break. A contrast between "the one" and "the many" *Adam* follows: one man (Adam) sinned in Eden—the many (a Semitic *vs. Christ* expression for "all") sinned and died in Adam; one man (Jesus Christ) performed an act of righteousness on the cross—the many (all who believe in Jesus Christ) are regarded as righteous and will live eternally.

The primary objection to this easy way of salvation, of justification by faith alone, is that it implies a patently false line of reasoning with a ridiculous conclusion: the more sin, the more God exercises his grace and gains greater glory for so doing—therefore, sin as much as possible for the glory of God! Paul's horrified repudiation of such reasoning rests on the doctrine of believers' union with Christ as dramatized through Christian baptism. In baptism, believers confess their death to sin through identification with Christ in his death, and also confess their coming alive to righteousness through identification with Christ in his resurrection. So far as God is concerned, then, they died when Christ died and rose when Christ rose. These events put believers under obligation to live as people who are dead to sin and alive to righteousness. They must form their self-image according to God's way of looking at them. *Read Romans 6:1–8:39.* *Union with Christ*

In the last part of chapter 6 Paul writes that freedom from the law does not imply freedom to sin, because freedom and slavery are relative terms. An unbeliever is free from the restrictions of Christian holiness but enslaved to the control of sin. On the other hand, a believer is free from the control of sin but enslaved to the restrictions of Christian holiness. In reality, captivity to Christian holiness brings the truest kind of freedom, freedom not to sin, freedom to live righteously. *Freedom and Slavery*

In chapter 7 Paul illustrates his argument from marriage law. A spouse is free to marry another person when the other spouse has died, because death has broken the marital bond. Similarly, the death of Christ and the union of believers with him in his death have broken their bond to the Mosaic law and freed them to belong to the risen Christ and bear fruit for God. Why then was the law given? It was given to prompt dependence on Christ for righteousness by increasing the awareness of human beings concerning their sin and moral incapability. Paul does not deny that God intended the Mosaic law to guide the conduct of Old Testament believers. But so far as justification is concerned, he does deny that God gave the law to be a means of achieving merit before him; rather, a means of inducing people to cast themselves on his grace. *Purpose of the Law*

The last part of chapter 7 classically describes the frustration of a person who wants to do good but cannot because of the demonic power of sin aggravated by the law. Frustration changes to triumph *From Frustration to Triumph* for believers, however, because they have the Spirit of Christ (chap. 8). As in Galatians, Paul contrasts the flesh and the Spirit. The Spirit of Christ empowers believers to conquer the sinful urge, assures them of salvation, will someday glorify them, and in the meantime prays for them. Chapter 8 climaxes with a burst of praise and confidence. The only one who has a right to accuse believers, because he is holy, is the very one who justifies them. God would not be righteous if he *did* condemn them now that they are in Christ.

The Election and Rejection of Israel   *Read Romans 9:1–11:36.* In discussing the problem of Israel, Paul maintains that God has a right to choose some and reject others as he wants. Sinners have no claim on God. But he does not exercise his prerogative arbitrarily. He has turned to Gentiles because Israel sought her own righteousness rather than his. Thus the invitation to salvation stands open to all, Jews and Gentiles alike. For several reasons the turning of God to Gentiles should not seem bad: (1) a remnant of Jews does believe; (2) Gentiles have a better opportunity than they had before; (3) jealousy over the widespread salvation of Gentiles will induce the Jews to repent; and (4) all Israel will yet be saved, that is, those Jews who are still living at the return of Christ will accept his messiahship and, as a result, receive salvation. Therefore, Gentile believers should not self-righteously exalt themselves over Jewish believers, lest they suffer the judgment that Jewish unbelievers have suffered.

Christian Commitment   Practical exhortations occupy the next main section of the epistle. For Paul, theology always affects life; and to maintain a high level of Christian conduct in the churches he never leaves his audience to guess the practical import of his doctrinal teaching. After an appeal that believers offer themselves to God as "living [as opposed to slain] sacrifices," Paul exhorts his readers not to imitate the outward conduct of non-Christians, but to live pleasingly before God out of renewed mental attitudes (12:1–2).

Individual consecration leads to the social ministries of preaching, teaching, serving, giving, and leading—all according to the various abilities God has given to believers and all to be performed modestly and harmoniously (12:3–8). Harmony within a church depends, however, on mutual love, which includes sincerity, hatred of evil, retention of right standards (goodness), affection, respect, industriousness, devotion to God, joy in hope, patience, prayer, generosity, and hospitality (12:9–13).

Similarly, believers should maintain good relations with unbelievers through prayer for their welfare, empathy with their joys, sympathy with their sorrows, and respectful and forgiving attitudes toward them. If the unbelievers still practice persecution, God himself will judge them and vindicate his own (12:14–21). Paul also commands submission to governmental authority by obedience and payment of taxes; but his words must not be taken as blind support of totalitarianism. The stated presupposition is that governing authorities are carrying out justice by punishing wrongdoers and praising rightdoers. Thus, resistance for purely political or selfish reasons deserves censure, but not resistance for moral and religious reasons (13:1–7). God requires love not only for one's fellow believers, but also for humanity in general. This includes payment of debts and avoidance of adultery, murder, theft, and covetousness (13:8–10). The prospect of Jesus' return sharpens these commands (13:11–14). As in 1 Corinthians, finally, Paul indicates that believers must allow one another freedom to differ on ritual questions so long as damage is not done to weaker, uninformed people (14:1–15:3). *Read Romans 12:1–15:13.*

Concluding Remarks

Stating his plans with more detail than in chapter 1, Paul now relates his hopes to deliver an offering to the church in Jerusalem and to evangelize Spain after visiting Rome. The commendation of Phoebe in 16:1–2 reflects the Christian practice in which a home church recommends one of its members to a church in the locality to which that member is moving or paying a visit. The greeting to Prisca (a shortened form of Priscilla) and Aquila in 16:3 implies that they have returned to Rome. We know from secular sources, too, that Claudius's edict expelling the Jews from Rome lapsed after he died. Greetings, a warning against false teachers, a benediction, further greetings, and a doxology complete the epistle. *Read Romans 15:14–16:27.*

FOR FURTHER DISCUSSION

Does Paul's doctrine of human sinfulness degrade the dignity and nobility of the human race?

Does Paul contradict himself in appealing to the Gentiles' good works performed out of conscience (2:12–16) and contending for the total depravity of Jews and Gentiles alike (3:9–20)? Or does he mean Christian Gentiles in 2:12–16?

Is transferring a penalty from a guilty to an innocent party morally and legally defensible?

How can God rightly blame the whole human race for the original sin of Adam?

How can God rightly attribute the righteousness of Christ to all believers?

Is justification possible without sanctification?

Does the inner struggle between right and wrong depicted in Romans 7:7–25 characterize Christians or non-Christians? (Compare Romans 8.)

How can God maintain his sovereignty and yet allow human beings enough freedom to be held responsible?

Are people saved because they decide to believe in Christ or because God decides to make them believe? Is there another alternative?

Do Paul's statements about the future of Israel relate to current events in the Middle East?

What should be the attitude of Christians toward government in the face of current social problems and international disputes?

FOR FURTHER INVESTIGATION

Barrett, C. K. *A Commentary on the Epistle to the Romans*. 2d ed. London: Black, 1991.

Bruce, F. F. *Romans*. 2d ed. Grand Rapids: Eerdmans, 1985.

Cranfield, C. E. B. *A Critical and Exegetical Commentary on the Epistle to the Romans*. 2 vols. Edinburgh: T & T. Clark, 1975, 1979. Advanced.

————. *Romans*. Grand Rapids: Eerdmans, 1985.

Dunn, J. D. G. *Romans*. 2 vols. Dallas: Word, 1988. Advanced.

Moo, D. J. *Romans 1–8*. Chicago: Moody, 1991.

Morris, L. *The Epistle to the Romans*. Grand Rapids: Eerdmans, 1988.

(Books on topics appearing in Romans)

Arminius, J. *Declaration of Sentiments*, I–IV, and *Apology Against Thirty-One Defamatory Articles*, Articles I, IV–VIII, XIII–XVII. For the Arminian view of divine sovereignty and human free will.

St. Augustine. *Confessions*. Especially the first several "books" for the problem of guilt.

Calvin, J. *Institutes of the Christian Religion*, Book I, chapter 15; Book II, chapters 1–5; Book III, chapters 21–24. For the Calvinistic view of divine sovereignty and human free will.

Calvin, J., and J. Sadoleto. *Reformation Debate: Sadoleto's Letter to the Genevans and Calvin's Reply.* Edited by J. C. Olin. New York: Harper & Row, 1966. For justification by faith as a disputed point during the Reformation.

Chafer, L. S. *He That Is Spiritual.* Grand Rapids: Zondervan [Dunham], 1918. On sanctification.

Lewis, C. S. *The Case for Christianity.* Part I. New York: Macmillan, 1950. Or *Mere Christianity.* Book I. London: G. Bles, 1952. On human moral consciousness.

Luther, M. *Commentary* [or *Lectures*] *on Romans.* On 3:21–31.

Walvoord, J. F. *Israel in Prophecy.* Grand Rapids: Zondervan, 1962. For comparison with Paul's discussion of Israel in Romans 9–11.

14

The Prison Epistles of Paul

❖ From which of his various imprisonments does Paul probably write his Prison Epistles?

❖ What are the interrelations of the Prison Epistles?

❖ What circumstances lead Paul to plead with Philemon on behalf of a runaway slave?

❖ Why does Paul write to the church in Colossae though he is unacquainted with them? What is the nature of

the "Colossian heresy" as inferred from his correctives?

❖ What is the destination of the probably misnamed "Ephesians"? How do its structure and distinctive theological emphasis compare with those of Colossians?

❖ What prompts the writing of Philippians? What are the attitudes and prospects of Paul at the time, and his concerns for the church in Philippi?

Paul's Imprisonments

Ephesians, Philippians, Colossians, and Philemon constitute the Prison (or Captivity) Epistles, so called because Paul is in prison when he writes them. There are two known imprisonments of Paul, one in Caesarea under the governorships of Felix and Festus (Acts 23:23–26:32), another in Rome while Paul awaits trial before Caesar (Acts 28:30–31). Supported by a small amount of early church tradition, some scholars have conjectured yet another imprisonment in Ephesus during Paul's extended ministry there. Paul does mention "frequent" imprisonments in 2 Corinthians 11:23, but these probably refer to overnight stays in jail, as at Philippi (Acts 16:19–40). The traditional view assigns all the Prison

The Gate of St. Paul at Rome stands in the southern part of the city.

Epistles to Paul's Roman imprisonment, but the Ephesian and Caesarean possibilities must at least be kept in mind for each of the Prison Epistles.

Philemon: Plea for a Runaway Slave

In the epistle to Philemon, Paul asks a Christian slavemaster named Philemon to receive kindly, perhaps even to release, his recently converted runaway slave Onesimus, now returning. A resident of Colossae, Philemon became a Christian through Paul ("you owe me even your own self," v. 19). This conversion probably took place in nearby Ephesus during Paul's ministry there. A church meets in the house of Philemon (v. 2). Early Christians had no church buildings and therefore met in homes. If the number of believers grew too large for one home to accommodate them, they used several homes.

Theme

Philemon the Slaveowner

An Outline of Philemon

INTRODUCTION: GREETING (1–3)

I. THANKSGIVING FOR PHILEMON (4–7)

II. PLEA FOR ONESIMUS (8–22)

CONCLUSION: GREETINGS AND BENEDICTION (23–25)

Onesimus
the Slave

Onesimus absconded with some of his master's money and fled to Rome, where somehow he came in contact with Paul.[1] The apostle converted Onesimus and convinced him that now as a Christian he should return to his master and live up to the meaning of his name, for "Onesimus" means "profitable" (vv. 10–12). With great tact and Christian courtesy, therefore, Paul writes to persuade Philemon not only to take back Onesimus without punishing him or putting him to death (a common treatment of runaway slaves), but also to welcome Onesimus "as a beloved brother . . . in the Lord" (v. 16).

Paul wants to retain Onesimus as a helper (v. 13). It has been suggested that the confident "you will do even more than I say" (v. 21) broadly hints that Philemon should liberate Onesimus; but perhaps Paul is suggesting only that Philemon loan Onesimus for missionary work. Paul promises to pay Philemon the financial loss caused by Onesimus's theft; however, the immediate mention of Philemon's greater spiritual debt to Paul invites Philemon to cancel the financial debt which Paul has just assumed (vv. 18–20). *Read Philemon 1–25.*

FOR
FURTHER
INVESTIGATION

Bruce, F. F. *The Epistles to the Colossians, to Philemon, & to the Ephesians.* Grand Rapids: Eerdmans, 1984.

Caird, G. B. *Paul's Letters from Prison.* New York: Oxford University Press, 1976.

Moule, C. F. D. *The Epistles of Paul the Apostle to the Colossians and to Philemon.* New York: Cambridge University Press, 1958. Advanced.

O'Brien, P. T. *Colossians, Philemon.* Waco, Tex.: Word, 1982. Advanced.

Colossians: Christ as the Head of the Church

Theme

In his epistle to the Colossians Paul highlights the divine person and creative and redemptive work of Christ against devaluation of Christ by a particular brand of heresy that threatens the church in Colossae. Then Paul draws out the practical implications of this high Christology for everyday life and conduct.

Ephesian
Origin

The ancient Marcionite prologue[2] to Colossians says that Paul writes this epistle from Ephesus. The tradition is doubtful, however, because it also says that Paul writes Philemon from Rome. Yet Colossians and Philemon are inseparably linked: both letters men-

---

1. See the following discussions of the place of origin for Colossians and Ephesians, written at the same time as Philemon.

2. An introduction to the epistle written from the standpoint of Marcionism, a brand of Gnosticism.

tion Timothy, Aristarchus, Mark, Epaphras, Luke, Demas, Archippus, and Onesimus (Col. 1:1 and Philem. 1; Col. 4:10–14 and Philem. 23–24; Col. 4:17 and Philem. 2; Col. 4:9 and Philem. 10ff.). The duplication of so many names must indicate that Paul writes and sends both letters at the same time and from the same place.

Furthermore, if Paul writes Colossians and Philemon from an Ephesian imprisonment, the slave Onesimus absconded with his master's money only 100 miles' distance to Ephesus. The shortness of this distance seems improbable, for Onesimus would have known that he might easily be captured so close to home. More likely, he fled far away to the larger city of Rome to hide himself among the crowds there. Moreover, Luke is with Paul when Paul writes Colossians (Col. 4:14); but the description of Paul's Ephesian ministry is not one of Luke's "we"-sections in Acts. Despite partial support from the Marcionite tradition, then, we should reject an Ephesian imprisonment as the place of origin for Colossians.

It is even more improbable that Colossians comes from the Caesarean imprisonment. Caesarea was much smaller than Rome and therefore a less likely destination for a runaway slave seeking to escape detection. Onesimus would scarcely have come in contact with Paul at Caesarea, for only Paul's friends could see him there (Acts 24:23). Also, the expectation of Paul that he will soon be released (he asks Philemon to prepare lodging for him, Philem. 22) does not tally with the Caesarean imprisonment, where Paul came to realize that his only hope lay in appealing to Caesar.

Caesarean Origin

Several considerations favor the Roman imprisonment: (1) it is most likely that to hide his identity Onesimus fled to Rome, the most populous city in the empire; (2) Luke's presence with Paul at the writing of Colossians agrees with Luke's accompanying Paul to Rome in Acts; (3) the difference in doctrinal emphases between Colossians, where Paul is not preoccupied with the Judaizing controversy, and the epistles to the Galatians, Romans, and Corinthians, where he strongly emphasizes freedom from the Mosaic law, suggests that he writes Colossians during a later period, such as his Roman imprisonment, when the Judaizing controversy no longer dominates his thinking (though the attack on Judaizers in Philippians 3, probably written later, weakens this third argument).

Roman Origin

The city of Colossae lay in the valley of the Lycus River in a mountainous district about 100 miles east of Ephesus (see the map

Occasion

on page 311). The neighboring cities of Laodicea and Hierapolis overshadowed Colossae in importance. The distant way in which Paul writes that he has "heard" of his audience's faith (1:4) and his inclusion of them among those who have never seen him face to face (2:1) imply that he neither founded the church in Colossae nor has visited it. Since the Colossians learned God's grace from Epaphras (1:6–7), Epaphras must have founded the church. Yet he is with Paul at the time of writing (4:12–13). We may surmise that Epaphras became a Christian through Paul's Ephesian ministry, evangelized the neighboring region of Colossae, Laodicea, and Hierapolis, and is now visiting Paul in prison to solicit his advice concerning a dangerous heresy threatening the Colossian church. Apparently Archippus has been left in charge of the church (4:17). Under this hypothesis we can understand why Paul assumes authority over the Colossian church even though he has never been there: since he is "grandfather" of the church through his convert Epaphras, his judgment has been sought.

A Gentile Church   The Christians in Colossae are predominantly Gentile. Paul classes them among the uncircumcised (2:13). In 1:27 the phrases "among the Gentiles" and "in you" seem to be synonymous. And the description of the Colossians as "once estranged and hostile in mind" (1:21) recalls similar phraseology in Ephesians 2:11ff., where Paul indubitably refers to Gentiles.

The Colossian Heresy   The epistle to the Colossians centers on the so-called Colossian heresy. We can infer certain features of this false teaching from the counter-emphases of Paul. In fact, he may borrow the false teachers' favorite terms, such as "knowledge" and "fullness," and turn them against the heresy by filling them with orthodox content. The heresy detracts from the person of Christ, so that Paul stresses the preeminence of Christ (1:15–19); emphasizes human philosophy, that is, human speculations divorced from divine revelation (2:8); contains elements of Judaism, such as circumcision (2:11; 3:11), rabbinic tradition (2:8), dietary regulations and Sabbath and festival observances (2:16); includes the worship of angels as intermediaries keeping the highest God (pure Spirit) unsullied through contact with the physical universe (a pagan feature, since although orthodox Jews have constructed a hierarchy of angels, they do not worship them or regard the materiality of the universe as evil—2:18); and flaunts an exclusivistic air of secrecy and superiority, against which

Paul stresses the all-inclusiveness and publicity of the gospel (1:20, 23, 28; 3:11).

The Colossian heresy, then, blends together Jewish legalism, Greek philosophic speculation, and Oriental mysticism. Perhaps the location of Colossae on an important trade route linking East and West has contributed to the mixed character of the false teaching. Most of its features will appear full-blown in later Gnosticism and in the Greek and Oriental mystery religions. But the presence of Judaistic features points to a syncretistic Judaism lacking the redeemer-motif of later, anti-Judaistic Gnosticism.

An Outline of Colossians

INTRODUCTION (1:1–12)
  A. Greeting (1:1–2)
  B. Thanksgiving (1:3–8)
  C. Prayer (1:9–12)

  I. THE PREEMINENCE OF CHRIST IN CHRISTIAN DOCTRINE (1:13–2:23)
     A. His creative and redemptive work (1:13–23)
     B. His proclamation by Paul (1:24–2:7)
     C. His sufficiency over against the Colossian heresy (2:8–23)

 II. THE PREEMINENCE OF CHRIST IN CHRISTIAN CONDUCT (3:1–4:6)
     A. Union with Christ in his death, resurrection, and exaltation (3:1–4)
     B. Application of death with Christ to sinful actions (3:5–11)
     C. Application of resurrection with Christ to righteous actions (3:12–4:6)

CONCLUSION (4:7–18)
  A. The coming of Tychicus and Onesimus (4:7–9)
  B. Greetings and final instructions (4:10–17)
  C. Farewell and benediction (4:18)

As seen in the outline, Colossians divides into two main sections: doctrine (chaps. 1–2) and exhortation (chaps. 3–4). Paul puts the doctrinal accent on Christology. The epistle opens with a greeting, thanksgiving, and prayer. Then begins the great Christological discussion. *Read Colossians 1:1–2:23.*

Doctrine, Especially Christology

Paul's laudatory statements about Christ mention:

- His kingdom (1:13);
- His redemptive work (1:14);
- His being the outward representation ("image") of God in human form (1:15);
- His supremacy over creation as its master and heir (since firstborn sons received more inheritance than other sons, "first-born of all creation" [1:15] need not imply that Jesus was the first to be created);
- His creatorship (1:16);
- His preexistence and cohesion of the universe (1:17);
- His headship over the new creation, the church; and
- His primacy in rising from the dead never to die again (1:18).

A number of scholars take verses 15–20 as a quotation from some early hymn. "The fullness of God" dwelling in Christ is the totality of divine nature. When Paul writes that his own sufferings complete "what is lacking in Christ's afflictions" (1:24), there is no implication that Christ suffered too little to provide a full atonement for sins. Paul means that sufferings endured in spreading the gospel are also necessary if people are to be saved and that Christ continues to suffer with his persecuted witnesses because of their union, or solidarity, with him. The term "mystery" ("this mystery . . . Christ in you," 1:27) refers to theological truth hidden from unbelievers but revealed to believers.

In his polemic against the Colossian heresy (2:8–23) Paul charges that this false teaching obscures the preeminence of Christ; that its ritual observances, taken from Judaism, only foreshadow spiritual realities in Christ; and that its asceticism and angel-worship foster pride and detract from the glory of Christ.

Exhortation The union of believers with Christ in his death, resurrection, and ascension forms the basis for practical exhortations. Believers are to adopt God's point of view by regarding themselves as dead in Christ to sin and alive in him to righteousness. *Read Colossians 3:1–4:18.* "Scythians" (3:11) were regarded as particularly uncouth barbarians. Since salt retards corruption, speech "seasoned with salt" (4:6) probably means speech that is not corrupt or obscene.

FOR FURTHER INVESTIGATION Bruce, F. F. *The Epistles to the Colossians, to Philemon, & to the Ephesians.* Grand Rapids: Eerdmans, 1984.

Houlden, J. L. *Paul's Letters from Prison.* Baltimore: Penguin, 1970.

Lohse, E. *Colossians*. Philadelphia: Fortress, 1971. Advanced.

Martin, R. P. *Colossians*. Grand Rapids: Zondervan, 1973.

Moule, C. F. D. *The Epistles of Paul the Apostle to the Colossians and to Philemon*. New York: Cambridge University Press, 1958. Advanced.

O'Brien, P. T. *Colossians, Philemon*. Waco, Tex.: Word, 1982. Advanced.

Schweizer, E. *The Letter to the Colossians*. Minneapolis: Augsburg, 1982.

Ephesians: The Church as the Body of Christ

Unlike most of Paul's epistles, Ephesians is not written in re- *Theme* sponse to a particular circumstance or controversy. It has an almost meditative quality. In the theme shared with Colossians—Christ the head of the church his body—Ephesians emphasizes the church as Christ's body, whereas Colossians emphasizes the headship of Christ. Colossians warns against a false doctrine which diminishes Christ; Ephesians expresses praise for the unity and blessings shared by all believers in Christ.

Paul must have written Ephesians and Colossians at approxi- *Relation to* mately the same time, because the subject matter in the two epistles *Colossians* looks related and because some verses about Tychicus appear in al- *Tychicus* most identical form both in Ephesians 6:21–22 and in Colossians 4:7–8. The indication that by word of mouth Tychicus will add further details about Paul's circumstances implies that Tychicus will carry both epistles at once to their destinations, Ephesus and Colossae, lying about 100 miles from each other. Paul's self-identification as "a prisoner of the Lord" indicates his imprisonment at the time of writing and his awareness of the Lord's purpose in that imprisonment.

Though Ephesians may be directed to the region around Ephesus rather than to Ephesus itself (see the discussion below), it is hardly probable that Paul writes from an Ephesian imprisonment. So far as the Caesarean imprisonment is concerned, his reference to preaching "boldly" as "an ambassador in chains" implies that he is still proclaiming the gospel in spite of his imprisonment (Eph. 6:20); yet in Caesarea only his friends could visit him (Acts 24:22–23). In Rome, however, he preached to a steady stream of visitors who came to his house-prison (Acts 28:30–31). Like the closely related epistles to the Colossians and Philemon, therefore, Ephesians seems to have been written during the Roman imprisonment.

Goodspeed's Theory   The American scholar E. J. Goodspeed theorized that an admirer of Paul wrote Ephesians toward the end of the first century. Goodspeed went so far as to suggest that the admirer was Onesimus, the converted slave about whom Paul wrote to Philemon.[3] According to this theory, the writer designed Ephesians to introduce a collection of Paul's genuine epistles by way of summarizing their theology. The collection was prompted by the prominence of Paul in Acts, written just recently. To the contrary, however, manuscript evidence is lacking that Ephesians ever stood first in the collection of his epistles, against expectation if Goodspeed's hypothesis were true. Moreover, very early church tradition assigns Ephesians to Paul himself.

Destination not Ephesus   The phrase "in Ephesus," which refers to the locale of the addressees (1:1), is missing in the most ancient manuscripts. Thus Paul omits the geographical location of the addressees altogether. Furthermore, the distant way in which he speaks of his having "heard" about their faith (1:15) and of their having "heard" about his ministry (3:2) combines with the absence of his usual terms of endearment to rule out Ephesus as the destination; for Paul labored there for more than two years and knew the Ephesian Christians intimately, as they also knew him.

Laodiceans?   Some early tradition identifies the church in Laodicea as the recipients of this epistle. The German scholar Adolf von Harnack suggested that early copyists suppressed the name Laodicea because of the condemnation of the Laodicean church in Revelation 3:14–22 and that later copyists substituted the name Ephesus because of Paul's close association with the church in that city. Paul does mention a letter to Laodicea in Colossians 4:16. But since no manuscript mentions Laodicea in Ephesians 1:1, the making of "Ephesians" into "Laodiceans" in early tradition probably represents an attempt to identify the letter to Laodicea mentioned in Colossians.

A Circular Epistle   More likely, "Ephesians" is a circular epistle addressed to various churches in the vicinity of Ephesus. Under this view, Paul's mention of the epistle to Laodicea in Colossians 4:16 may refer to "Ephesians" but would not imply that the epistle is addressed only to the church of Laodicea. Rather, in its circulation to the churches throughout the region the epistle has reached Laodicea and is about

---

3. *The Key to Ephesians (Chicago: University of Chicago Press, 1956) and other works by Goodspeed and by those following his lead.*

to go to Colossae. A circular destination for the epistle then explains the omission of a city name in the address. If a single copy of the letter circulated from Ephesus and came back to Ephesus, the name of that city could easily have become linked to the epistle, as happened.

Like Colossians, Ephesians falls into two parts. Ephesians 1–3 *Structure* contains doctrine and discusses the spiritual privileges of the church. Ephesians 4–6 contains exhortation and discusses the spiritual responsibilities of Christians.

An Outline of Ephesians

INTRODUCTION: GREETING (1:1–2)

I. THE SPIRITUAL PRIVILEGES OF THE CHURCH (1:3–3:21)
  A. Praise for spiritual blessings planned by the Father, accomplished by the Son, and applied by the Spirit (1:3–14)
  B. Thanksgiving and prayer for increased comprehension of divine grace (1:15–23)
  C. The regeneration of sinners by divine grace alone (2:1–10)
  D. The reconciliation of Gentiles with God and with Jews in the church (2:11–22)
  E. Paul's sense of privilege in proclaiming the gospel (3:1–13)
  F. Prayer for stability through increased comprehension (3:14–19)
  G. Doxology (3:20–21)

II. THE SPIRITUAL RESPONSIBILITIES OF THE CHURCH (4:1–6:20)
  A. Maintenance of unity through diversity of edifying ministry (4:1–16)
  B. Moral conduct (4:17–5:14)
  C. The filling with the Spirit (5:15–21)
  D. A code for Christian households (5:22–6:9)
    1. Submission of wives to husbands (5:22–24)
    2. Love of husbands to wives (5:25–33)
    3. Obedience of children to parents (6:1–3)
    4. Reasonableness of fathers with children (6:4)
    5. Obedience of slaves to masters (6:5–8)
    6. Fairness of masters to slaves (6:9)
  E. Spiritual warfare utilizing the whole armor of God against satanic forces (6:10–20)

CONCLUSION: THE COMING OF TYCHICUS, A FINAL GREETING, AND A BENEDICTION (6:21–24)

Heavenly Blessings   After a greeting (1:1–2) Paul launches into a doxology of praise to God for spiritual blessings in Christ "in the heavenly places" (1:3–14). That is to say, the union of believers with Christ entails a share in his heavenly exaltation as well as in his earthly death, burial, and resurrection. The doxology delineates the parts played in salvation by all three members of the Trinity: the Father chose believers (the doctrine of election, 1:4); the Son redeemed them (1:7); the Holy Spirit "sealed" them, that is, the gift of the Spirit is God's downpayment, or guarantee, that he will complete their salvation at the return of Christ (1:13–14). Following the doxology is a thanksgiving and prayer that believers may comprehend and appreciate the immensity of God's grace and wisdom (1:15–23). *Read Ephesians 1:1–23.*

Divine Grace   To help his audience appreciate the immensity of God's grace, Paul contrasts their domination by sin before conversion and their freedom from that tyranny after conversion. He also emphasizes that salvation is wholly unearned; it comes by God's grace, through faith, and apart from meritorious good works. God's action does produce good works, but they are a consequence rather than a means of salvation. His grace reveals itself especially in the redemption of Gentiles from paganism and in their equality with Jews in the church. The dividing wall of hostility between the two groups, symbolized by the wall in the temple courtyards beyond which Gentiles were not allowed to go, does not exist in the church.[4] But however grand the plan of salvation, Paul and his audience face the unpleasant reality of present persecution. He writes that his awareness of divine grace and of his privilege in spreading the good news prevents discouragement. Similar awareness on the part of his audience will also prevent their discouragement. The section therefore closes with another doxology and prayer that the audience may be stabilized by increased spiritual knowledge. *Read Ephesians 2:1–3:21.*

Unity and Diversity   The practical exhortations begin with a plea for outward unity growing out of the already existing spiritual unity of the church. Yet this unity includes a diversity of function for the growth of the body, or church. Each believer has a ministerial function. Leaders in the church are to equip other believers for the carrying out of their various functions. *Read Ephesians 4:1–16.*

---

4. *Alternatively, the dividing wall represents the old barrier between God and human beings, now broken down by Christ.*

Miscellaneous instructions on holiness follow: tell the truth; be righteously indignant when necessary, but do not sin by failing to control your anger; do not steal; avoid obscene speech and risqué humor. The section closes with a metrical triplet that may have come from an early baptismal hymn, sung at the moment of rising from the water:

Holy Conduct

> Awake, sleeper,
> And rise from the dead,
> And the Christ will shine on you.

Read Ephesians 4:17–5:14.

Paul's exhortation to be filled with the Holy Spirit indicates that such a filling will show itself in avoiding drunkenness (contrast the drunken orgies of Hellenistic cults) and in joyful singing, witnessing, and submission to one another. In particular, wives should submit themselves to their husbands as the church is submissive to Christ its head. Husbands should love their wives as Christ loved the church his body. Children should obey their parents. Fathers should be reasonable with their children. Slaves should obey their masters. And masters should be kind to their slaves.

The Filling with the Spirit

Paul unites the metaphors of head and body with a picture of the church as the bride and wife of Christ, who is the groom and husband. Just as husband and wife become physically one ("one flesh") in the relationship of marriage, so Christ and the church are one in the Spirit. Scholars have suggested different sources for Paul's metaphor of the church as Christ's body: the Stoic notion that the universe is a body with many different parts, the rabbinic idea that human beings are the members of Adam's body in a literal sense, the symbolic or sacramental union of believers with Christ's body when they eat the bread of the Lord's Supper, a Hebrew concept of corporate personality, and Paul's own doctrine of the union between believers and Christ.

Before saying farewell, Paul urges his audience to don the spiritual armor provided by God and to fight the satanic powers which dominate the world. Perhaps the sight of the soldier to whom Paul is handcuffed while dictating Ephesians in his house-prison suggests "the full armor of God." The word for "shield" denotes the large kind that covers the whole body, not the small circular shield used by Greeks. "Flaming missiles" refers to darts and arrows dipped in

The Armor of God

401

pitch or some other combustible material, set aflame, and hurled or shot toward the enemy. *Read Ephesians 5:15–6:24.*

FOR FURTHER INVESTIGATION

Barth, M. *Ephesians.* 2 vols. Garden City, N.Y.: Doubleday, 1974. Advanced.

Bruce, F. F. *The Epistles to the Colossians, to Philemon, & to the Ephesians.* Grand Rapids: Eerdmans, 1984.

Lincoln, A. T. *Ephesians.* Dallas: Word, 1990. Advanced.

Mitton, C. L. *Ephesians.* Grand Rapids: Eerdmans, 1981.

Stott, J. R. W. *God's New Society. The Message of Ephesians.* Leicester: Inter-Varsity, 1979.

Philippians: A Friendly Note of Thanks

Theme and Occasion

The church at Philippi appears to be Paul's favorite. He has received regular assistance from it (Phil. 4:15–20; 2 Cor. 11:7–9). The epistle to the Philippians is thus the most personal of any that he wrote to a church. In fact, it is a thank-you note for their most recent financial gift (4:10, 14), which they sent through Epaphroditus (2:25).

During his trip or after his arrival with the offering, Epaphroditus fell almost fatally ill (2:27). Back home the Philippians heard of his illness, and word came to Epaphroditus that they were concerned about him. Paul senses that Epaphroditus wants to return to Philippi and therefore sends him with the epistle (2:25–30).

Purpose

The return of Epaphroditus not only enables Paul to write his gratitude for the financial assistance given by believers in Philippi. It also gives him opportunity to counteract a tendency toward divisiveness in their church (2:2; 4:2), to warn against Judaizers (chap. 3), and to prepare the church for approaching visits by Timothy and, God willing, by Paul himself (2:19–24).[5]

Caesarean Origin

Paul is in prison at the time of writing ("my imprisonment," 1:7, 13). But to which of his imprisonments does he refer? Probably not the Caesarean, because there he would not be able to preach so freely as is implied in 1:12–13 (compare Acts 24:23). Also, he would know that release in Caesarea would mean almost instant lynching by Jews in the territory; his only prospect of safety would lie in appealing to Caesar and thus going to Rome under guard. Yet in Philippians 1:25; 2:24 (and Philem. 22) Paul hopes for quick release.

---

5. "Epaphroditus" is the full form of the name "Epaphras," which appears in Colossians. But we do not have enough evidence to identify Epaphras, founder of the church in Colossae, with Epaphroditus, messenger of the church in Philippi.

Presenting a better possibility is an imprisonment in Ephesus. *Ephesian Origin*
Paul writes that he hopes to send Timothy to Philippi (2:19, 23);
and Luke writes that Paul sent Timothy and Erastus to Philippi
from Ephesus (Acts 19:22). (But if the two passages are really parallel, why does Paul omit mentioning Erastus in Phil. 2:19–24?)
The polemic against Judaizers in chapter 3 looks like Paul's earlier
polemics around the time he spent in Ephesus. (It remains possible,
however, that a later Judaizing threat revives his earlier polemics.)

Furthermore, inscriptions testify that a detachment of the
Praetorian Guard was once stationed in Ephesus, and Paul mentions the Praetorian Guard in 1:13. Similarly, "Caesar's household"
(4:22) might refer to imperial civil servants at Ephesus. According to
Acts, Luke accompanied Paul to Rome but not to Ephesus. That
Paul does not mention Luke in Philippians as he does in Colossians
4:14 and Philemon 24 therefore suggests that he writes Philippians
from an Ephesian imprisonment. (But if he writes toward the end of
his Roman imprisonment, at least two years long, Luke might have
left Paul by then, so that this argument from silence is not decisive.)

It is also argued for an Ephesian imprisonment that if Paul writes
Philippians from Rome at a later date, he could hardly state that his
readers have for some time "lacked opportunity" to support him financially (4:10). So much time has elapsed by the time of the
Roman imprisonment that they would have had prolonged opportunity; but an earlier Ephesian imprisonment allows for such a statement. (On the other hand, we do not know all the financial
circumstances of Paul and the Philippians. To avoid the charge of
embezzlement, Paul may have refused personal gifts during the period he was collecting money for the church in Jerusalem. Such a refusal may be the reason the Philippians have "lacked opportunity.")

Generally considered the strongest argument in favor of an
Ephesian imprisonment over against the Roman is that Philippians
presupposes too many journeys between Rome and Philippi (about
a month's journey apart), whereas the short distance between
Ephesus and Philippi makes the numerous journeys more conceivable within a short period of time. The journeys presupposed in
Philippians are as follows:

- The carrying of a message from Rome to Philippi that Paul
  has been imprisoned in Rome;
- Epaphroditus's bringing of a gift from Philippi to Rome;
- The delivery back to Philippi of word that Epaphroditus has
  fallen ill; and

- The return of a report that the Philippians are concerned about Epaphroditus.

In reality, however, this argument for Ephesus and against Rome lacks substance. Time for the journeys between Rome and Philippi would require only four to six months *in toto*. Allowance for intervals between the journeys still keeps the whole amount of required time well within the two years that we know Paul spent in Rome (Acts 28:30). And he almost certainly spent more than two years there; for even by their end his trial had not yet started, but a transfer from his own rented house (Acts 28:16, 23, 30) to the barracks of the Praetorian Guard on the Palatine (Phil. 1:13) and his expectation of soon release (1:19–26) and of a subsequent visit to Philippi (2:23–24) would favor that his trial is finally in progress and near conclusion and therefore that he is writing after the two years mentioned in Acts.

Moreover, the Philippians may have known before Paul arrived in Rome that he was going there as a prisoner, so that Epaphroditus could already have started toward Rome. Or, since the shipwreck delayed Paul at Malta, Epaphroditus may even have arrived in Rome before Paul. The Christians in Rome knew beforehand of Paul's coming, for they met Paul outside the city and escorted him the rest of the way (Acts 28:15–16). Had Epaphroditus informed them? Only the second, third, and fourth journeys are necessarily presupposed, then; and the temporal factor does not at all hinder the view that Paul writes to the Philippians from Rome.

Against an Ephesian imprisonment, Paul fails to mention the offering for Jerusalem, though it was very much on his mind throughout his third missionary journey, during which he ministered in Ephesus; and his writing about monetary matters in Philippians would have made a reference to the offering almost certain had he been writing from Ephesus during that period. Also, we must bear in mind that an Ephesian imprisonment of Paul is largely conjectural and not at all mentioned in Acts even though Luke goes into great detail about Paul's ministry in Ephesus (Acts 19).

Roman Origin   In favor of Rome, "Praetorian Guard" (1:13) and "Caesar's household" (4:22) most likely point to Rome.[6] According to 1:19ff., Paul's life is at stake in the trial. The trial must therefore be before Caesar

---

6. *Since the Praetorian Guard in Rome numbered about nine thousand, but in Ephesus far fewer, the fact that the "whole" Praetorian Guard has heard of Paul's imprisonment for Christ (1:13) is thought by some to favor Ephesus over Rome. But the success of Paul's witness else-*

in Rome, for in any other location Paul could always exercise his right of appeal to Caesar. The early tradition of the Marcionite prologue likewise assigns the epistle to Rome. For all these reasons and because of the weakness of arguments to the contrary, the traditional view that Paul writes Philippians from Rome remains the best.

An Outline of Philippians

INTRODUCTION: GREETING (1:1–2)

I. PERSONAL MATTERS (1:3–26)
   A. Paul's thanksgiving, prayer, and affection for the Christians in Philippi (1:3–11)
   B. Paul's preaching in prison, prospect of release, and readiness to die (1:12–26)

II. EXHORTATIONS (1:27–2:18)
   A. To worthy conduct (1:27–30)
   B. To unity by humility, with the example of Christ's self-emptying (2:1–18)

III. THE SENDING OF TIMOTHY AND EPAPHRODITUS TO PHILIPPI (2:19–30)

IV. WARNING AGAINST THE JUDAIZERS, WITH A FAMOUS AUTOBIOGRAPHICAL PASSAGE (3:1–21)

V. EXHORTATIONS (4:1–9)
   A. Unity between Euodia and Syntyche (4:1–3)
   B. Joy and trust (4:4–7)
   C. Nobility of thought (4:8–9)

VI. THANKS FOR FINANCIAL ASSISTANCE (4:10–20)

CONCLUSION: GREETINGS AND A BENEDICTION (4:21–23)

The character of Philippians as a thank-you note makes for some informality. Throughout, the dominant emotional note is one of joy. In the first chapter—after the customary greeting, thanksgiving, and prayer—Paul describes the ministry he is carrying on despite his imprisonment, even because of it. The palace guard and Roman officialdom in general are hearing the gospel. Moreover, the bold-

Joy in Hardship

---

where suggests that the whole guard in Rome may indeed have heard, especially if Paul has succeeded in converting some of them. Or "praetorium" may refer to the emperor's palace rather than to a large group of soldiers making up the guard.

ness of Paul's witness has inspired other Christians, even those who do not like him. The latter are not false teachers, however, for he calls them "brethren." *Read Philippians 1:1–30.*

Read Philippians 2:1–30. This chapter is famous for the passage on Jesus' self-emptying, or humiliation, and exaltation (2:6–11). Many scholars think that Paul is quoting an early Christian hymn. Whether or not a hymn, however, the passage is incidental to an exhortation to ecclesiastical unity through humility, of which Jesus provides the great example. The ancient world despised humility; Christian teaching makes it a virtue. The passage mentions the existence of Christ before his incarnation—that is, his preexistence—

Kenosis and the emptying of himself. The Greek verb "to empty," *kenoun*, has given rise to the *kenosis*-theory of the incarnation, the incarnation as an emptying (*kenosis* being a noun cognate to the verb). But of what did Christ empty himself? Of divine metaphysical attributes, such as omnipotence, omniscience, and omnipresence (though not of divine moral attributes, such as love and justice)? But he often displayed these metaphysical attributes according to the gospel accounts of his earthly ministry. Of the independent exercise of those attributes (compare John 5:19)? But had he ever acted independently of the Father? Or simply of the outward glory of his deity? But does not "himself" require something inward? Perhaps then the self-emptying does not refer to incarnation at all, but to Jesus' expiring on the cross. If so, there is synonymous parallelism with a reference to death in the following verse and a possible allusion to Isaiah 53:12: "he poured out [that is, emptied] his soul [a Hebrew equivalent of 'himself'] to death."

"Finally, my brothers" (3:1) sounds so much like the closing part of an epistle (yet two more chapters follow) and Paul changes tone so suddenly that some scholars posit a long interpolation, beginning in 3:2, from another epistle. But the theory lacks manuscript evidence. It is better to suppose a break in dictation, perhaps with fresh news from Philippi about a threat of false teachers there. Paul intended to close, but now thinks it necessary to prolong the epistle with a warning against the Judaizers.

Against Chapter 3 contains another famous passage: Paul's autobiograph-
Judaizers ical review of his Jewish background and the revolution in his scale of values when Christ became the goal of his life (3:3–14). Again, however, the passage is incidental—this time to a warning against the Judaizers, who practice, according to Paul's sarcastic term, "mu-

tilation" instead of circumcision (3:2). Paul also calls them "dogs," regarded then as despicable creatures, the very term by which Jews often referred to Gentiles. Still another designation is "evil-workers," an ironic counterthrust at their belief in salvation at least partly by good works. Contrastingly, circumcision consists of inward faith in Christ Jesus alone, no reliance on one's own merit mixed in.

Paul's Jewish background was impeccable: (1) circumcision on the eighth day, exactly as prescribed by the Mosaic law (Lev. 12:3); (2) Israelite ancestry; (3) tribal origin in Benjamin, from which came the first king of Israel, Saul (another name of Paul); (4) Hebraistic rather than Hellenistic practice and heritage;[7] (5) Phariseeism; (6) zealousness to the point of persecuting the church; (7) observance of the law so scrupulously that others could find nothing to fault. But the entrance of Christ into his life caused Paul not merely to dismiss, but to renounce as liabilities, all his former assets as such a Jew. And he continues to do so, growing to regard them as "rubbish" (3:8), that he might experience increasing union with Christ in Christ's resurrection, sufferings, and death. Realizing that his audience might misunderstand him to claim perfection, Paul disclaims it and expresses the ardor with which, forgetting the past, he is pursuing a heavenly goal (3:12–16). "Forgetting" does not mean banishing from memory (if that were possible), but disregarding as to present potency.

Pauline Autobiography

The discussion again comes round to the Judaizers, who oppose the cross of Christ by requiring works of the law, who worship their belly by insisting on adherence to the dietary restrictions of the law, who glory in their shame by exposing nakedness for the rite of circumcision, and who set their minds on earthly things by occupying themselves with outward forms and ceremonies (3:17–19).[8] Chapter 3 closes with a reference to the Christian "commonwealth" or "citizenship" in heaven, a figure of speech particularly meaningful to the Philippians, whose own city was a colony populated mainly with Roman citizens living away from their true home in Italy. *Read Philippians 3:1–4:23.*

The various exhortations in chapter 4 include a plea for unity between two women of the church, Euodia and Syntyche, former helpers of Paul. The man who is to aid their reconciliation is a "true

Exhortations

---

7. Compare page 79.

8. Some scholars see antinomian and perfectionist Gnostics as the target of these remarks; but Paul's appeal to his own Judaistic, indeed Pharisaical, background favors identification with the Judaizers throughout chapter 3.

yokefellow," unknown by name unless that is his name with a play on its meaning: "*Syzygos* [Greek for 'yokefellow, comrade'], truly so called" (4:3). At any rate, Paul asks him to live up to his name or description by promoting the reconciliation. Exhortations to joy, patience, trust, prayer, thanksgiving, and nobility of thought follow with promises of God's presence and peace and of Jesus' return.

Thanks and Conclusion Then Paul expresses thanks for the Philippians' recent gift to him as well as for previous contributions. Throughout this section he maintains disinterest in money for its own sake and for his personal benefit, but indicates a concern for and confidence in the reward of the Philippians for having given so generously. Finally, greetings and a benediction conclude the epistle.

FOR FURTHER DISCUSSION *Should Paul and the early Christians have crusaded against slavery? Why did they not? What should be the involvement or noninvolvement of the church in curing social ills—within the church, outside the church, officially, individually?*

Compare current neo-mysticism and intellectualism with the Colossian heresy.

Why do people tend to react against the Ephesian emphasis on salvation through the sheer grace of God by constructing their own systems of salvation by meritorious works?

What was the key to Paul's joy in hardship, as expressed in Philippians?

FOR FURTHER INVESTIGATION Bruce, F. F. *Philippians*. Peabody, Mass.: Hendrickson, 1989.

Hawthorne, G. F. *Philippians*. Waco, Tex.: Word, 1983. Advanced.

Martin, R. P. *The Epistle of Paul to the Philippians*. 2d ed. Grand Rapids: Eerdmans, 1988.

O'Brien, P. T. *The Epistle to the Philippians*. Grand Rapids: Eerdmans, 1991.

Silva, M. *Philippians. Chicago: Moody, 1989.*

15

The Pastoral Epistles of Paul

❖ *What are the Pastoral Epistles, and why are they so called?*

❖ *What are the pros and cons of Pauline authorship of the Pastorals?*

❖ *If Paul wrote them, where do the Pastorals fit in the chronology of his life?*

❖ *What instructions do the Pastorals give for the ongoing life of the church and the maintenance of Christian belief?*

First and Second Timothy and Titus constitute the Pastoral Epistles, so called because Paul writes them to young pastors. They contain instructions concerning the administrative responsibilities of Timothy and Titus in churches.

Theme

Modern higher critical scholarship casts more doubt on the authenticity of these epistles than on any of the others claiming authorship by Paul. According to the view which denies his authorship, a pseudonymous writer of the second century is using the authority of Paul's name to combat the rising tide of Gnosticism. It is said either that the Pastorals are wholly pseudonymous (but why then the presence of very personal items about Paul, which have the ring of authenticity?) or, more often, that an admirer of Paul incorporates authentic Pauline fragments in writing the epistles after Paul's lifetime.

Authenticity

Fragmentary Theory

Disagreement exists concerning what sections of the Pastorals contain the supposed fragments written by Paul.[1] Moreover, it is unlikely that mere fragments of genuinely Pauline epistles would be preserved, especially since most of them are of a personal nature and lack theological attractiveness. It is still more unlikely that they would later be incorporated into longer pseudonymous epistles in a haphazard way. And why would a forger concentrate almost all the fragments in 2 Timothy instead of distributing them evenly throughout the Pastorals? For that matter, why does he write *three* Pastorals? Their contents do not differ enough to indicate why he should be writing three instead of one.

Pseudonymity

In favor of authorship by Paul stands the claim in the first verse of each pastoral that he is writing. Against this claim it is argued that in ancient times and in the early church pseudonymous writing was an accepted literary practice ("pious forgery"). But 2 Thessalonians 2:2; 3:17 warn against forgeries in Paul's name, and the early church expelled an elder from ecclesiastical office for writing pseudonymously[2] and exercised itself over questions of authorship, as shown, for example, by debate on the authorship of Hebrews and by hesitancy in adopting a book of unknown authorship into the New Testament canon.

Furthermore, it is very improbable that a late admirer of Paul would have called him "the foremost of sinners" (1 Tim. 1:15). The Pastorals are much closer in style and content to Paul's other epistles than are noncanonical and indubitably pseudonymous books to the authentic writings of those in whose names they were forged. Added to the claim of the Pastorals themselves that Paul is writing them and to the concern of the early church over questions of authorship is the very strong and early tradition of Pauline authorship. Only Romans and 1 Corinthians have stronger attestation.

Vocabulary and Style

Doubt about Paul's authorship stems primarily from differences in vocabulary and grammatical style that appear when the Pastorals are compared with other Pauline epistles. Comparisons consist of statistical tables, sometimes drawn up with the aid of computers. But this "scientific" objection to Pauline authorship does not take sufficient account of differences in vocabulary and style as caused by differences in subject matter and addressees and by changes in a

---

1. *The fragments most commonly claimed are 2 Timothy 1:16–18; 3:10–11; 4:1–2a, 5b–22; Titus 3:12–15.*

2. *See Tertullian,* On Baptism *17.*

person's writing style because of environment, age, experience, and the sheer passage of time. Perhaps even more significant is the possibility that stylistic differences stem from different amanuenses and from Paul's giving greater freedom to his amanuenses in the exact wording of his thoughts at some times than at other times. An appeal to amanuenses is sometimes scorned as too easy and scientifically uncontrollable. But it is historically realistic, for we know positively that Paul dictated his epistles and that ancient authors gave their amanuenses varying amounts of freedom.

Yet again, the generally accepted Pauline epistles, or extended passages within them, sometimes exhibit the same kinds of stylistic differences that assertedly disprove Paul's authorship of the Pastorals. And most of the words occurring only in the Pastorals among his epistles also occur in the Septuagint and in extrabiblical Greek literature of the first century, so that the words must have belonged to his and his amanuenses' vocabulary.

Doubters of Pauline authorship also contend that the Gnostic heretic Marcion omitted the Pastorals from his New Testament canon because Paul did not write them. But Marcion had a propensity for rejecting parts of the New Testament accepted by orthodox Christians. He rejected Matthew, Mark, and John, for example, and excised portions of Luke. The statement that "the law is good" (1 Tim. 1:8) must have offended Marcion's radical rejection of the Old Testament, and the disparaging reference to "what is falsely called 'knowledge [Greek: *gnōsis*]'" (1 Tim. 6:20) must also have offended him because of his calling his own system of doctrine *gnôsis*—ample reasons from his standpoint for omitting the Pastorals without any implication that they are pseudonymous.

Marcion's Omission

Some also assert that the Pastorals attack a kind of Gnosticism that arose only after Paul's lifetime. To be sure, the asceticism criticized in 1 Timothy 4:3 ("forbidding people to marry and teaching them to abstain from foods") sounds like a branch of later Gnosticism. Nevertheless, the prominent Jewish element in the false teaching—"those of the circumcision," "Jewish myths," "disputes about the law" (Titus 1:10, 14; 3:9)—disproves that the Pastorals necessarily attack later Gnosticism; for later Gnosticism, though it borrowed its cosmological myth from Judaism, was opposed to the other features of Judaism.

Gnosticism

The Pastorals strike rather at the mixed kind of heresy rebutted earlier in Colossians and now known to have originated in syncretistic Judaism of a pre-Christian variety. Thus, an early date for the Pastorals is preferable; and an early date favors authorship by Paul, since a pious forger would not likely have succeeded in using Paul's name so close to Paul's lifetime.

Ecclesiastical Structure

It is claimed that the Pastorals reflect a more highly organized ecclesiastical structure than had developed during the lifetime of Paul. But they mention only elders (or bishops), deacons, and widows, all of whom figure earlier in the New Testament period as distinct classes within the church (see, for example, Acts 6:1; 9:39, 41; 1 Cor. 7:8; Phil. 1:1). Moreover, the pre-Christian Dead Sea Scrolls describe an officer in the Qumran community who bears remarkable similarity to the bishops who appear in the Pastorals. Instructions for the appointment of elders by Timothy and Titus (1 Tim. 5:22; Titus 1:5) are due, not to advanced, hierarchical church government, but to the starting of new churches under missionary conditions, just as Paul and Barnabas at a very early date appointed elders for the new churches in South Galatia (Acts 14:23).

Orthodoxy

In the same way it is argued that the Pastorals' emphasis on orthodoxy of doctrine implies a post-Pauline stage of theological development when Christian doctrine was considered complete and therefore to be defended from corruption rather than widened in scope. But the defense of traditional Christian orthodoxy characterized Paul's epistles from the very earliest. Galatians as a whole and the fifteenth chapter of 1 Corinthians provide outstanding examples.

Conflicting Data

Finally, some maintain that the Pastorals give historical and geographical data which do not harmonize with Paul's career as recorded in Acts and the other epistles. These are supposed to be the tell-tale mistakes of a pious forger. The conflicting data are that Paul left Timothy in Ephesus when he traveled on to Macedonia (1 Tim. 1:3; contrast Acts 20:4–6), that Demas has deserted Paul (2 Tim. 4:10—yet Demas is still with Paul in Philem. 24), and that Paul left Titus in Crete (Titus 1:5) and went to Nicopolis (Titus 3:12) while Titus proceeded to Dalmatia (2 Tim. 4:10—whereas in Acts, Paul visits neither Crete nor Nicopolis).

Two Roman Imprisonments

The answer to this argument is the hypothesis that Paul was acquitted and released from his first Roman imprisonment; that he enjoyed a period of freedom, into which the travel data of the Pastorals fit; and that he was later reimprisoned and condemned to die as a martyr for the Christian faith. Thus, the historical and geographical data of the Pastorals refer to events that took place after the close of

Acts. The Pastorals themselves constitute evidence favoring this hypothesis, but independent support comes from Paul's expectation of being released in Philippians 1:19, 25; 2:24, written most likely during the first Roman imprisonment, in contrast with Paul's failure to entertain any possibility of release in 2 Timothy 4:6–8, written during the hypothesized second Roman imprisonment.

We may conclude that Paul wrote 1 Timothy and Titus between the imprisonments and 2 Timothy during the second imprisonment, just before his martyrdom. Whether or not he ever reached Spain, as planned in Romans 15:24, 28, remains unknown. First Clement 5:7 says that he "reached the limits of the West," a statement that may be interpreted as a reference either to Rome or to Spain at the far western end of the Mediterranean Basin. *Order of Writing*

In addition to instructions concerning the administrative responsibilities of Timothy and Titus in the churches, Paul summons Titus to come to him in Nicopolis on the west coast of Greece. And in 2 Timothy, Paul, reminiscing over his past career and expecting his execution soon, asks Timothy to come to him in Rome before winter (1:17; 4:6–9, 21). Paul fears that otherwise he may never see Timothy again, for navigation ceases during winter and the execution might occur in the meantime. *Subsidiary Purposes*

First Timothy
An Outline of First Timothy

INTRODUCTION: GREETING (1:1–2)

I. WARNING AGAINST HERESY, WITH PERSONAL REMINISCENCES (1:3–20)

II. THE ORGANIZATION OF THE CHURCH BY TIMOTHY (2:1–3:13)
A. Public prayer (2:1–8)
B. Modesty and subordination of women (2:9–15)
C. Qualifications for bishops (3:1–7)
D. Qualifications for deacons (3:8–13)

III. THE ADMINISTRATION OF THE CHURCH BY TIMOTHY (3:14–6:19)
A. Preserving the church as the bastion of orthodoxy against heterodoxy (3:14–4:16)
B. Pastoring members of the church (5:1–6:2b)
1. Men and women, young and old (5:1–2)
2. Widows (5:3–16)
3. Elders, with an aside regarding Timothy (5:17–25)

4. Slaves (6:1–2b)
C. Teaching and urging of Christian duties (6:2c–10)
D. Leading by example (6:11–16)
E. Warning the wealthy (6:17–19)

CONCLUSION: A FINAL CHARGE TO TIMOTHY AND A BENEDICTION
(6:20–21)

Orthodoxy

First Timothy proceeds from a greeting to a warning against false teachers who mishandle the law. Paul then recalls his own experience of conversion and commission to apostleship and charges Timothy to cling tenaciously to orthodox Christian faith.

Hymenaeus and Alexander

Timothy must take warning from two false teachers whom Paul has ejected from the church into the world, which he calls Satan's territory ("whom I have given over to Satan that they may learn not to blaspheme," 1:20). *Read 1 Timothy 1:1–20.* The clause, "Trustworthy is the statement," leading into the declaration, "Christ Jesus came into the world to save sinners" (1:15), is a formula that introduces and caps early Christian confessions, slogans, and hymns (see also 1 Tim. 3:1; 4:9–10; 2 Tim. 2:11–13; Titus 3:5–8a).

Prayer and Moderation

Chapter 2 begins with an exhortation to public prayer for all people, especially for governmental authorities. There follow instructions that Christian women dress moderately rather than extravagantly and that in the church they not occupy authoritative teaching positions over men. It is disputed whether Paul means the prohibition to be taken universally, as he has been traditionally understood, or only locally because of the influence of false teachers on Christian women in Ephesus (compare 1:3–7). The statement, "Yet she will be saved through childbearing" (2:15), probably means that despite her suffering of birthpangs, a lingering result of the original curse on human sin (Gen. 3:16), the Christian woman is still saved from the eternal judgment of God against sin; in other words, the continuation of pain in giving birth to children does not contradict the salvation of Christian mothers. Under this view "through" means "through the midst of" rather than "by means of (bearing children)."[3]

Bishops and Deacons

Paul now lists the qualifications for bishops and deacons. "Bishop" (*episcopos*) means "overseer, superintendent," and alludes to the

---

3. *Other interpretations are (1) that believing women are saved through the supreme childbirth, that of Christ; (2) that Christian women work out their salvation by bearing and rearing children in a godly manner; and (3) that Paul does not promise eternal salvation, but deliverance from the physical dangers of childbearing.*

office filled by men called "elders" (*presbyters*). Thus, though "bishop" and "elder" go back to different Greek words, they are largely synonymous. "Deacon" means "servant, helper" and refers to the bishops' assistants, who take care of the mundane matters of church life, particularly the distribution of charity. The listing of qualifications for "women" in 3:11 may imply a female order of deaconesses or may refer to deacons' wives, expected to help in the charitable work of their husbands. Closing the section is a quotation from an early Christian hymn or creed which traces the career of Christ from incarnation to ascension ("who was revealed in flesh . . . taken up in glory," 3:16). *Read 1 Timothy 2:1–3:16.*

A further warning against false doctrine is followed in chapter 5 *Propriety* by discussions of Timothy's proper relation to different age groups in the church, the status of widows, and the treatment of elders. As a young man, Timothy is to treat other young men as brothers, older men as fathers, older women as mothers, and young ladies as sisters.

Widows should be supported by their families. But godly widows *Widows* sixty or more years old and unsupported by a family should receive economic assistance from the church. Younger widows should marry lest they fall into the temptation of resorting to an immoral life as means of support.

Faithful elders, especially those who preach and teach, merit fi- *Elders* nancial support. Elders are not to be impeached except on the testimony of two or three witnesses, but those who are duly convicted must be rebuked publicly. Timothy is not to ordain ("lay hands on") a man to eldership hastily, that is, without first proving his character over a period of time (unless the reference is to restoring disciplined members of the church). The epistle closes with miscellaneous instructions about Christian slaves, false teachers, wealthy Christians, and Timothy's own spiritual responsibilities. *Read 1 Timothy 4:1–6:21.*

Titus
An Outline of Titus

INTRODUCTION: GREETING (1:1–4)

  I. THE APPOINTMENT AND QUALIFICATIONS OF BISHOPS (1:5–9)

  II. THE SUPPRESSION OF FALSE TEACHERS (1:10–16)

  III. THE TEACHING OF GOOD CONDUCT (2:1–3:8a)

Conclusion (3:8b–15)

    A. Summary (3:8b–11)

    B. Request for Titus to come to Nicopolis and other instructions (3:12–14)

    C. Greetings and a benediction (3:15)

Place and Purpose   Paul writes this epistle from Nicopolis, on the west coast of Greece, to Titus, whom he has left on the island of Crete to organize the church there. As in 1 Timothy, he warns against false teachers and issues instructions to various classes of Christians on proper conduct. The doctrinal basis for these instructions is God's grace, which brings salvation, leads to godly living, and offers the "blessed hope" of Jesus' return (2:11–14). The experiential basis for these instructions is regeneration by the Holy Spirit (3:3–7). *Read Titus 1:1–3:15.*

Second Timothy
An Outline of Second Timothy

Introduction: Greeting (1:1–2)

   I. Exhortation to Strength of Ministry, Against Timothy's Tendency to Timidity (1:3–2:7)

   II. Exhortation to Orthodoxy, Against False Teaching and Practice (2:8–4:8)

Conclusion (4:9–22)

    A. A request for Timothy to come soon (4:9–13)

    B. News about Paul's trial (4:14–18)

    C. Greetings, with a further plea for Timothy to come and a benediction (4:19–22)

Reminiscence and Exhortation   This last epistle of Paul opens with reminiscences of God's call to Timothy and to Paul interspersed with exhortations and a sidelight on some who have forsaken Paul in prison and others who have stood by him. Further directions to Timothy draw comparisons with the hard work and self-discipline required of soldiers, athletes, and farmers. Against heretical teaching, Paul stresses that "all scripture is inspired by God and profitable" (3:16). A final charge to preach the Word of God, a statement of readiness to die, and personal news and requests conclude Paul's farewell epistle. *Read 2 Timothy 1:1–4:22.*

According to Targum Jonathan on Exodus 7:11 and early *Jannes and* Christian literature outside the New Testament, Jannes and Jambres *Jambres* (3:8) were two of Pharaoh's magicians who opposed Moses. The parchments that Paul asks Timothy to bring (4:13) must have had important contents, for parchment was expensive. Perhaps they included Paul's legal papers, such as his certificate of Roman citizenship, copies of the Old Testament Scriptures, and records of Jesus' life and teachings.

We are probably to understand the deliverance of Paul "out of the *A Lion* lion's mouth" figuratively rather than literally, for the lion was a common metaphor for extreme danger (4:17; compare Ps. 22:21). More specifically, the lion has been taken as a symbol for the devil, as in 1 Peter 5:8, or for the Emperor Nero.

What differences are noticeable between the structure of modern **FOR** *churches and the early church as reflected in the Pastorals? How do we* **FURTHER** *account for these differences?* **DISCUSSION**

How binding on the modern church are the ecclesiastical structure and functional style of the ancient church? Conversely, do changing circumstances and different cultures allow the church freedom of operation and innovation—and if so, within what limits, provided there are limits?

Evaluate the charge that Paul's concern for orthodoxy in the Pastorals sounds negative and overly defensive.

Barrett, C. K. *The Pastoral Epistles in the New English Bible*. Oxford: Clarendon, **FOR**
  1963. **FURTHER**
Dibelius, M., and H. Conzelmann. *The Pastoral Epistles*. Philadelphia: Fortress, **INVESTIGATION**
  1972. Advanced.
Fee, G. D. *First & Second Timothy, Titus*. Peabody, Mass.: Hendrickson, 1989.
Guthrie, D. *The Pastoral Epistles*. 2d ed. Grand Rapids: Eerdmans, 1991.
Hanson, A. T. *The Pastoral Epistles*. Grand Rapids: Eerdmans, 1982.
Kelly, J. N. D. *A Commentary on the Pastoral Epistles*. New York: Harper & Row,
  1963.
Quinn, J. D. *The Letter to Titus*. New York: Doubleday, 1990. Advanced.
For a summary chart of the Pauline epistles, see "A Chart of the Books in the
  New Testament," pages 480–81.

Excursus: A Résumé of Paul's Theology

Since Paul's theology is distributed throughout a number of epis- *Origins* tles written in a variety of missionary circumstances, it remains for us to summarize his thought. Some early scholars believed that for the content and form of his theology Paul borrows extensively from Greek concepts and from the mystery religions. There is general agreement now, however, that his debt to the Old Testament and rabbinic Judaism far exceeds his debt to Greek and mystical sources.

Those same scholars also believed that Paul is the great innovator, who transforms Jesus from what he actually was, a prophetic rabbi and martyr, into a cosmic Savior with divine attributes. But closer study has shown that Paul draws on earlier Christian tradition: hymns, creeds, baptismal confessions, catechetical instructions concerning Christian conduct, and oral and written traditions about Jesus' life and teaching prior to the writing of the gospels. A study of the gospels, Acts, and the non-Pauline epistles leads to this same conclusion: Paul develops an already existing Christian theology which originated with Jesus and grew out of the Scriptures of the Old Testament.

God and Creation From Judaism and the Old Testament comes Paul's belief in one true God who is omnipotent, holy, and gracious. This God is a person. Those who know him through Christ may address him affectionately as Father ("Abba"). But there is multiplicity within the personality of the one God; so Paul writes in the trinitarian terms of Father, Son, and Holy Spirit (though philosophical development of the doctrine of the Trinity will not come until after the writing of the New Testament). God the Father created the universe and all beings in it through and for his Son. In all its materiality, then, the universe is inherently good; sin is an intruder. Every human being sinned in Adam, and sin has such a firm grip on human beings that the good law of God provokes transgression rather than obedience. The result is death, both physical and spiritual. As part of the material creation, the human body is inherently good; but because sin works itself out through the body, Paul calls the sinful urge "the flesh."[4]

Christ and Redemption Jesus, the eternally preexistent Son of God, came from heaven to rescue human beings from sin and its consequences. Thus, he became a human being himself and died to satisfy both God's anger against sin and God's love for sinners. To demonstrate his satisfaction, God raised Jesus from the dead and exalted him as Lord in

---

4. *"The flesh" does not always refer to the propensity to sin, however; other meanings include bodily flesh, the human race, natural human descent or relationship, and human nature as such (whether weak and sinful or not).*

heaven. Now the "call" of God comes to those people whom he has elected, or chosen, beforehand. Yet his election of some for salvation does not contradict the open invitation to all. People accept this invitation by sincere sorrow for sin (repentance) and faith in Jesus Christ, which includes mental assent to what Christianity says about his identity, exclusive trust in his death and resurrection for the remission (removal) of sins, and moral commitment to the kind of life he demands. Repentant believers immediately come to be "in Christ," so that their sin is transferred to Christ and the righteousness of Christ is transferred to them. Solidarity with Christ replaces solidarity with Adam. In this way God can lovingly treat believers as righteous (the doctrine of justification) while still upholding his own standard of justice. As Lord, Jesus "redeems" believers, that is, sets them free from slavery to sin by paying a price, just as the LORD redeemed Israel from bondage in Egypt at the Exodus. God and believers are reconciled, their broken fellowship restored. All these events happen by divine grace: the favor of God toward ill-deserving human beings, without meritorious good works on their part.

The Spirit, Christians, and the Church

To believers God gives his Spirit as a guarantee of future and eternal glory and as an aid to individual and corporate Christian living. The Spirit enables them to conquer the sinful urge ("the flesh"), to live virtuously, to pray, and to minister to others. The body, once dominated by the flesh, becomes a temple of the Spirit and is destined for the resurrection to life eternal. But just as the body of an individual Christian is a temple of the Holy Spirit, so also is the church as a whole. Indeed, the body with its various parts becomes Paul's great metaphor for the church in her organic unity, diversity of function, and subordination to Christ the head. And churches (from the Greek word *ecclesia*) are not buildings, but local assemblies of those who belong to the kingdom of God. These are the holy ones ("saints"), the brothers and sisters ("brethren") into whose hearts have shone the open secrets ("mysteries") of the gospel. By baptism they confess their union with Christ in his death, burial, and resurrection, and the continuance of that union by the Lord's Supper, which looks forward to a messianic banquet at the Second Coming as well as backward to the death of Christ.

Eschatology

The forces of evil—Satan, demonic spirits, and human beings dominated by them—control this present age. But their domination will not last forever; the Day of the Lord is coming. Then *he* will take control. When the man of lawlessness (Antichrist) leads a great rebellion against God, Christ the Lord will return to judge the wicked, vindicate the godly, and restore the nation of Israel. For this event Christians must watch. It is their confident "hope." After the Day of the Lord, the age to come begins, a never-ending succession of ages called eternity, in which God will enjoy his people and they him—forever.[5]

FOR FURTHER DISCUSSION

Why did not Paul and other early Christian authors write systematic theological books rather than occasional letters and tracts?

What particular aspects of his theology kept Paul from becoming an armchair theologian and for the sake of evangelism compelled him to travel far and wide at great personal cost?

FOR FURTHER IN-VESTIGATION

Beker, J. C. *Paul the Apostle*. Philadelphia: Fortress, 1980.

Bruce, F. F. *Paul*. Grand Rapids: Eerdmans, 1977.

Davies, W. D. *Paul and Rabbinic Judaism*. 2d ed. New York: Harper & Row, 1967.

Hunter, A. M. *Paul and His Predecessors*. Philadelphia: Westminster, 1961.

——. *The Gospel According to St. Paul*. Philadelphia: Westminster, 1967.

Longenecker, R. N. *Paul, Apostle of Liberty*. New York: Harper & Row, 1964.

Machen, J. G. *The Origin of Paul's Religion*. Grand Rapids: Eerdmans, 1925.

Neyrey, J. H. *Paul in Other Words*. Louisville: Westminster; John Knox, 1990.

Ridderbos, H. *Paul*. Grand Rapids: Eerdmans, 1975.

Sanders, E. P. *Paul and Palestinian Judaism*. Philadelphia: Fortress, 1977.

Schweitzer, A. *The Mysticism of Paul the Apostle*. New York: Seabury, 1968.

Stewart, J. S. *A Man in Christ*. New York: Harper & Row, n.d.

5. *Paul draws the three terms, "this (present) age," "the Day of the Lord," and "that [or, 'the coming'] age," from rabbinic parlance and fills them with Christian content.*

16

Hebrews:
Jesus as Priest

❖ *Who are the leading candidates for the authorship of Hebrews?*

❖ *To what people was Hebrews written, where did they live, and what was their spiritual state?*

❖ *What is the distinctive Christological emphasis in Hebrews, and how does it relate to the dissuasion of the addressees from apostasy?*

The author of Hebrews portrays Jesus Christ distinctively as a priest who, having offered none other than himself as the completely sufficient sacrifice for sins, now ministers in the heavenly sanctuary. The purpose of this portrait, which emphasizes the superiority of Christ over every aspect and hero of Old Testament religion, is to prevent the first audience of the epistle from apostatizing from Christianity back to Judaism. *Theme*

Early church tradition exhibits uncertainty over the authorship of this anonymous epistle. Nevertheless, at a very early date Hebrews was known and used by 1 Clement (c. A.D. 95). *Authorship*

In the eastern part of the Roman Empire, Paul was usually regarded as author of the epistle. Its theology does resemble that of Paul when we compare the preexistence and creatorship of Christ in Hebrews 1:1–4 with Colossians 1:15–17, the humiliation of Christ in Hebrews 2:14–17 with Philippians 2:5–8, the new covenant in Hebrews 8:6 with 2 Corinthians 3:4–11, and the distribution of *Paul* gifts by the Holy Spirit in Hebrews 2:4 with 1 Corinthians 12:11. The western segment of the church doubted Pauline authorship, however, and even excluded Hebrews from the canon at first because of the uncertain authorship. This fact shows that the early church did not gullibly accept books into the canon without first examining their credentials as to authorship, trustworthiness, and doctrinal purity.

The western church had good reasons to doubt authorship by Paul. None of his acknowledged epistles are anonymous, as Hebrews is. The polished Greek style of Hebrews differs radically from Paul's rugged style, more than can be reasonably explained by a difference in amanuenses. And Paul constantly appeals to his own apostolic authority, but the author of Hebrews appeals to the authority of those who were eyewitnesses to Jesus' ministry (Heb. 2:3; but compare Acts 13:31).

Barnabas Others have suggested Barnabas, whose Levitical background (Acts 4:36) fits the interest in priestly functions evident throughout Hebrews and whose association with Paul would explain the similarities to Pauline theology. But as a resident of Jerusalem (Acts 4:36–37), Barnabas probably heard and saw Jesus, whereas the author of Hebrews includes himself among those who had to depend on others for eyewitness testimony (Heb. 2:3).

Luke Luke, another companion of Paul, is also a candidate for the authorship of Hebrews because of similarities between the polished Greek style of Hebrews and that of Luke-Acts. But Luke-Acts is Gentile in outlook, Hebrews very Jewish.

Apollos Martin Luther suggested Apollos, whose acquaintance with Paul (1 Cor. 16:12) and being tutored by Priscilla and Aquila (Acts 18:26) would account for the likenesses in Hebrews to Pauline theology. Apollos's learning or eloquence (Acts 18:24, 27–28) could have produced the refined literary style of Hebrews. And his Alexandrian background fits Hebrews' frequent and nearly exclusive use of the Septuagint in Old Testament quotations, for the Septuagint was produced in Alexandria, Egypt.[1] But the lack of early tradition favoring Apollos leaves doubt.

---

1. *Some scholars draw a parallel between the allegorical interpretation of the Old Testament by the Jewish philosopher Philo, a contemporary of Apollos and fellow native of Alexandria, and the treatment of the Old Testament in Hebrews. But Hebrews treats the Old Testament as typological history rather than as allegory.*

To suppose that Paul's companion Silvanus (Silas) authored the *Silvanus* epistle would again explain the similarities to Pauline theology. Not much more can be said for or against authorship by Silvanus.

The same is true of the suggestion that Philip wrote Hebrews. *Philip*

Because of her close association with Paul, Adolf von Harnack *Priscilla* suggested Priscilla and ingeniously argued that she left the book anonymous because of the cultural unacceptability of female authorship.

Likenesses between Hebrews and 1 Clement make Clement of *Clement* Rome a possibility. But there are many differences in outlook, too; and Clement probably borrowed from Hebrews. With the early church father, Origen, we may conclude that only God now knows who wrote Hebrews.

Despite the traditional heading, "To the Hebrews," some have *Addressees* thought that Hebrews was originally addressed to Gentile Christians. For support, an appeal is made to the polished Greek style of the epistle and its extensive use of the Septuagint, with only an occasional departure from that Greek translation of the Old Testament. But these phenomena imply nothing about the original addressees; they indicate only the background of the author. The frequent appeal to the Old Testament, the presupposed knowledge of Jewish ritual, the warning not to apostatize back to Judaism, and the early traditional title all point to Jewish Christians as the original recipients.

Prima facie, it might seem most likely that these Jewish Christians *Destination* lived in Palestine. But according to 2:3 they neither saw nor heard Jesus for themselves during his earthly ministry, as many Palestinian Christians doubtless did; and according to 6:10 they materially assisted other Christians, whereas Palestinian Christians were poor and had to receive aid (Acts 11:27–30; Rom. 15:26; 2 Cor. 8:1–9:15). Furthermore, the readers' knowledge of Jewish ritual appears to have come from the Old Testament in its Septuagintal version rather than from attendance at the temple services in Jerusalem; and the statement, "Those from Italy greet you" (13:24), sounds as though Italians away from Italy are sending greetings back home. If so, Rome is the probable destination. Substantiating this conclusion is the fact that evidence for the knowledge of Hebrews appears first in Rome (1 Clement).[2]

---

2. See further W. Manson, The Epistle to the Hebrews *(London: Hodder & Stoughton, 1951)*.

H. Montefiore has proposed that Apollos wrote Hebrews in A.D. 52–54 at Ephesus and sent it to the church in Corinth, especially to its Jewish Christian members.[3] He draws many parallels between Hebrews and Paul's Corinthian correspondence. In his view, "those from Italy" (13:24) are Priscilla and Aquila, who originally moved to Corinth from Rome but subsequently accompanied Paul from Corinth to Ephesus. It remains a difficulty, however, that the author of Hebrews does not mention Priscilla and Aquila by name rather than by a generalizing phrase, especially since he has just mentioned Timothy by name.

Purpose   Wherever the addressees lived, they are well known to the author. He writes about their generosity (6:10), their persecution (10:32–34; 12:4), their immaturity (5:11–6:12), and his hope of revisiting them soon (13:19, 23). Two additional details may be significant: (1) the addressees are exhorted to greet not only the leaders and fellow Christians in their own assembly, but also "*all* the saints" (13:24); (2) they are rebuked for not meeting together often enough (10:25). Possibly, then, they are a Jewish Christian group or house church who have broken away from the main body of Christians in their locality and who stand in danger of lapsing back into Judaism to avoid persecution.[4] The main purpose of the epistle is to prevent such apostasy and to bring them back into the mainstream of Christian fellowship.

Date   The use of Hebrews in 1 Clement requires a date of writing before c. A.D. 95, the date of 1 Clement. It is sometimes argued further that the present tense of verbs in Hebrews describing sacrificial rituals implies a date before A.D. 70, when Titus destroyed the temple and sacrifices ceased to be offered. But other writings that most certainly date from after A.D. 70 continue to use the present tense about Mosaic rituals (1 Clement, Josephus, Justin Martyr, the Talmud). Furthermore, Hebrews does not describe the ritual of the temple, but the ritual of the pre-Solomonic "tabernacle"; therefore, the present tense is merely vivid literary style and cannot very well imply anything about the date of Hebrews. What does favor a date of writing before A.D. 70, however, is the lack of any reference in Hebrews to the destruction of the temple as a divine indication that the Old Testament sacrificial system has been outmoded. The

---

3. *A Commentary on the Epistle to the Hebrews (London: Black, 1964).*

4. *The immediate fading of a sure tradition concerning authorship may be due to separatism on the part of the original addressees. Others identify them as converted Jewish priests (Acts 6:7) or converts from the Qumran sect, which produced the Dead Sea Scrolls.*

author would probably have used such a historical argument were he writing after that event.

As do other epistles, Hebrews concludes with personal allusions; but unlike other epistles, it has no introductory greeting. The oratorical style and remarks such as "time would fail me to tell" (11:32) might seem to indicate a sermon. But the statement, "I have written to you briefly" (13:22), requires us to think that Hebrews is an epistle after all, written in sermonic style. *Literary Form*

To keep his audience from lapsing back into Judaism, the author of Hebrews emphasizes the superiority of Christ over all else, especially over various features of Judaism arising out of the Old Testament. The phrase "better than" epitomizes this dominant theme of Christ's superiority, a theme punctuated throughout the book by exhortations not to apostatize. *Christ's Superiority*

An Outline of Hebrews

I. THE SUPERIORITY OF CHRIST OVER THE OLD TESTAMENT PROPHETS (1:1–3a)

II. THE SUPERIORITY OF CHRIST OVER ANGELS (1:3b–2:18), AND A WARNING AGAINST APOSTASY (2:1–4)

III. THE SUPERIORITY OF CHRIST OVER MOSES (3:1–6), AND A WARNING AGAINST APOSTASY (3:7–19)

IV. THE SUPERIORITY OF CHRIST OVER JOSHUA (4:1–10), AND A WARNING AGAINST APOSTASY (4:11–16)

V. THE SUPERIORITY OF CHRIST OVER THE AARONITES (AARON AND HIS PRIESTLY DESCENDANTS), AND WARNINGS AGAINST APOSTASY (5:1–12:29)

A. Christ's human sympathy and divine appointment to priesthood (5:1–10)

B. Warning against apostasy with exhortation to maturation (5:11–6:20)

C. The Melchizedek pattern of Christ's priesthood (7:1–10)

D. The transitoriness of the Aaronic priesthood (7:11–28)

E. The heavenly realities of Christ's priesthood (8:1–10:18)

F. Warning against apostasy (10:19–39)

G. Encouragement from Old Testament heroes of faith (11:1–40)

H. Encouragement from the example of Christ (12:1–11)

I. Warning against apostasy with the example of Esau (12:12–29)

VI. Practical Exhortations (13:1–19)

Conclusion: Greetings, News of Timothy's Release, and Benedictions (13:20–25)

Over the Prophets Christ is better than the Old Testament prophets because he is the Son of God, the heir of the universe, the creator, the exact representation of divine nature, the sustainer of the world, the purifier from sins, the exalted one—and therefore God's last and best word to the human race (1:1–3a).

Over the Angels Christ is also better than the angels, whom Jews regarded as mediators of the Mosaic law on Mount Sinai (Acts 7:53; Gal. 3:19); for Christ is the divine Son and eternal creator, but angels are mere servants and created beings (1:3b–2:18). Even his becoming lower than the angels through incarnation and death was only temporary. He had to become a human being to qualify as the one who by his death could lift fallen humanity to the dignity in which God originally created them. For that sacrificial act, Christ has received great honor. In the middle of this discussion occurs an exhortation not to drift away from Christian profession (2:1–4). *Read Hebrews 1:1–2:18.*

Over Moses As the divine Son *over* God's household, Christ is better than Moses, a mere servant *in* God's household (3:1–6). The exhortation, therefore, is to avoid incurring God's judgment as a result of unbelief. Providing a warning example is the generation of Israelites who came out of Egypt under Moses but died in the wilderness because of God's anger against their rebellion (3:7–19).

Over Joshua Christ is better than Joshua; for though Joshua brought Israel into Canaan, Christ will bring believers into the eternal resting place of heaven, where God rests from his work of creation (4:1–10). It is obvious that Joshua did not bring Israel into this heavenly rest; for long after Joshua lived and died, David spoke of Israel's resting place as yet to be entered (Ps. 95:7–11).[5] The comparison between Jesus and Joshua is all the more pointed in the Greek text because the

---

5. *According to another interpretation, the "rest" into which Jesus leads Christians is not future heavenly rest from the good works of Christian living, but present spiritual rest or cessation from self-righteous works of the law, because Christ has already accomplished redemption. Yet the closely connected warning against apostasy, with its direct consequences, and the parallel between God's resting from his good work of creation and our resting from work both favor the interpretation given above. According to still another view, the rest is not salvation itself (whether present or future), but successful Christian living as typified by the conquest of Canaan under Joshua. But this interpretation, too, tends to cut the connection with warnings not to apostatize.*

Hebrew name "Joshua" has "Jesus" as its Greek form. In other words, the Greek text knows no distinction between the names of the Old Testament Joshua and the New Testament Jesus.

The author now exhorts his audience to enter the heavenly rest by fidelity to their Christian profession (4:11–16). Later emphasis on the all-sufficiency of Jesus' sacrifice eliminates any implication that continuance of good works in the Christian life merits salvation. Good works and the avoidance of apostasy are necessary, however, to demonstrate genuineness of Christian profession. We find in 4:12 the famous comparison of God's Word to a double-edged sword that pierces and lays bare a person's innermost being. Christians must therefore prove that their outward profession springs from inward reality. *Read Hebrews 3:1–4:16.*

Over Aaron

Christ is better than Aaron and his successors in the priesthood (5:1–12:29). The author of Hebrews first indicates two points of similarity between the Aaronic priests and Christ: (1) like Aaron, Christ was divinely appointed to priesthood; and (2) by sharing our human experiences, Christ has a sympathy for us at least equal to that of Aaron (5:1–10). The outstanding example of Jesus' human feelings is his instinctive shrinking from death while praying in Gethsemane. Next comes a lengthy exhortation (5:11–6:20) to grow out of spiritual infancy into maturity by advancing beyond elementary doctrines of the Jewish faith that form the foundation for Christian belief but gain new significance in their Christian context. Failure to grow increases the danger of apostasy; and if a Christian apostatizes—that is, renounces Christ willfully and utterly—all possibility of salvation forever ceases to exist. The author describes his audience as Christians from the standpoint of their present profession (not knowing their hearts, how else can he describe them?), but goes on to point out that apostasy would both demonstrate the unreality of that profession and incur an irrevocable judgment for false profession. Apostasy, it should be noted, carries a much stronger meaning than temporary disobedience. *Read Hebrews 5:1–6:20.*

Points of Christ's superiority over Aaron are that (1) Christ became priest with a divine oath, but the Aaronites did not; (2) Christ is eternal, whereas the Aaronites died and had to be succeeded; (3) Christ is sinless, but the Aaronites were not; (4) the priestly functions of Christ deal with heavenly realities, those of the Aaronites only with earthly symbols; (5) Christ offered himself voluntarily as a sacrifice that will never need to be repeated, whereas the repetitiousness of animal offerings exposes their ineffectiveness as inferior creatures to take away sins; and (6) the Old Testament itself, written during the period of the Aaronic priesthood, predicted a new covenant that would make obsolete the old covenant under which the Aaronites have functioned (Jer. 31:31–34).

Excursus on the Theological Debate over 6:1–12

Interpretive dispute has raged around the warning in 6:1–12:

(1) Those who believe that the passage teaches the terrifying possibility of a true Christian's reverting to a lost condition struggle against the stated impossibility of restoration (6:4), against those New Testament passages which assure believers, the elect, of eternal security (John 6:39–40; 10:27–29; Rom. 11:29; Phil. 1:6; 1 Peter 1:5; 1 John 2:1), and against the entire doctrine of regeneration.

(2) Those who think that the author of Hebrews poses a hypothetical rather than a realistic possibility find the repetition of this urgent warning here and elsewhere in Hebrews (especially 10:26–31) embarrassing.

(3) Those who tone down the severity of the threatened judgment from loss of salvation to loss of reward (with a bare retention of salvation; compare 1 Cor. 3:12–15) run against the implication of 6:9 that the threatened judgment is the opposite of salvation: "Even though we speak in this way, yet concerning you, beloved, we are persuaded of better things that belong to salvation" (compare 10:27: "a fearful prospect of judgment, and a fury of fire which is going to consume the adversaries").

(4) Those who view the warning as addressed to near Christians rather than to full Christians must minimize the force of the phrases "those who have once been enlightened [compare 10:32; 2 Cor. 4:4, 6; 1 Peter 2:9 et passim], who have tasted the heavenly gift [compare Christ's tasting death for every person (2:9), certainly a full experience], and have become partakers of the Holy Spirit [compare Christ's partaking of human nature (2:14), surely not a partial incarnation], and have tasted the goodness of the word of God and the powers of the age to come [compare 1 Peter 2:3]." They also find difficult the appeal for maturity instead of conversion, the warning against "apostasy" (6:6) instead of failure to con-

fess Christ initially, and the distinctively Christian address "beloved" (6:9; compare 10:30: "The Lord will judge *his people*").

(5) Perhaps the most promising interpretation takes the warning as directed to professing Christians, with the implication that they must show the genuineness of their profession by withstanding pressure to apostatize. Whereas assurances of eternal security assume a true profession of faith, warnings like this one take into account the phenomenon of false professions and the fact that only God knows in advance the difference between true professions and false.

Taking his cue from the statement in Psalm 110:4 that the messianic king will be a priest after the pattern of Melchizedek, the author of Hebrews draws several parallels between Christ and that shadowy Old Testament figure, to whom Abraham gave a tenth of the spoils of battle after rescuing Lot (Gen. 14:1–24). Melchizedek was a priest of God; so also is Christ. The name "Melchizedek" means "King of Righteousness" (more literally, "my king is righteous"); the man by that name was king of "Salem" (perhaps a short form of "Jerusalem"), which means "peace" (in the sense of full divine blessing); and righteousness and peace are characteristics and results of Christ's priestly ministry. Absence in the Old Testament of a recorded genealogy for Melchizedek and of accounts of his birth and death typifies the eternality of Christ as God's Son, in contrast with the dying of all Aaronic priests. The superiority of Christ over Aaron is further symbolized by Melchizedek's receiving a tenth of the spoils of battle from Abraham, whose descendant Aaron was. Solidarity with one's ancestors is here presupposed. The same superiority appears again in Melchizedek's blessing Abraham, rather than vice versa; for the greater person blesses the lesser. *Read Hebrews 7:1–10:18.* *Melchizedek*

Hebrews closes with a long hortatory section and final greetings (10:19–13:25). The author urges his readers to use the superior method of approaching God through Christ rather than the outdated Old Testament method, especially in collective worship, which they have been neglecting (10:19–25). He warns them again, as in chapter 6, of the terrifying judgment that comes on those who willfully and utterly repudiate their Christian profession, but states his confidence, based on their previous endurance of persecution, that they will not fall into apostasy (10:23–31). Then he encourages *Exhortation* them to continued steadfastness by citing as examples the Old Testament heroes of faith,[6] by linking his audience with them, and finally by citing Jesus as the most outstanding example of patient endurance of suffering and ultimate reception of reward (10:32–12:3). Suffering is good discipline and a sign of sonship (12:4–13). Esau becomes a warning example of the faithless apostate (12:14–17). And finally, the writer stresses again the superiority of the new covenant, based on the blood of Christ (12:18–29), and exhorts his audience to mutual love, hospitality (especially needed in those days by itinerant preachers), sympathy, the healthy and moral use of sex within marriage, avoidance of avarice, imitation of godly church leaders, avoidance of false teaching, acceptance of persecution, thanksgiving, generosity, obedience to ecclesiastical leaders, and prayer. *Read Hebrews 10:19–13:25.*

FOR FURTHER DISCUSSION

How important is it to determine the authorship of Hebrews and the date, geographical destination, and original audience of the epistle?

What would be a likely apology by the author of Hebrews to the modern charge that salvation by sacrificial blood is a primitive religious concept?

If God accurately sees the inward state of a professing Christian but other people judge with only relative certainty by observing outward profession, in what ways do Christians know their own individual state, and with what degree of certainty?

FOR FURTHER INVESTIGATION

Attridge, A. W. *Hebrews.* Philadelphia: Fortress, 1989. Advanced.

Bruce, F. F. *The Epistle to the Hebrews.* 2d ed. Grand Rapids: Eerdmans, 1990.

Guthrie, D. *The Epistle to the Hebrews.* Grand Rapids: Eerdmans, 1983.

Hagner, D. A. *Hebrews.* Peabody, Mass.: Hendrickson, 1990.

Lane, W. L. *Hebrews.* 2 vols. Dallas: Word, 1991. Advanced.

---

6. *Chapter 11 is sometimes considered the great faith chapter of the New Testament, just as 1 Corinthians 13 is considered the great love chapter and 1 Corinthians 15 the great resurrection chapter.*

17

The Catholic, or General, Epistles

- ❖ Why are the Catholic, or General, Epistles so called?

- ❖ Which James writes the epistle bearing this name? Whom does he address? What is the practical value of his epistle? How does his doctrine of works compare with Paul's doctrine of faith?

- ❖ What is the nature of the persecution being suffered by the addressees of 1 Peter? How does Peter encourage them? Where is the "Babylon" from which he writes?

- ❖ How are we to evaluate modern doubts over the Petrine authorship and canonicity of 2 Peter? What theme does the epistle have in common with Jude, and what is the relation between these two epistles?

- ❖ Who is Jude? Why does he change his mind regarding the contents of his epistle? How are we to understand his quotations of pseudepigraphical sources?

- ❖ To whom and against whom does John address his first epistle?

- ❖ What are the Johannine criteria of genuine Christianity?

- ❖ Who are "the elect lady and her children" whom John warns in his second epistle not to entertain false teachers?

- ❖ What roles do Gaius, Diotrephes, and Demetrius play in the ecclesiastical dispute around which 3 John revolves?

The term *catholic*, meaning "general, universal," came to be applied by the early church to James, 1–2 Peter, 1–3 John, and Jude, because these epistles (with the exceptions of 2–3 John) lack indications of limited address to a single locality. They are

Catholic

titled according to their traditional authors, like the gospels, but unlike Paul's epistles and Hebrews, which take their titles after the traditional addressees.

James: Salvation by Works

The epistle of James is the least doctrinal and most practical book in the New Testament. We are dealing, then, with a manual of Christian conduct that assumes a foundation of faith.

The Author   This epistle bears the name of its author James (Greek for the Hebrew name "Jacob"), a leader in the early Jerusalem church (Acts 15:12ff.; 21:18; Gal. 2:9, 12) and usually considered to be a brother of Jesus, but only a half brother because of the Virgin Birth.[1] It is possible, however, that James is an older stepbrother of Jesus by a conjectural marriage of Joseph preceding his marriage to Mary. This view, which excludes any blood relationship to Jesus, might better explain the failure of Jesus' brothers to believe in him during his lifetime (Mark 3:21; John 7:2–8); and a lack of concern for Mary because she was only their stepmother might also better explain why Jesus, from the cross, committed his mother to the beloved disciple (John 19:25–27). But the reason may have been that Mary's discipleship alienated her from her other children, who still did not believe in Jesus.

To maintain the doctrine of Mary's perpetual virginity, the traditional Roman Catholic view is that "brother" means "cousin." But the associations between Jesus and his brothers in Matthew 13:55; Mark 6:3; and John 2:12; 7:2–10 imply a closer relation than that of cousins, and probably also closer than that of stepbrothers. The view that the James who wrote this epistle was Jesus' half brother therefore remains the most probable.

Though not a believer in Jesus during his public ministry, James saw the risen Christ (1 Cor. 15:7) and was among those who were awaiting the Holy Spirit on the Day of Pentecost (Acts 1:14). Therefore James (and the other brothers of Jesus) must have come to belief some time during the last stage of Jesus' time on earth. Though James himself carefully practiced the Mosaic law (Acts

---

1. *James the son of Zebedee and one of the twelve apostles suffered martyrdom in A.D. 44 (Acts 12:2), probably too early for us to think that he wrote the epistle. The tone of authority in the epistle of James fairly well rules out lesser-known Jameses in the New Testament: the son of Alphaeus, the son of Mary (not the mother of Jesus), and the father of Judas (not Iscariot). See a concordance for references.*

21:17–26; Gal. 2:12), at the Jerusalem Council he supported Paul's position that Gentile converts should not have to keep the law (Acts 15:12–21; compare Gal. 2:1–10).

The subject matter of James and its Jewish tone, especially its stress on God's law, harmonize with what we know of James the Lord's brother from Acts, Galatians, and other sources. There are also some significant verbal parallels between the epistle of James and the words of James in Acts 15, such as the term "greeting" (Greek: *chairein*, used at the start of epistles only in James 1:1 and Acts 15:23, the decree drafted under James's leadership), the term "visit," or "concerned himself about" (James 1:27 and Acts 15:14, the speech of James before the Jerusalem Council), and others (compare James 2:5, 7 with Acts 15:13, 17). Those who regard the epistle as a late first- or early second-century pseudonymous work maintain that a simple Galilean, such as James, could not have written its well-styled Greek. But this objection overestimates the literary quality of the Greek style in James and, more importantly, fails to consider that Palestinian Jews, especially Galileans, who lived in a predominantly Gentile region, knew and used Greek along with Aramaic and Hebrew.[2]

Canonicity The epistle of James encountered some difficulty in gaining canonical status. Several factors explain the hesitancy of the early church: the brevity of the epistle; its dominantly practical rather than doctrinal character; and the limitation of its address to Jewish Christians—all of which doubtless retarded wide circulation. An uncertainty about the identity of James in 1:1 (for several men by that name appear in the New Testament) also cast initial doubt on the epistle's canonicity. The mistaken impression (voiced by Martin Luther) that the doctrine of works in James contradicts Paul's doctrine of faith did not seriously disturb the early church so far as we can tell. When it came to be realized that the author was almost surely James the Lord's brother, the final verdict proved favorable to canonicity.

Jewish Christian Address James writes "to the twelve tribes in the Dispersion" (1:1). This designation may be taken metaphorically, as in 1 Peter 1:1,[3] for the predominantly Gentile church scattered throughout the Roman Empire. In James, however, the reference is more probably to Jewish

---

2. See J. N. Sevenster, Do You Know Greek? *(Leiden: Brill, 1968).*
3. *See page 440.*

Christians living outside Palestine, as favored by a number of items: the specificity of reference to "the twelve tribes"; the use in 2:2 of the Greek word for synagogue, usually translated here in its untechnical sense of "assembly"; the five quotations of and numerous allusions to the Old Testament; Jewish idioms, such as "Lord of Sabaoth [hosts]" (5:4); stress on several permanent principles of the Jewish law (2:8–13; 4:11–12) and on monotheism (2:19); and the omission of any polemic against idolatry. Idolatry did not characterize Jews of the first century, and it had not characterized them since the Babylonian exile; but it was commonly practiced by Gentiles.

Date   Josephus puts the martyrdom of James in A.D. 62,[4] so the epistle of James must be dated earlier. Some scholars advance arguments for a date so early (A.D. 45–50) that the epistle could be considered the first New Testament book to have been written. For example, the lack of any reference to the Judaizing controversy is said to imply a date before that controversy arose just prior to the Jerusalem Council of about A.D. 49; and the Jewish tone of this epistle is said to imply a date before Christianity had expanded to include Gentiles. But a limitation of the address to Jewish Christians and the strongly Jewish outlook of James himself can account for both phenomena. We should therefore content ourselves with an indeterminate date before James's martyrdom.

Relation to Jesus' Teaching   Notably, James contains numerous allusions to sayings of Jesus recorded in the gospels, especially material associated with the Sermon on the Mount. For example, the contrast in 1:22 between hearers and doers of the Word recalls the parable of the wise person, who builds on a solid foundation by hearing and doing the words of Jesus, and the foolish person, who builds on the sand by hearing but failing to do his words (Matt. 7:24–27; Luke 6:47–49).

Topics   It is difficult to outline James. On the one hand, the epistle has the rambling and moralistic style of Proverbs and other wisdom literature. On the other hand, its precepts are delivered with the fire and passion of a prophetic sermon. After the initial greeting (1:1), one can only list a series of practical exhortations on various topics dealing with Christian conduct in everyday life:[5]

- Rejoice in trials (1:2–4).

---

4. *Antiquities* 20.9.1 §§197–203. *Less likely is the date* A.D. *68 given by Hegesippus, as recorded in Eusebius,* Ecclesiastical History *2.23.18.*

5. *The usual outline of only a few major points would violate the style of James.*

- Believingly ask God for wisdom (1:5–8).
- Do not desire wealth (1:9–11).
- Distinguish between trials, which come from God, and temptations, which come from human lusts; for God gives only good gifts (1:12–18).
- Be doers of the Word in speech and action, not mere hearers (1:19–27).
- Do not show partiality toward the rich, but love all equally and as yourselves (2:1–13). As in the Old Testament, the emphasis in "the rich" lies as much on their wicked persecution of the righteous as on their wealth, just as "poor" often means "pious and persecuted" as well as "poverty stricken."
- Demonstrate the genuineness of your faith by good works (2:14–26). James writes of justification by works *before other human beings*, who need outward evidence because they cannot see into the heart. He is not contradicting Paul, who writes of justification by faith *before God*, who does not need outward evidence because he *can* see into the heart. Some scholars who think that James wrote the epistle late in his lifetime argue for his correcting an antinomian perversion of Paul's doctrine of justification by faith. Others, failing to see that James and Paul complement each other (Paul, too, emphasizes good works as a consequence of true faith), hold that James or a later forger is attacking not merely a distortion of Paul's doctrine, but that doctrine itself. *Read James 1:1–2:26.* *Works and Faith*
- Exhibit the characteristics of genuine wisdom required of Christian teachers: control of the tongue, that is, of its speech; meekness, which avoids quarrelsomeness; and purity, which avoids worldliness (3:1–4:10). *Controlling the Tongue*
- Do not slander one another (4:11–12).
- Do not plan overconfidently by failing to take into account God's will and the possibility of death (4:13–17).
- Be patient until Jesus returns, for then God will punish your rich and powerful persecutors (5:1–11).
- Do not use oaths, but speak straightforwardly and honestly (5:12).
- Share your concerns and joys with one another (5:13–18). In particular, let the elders of the church believingly pray for the healing of the sick as they anoint them with oil in the name of the Lord. If a sick person has sinned and confesses, healing *Anointing the Sick*

will demonstrate that God has forgiven. (The reverse—that sickness is always a direct chastisement for sin and that failure to recover always implies unforgiveness by God—does not logically follow.) Since olive oil was a common household remedy, James may have its medicinal properties in mind, as though to say, "Treat with medicine and pray for recovery." The command to anoint with oil underlies the Roman Catholic sacrament of extreme unction, in which a priest anoints the eyes, ears, nostrils, hands, and feet of a person about to die as a medium of forgiveness if the person cannot consciously engage in confession to receive priestly absolution. But James speaks of "elders," not priests. Nor does he speak of people already in the throes of death. Similarly, the command, "Confess your sins to one another" (5:16), is a Roman Catholic prooftext for auricular confession. But James writes "to one another" and may refer to resolving differences among Christians rather than to exposing one's private sins either to a priest or to the whole church.

Confessing Sins

Preventing Apostasy

- Keep fellow professing Christians from apostatizing and incurring eternal judgment (5:19–20).[6] *Read James 3:1–5:20.* The sinners who are to be turned from the error of their ways are fellow Christians whose straying tends toward apostasy. The death of their soul means eternal death, should they apostatize. And covering a multitude of sins means God's forgiveness of strayers' sins when others have induced them to repent.

FOR FURTHER INVESTIGATION

Davids, P. H. *Commentary on James*. Grand Rapids: Eerdmans, 1982. Advanced.

———. *James*. Peabody, Mass.: Hendrickson, 1989.

Dibelius, M., and H. Greeven. *James*. Philadelphia: Fortress, 1975. Advanced.

Laws, S. *A Commentary on the Epistle of James*. San Francisco: Harper & Row, 1980.

Martin, R. P. *James*. Dallas: Word, 1988. Advanced.

Moo, D. J. *James*. Grand Rapids: Eerdmans, 1987.

Romans 4, for comparison with James 2:14–26 on faith and works.

---

6. *See the remarks on apostasy in connection with Hebrews, pages 428–29.*

First Peter: Salvation and Suffering

The audience to whom this epistle was first directed were suffer- *Theme*
ing persecution. The emphasis therefore falls on proper Christian
conduct in the face of anti-Christian hostility and on the compen-
satory gift of salvation that will reach completion in the future.

The author identifies himself as Peter (1:1). This identification *Authorship*
agrees remarkably with two phenomena: (1) a number of phrases in
1 Peter recall the phraseology of Peter's sermons as recorded in Acts[7]
and (2) allusions to Jesus' sayings and deeds as recorded in the
gospels come from stories in which Peter played a special part or
from sayings in which he would have taken a special interest.[8]
Therefore, though some modern scholars have theorized that
1 Peter is a baptismal sermon or liturgy (1:3–4:11) transformed into
an epistle by the addition of 1:1–2 and 4:12–5:14 and hence probably non-Petrine, we should accept the epistle's own claim to have
been written by the apostle Peter, a claim supported by early church
tradition.

The theme of persecution which runs throughout the epistle sug- *Date*
gests that Peter wrote it around A.D. 63–64, shortly before his martyrdom in Rome under Nero about A.D. 65.

The persecution lying behind 1 Peter seems not to have origi- *Persecution*
nated from an imperial ban on Christianity, for Peter still speaks of
the government as a protector (2:13–17; 3:13). The empire-wide
ban came later. The present persecution rather takes the forms of
slanderous accusations, social ostracism, mob riots, and local police
action. Scholars who deny Petrine authorship usually date the epistle during the persecutions under Domitian (A.D. 81–96) or Trajan
(A.D. 98–117). But in these later persecutions the dominant issue
was Christians' refusal to sacrifice to the emperor. Since this issue
does not come up in 1 Peter, the early date, with Petrine authorship,
is preferable.

---

7. Compare, for example, Acts 2:23 and 1 Peter 1:20 on the foreordination of Christ's
death; Acts 10:42 and 1 Peter 4:5 on the judgment of "the living and the dead"; and the distinctive use of the Greek word xylon (literally, "wood") for the cross in Acts 5:30; 10:39 and
1 Peter 2:24.

8. For example, the exhortation in 2:13–17 to live as free persons, but at the same time to live
in subjection to civil authority in order to avoid giving offense, goes back to the story in Matthew
17:24–27, according to which Jesus said that he and his disciples were really free from human authority, but to avoid giving offense he would pay the temple tax with "Peter's Penny," to be found by
Peter in the mouth of a fish. For further examples, see R. H. Gundry, "'Verba Christi' in 1 Peter:
Their Implications Concerning the Authorship of 1 Peter and the Authenticity of the Gospel
Tradition," New Testament Studies, 13 (1967): 336–50.

Ancient Babylon, the glorious Chaldean capital of Old Testament times, was in ruins and almost uninhabited in the days of Peter and Paul.

Silvanus   Either Silvanus acts as Peter's amanuensis for this epistle ("I have written . . . through Silvanus," 5:12) and so may produce the fair style of its Greek or, since we must not think of Palestinian Jews like Peter as incapable of handling that language well,[9] Silvanus simply carries the letter (hence Paul's commending him as a "faithful brother"). Or Silvanus performs all these services. His name, a Latin one, sounds like the Aramaic "Silas" and probably refers to the Silas who accompanied Paul on his second missionary journey; for Paul mentions a "Silvanus" as his companion during that journey (2 Cor. 1:19; 1 Thess. 1:1; 2 Thess. 1:1), and Luke's narrative of the journey uses "Silas" (nine times in Acts 15:40–18:5). The similarity of Peter's ethical exhortations to those in Pauline literature suggests that Peter is influenced by Paul's writings, perhaps known to him through Silvanus, or that both apostles draw from a common stock of more or less stereotyped catechetical instruction—oral or written, prebaptismal or postbaptismal.

9. See note 2 on page 433.

A Roman head in marble, from about A.D. 125–150, found in the Jordan Valley. Notice how the hair is elaborately waved with several plaits above the waves. Perhaps 1 Peter 3:3 refers to this kind of ostentation.

Roman Origin

Peter writes from "Babylon" (5:13), probably not the city by that name in Mesopotamia, but Rome. (Mesopotamian Babylon had lost almost all its inhabitants by the beginning of the Christian era.) "Babylon" occurs as a symbolic name for Rome in Revelation 17:4–6, 9, 18; for Rome was the ruling city in the New Testament period (v. 18), the city of seven hills (v. 9—Babylon in Mesopotamia being situated on a plain, its ruins still visible today), and the persecutor of the church (v. 6). Rome is called "Babylon" because it is the world capital of idolatry, a position once held by the Mesopotamian city.[10] Extrabiblical references to Rome as "Babylon" also suggest that Peter is using a well-known designation, and the early church fathers understood "Babylon" as a reference to Rome.

Tradition knows of no church in Mesopotamian Babylon or of Peter's ever going there, but tradition does indicate that Peter died in Rome. When John Mark's presence in Rome during Paul's imprisonment there (Col. 4:10) is connected with his presence with Peter at the writing of 1 Peter (1 Peter 5:13), another formidable argu-

---

10. *Compare the calling of Jerusalem "Sodom and Egypt" because of Jerusalem's wickedness (Rev. 11:8).*

439

ment for the Roman origin of this epistle appears. Finally, the order of provinces in the address (1:1) suggests that the bearer of the epistle comes from Rome in the West, makes a circuit of certain provinces in Asia Minor with the epistle, and returns westward to Rome. The route can be traced on a map through Pontus, Galatia, Cappadocia, Asia, and Bithynia (see page 345).

Addressees   At first glance the phrases "exiles of the Dispersion" (1:1), "among the Gentiles" (2:12), and "the Gentiles" (as a third party, 4:3) seem to imply that the original addressees were Jewish Christians. But references to their idolatry prior to conversion (4:3; Jews of the first century did not practice idolatry) and "passions of your former ignorance" and "futile way of life" (1:14, 18; compare Eph. 4:17, where similar phraseology applies to Gentiles) clearly indicate the predominantly Gentile background of the intended audience. This conclusion is confirmed by 2:10: "once you were not a people [this could hardly be said of the Jews, God's covenant nation], but now you are the people of God." Just as Peter uses the term "Babylon" figuratively for Rome, then, he also uses the term "Gentiles" figuratively for non-Christians and the phrase "exiles of the Dispersion" for Gentile Christians scattered throughout the world. Because the church has currently displaced Israel, Jewish designations can apply to the predominantly Gentile church.

An Outline of First Peter

INTRODUCTION: GREETING (1:1–2)

I. PRAISE FOR THE HEAVENLY INHERITANCE OF PERSECUTED CHRISTIANS (1:3–12)

II. EXHORTATION TO PERSONAL HOLINESS (1:13–21)

III. EXHORTATION TO MUTUAL LOVE (1:22–25)

IV. EXHORTATION TO ADVANCEMENT IN SALVATION (2:1–10)

V. EXHORTATION TO CHRISTIAN CONDUCT IN NON-CHRISTIAN SOCIETY (2:11–4:19)
A. Good deeds (2:11–12)
B. Good citizenship (2:13–17)
C. Submission of slaves, with the example of Christ (2:18–25)
D. Submission of wives (3:1–6)
E. Considerateness of husbands (3:7)

F. Sympathetic and loving unity (3:8–12)

G. Innocent suffering, with the example of Christ and his vindication in hell (3:13–4:6)

H. Loving Service (4:7–11)

I. Joyful suffering (4:12–19)

VI. EXHORTATION TO HUMILITY IN THE CHURCH AND RESISTANCE TO PERSECUTION (5:1–11)

CONCLUSION: SILVANUS'S FUNCTION AS AMANUENSIS OR CARRIER OR BOTH; GREETINGS; AND BENEDICTION (5:12–14)

Suffering and Reward

After his greeting, Peter praises God for the prospect of a glorious heavenly inheritance that makes present persecution bearable. Christ also had to suffer before glorification, something the Old Testament prophets did not understand because they did not discern the distinction between Jesus' first coming, for death, and his second coming, for dominion. *Read 1 Peter 1:1–12.*

Good Conduct

In view of future glory, it is imperative for Christians to be holy in conduct. They have been liberated ("redeemed") from slavery to sin by Jesus' blood, which is the evidence of his life sacrificed for sinners. It is imperative for Christians also to love one another, because they have all been born into the family of God through his Word, and to grow like newborn infants and be built up like a temple, with Christ as the corner- or capstone. Furthermore, Christians are to make a favorable impression on the unbelieving world by good behavior. This entails exemplary citizenship, obedience of slaves to masters without talking back, Christian wives' adorning themselves with obedience to their husbands rather than with gaudy fashions, the honoring of wives by their husbands, and, once again, mutual love in the Christian fellowship. *Read 1 Peter 1:13–3:22.*

Descent into Hell

The preaching of Christ to the spirits in prison (3:18–20) most probably means that during the time between his death and resurrection he descended in disembodied form into hell[11] to proclaim his triumph over the demonic spirits whom God had imprisoned there because of their corrupting the human race at the time of Noah, just before the Flood. The preaching need not refer to an

---

11. *A slight variation is that the prison is not hell, but the atmosphere of the earth, to which demonic spirits are now confined. Compare Ephesians 2:2; 6:12; but for the above view, see 2 Peter 2:4; Jude 6.*

offer of salvation. When unqualified, the term "spirits" refers in the Bible to supernatural beings, not to departed human spirits. The point of the passage is that just as God vindicated Christ before the very spirits who had tried to thwart the history of redemption, so also God will someday vindicate Christians before their persecutors.

An alternative interpretation is that the preincarnate Christ offered salvation through Noah's preaching to members of the antediluvian generation, who are now confined to hell because they rejected the message. In this interpretation the point of the passage lies in the parallel between God's past vindication of Noah (rather than of Christ) and his future vindication of Christians. But the succession of mainly verbal phrases about Christ—"put to death," "made alive in spirit," "went," "preached," "the resurrection of Jesus Christ," "has gone into heaven," "is at the right hand of God"— makes a backward reference to the activity of Christ millennia before his incarnation exceedingly awkward.

Baptism   In comparing baptism to the Flood, Peter carefully indicates that contact with baptismal water does not remove sin ("not the removal of dirt from the flesh"); rather, the inward attitude of repentance and faith, which shows itself by submission to the baptismal rite ("an appeal to God for a good conscience," 3:21), leads to remission.

Exhortations   The next section begins with a summary exhortation not to sin. Suffering in the flesh (4:1) refers to physical persecution. Since Christ suffered such persecution, his followers should be prepared to do so, too. This suffering does not cause a person to stop sinning; rather, it is ceasing to sin that causes the suffering of persecution. Ceasing to sin means not pursuing "debaucheries, lusts, drunkenness, orgies, drinking parties, and forbidden idolatries" (4:3). The surprise of unbelievers that Christians no longer join them in such activities turns into taking offense that the Christians no longer do so. The result is persecution: malignment that leads to physical suffering. "The dead" to whom the gospel was preached (4:6) are not "the spirits in prison" of 3:18–20. They are Christians who have been martyred ("judged in the flesh [by their persecutors]") and consequently enjoy heavenly life as disembodied spirits ("live in spirit"). The final exhortations are to rejoice in suffering for Christ, to make sure that suffering is incurred by Christian testimony rather than by bad conduct, to show humility, and to resist with courage satanically instigated persecution. *Read 1 Peter 4:1–5:14.*

Best, E. *First Peter*. Grand Rapids: Eerdmans, 1982.

Davids, P. H. *The First Epistle of Peter*. Grand Rapids: Eerdmans, 1990. Advanced.

Marshall, I. H. *First Peter*. Downers Grove, Ill.: InterVarsity, 1991.

Selwyn, E. G. *The First Epistle of St. Peter*. London: Macmillan, 1955. Advanced.

1 Enoch 6–21, 67–69; Jubilees 10, in R. H. Charles's or J. H. Charlesworth's edition of the Old Testament Pseudepigrapha (for comparison with Christ's preaching to the spirits in prison according to 1 Peter 3:19).

*FOR
FURTHER
INVESTIGATION*

Second Peter: In Defense of Orthodoxy

Heretical teachers who peddled false doctrine and practiced easy morality were beginning to make serious inroads into the church. Second Peter polemicizes against them, particularly against their denial of Jesus' return, and affirms the true knowledge of Christian belief to counter their heretical teaching.

Theme

Widespread doubt exists among modern scholars that the apostle Peter wrote this epistle. The early church exhibited some hesitancy in accepting it into the canon. This hesitancy can be explained by the comparative brevity of the epistle, however; and such brevity may have curtailed its distribution and limited people's acquaintance with it. The early church did finally accept it as a genuine and canonical writing of Peter. We should note, moreover, that two books of the New Testament apocrypha, the Gospel of Truth and the Apocryphon of John, contain probable quotations from or allusions to 2 Peter and thus show an acceptance of 2 Peter as authoritative already in the second century.[12] Similarly, the very early (third century) Bodmer papyrus designated P[72] shows acceptance of 2 Peter as canonical; for in that manuscript 2 Peter shares with 1 Peter and Jude a blessing on readers of these sacred books and gets even more elaborate ornamentation than the other two epistles.

*Authenticity
and Canonicity*

The style of 2 Peter differs from that of 1 Peter. But a difference in amanuenses may provide the reason. Remarkable similarities of phraseology between 2 Peter and 1 Peter and the Petrine speeches in Acts point to a common source, the apostle Peter.[13]

---

12. See A. Helmbold, The Nag Hammadi Gnostic Texts and the Bible *(Grand Rapids: Baker, 1967), 90–91.*

13. *See* E. M. B. Green, 2 Peter Reconsidered *(London: Tyndale, 1961), 12–14, and the entire monograph for a full discussion of all aspects of the problem. See also D. Guthrie,* New Testament Introduction *(Downers Grove, Ill.: Inter-Varsity, 1971), 814–63; and for conceptual similarities to the pre-Christian Dead Sea Scrolls, W. F. Albright,* From the Stone Age to Christianity, *2d ed. (Garden City, N.Y.: Doubleday, 1957), 22–23.*

Relation to Jude

It is also argued that 2 Peter borrows from Jude, especially in description of false teachers, and that a man of Peter's apostolic stature would not have borrowed from a comparatively insignificant writer, such as Jude. But one may question the last part of this argument. Literary history is filled with examples of prominent writers who borrowed from obscure ones. Shakespeare did, and the practice was especially common in the ancient world. Furthermore, a number of scholars have argued cogently that Jude wrote his epistle later and borrowed from 2 Peter. For example, the fact that 2 Peter speaks of the coming of the false teachers predominantly in the future tense and Jude in the past tense might indicate that 2 Peter was written before the spread of heresy, Jude afterward. It is also possible that their similar phraseology comes from a common source unknown to us.

Allusion to Paul's Epistles

In further objection to Petrine authorship, the reference to Paul's epistles in 2 Peter 3:15–16 is said to imply that all of them had been written, collected, and published; yet these things could have happened only after the martyrdoms of Peter and Paul, for Paul was writing up to the very end of his life. But the reference to his epistles need imply the existence of only those epistles which he had written up to the time that Peter wrote his second epistle. Peter's knowledge of them probably came from his travels, from the circulation of Paul's epistles, and from Silvanus (or Silas), who was both Paul's missionary companion and Peter's helper (1 Peter 5:12). The description of Paul as "our beloved brother" (2 Peter 3:15) is what an apostolic contemporary and equal would write, not what a later pseudonymous author would write about an ecclesiastical hero of a preceding generation. Despite modern doubt, then, we may accept the final verdict of the early church that shortly after the apostle Peter wrote his first epistle and shortly before his martyrdom about A.D. 65, he wrote this second epistle which bears his name.

An Outline of Second Peter

INTRODUCTION: GREETING (1:1–2)

   I. THE TRUE KNOWLEDGE OF CHRISTIAN BELIEF (1:3–21)

     A. The moral undergirding of Christian belief with correct conduct (1:3–11)

     B. The historical reliability of Christian belief, supported by eyewitness testimony and fulfilled prophecy (1:12–21)

   II. FALSE TEACHERS (2:1–22)

A. Their coming appearance in the church (2:1–3)
B. Their future judgment (2:4–10a)
C. Their immoral ways (2:10b–22)

III. THE PAROUSIA AND FINAL DISSOLUTION (3:1–18a)
A. Its certainty in spite of delay and denials by false teachers (3:1–10)
B. Its call to godliness (3:11–18a)

CONCLUSION: DOXOLOGY (3:18b)

Second Peter affirms the true knowledge of Christian belief in op- *Reliability of* position to false teaching. After the salutation, Peter glories in the *Orthodoxy* magnitude of God's promises to believers, by which they come to share the divine nature, and points out the resultant necessity of nurturing Christian virtues. Correct conduct must undergird correct belief. He reminds his audience of the reliability of the Christian faith, as supported by eyewitness testimony to the events of Jesus' life (Peter singles out his own observation of the Transfiguration, 1:16–18) and as proved by the fulfillment of divinely inspired prophecy. *Read 2 Peter 1:1–21.* "No prophecy of scripture is a matter of one's own interpretation" (1:20) probably means that the Old Testament predictions of messianic events did not arise out of the prophets' own interpretation of the future, but from the influence of the Holy Spirit. Compare 1:21: "for no prophecy was ever brought about by human will, but people moved by the Holy Spirit spoke from God."[14]

The mention of true prophecy at the end of chapter 1 leads to a *Judgment on* condemnation of false prophecy. Current and future false teachers *Heterodoxy* stand in the tradition of false prophets in the Old Testament and will incur the same judgment from God on themselves. Though they promise freedom, their licentious living demonstrates their depravity and slavery to lust. True Christians, however, should recall the predictions of judgment at the Second Coming—a judgment after the pattern of the Flood, but with fire instead of water. The delay in Jesus' return should not be misinterpreted as cancellation. It is due, rather, to God's patience in giving each generation more time for repentance. After all, what is a thousand years to the eter-

---

14. Other interpretations are that (1) prophetic predictions should not be interpreted in isolation from other Scriptures; (2) prophetic predictions were not addressed exclusively to the generation contemporary with their issuance; (3) the Holy Spirit interprets prophecy as well as inspires it; (4) by themselves Christians do not have the ability or right to interpret Scripture, but need ecclesiastical direction.

nal God? Since the present scheme of things will be destroyed, Christians should live uprightly, that is, according to the eternal values that are fostered by anticipating Jesus' return. The classification of Paul's epistles among "the other scriptures" (3:15–16) shows that they are already regarded as inspired. *Read 2 Peter 2:1–3:18.*

FOR FURTHER INVESTIGATION

Bauckham, R. J. *Jude, 2 Peter.* Waco, Tex.: Word, 1983. Advanced.

Green, E. M. B. *The Second Epistle of Peter & the Epistle of Jude.* Grand Rapids: Eerdmans, 1987.

Kelly, J. N. D. *The Epistles of Peter & Jude.* Peabody, Mass.: Hendrickson, 1988.

Jude: Danger! False Teachers!

Theme

Like 2 Peter, the epistle of Jude polemicizes against false teachers who have penetrated the church—in greater numbers, it would appear, than at the time 2 Peter was written.[15] The particular heresies receive no detailed description or rebuttal, but the heretics themselves draw vehement castigation.

The Author

The author of this epistle identifies himself as Jude, "the brother of James" (v. 1). He is probably not referring to the apostle James of the well-known trio, Peter, James, and John. Herod Agrippa I martyred the apostle James at an early date (Acts 12:1–2). The writer refers instead to James the leader of the church in Jerusalem (Acts 15; Galatians 1–2) and the half brother of Jesus. Thus Jude, too, is a half brother of Jesus, but modestly describes himself as "a servant of Jesus Christ" (v. 1). The date of this epistle is uncertain, but it is late enough for heretics to have made serious inroads into the church.

An Outline of Jude

Introduction: greeting (1–2)

I. The Entrance of False Teachers into the Church (3–4)

II. The Ungodly Character and Coming Judgment of the False Teachers (5–16)

III. Resistance Against the False Teachers (17–23)

Conclusion: benediction (24–25)

False Teachers

Jude intended to write a doctrinal treatise, but the infiltration of false teachers into the church has compelled him to change his epistle into an exhortation to fight vigorously for the truth of the gospel. In vivid terms he describes both the wickedness of the false teachers

---

15. *The point is disputed; see page 444.*

Enoch fragment from the Dead Sea Scrolls.

and their doom by citing past examples of divine judgment: the generation of Israel who perished in the wilderness for their faithless ways, the fallen angels (probably the demonic spirits who corrupted the human race just before the Flood [Gen. 6:1–4; 1 Peter 3:18–20]), and Sodom and Gomorrah. The false teachers' lack of reverence for spiritual things and for superhuman beings stands in contrast to the care which Michael the archangel exercised when disputing with Satan over Moses' corpse. The letter closes with a stirring doxology. *Read Jude 1–25.*

In verses 14–15 Jude quotes the pseudepigraphical apocalypse of 1 Enoch ("Enoch . . . prophesied, saying, 'Behold, the Lord came with many thousands of his holy ones . . . ,'" 1 Enoch 1:9). In an allusion to the dispute between Michael and Satan (v. 9), Jude seemingly refers to another pseudepigraphical book, the Assumption of Moses. Though the full text of the Assumption of Moses has not survived and the extant fragments do not contain this story, it seems likely that Jude's reference draws from that source. We should not be surprised that a canonical writer quotes noncanonical writings. Paul refers to a rabbinic midrash (exposition) on the water-giving rock that "followed" Israel in the wilderness (1 Cor. 10:4), quotes heathen poets in his sermon at Athens (Acts 17:28), and appar-

Pseudepigraphical References

447

ently borrows the names of Pharaoh's magicians who opposed Moses (Jannes and Jambres, 2 Tim. 3:8) from some noncanonical source. Quotations from such material do not imply belief in its divine inspiration. Nor do they have to imply the historicity of the material; for the New Testament writers may simply be illustrating a point, just as John Milton (to take one of many possible examples) utilizes Greek myths without implying a belief in the historicity of their contents.

FOR FURTHER INVESTIGATION See the bibliography for 2 Peter, page 446.

First John: Fatherly Instruction to "Little Children"

Theme For early Christians, heresy in the church posed the problem of distinguishing orthodoxy from heterodoxy, faithful ministers of the Word from false teachers. The epistle of 1 John formulates several criteria—righteousness, love, and correct Christology—for testing the Christian profession of teachers and of oneself.

Literary Form and Address Written probably toward the end of the first century by the apostle John, 1 John has no introduction, author's greetings, or concluding salutations. Yet the statements, "I am writing" (2:1) and "These things I have written to you" (2:26), show that 1 John was not originally an oral sermon, but a written composition. It might have been a general tract for the whole church. But the affectionate "my little children," by which the writer repeatedly addresses his audience, implies a limited circle of Christians with whom he is closely acquainted. According to early church tradition John lived in Ephesus during his old age. Therefore, 1 John is probably a general letter written in sermonic style to Christians he came to know in Asia Minor in the region surrounding Ephesus (compare Paul's circular *Purpose* letter to the "Ephesians" and the sermonic style of Hebrews).[16] John clearly states his purpose in writing to strengthen the audience's knowledge, joy, and assurance in the Christian faith (1:3–4; 5:13) over against false teaching (2:1ff.; 4:1ff.).

Antignostic Polemic The heresy of Gnosticism was probably growing in Christendom by the time John wrote. According to early tradition John hurriedly left a public bath in Ephesus when he heard that the Gnostic leader

---

16. *It is also possible that 1 John represents a Western Asiatic letter-form which lacked an opening address and a closing greeting.*

Cerinthus had entered.[17] Building on the notion that matter is inherently evil, Cerinthus distinguished between an immaterial, divine Christ-spirit and a human Jesus with a physical body, and said that the Christ-spirit came on the human Jesus right after his baptism and left just before the Crucifixion.

Cerinthianism

Against this Cerinthian doctrine John stresses that it was the one person "Jesus Christ" who began his public manifestation by being baptized and finished it by being crucified: "This is the one who came by water and blood, Jesus Christ; not by the water only, but by the water and by the blood" (5:6). That is, Jesus Christ really died as well as entered his ministry by the water of baptism. The water may also refer to the water which flowed with the blood from his pierced side and proved the reality of his death (John 19:34).

Working on the same presupposition that anything material and physical must necessarily be evil, other Gnostics tried to avoid the incarnation and bodily death of Jesus Christ by saying that he only seemed to be human (so-called doceticism, from the Greek verb *dokein*, "to seem"). Therefore John emphasizes the reality of the Incarnation: "What we have heard, what we have seen with our eyes, what we observed and our hands touched, . . . and we have seen" (1:1–2). Ironically from the modern standpoint, the first Christological heresy attacked the humanity of Jesus rather than his deity.

Docetism

To accomplish the purpose of strengthening his audience by combating heresy with truth, John discusses three criteria for determining genuine Christian profession: (1) righteous living; (2) love for other believers; (3) belief in Jesus as the incarnate Christ. Just as the criterion of belief in Jesus as the incarnate Christ is directed against Gnosticism, so also is the criterion of righteous conduct directed against the moral laxity of Gnostics and the criterion of love toward fellow Christians directed against the haughty exclusivism of Gnostics.

Criteria of True Christian Profession

---

17. Irenaeus, Against Heresies 3.3.4: *"There are also those who heard from him [Polycarp] that John, the disciple of the Lord, going to bathe at Ephesus, and perceiving Cerinthus within, rushed out of the bath-house without bathing, exclaiming, 'Let us fly, lest even the bath-house fall down, because Cerinthus, the enemy of the truth, is within'"* (translation from the edition of Roberts and Donaldson).

An Outline of First John

PROLOGUE: THE EYEWITNESSED INCARNATION OF CHRIST AS THE BASIS FOR CHRISTIAN FELLOWSHIP (1:1-4)

    I. THE CRITERION OF RIGHTEOUS CONDUCT (1:5–2:6)

    II. THE CRITERION OF MUTUAL CHRISTIAN LOVE (2:7–17)

    III. THE CRITERION OF INCARNATIONAL CHRISTOLOGY (2:18–28)

    IV. THE CRITERION OF RIGHTEOUS CONDUCT (2:29–3:10a)

    V. THE CRITERION OF MUTUAL CHRISTIAN LOVE (3:10b–24a)

    VI. THE CRITERION OF INCARNATIONAL CHRISTOLOGY (3:24b–4:6)

    VII. THE CRITERION OF MUTUAL CHRISTIAN LOVE (4:7–5:3)

    VIII. THE CRITERION OF RIGHTEOUS CONDUCT (5:4–21)

After claiming firsthand knowledge of Jesus' life (1:1–4), John insists that true Christians, though not sinless, live righteously (1:5–2:6), love one another instead of the world (2:7–17), and believe the truth concerning Jesus Christ. Thus they reject false teachers, called "antichrists" because they are precursors of *the* Antichrist, who will appear during the Tribulation just before the end of this age (2:18–28). Then John discusses the criteria again, and yet again. *Read 1 John 1:1–5:21.*

Sinlessness?   The strong language in chapter 3 about Christians' not sinning cannot denote flawlessness, for 1:8 reads: "If we say that we have no sin, we deceive ourselves and the truth is not in us" (compare 1:10; 2:1). The Greek present tense may indicate that the conduct of true Christians is not *predominantly* sinful. Or John may mean that Christians cannot sin *as* Christians. When they do sin, they temporarily deny their Christian nature. Not that they cease to be Christians, but they cease to act like the Christians they are. The Gnostics pride themselves on their "Christian freedom" to do anything they please, including freedom to sin.

The enigmatic mention of a sin leading to death, a sin undeserving of intercessory prayer (5:16–17), probably refers to the final apostasy warned against in Hebrews, exhibited by the Gnostic heretics, and resulting in irrevocable condemnation. Alternatively, John refers to physical (not eternal) death as a chastisement for disobedient Christians (compare 1 Cor. 5:5; 11:27–34).

Second and Third John: Fatherly Instruction to Christian People

The attestation of 2 and 3 John in patristic writings is some-what weak, doubtless because of the brevity of these letters. The earliest church fathers exhibited no doubt that the apostle John wrote them. In both letters John identifies himself as "the elder," not in the sense of an officer in a local church, but in the sense of an elder statesman of the church at large, that is, an apostle (compare 1 Peter 5:1). The term stands in contrast with John's favorite designation of his audience, "my little children." *Canonicity and Authorship*

An Outline of Second John

INTRODUCTION: GREETING (1–3)

I. EXHORTATION TO CHRISTIAN LOVE (4–6)

II. WARNING AGAINST FALSE DOCTRINE AND ENTERTAINMENT OF FALSE TEACHERS (7–11)

CONCLUSION: HOPE FOR A COMING VISIT, AND ANOTHER GREETING (12–13)

The themes of Christian love and truth dominate 2 John. The purpose is to warn against showing hospitality to any false teacher ("do not take him into your house and do not say hello to him," v. 10). The addressees are "the elect [or chosen] lady and her children" (v. 1). Some interpreters consider them to be personal acquaintances of the apostle. It is far more likely that "the elect lady" personifies a local church and that "her children" represent the individual members of that church, for the lady and her children are beloved by "all who know the truth" (v. 1). It is improbable that one family enjoyed such a wide reputation in Christendom, but quite conceivable that a prominent church did. Furthermore, neither the lady's children nor her nephews (v. 13) are mentioned by personal names;[18] and the pronoun "you" in verses 8, 10, and 12 is plural. These data, plus the warning against false teachers and the command to love one another, are more appropriate to a church than to a family (compare 1 John). Where the church was located we do not know. *Read 2 John 1–13.* *Themes, Purpose, and Address*

---

18. Some have treated the words "elect" and "lady" as proper names of a woman, giving "Electa" or "Kyria" or both. But "elect" can hardly be a proper name, for the lady's sister is also "elect" (v. 13). Two sisters would not have the same name "Electa"! Also, considerations in the text above militate against taking "lady" either as the name or as the description of an individual Christian woman.

An Outline of Third John

INTRODUCTION: GREETING (1)

I. COMMENDATION OF GAIUS'S HOSPITALITY TO TRAVELING CHRISTIAN WORKERS (2–8)

II. CONDEMNATION OF THE REBELLION OF DIOTREPHES AGAINST APOSTOLIC AUTHORITY AND OF HIS REFUSAL OF HOSPITALITY TO TRAVELING CHRISTIAN WORKERS (9–11)

III. COMMENDATION OF DEMETRIUS, PROBABLE CARRIER OF THE LETTER AND ENVOY OF JOHN (12)

CONCLUSION: THE PROSPECT OF A COMING VISIT, AND FINAL GREETINGS (13–15)

Theme, Address, and Purpose

Third John focuses on an ecclesiastical dispute. The place where the recipient lives remains unknown, but it is most likely the region around Ephesus. John sends the letter to Gaius (1) to commend Gaius's hospitality to "the brothers" (probably itinerant teachers sent by John); (2) to rebuke Diotrephes, a self-assertive leader in the church, for his lack of hospitality toward "the brothers," for his dictatorial ways, and for his opposition to the apostolic authority of John; and (3) to praise Demetrius, who probably carries the letter. Demetrius may need a recommendation because he is moving from the Ephesian church, with which John is associated, to the church where Gaius lives (compare the commendation of Phoebe in Rom. 16:1–2) or because he is one of the itinerant teachers of the kind to whom Diotrephes has refused hospitality. Indeed, Diotrephes has expelled from the church those who dared to give them food and lodging. John indicates that he has written another letter to the whole church to which Gaius belongs (v. 9). This other letter may be 2 John, the circular 1 John, or an epistle that has since been lost. Verse 10 contains the threat of a personal visit by John for a direct confrontation with Diotrephes. *Read 3 John 1–15.*

Is there anything specifically Christian (rather than merely Jewish) about the epistle of James? If any, why so little?

What relevance can an epistle that arose out of persecution, as 1 Peter did, have for the church in a free society?

How should false teachers in the church be treated? And how serious a deviation is required to merit the opprobrious epithet "false teacher" or "heretic"?

What are the theological connections between righteousness, love, and orthodoxy in 1 John?

Brown, R. E. *The Epistles of John.* Garden City, N.Y.: Doubleday, 1982. Advanced.

Bruce, F. F. *The Epistles of John.* Grand Rapids: Eerdmans, 1992.

Law, R. *The Tests of Life.* Edinburgh: T. & T. Clark, 1909.

Marshall, I. H. *The Epistles of John.* Grand Rapids: Eerdmans, 1978.

Smalley, S. S. *1, 2, 3 John.* Waco, Tex.: Word, 1984. Advanced.

Talbert, C. H. *Reading John.* New York: Crossroad, 1992.

Thompson, M. M. *John I–III.* Downers Grove, Ill.: InterVarsity, 1992.

FOR FURTHER DISCUSSION

FOR FURTHER INVESTIGATION

PART V

The Apocalypse

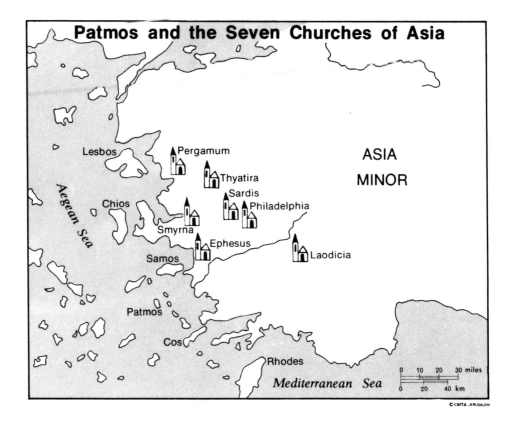

Patmos and the Seven Churches of Asia

Lesbos

Pergamum

Thyatira

Chios

Sardis

Philadelphia

Smyrna

ASIA

MINOR

Aegean Sea

Ephesus

Samos

Laodicia

Patmos

Cos

Rhodes

Mediterranean Sea

| 0 | 10 | 20 | 30 miles |
| 0 | 20 | | 40 km |

© carta, JERUSALEM

18

Revelation: Jesus Is Coming!

- ❖ Why does the style of Revelation differ from that of the gospel and epistles of John if John authored them all?

- ❖ What historical circumstance prompted the writing of Revelation?

- ❖ What are the main interpretative approaches to Revelation, and their strengths and weaknesses?

- ❖ What local background enlivens our understanding of the seven messages to churches in Asia?

- ❖ What meanings do the apocalyptic symbols in Revelation have?

- ❖ What are the sources of the plagues described in Revelation?

- ❖ Who are the 144,000, the two witnesses, the woman, the child, the beast, and the false prophet?

- ❖ With what events does Revelation say that present history will conclude and the eternal state begin?

The Apocalypse (Greek for "uncovering"), or book of Revelation, contains more extended prophecies about the future than any other part of the New Testament. These prophecies focus on the eschatological triumph of Christ over the anti-Christian forces of the world—beginning with the Tribulation, climaxing with the Second Coming, and reaching completion with the full realization of God's kingdom—all to the great encouragement of Christians who face the antagonism of an unbelieving society.

Theme

The acropolis and theater at Pergamum, city of one of the seven churches of Asia.

Canonicity and Authorship   Revelation is strongly attested as canonical and apostolic in the earliest post-New Testament period of church history, from Hermas in the early second century through Origen in the first half of the third century. Doubts arose later, largely because of Dionysius's argument that differences between Revelation and the gospel and epistles of John exclude common authorship: the apostle John cannot therefore have written Revelation. It is true that from a grammatical and literary standpoint the Greek style of Revelation is inferior to that of the gospel and epistles. But in part the "bad grammar" may be deliberate, for purposes of emphasis and allusion to Old Testament passages in Hebraic style, rather than due to ignorance or blundering. In part the "bad grammar" may also stem from an ecstatic state of mind, due to John's having received prophecies in the form of visions. Or writing as a prisoner on the island of Patmos in the Aegean Sea, he did not have the advantage of an amanuensis to smooth out his rough style, as he probably did have for his gospel and epistles.

Date   Concerning the date of writing, one view maintains that Nero's persecution of Christians after the burning of Rome in A.D. 64 evoked Revelation as an encouragement to endure the persecution.

Supporting this view is the observation that the numerical value of the Hebrew letters spelling Nero Caesar comes to 666, the very number that appears in Revelation 13:18 as symbolic of "the beast." Technical problems cast some doubt on the numerical value of Nero's name and title; but more seriously, an allusion to Nero Caesar in 666 need not imply a writing at the time of Nero. It could refer back to him from a later date.

It is also argued in favor of an early (Neronian) date that the smoother literary style of the gospel and epistles of John exhibit an improvement in his command of the Greek language and thus imply that Revelation dates from an earlier period when he was still struggling with Greek as a language not very familiar to him. But there are other explanations for the rough style in Revelation (as noted above); and archaeological discoveries and literary studies have recently demonstrated that along with Aramaic and Hebrew, Greek was commonly spoken among first-century Palestinians. Thus John must have known and used Greek since his youth.[1]

More often, Revelation has been dated during the reign of Domitian (A.D. 81–96). Though Domitian did not persecute Christians on a wide scale, his attempt to enforce emperor worship presaged the violent persecutions to come. Revelation is designed, then, to prepare Christians for resistance. The early church father Irenaeus explicitly dates the writing of Revelation during Domitian's emperorship.[2] The testimony of Irenaeus gains importance from his having been a protégé of Polycarp (A.D. 60–155), the bishop of Smyrna who had sat under the tutelage of John himself. On the other hand, if against the usual interpretation of Revelation 17:9–11 we start numbering the heads of the beast with Nero because he was the first emperor to persecute Christians, then the sixth, during whose reign John writes Revelation, is Titus, the predecessor of Domitian (A.D. 79–81), and Revelation looks forward to the Domitianic and following persecutions.

In a style typical of apocalyptic literature, Revelation uses highly symbolic language for the description of visions. The visions portray the end of history when evil will have reached its limit and God will intervene to commence his reign, judge the wicked, and reward the righteous. All this is presented, not to satisfy idle curiosity about the future, but to encourage the people of God to endure in a world

Apocalyptic Style

---

1. See note 2 on page 433.
2. *Irenaeus*, Against Heresies 5.30.3.

dominated by wickedness. Very often John borrows phraseology from the Old Testament, especially from Daniel, Ezekiel, and Isaiah.

The extravagant figures of speech used throughout the Apocalypse may sound strange to modern ears, but they convey the cosmic proportions of the described events far more effectively than prosaic language could ever do. The strange figures compare in style to the creations of our own contemporary cartoonists, which we readily accept and understand.

Interpretations   Interpreters usually follow one of four main approaches to Revelation:

Idealism   (1) Idealism, which strips the symbolic language of any predictive value and reduces the prophecy to a picture of the continuous struggle between good and evil, the church and paganism, and of the eventual triumph of Christianity. This approach contains a kernel of truth, but arises mainly from a predisposition against genuinely predictive prophecy and from embarrassment over the extravagance of apocalyptic language.

Preterism   (2) Preterism, which shares the predisposition behind idealism but limits Revelation to describing the persecution of Christianity by ancient Rome and to what was expected to happen by way of the destruction of the Roman Empire and the vindication of Christians at the supposedly near return of Christ. Of course, under this view Revelation turns out to be mistaken: Jesus did not return quickly, though the Roman Empire did fall and Christianity did continue. Consequently, preterists may try to salvage the significance of the book for modern times by resorting also to idealism. Preterists are prone to infer a utilization of pagan mythology throughout Revelation.

Historicism   (3) Historicism, which interprets Revelation as a symbolic pre-narration of church history from apostolic times until the Second Coming and the Last Judgment. Thus, the breaking of seven seals represents the fall of the Roman Empire, locusts from the bottomless pit stand for Islamic invaders, the beast represents the papacy (according to the Protestant Reformers), and so on. But the explanations of individual symbols vary so widely among interpreters of this school that doubt is cast on the interpretative method itself. For though prophetic language is somewhat opaque before the predicted events come to pass, the fulfilling events should clarify the language well enough to prevent the breadth of interpretative variation that exists among historicists.[3] Generally, historicists hold to postmillennialism, the belief that Christ will return *after* a lengthy golden age (the Millennium) resulting from conversion of the world to Christianity—a view popular in the nineteenth century; or they hold to amillennialism (the more usual view today), which denies a future thousand years' reign of Christ over the earth and transmutes that reign into his present rulership while seated at God's right hand in heaven.

(4) Futurism, which holds that Revelation describes a coming *Futurism* painful and chaotic time called "the Tribulation" immediately followed by the return of Christ, the advent of God's kingdom, the Last Judgment, and the eternal state. Futurists usually calculate the Tribulation, or Daniel's seventieth week (Dan. 9:24–27), as seven years in length, with perhaps only the latter three and one-half years intensely distressing. Also, they usually hold to the premillennial view that upon his return Christ will rule the world with the saints for one thousand years, crush a satanically inspired rebellion at the close of this millennium, and preside at the Last Judgment before the eternal state begins.

Disagreement exists among futurists (or premillennialists) over *The Rapture* whether the nation of Israel will enjoy restoration during the *Question* Tribulation and the Millennium (dispensationalism) and whether the church will stay on earth throughout the Tribulation (posttribulationism), will be evacuated from the earth by a preliminary coming of Christ before the Tribulation (pretribulationism), or at its halfway mark (midtribulationism), or whether only the godly part of the church will be evacuated beforehand (partial rapturism).[4] Most futurists hold either to pretribulationism or to posttribulationism. Broadly speaking, the more strictly an interpreter separates God's dealings with the church from his dealings with Israel, the more inclined that interpreter is to see the church removed from the Tribulation. Entire loss (or nearly so) of a distinction between the church and Israel usually results in historicism, the denial that there will be a future period of seven years' tribulation, so that it becomes meaningless to ask whether the Rapture will occur before,

---

3. For example, historicists have variously identified the locusts from the abyss in 9:1ff. with the Vandals, Goths, Persians, Mohammedans, heretics, and others.

4. On the term rapture, *see page 355.*

during, or after the Tribulation. But some historicists believe in a millennium following Jesus' return.

Perspective   The view adopted here blends preterism with futurism: John writes for the Christians of his own time. They might have turned out to be the last generation. But since they did not, what John writes will apply to the generation which does turn out to be the last; and every generation of Christians should read Revelation with the possibility in mind that they will be that one. More particularly, the ancient struggle between Christianity and the Caesars corresponds to the struggle between God's people and the Antichrist in the coming tribulation.

Origin,   After an address, the first chapter of Revelation contains an ac-
Address,   count of John's vision of Christ on a certain Sunday ("Lord's day,"
and Contents   1:10) while John was in exile on Patmos because of his Christian testimony. Early church tradition seems to imply that he was later released from Patmos and spent his last years in Ephesus. Chapters 2–3 contain seven messages dictated to John by Christ and addressed to seven churches in Asia in and around Ephesus.[5] (As before in the New Testament, "Asia" refers to a Roman province in western Asia Minor.) Then follows a vision of God, his heavenly court, and an appearance of Christ (chaps. 4–5). For the most part, chapters 6–19 describe plagues that will take place during the Tribulation and the subsequent return of Christ. Finally, John tells about the reign of Christ and the saints for a thousand years, the Last Judgment, and the New Jerusalem (chaps. 20–22).

An Outline of Revelation

INTRODUCTION (1:1–8)
    A. Title and means of revelation (1:1–2)
    B. A blessing on the public reader and audience (1:3)
    C. Greeting (1:4–5a)
    D. Doxology (1:5b–6)
    E. Statement of theme (1:7–8)

   I. CHRIST THE ROYAL PRIEST TENDING SEVEN LAMPSTANDS (CHURCHES) AND HOLDING SEVEN STARS (ANGELS OR MESSENGERS OF THE CHURCHES) (1:9–20)

---

5. *These messages are somewhat incorrectly called "letters," since that designation would imply separate communications to each church, whereas John is to write and send the entire contents of Revelation with the seven messages embedded within it (1:11).*

II. THE SEVEN MESSAGES TO CHURCHES IN ASIA (2:1–3:22)
  A. A message to the church in Ephesus (2:1–7)
  B. A message to the church in Smyrna (2:8–11)
  C. A message to the church in Pergamum (2:12–17)
  D. A message to the church in Thyatira (2:18–29)
  E. A message to the church in Sardis (3:1–6)
  F. A message to the church in Philadelphia (3:7–13)
  G. A message to the church in Laodicea (3:14–22)

III. THE HEAVENLY COURT (4:1–5:14)
  A. The worship of God by four living creatures and twenty-four elders (4:1–11)
  B. The appearance of Christ the Lamb to take a scroll with seven seals, and further praise (5:1–14)

IV. THE PLAGUES OF THE TRIBULATION (6:1–16:21)
  A. The first six seals (6:1–17)
    1. The first seal: militarism (6:1–2)
    2. The second seal: warfare (6:3–4)
    3. The third seal: famine (6:5–6)
    4. The fourth seal: death (6:7–8)
    5. The fifth seal: persecution and martyrdom (6:9–11)
    6. The sixth seal: celestial phenomena (6:12–17)
  B. The sealing of 144,000 for protection (7:1–8)
  C. A white-robed multitude of saints who came out of the Tribulation (7:9–17)
  D. The seventh seal: silence in heaven, thunder, lightning, and an earthquake (8:1–5)
  E. The first six trumpets (8:6–9:21)
    1. The first trumpet: hail, fire (or lightning), blood, and a burning of one-third of the earth (8:7)
    2. The second trumpet: the throwing of an erupting volcano into the sea, the turning into blood of one-third of the sea, and the destruction of one-third of life and ships at sea (8:8–9)
    3. The third trumpet: the falling of a meteorite on one-third of the water supply on land, turning it poisonous and causing widespread loss of life (8:10–11)
    4. The fourth trumpet: a darkening of sun, moon, and stars by one-third (8:12)
    5. Announcement that the last three trumpets constitute the three woes (8:13)

6. The fifth trumpet: locusts from the bottomless pit (9:1–12)
7. The sixth trumpet: the slaughter of one-third of human population by barbaric horsemen (9:13–21)

F. The canceling of seven thunders to avoid further delay (10:1–7)

G. John's eating a scroll of prophecies about the nations (10:8–11)

H. The two witnesses (11:1–13)

I. The seventh trumpet: a transfer of the world to Christ's rule, lightning, thunder, an earthquake, judgment, and reward (11:14–19)

J. Protection from the dragon of the woman who bears a male child (12:1–17)

K. Two beasts (13:1–18)
1. The beast out of the sea with seven heads and ten diadems (13:1–10)
2. The beast out of the earth with two horns (13:11–18)

L. The 144,000 with Christ the Lamb on Mount Zion (14:1–5)

M. Three angelic messages (14:6–12)
1. The eternal gospel (14:6–7)
2. The fall of Babylon (Rome) (14:8)
3. A warning against worship of the beast (14:9–12)

N. Two harvests (14:14–20)
1. By "one like a son of man" (14:14–16)
2. By an angel, with much bloodshed (14:17–20)

O. The seven bowls (15:1–16:21)
1. Preparation (15:1–16:1)
2. The first bowl: malignant sores (16:2)
3. The second bowl: a turning of the sea into blood and death to all life at sea and in it (16:3)
4. The third bowl: a turning of all rivers and springs into blood (16:4–7)
5. The fourth bowl: scorching heat (16:8–9)
6. The fifth bowl: darkness and pain (16:10–11)
7. The sixth bowl: a gathering of Eastern hordes for the Battle of Armageddon (16:12–16)
8. The seventh bowl: "It is done," an earthquake, thunder, lightning, and the downfall of pagan powers (16:17–21)

V. The Fall of Babylon (Rome) and the Return of Christ
   (17:1–19:21)
   A. A description of the harlot Babylon, with emphasis on her
      paganism and a prediction of her downfall (17:1–18)
   B. The destruction of Babylon, with emphasis on her commer-
      cialism (18:1–19:5)
   C. The marriage supper of the Lamb (19:6–10)
   D. The descent of Christ (19:11–16)
   E. The defeat of wicked hordes and the casting of the beast and
      the false prophet into a lake of fire (19:17–21)

VI. The Kingdom of Christ and of God (20:1–22:5)
   A. The binding of Satan for one thousand years (20:1–3)
   B. The millennial reign of Christ and the saints (20:4–6)
   C. The loosing of Satan, a rebellion, and its defeat (20:7–10)
   D. Judgment at the great white throne (20:11–15)
   E. The new Jerusalem, new heaven, and new earth
      (21:1–22:5)

Conclusion (22:6–21)
   A. The trustworthiness of Revelation, with warnings and an in-
      vitation (22:6–20)
   B. Benediction (22:21)

Read Revelation 1:1–3:22. The seven spirits of God mentioned in
the introductory remarks (1:4; compare 4:5) are probably not seven
different spirits, but the one Holy Spirit parceled out in fullness to
each of the seven churches addressed. John does not intend his description of Christ to be taken with strict literalness, which would
prove grotesque. The figures of speech are rather to be translated
into the various characteristics and functions of Christ. His clothing
represents royal priesthood, his white hair eternal age, his flaming
eyes the piercing gaze of omniscience, his bronze-like feet the judgmental activity of stamping down, his thunderous voice divine authority, the two-edged sword his word, and his shining face the
glory of his deity.

   The seven golden lampstands symbolize the seven addressed
churches, for whom Christ cares. The seven stars in his hand represent the "angels" of the seven churches, either guardian angels for
each local assembly or human "messengers" (another possible translation) sent from the churches to visit John on Patmos. The translation "messengers" is favored by their being addressed and exhorted

*Introduction
and First
Vision*

465

throughout chapters 2–3. How could John write to angels and exhort them?

The command given to John, "Write the things which you have seen, and the things which are, and the things which are going to take place after these things" (1:19), is sometimes taken as a built-in, threefold outline of Revelation: (1) past things, or John's vision of Christ (chap. 1); (2) present things, or the messages to seven churches representing the entire age of the church (chaps. 2–3); and (3) future things, or the return of Christ with preceding and following connected events (chaps. 4–22). But at the time Christ speaks the words recorded in 1:19, "the things that are" still have to do with the vision of him, for dictation of the messages has not yet started. After the introduction, chapters 1–3 describe a single vision. The statement in 1:19 should not be taken as a formal outline of the book, then, but as a simple statement that John is to write the things he has just seen, is seeing, and is going to see.

The Seven Messages Each of the seven messages contains an address, self-designation, analysis (with commendation and/or rebuke), exhortation, and promise. Christ carefully chooses his self-designating titles to suit the condition of each church. For example, to the suffering church at Smyrna he is the one "who died and came to life" (2:8).

Ephesus The Nicolaitans were opposed by the Ephesian church and have been identified as heretical followers of Nicolaus of Antioch (an identification perhaps based on a similarity of the names). This Nicolaus was one of the seven men chosen to wait on tables in the early church at Jerusalem (Acts 6:5). Did he turn apostate? We gather from scattered statements in Revelation 2–3 that the Nicolaitans participated in pagan worship and immorality. Perhaps the commendable opposition to them by the Ephesian church led to a divisiveness that made the orthodox Christians lose their former love ("first love") toward one another.

Smyrna The "ten days" of persecution for the church in Smyrna (2:10) refers to a short period of testing, like the ten days of testing for Daniel and his three friends in Babylon (Dan. 1:12, 14).

Pergamum "Satan's throne" in Pergamum (2:13) alludes to the centrality of that city for worship of the emperor in Asia, and to a huge altar to Zeus located on a nearby hill and dominating the city. The "manna" that is promised to overcomers symbolizes eternal life (2:17). Compare Jesus' self-designation as the "bread of life" in typological fulfillment of the Old Testament manna (John 6). The symbolism of

Ruins of the
Temple of Artemis
at Sardis.

Site of the temple
of Zeus at
Pergamum.

the "white stone" inscribed with a new name and given to overcomers (also 2:17) signifies their right to enter eternal life, but the specific background is difficult to ascertain (see the commentaries).

Thyatira   Numerous trade guilds in the industrial city of Thyatira caused many Christian members of the guilds to participate in heathen festivities that formed part of the guilds' activities. It appears that a false prophetess, sarcastically called "Jezebel" after King Ahab's wicked Tyrian wife, was practicing and encouraging this licentious kind of freedom (2:20; compare 1 Kings 16–22; 2 Kings 9:30–37).

Sardis   Sardis was noted for its immorality. The effect on the church: only "a few people in Sardis . . . have not soiled their garments" (3:4). The city was noted also for its dyeing of woolen garments. Therefore Christ promises that overcomers will walk with him, by contrast, "in *white* garments" (3:4–5).

Philadelphia   Because of frequent earthquakes the population of Philadelphia was small. The church there was correspondingly small ("You have a little power," 3:8). As the one who has authority to admit or deny entrance into the messianic kingdom ("he . . . who has the key of David," 3:7), the Lord promises admittance to the Philadelphian Christians, whom he does not criticize at all. Pretribulationists take the promise to the church at Philadelphia, "I also will keep you from the hour of testing" (3:10), as an indication that true Christians will be removed from the world before the Tribulation. Posttribulationists, comparing the phraseology of John 17:15 ("I do not ask that you should take them out of the world, but that you should keep them from the evil one"), regard the promise as one of protection on earth from the wrath of God.

Laodicea   Laodicea was a prosperous center of banking, a place for the manufacture of clothing from the raven-black wool of sheep raised in the region, and a center for medical studies. In particular, a famous Phrygian powder used to cure eye diseases came from the region. So self-sufficient was Laodicea that after a destructive earthquake in A.D. 60, the city did not need the financial aid which Rome gave to neighboring cities for reconstruction. In allusion to these facts, Christ castigates the Laodicean Christians for their spiritual poverty and nakedness in the midst of affluence and advises them to acquire spiritual wealth, to clothe themselves with *white* clothing (righteousness), and to treat their defective spiritual eyesight, or distorted sense of values, with spiritual medicine (3:18). Cold water is refreshing; hot water is useful. But the Laodiceans

At Hierapolis these formations are produced by lime from ancient hot springs. Such hot springs also provided lukewarm drinking water for the nearby Laodiceans.

were like the water from nearby hot springs, which after flowing through an aqueduct was tepid and nauseating.

The churches addressed in the seven messages existed as local assemblies in Asia during the first century. They also represent types of churches that have existed throughout church history. It has been suggested even further, though not all agree, that the dominant characteristics of the seven churches in the order of their mention represent distinctive characteristics and developments within Christendom during successive eras of church history:

The Seven Churches and Church History

- Ephesus, the hardworking apostolic church;
- Smyrna, the heavily persecuted postapostolic church;
- Pergamum, the increasingly worldly church after Emperor Constantine made Christianity virtually the Roman state religion;
- Thyatira, the corrupt church of the Middle Ages;

- Sardis, the church of the Reformation with a reputation for orthodoxy but a lack of spiritual vitality;
- Philadelphia, the church of modern revivals and global missionary enterprise; and
- Laodicea, the contemporary church made lukewarm by apostasy and affluence.

This interpretation suffers, however, from the criticisms that Thyatira receives some higher marks than are usually given to the church of the Middle Ages, that the church of the Reformation hardly merits the message of almost total rebuke directed to Sardis, that the open door mentioned in the message to Philadelphia probably refers to entrance into the messianic kingdom rather than to missionary enterprise, and that the lengthening of church history demands frequent readjustments of the interpretation.

John's Rapture   A difference of opinion exists concerning John's being caught up to heaven in 4:1. Posttribulationists treat it as a purely personal experience for the reception of further visions; many pretribulationists regard it as symbolizing a rapture of the entire church before the Tribulation. Moreover, pretribulationists usually regard the twenty-four "elders" surrounding God's throne as representing the just-raptured church. To posttribulationists they are no more than human or angelic leaders in the heavenly worship of God and Christ. *Read Revelation 4:1–5:14.*

The Seven-Sealed Scroll   The scroll with seven seals that keep it rolled up along its exposed edge is a title deed to the world. Only the one who owns the world has the right to take the scroll, break its seals, open it, and claim his property. At first that one does not appear; so John weeps, for until the rightful owner appears the forces of wickedness, who have usurped control of the world, will persecute the saints. John hears mention of the Lion of the tribe of Judah, the messianic conqueror from David's tribe, but what he then sees is a lamb, Jesus, bearing the scars of crucifixion but standing in resurrection rather than lying slain on an altar (compare John 20:24–29). Jesus' taking the scroll, breaking its seals, and unrolling it will therefore represent his seizing control of the world from the persecutors of God's people. This activity peaks at the Second Coming and establishment of God's kingdom on earth.

Seals, Trumpets and Bowls   Chapters 6–16 contain three series of seven plagues each: seals, trumpets, and bowls. Some interpreters think that their fulfillment will be consecutive, the plagues under the trumpets coming to pass

470

after those under the seals, the plagues in the bowls after those of the trumpets, and the Second Coming forming a climax. In this scheme the trumpets constitute the seventh seal; the bowls, the seventh trumpet; and the Second Coming, the seventh bowl:

Seals 1 2 3 4 5 6 7

         Trumpets 1 2 3 4 5 6 7

                  Bowls 1 2 3 4 5 6 7

                           Second Coming

But the fact that the contents of the seventh in each series are practically identical and seem to indicate finality—thunder, lightning, an earthquake, and various indications that the end has come—favors that the seals, trumpets, and bowls are at least partly concurrent in their fulfillment. Thus, the plagues of the seals will be spread out over the whole tribulation, those of the trumpets over its last part, and those of the bowls concentrated at the end, so that the seventh in each series is identical and encompasses the Second Coming and its immediate accompaniments:

                           Second Coming

    Seals 1   2   3   4   5   6   7

        Trumpets 1 2 3 4 5 6 7

               Bowls 1234567

For the most part, the contents of the seals appear to stem from human depravity: ***Seals***

Seal 1: militarism, perhaps on the part of the Antichrist;

Seal 2: warfare, resulting from militarism;

Seal 3: famine, resulting from warfare;

Seal 4: death, resulting from famine and other ravages of war (the first four seals represented by "The Four Horsemen of the Apocalypse");

Seal 5: persecution and martyrdom of the saints (the last generation of the church according to posttribulationism; others who have turned to God after the rapture of the church according to pretribulationism);

Seal 6: the celestial phenomena which Jesus said would immediately precede his return (Mark 13:24–26; Matt. 24:29–30; Luke 21:25–27);

Seal 7: silence in heaven, thunder, lightning, and an earthquake.

Read Revelation 6:1–8:5.

144,000   Many interpreters regard the 144,000 Israelites who are marked for protection during the Tribulation as symbolic of the church. Just as in chapter 5 John *heard* Jesus announced as a lion but *saw* him as a lamb, so here John *hears* the church announced as the tribes of Israel but *sees* them as an international multitude of redeemed people. Pretribulationists usually cast the 144,000 in the role of Israelite evangelists who spread the gospel throughout the world in the absence of the church, with the result that a vast multitude of Gentiles believe and are saved. Others regard the 144,000 as orthodox Jews whom God will protect during the Tribulation, especially when they are being persecuted for refusal to worship an image of the Antichrist placed in a rebuilt temple at Jerusalem. This Jewish remnant will thus survive to become the nucleus of a reestablished Davidic kingdom during the Millennium.

Trumpets   The trumpets appear to stem primarily from satanic and demonic activity:

Trumpet 1: hail, fire (or lightning), and blood, resulting in the burning of one-third of the earth;

Trumpet 2: the throwing of an erupting volcano ("burning mountain") into the sea, resulting in the turning into blood of one-third of the sea and in death and destruction to one-third of life and ships at sea;

Trumpet 3: the falling of a meteorite, described as a blazing star named "Wormwood," on one-third of the water supply on land (rivers and springs), turning them bitter and poisonous with widespread loss of life;

Trumpet 4: the darkening of the sun, moon, and stars by one-third;

Trumpet 5: the opening of the bottomless pit by a star (probably Satan) that has fallen from heaven to earth, resulting in demonic torment of human beings, the demons being likened to locusts with the stinging tails of scorpions;

Trumpet 6: the slaughtering of one-third of human population by barbaric horsemen;

Trumpet 7: the turning of the kingdoms of the world into the kingdom of Christ, lightning, thunder, an earthquake, and the time of judgment and reward.

It is obvious that much of the language in these descriptions is meant to be taken symbolically. Nonetheless, symbolic language may point to literal reality; so an interpreter must avoid overspiritualization. The burning mountain, or volcano, and the blazing star, or meteorite, probably refer to fallen angels, perhaps to Satan himself, as does the star that falls from heaven to earth under the fifth trumpet. *Read Revelation 8:6–11:19.*

The two witnesses in the first part of chapter 11 probably minister during the latter three and one half years (1,260 days, or 42 months) of the Tribulation, because during the time of their preaching the Gentiles "will tread under foot the holy city" (11:2; compare Dan. 9:27). Futurists often identify the two witnesses with Moses and Elijah, who will reappear and represent the law and the prophets. Elijah's return for ministry to Israel was predicted in Malachi 4:5 and confirmed by Jesus (Matt. 17:11; Mark 9:12a). Moses and Elijah appeared together on the Mount of Transfiguration during Jesus' first advent; and the miracles of the two witnesses in Revelation 11:6 correspond to the Old Testament miracles of Moses (turning water to blood and smiting the earth with plagues—compare Exodus 7–12) and Elijah (striking their enemies with lightning, or "fire"—compare 2 Kings 1:9–12—and producing drought —compare 1 Kings 17:1). Sometimes the two witnesses are identified with Enoch and Elijah, the only biblical characters to avoid physical death (by translation to heaven) and therefore to be sent back during the Tribulation to preach until martyred. But believers still alive at the Second Coming will all avoid physical death; so we need not suppose that both Enoch and Elijah must die to maintain a general rule of physical death as part of the curse on sin. Interpreted still differently by a large number of commentators, the two witnesses stand for the collective Moses- and Elijah-like testimony of God's people on earth during the Tribulation.

Two Witnesses

Chapter 12 poses uncertainties of interpretation. Perhaps it is best to understand the woman as representing Jesus' first disciples, and her pain in childbirth as their sorrow when he died (see John 16:19–22 for this comparison). The catching up of the child to God then represents Jesus' ascension (John 20:17). Since the saints are subject to severe persecution (13:7), the woman's refuge in the wilderness, "where she had a place prepared by God" (12:6), does not refer to protection from persecution, but to salvation in Christ (see John 14:1–3, where we are to think of prepared abiding places in Christ, as in John 15:1ff.). The wilderness represents the place of

Woman and Child

redemption, just as at the Exodus. Satan's downfall occurred at the Cross (John 12:31). *Read Revelation 12:1–17.*

Beast and False Prophet   The beast and the false prophet of chapter 13 have been interpreted to represent the Roman Empire (revived) and the Antichrist, respectively. More probably, the beast represents the empire personified in its ruler the Antichrist, and the false prophet represents a minister of propaganda in the idolatrous cult of Antichrist (compare Dan. 9:27; Mark 13:14; Matt. 24:15; 2 Thess. 2:3–4, 9). In 19:20 both the beast and the false prophet appear to be individuals, because each is thrown into a lake of fire: "and the beast was seized, and with him the false prophet who had performed the signs in his presence, by which he deceived . . . the ones worshiping his image; these two were thrown alive into the lake of fire." *Read Revelation 13:1–14:20.*

144,000   The 144,000 appear again in chapter 14, this time on Mount Zion with Christ the Lamb, and celebrate their triumphant passage through the Tribulation. The celebration implies a time at the close of the Tribulation, after Christ's return, and constitutes one indication among many that John's visions dart back and forth chronologically .

Harvests   The two harvests reaped in 14:14–20 may both symbolize judgment at the Second Coming. Or the first harvest, reaped by "one like a son of man" sitting on a white cloud, represents the rapture of the church at the coming of Christ after the Tribulation; and because of the phrase mentioning "the wrath of God," the second reaping represents the immediately following outburst of judgment at Armageddon.

Bowls   John explicitly states that the bowls represent plagues originating in the wrath of God, which is probably concentrated at the end of the Tribulation ("seven plagues, which are the last," 15:1):

Bowl 1: malignant sores;

Bowl 2: the turning of the sea to blood, resulting in death to all life at sea and in it (an intensification of the second trumpet);

Bowl 3: the turning of all rivers and springs to blood (an intensification of the third trumpet);

Bowl 4: scorching heat;

Bowl 5: darkness and pain;

Bowl 6: the gathering of hordes to invade the Roman Empire from the East, the Battle of Armageddon;

Bowl 7: "It is done," an earthquake, thunder, lightning, and the downfall of pagan powers.

Read Revelation 15:1–16:21.

The collapse of the Roman Empire is now celebrated. "Babylon" is symbolic for Rome, since Rome has taken the place of that Mesopotamian city as the world's center of idolatry, immorality, and persecution of God's people.[6] Chapter 17 puts emphasis on the false religion of pagan Rome; chapter 18 on her commercialism and materialism. Much of the phraseology in these chapters comes from prophecies against Babylon in Isaiah 13–14, 46–48 and especially Jeremiah 50–51 and the prophecy against Tyre in Ezekiel 26–28. *Read Revelation 17:1–18:24.*

Fall of Babylon

The marriage supper of the Lamb represents a uniting of the saints with their Savior at the long-awaited messianic banquet. Pretribulationists see the event as having taken place in heaven during the Tribulation, since all the church will have been taken to heaven by that time. Posttribulationists see it as on the verge of taking place at the return of Christ following the Tribulation, because the last generation of the church will still be on earth.

Marriage Supper

At his coming, Christ destroys the gathered armies of the wicked nations. The beast and the false prophet are thrown into the lake of fire. Satan is confined for one thousand years. The righteous dead rise and share in Christ's millennial rule over the earth. John makes special mention of the martyrs to encourage willingness on the part of God's people to undergo martyrdom, if necessary, in maintaining fidelity to Christ. Satan, loosed after the thousand years, instigates a revolt against the rule of Christ among the many who have had to submit outwardly to his political dominion but have not submitted in their hearts. The revolt is crushed, and the Last Judgment takes place. *Read Revelation 19:1–20:15.*[7]

Parousia

Millennium

Judgment

The New Jerusalem, spotless bride and wife of the Lamb—in other words, the church[8]—contrasts sharply with the harlot Babylon (Rome) of preceding chapters. That "the kings of the earth bring

New Jerusalem

---

6. *See the discussion on page 439 concerning the application of "Babylon" to Rome in 1 Peter.*

7. *Amillennialists refer the binding of Satan to the work of Christ during his first advent, the first resurrection to the spiritual coming alive of those who believe in Christ, the thousand years' reign with Christ to the present spiritual kingship of Christ and the saints (one thousand being figurative for a long period of time), the crushing of the revolt to the Second Coming, and the second resurrection to the physical resurrection of both the righteous and the wicked (thus a general resurrection) at the Second Coming.*

8. *For an interpretation of the New Jerusalem as the saints themselves, not their eternal habitat, see R. H. Gundry, "The New Jerusalem: People as Place, Not Place for People,"* Novum Testamentum, *29 (1987): 254–64.*

their glory into it" (21:24) may indicate a descent of the New Jerusalem to earth at the beginning of the millennial kingdom. But the abolishing of death, grief, crying, pain, and all "the first things" associated with the world in which evil resides (21:4) points to the eternal state after the Millennium and the final elimination of sin with all its results.

Conclusion   And so the New Testament ends with the beatific vision ("they will see his face," 22:4), an invitation to eternal life (22:17), a curse on anyone who adds to or subtracts from the prophecies of Revelation (22:18–19), a promise of and prayer for Jesus' return (22:20), and a benediction (22:21). *Read Revelation 21:1–22:21.*

FOR FURTHER DISCUSSION

In view of almost two thousand years of church history, how are we to understand "what must soon take place" and "the time is near" (1:1, 3)?

Why is predictive prophecy at least partly opaque in meaning till after its fulfillment?

Assign the various branches of Christendom, including denominations, to the categories represented by the seven churches in Asia.

What guidelines might help settle the question of literal versus figurative interpretation of the Apocalypse?

What developments in recent and current history may be a stage-setting for events predicted in Revelation, or should we even attempt to engage in such speculation?

Why are so few clearly understandable details about heaven and hell given us? Is the assumption of the question false?

FOR FURTHER INVESTIGATION

Beasley-Murray, G. R. *The Book of Revelation.* Grand Rapids: Eerdmans, 1981.

Caird, G. B. *A Commentary on the Revelation of St. John the Divine.* New York: Harper & Row, 1966.

Hemer, C. J. *The Letters to the Seven Churches of Asia in Their Local Setting.* Sheffield: JSOT, 1986. Advanced.

Morris, L. *Revelation.* 2d ed. Grand Rapids: Eerdmans, 1987.

Mounce, R. H. *The Book of Revelation.* Grand Rapids: Eerdmans, 1977.

Sweet, J. *Revelation.* 2d ed. London: SCM; Philadelphia: Trinity, 1990.

Walvoord, J. F. *The Revelation of Jesus Christ.* Chicago: Moody, 1966.

In Retrospect

Jesus Christ came into the world at a time of religious and philosophical malaise. Under the heel of Roman domination, his own people the Jews were looking for a political Messiah. When for the most part he avoided the politically loaded term "Messiah" and presented himself as the Son of man who must suffer and die as the Servant of the LORD before being exalted to dominion, not even his own disciples understood him. The Jews in general and the Sanhedrin in particular rejected him for Barabbas, a political revolutionary. Unjustly charged with sedition himself, Jesus died by Roman crucifixion.

But the Resurrection vindicated Jesus before his disciples. After his ascension and the outpouring of the Holy Spirit on the Day of Pentecost, they began to proclaim him as Lord and Savior. Apparently they expected him to return within a short time and in a continued but understandable spirit of Jewish nationalism set about evangelizing their fellow Jews in preparation for a soon-to-be-established kingdom in which Israel would dominate the Gentiles. The Second Coming was delayed, however, and converted Hellenistic Jews, having less anti-Gentile bias than most Hebraistic Jewish Christians, sent Barnabas and Paul from Antioch, Syria, on the first concerted effort to win Gentiles. Success inspired further missions, and the gospel eventually spread across the Roman Empire.

Evangelistic success necessitated the organization of local groups of converts for instruction and worship. The structure of the institutional church began to take shape. Doctrinal and ethical instruction was amplified by those elements in the Old Testament not outmoded through New Testament fulfillment and by the recall, application, and elaboration of Jesus' teaching and example. These led to deeper reflection on the person and work of Christ, on the significance of the church, and on the eschatological future.

Except for some scattered and now-lost writings, the earliest communication of Christian doctrine and ethics was oral. The geographical spread of the gospel created the need for instruction from a distance, however; so the writing of the New Testament epistles started. Somewhat later the writing of the gospels and Acts began as a literary means of evangelizing unbelievers, confirming the faith of believers, and providing an authoritative record of Jesus' life and ministry as the availability of eyewitnesses diminished through their deaths and through movement of the gospel away from Palestine, where most of the remaining eyewitnesses resided. Toward the close of the first century the last surviving apostle, John, contributed the last of the New Testament writings with both the literary forms of gospel and epistle, and added a book unique in form within the New Testament—the visionary, forward-looking Apocalypse. Then began the process of collection and canonization. For a final conspectus of New Testament literature, see the chart on pages 480–81.

A CHART OF THE BOOKS IN THE NEW TESTAMENT

Book	Author	Time of Writing (A.D.)[1]	Place of Writing	Addressees	Themes and Distinctive Emphases
Galatians	Paul	49, just after Paul's 1st missionary journey	Antioch in Syria	Christians in Pisidian Antioch, Iconium, Lystra, and Derbe, South Galatia	Justification by divine grace through faith in Jesus Christ—against the Judaizing doctrine of meritorious works of the law
1 Thessalonians	Paul	50–51, during the 2d missionary journey	Corinth	Christians in Thessalonica	Congratulations upon conversion and Christian growth and exhortations to further progress, with emphasis on comfort from end expectancy toward the Parousia
2 Thessalonians	Paul	50–51, during the 2d missionary journey	Corinth	Christians in Thessalonica	Quieting of a fanatical belief (engendered by persecution) in the immediacy of the Parousia
1 Corinthians	Paul	55, during the 3d missionary journey	Ephesus	Christians in Corinth	Problems of manners, morals, and beliefs within the church
2 Corinthians	Paul	56, during the 3d missionary journey	Macedonia	Christians in Corinth	Paul's inner feelings about his apostolic ministry; the offering for the church in Jerusalem
Romans	Paul	57, during the 3d missionary journey	Corinth	Christians in Rome	Justification by divine grace through faith in Jesus Christ
James	James the half-brother of Jesus	40s or 50s	Jerusalem	Jewish Christians of the Dispersion	Exhortations to Christian conduct in everyday life
Mark	John Mark	late 50s or early 60s	Rome	Non-Christian Romans	Jesus as the powerful Son of God
Matthew	Matthew	late 50s or early 60s	Antioch in Syria	Jewish Christians in Syria	Jesus as builder of the church
Philemon	Paul	61–62	Rome	Philemon, his family, and the church in his house—all in Colossae	Mercy for a runaway slave, Onesimus, who had become a Christian
Colossians	Paul	61–62	Rome	Christians in Colossae	The preeminence of Christ
Ephesians	Paul	61–62	Rome	Christians in the region around Ephesus	The spiritual privileges and responsibilities of the church
Luke	Luke	62	Rome	Non-Christian Gentiles, especially those with some culture and interest in Christianity	The historical reliability of the gospel

Book	Author	Date	Place of writing	Recipients	Purpose
Acts	Luke	62	Rome	Non-Christians Gentiles, especially those with some culture and interest in Christianity	The historical reliability of the gospel
Philippians	Paul	62	Rome	Christians in Philippi	Thanks for financial assistance with personal news and exhortations
1 Timothy	Paul	63–64	Macedonia	Timothy in Ephesus	The organization and administration of churches by Timothy
Titus	Paul	63–64	Nicopolis	Titus in Crete	The organization and administration of the churches in Crete by Titus
1 Peter	Peter	63–64	Rome	Christians in Asia Minor	The salvation and conduct of suffering Christians
2 Peter	Peter	65	Rome	Christians in Asia Minor	The true knowledge of Christian belief versus false teachers and their denial of the Parousia
2 Timothy	Paul	65	Rome	Timothy in Ephesus	The commission of Timothy to carry on Paul's work
Hebrews	Unknown (Apollos?)	60s	unknown	Jewish Christians in Rome	The superiority of Christ as a deterrent against apostasy from Christianity back to Judaism
Jude	Jude the half-brother of Jesus	60s or 70s	unknown	Christians everywhere	Warning against false teachers in the church
John	John	late 80s or early 90s	Ephesus	Christians in the region around Ephesus	Believing in Jesus as the Christ and Son of God for eternal life
1 John	John	late 80s or early 90s	Ephesus	Christians in the region around Ephesus	The criteria of true Christian belief and practice over and against Gnosticism
2 John	John	late 80s or early 90s	Ephesus	A church near Ephesus	Christian love and Christian truth
3 John	John	late 80s or early 90s	Ephesus	Gaius, a Christian in the region around Ephesus	An ecclesiastical dispute involving Gaius, Diotrephes, Demetrius, and John himself
Revelation	John	late 80s or early 90s	Patmos	Seven churches in western Asia Minor	Visions of the eschatological triumph of Christ over the anti-Christian forces of the world

¹Datings are approximate and often disputed. They presuppose the discussions throughout this book. Places of writing and identification of authors are also disputed.

Scripture Indexes

Old Testament

Genesis

1:1	262
4:24	190
6:1–4	447
14:1–24	429
17:12–14	217
19:26	238
21:4	217
26:12	136n
28:12	264
38:8	150
42:17–18	183

Exodus

2:15	162
20:4–6	149
3:14	257, 275, 284
3:6	150
4:19–20	162
7–12	473
7:11	417
12:1–51	152
12:22	287
12:43–46	280
13:9, 16	195
33:19, 22	140
34:29	162
34:29–30	188
34:5–7	140

Leviticus

6:1–5	240
10:9	216
11	141
12	218
12:3	217
13–14	134
13:45–46	238
15	139n
18:16	140
18:6–18	176n, 319
19:18	281
20:21	140
23:4–8	152
23:4–43	69n
25:8–55	177

Numbers

5:2–4	238
5:6–7	240
6:1–21	325
6:2–4	216
6:9–12	328
9:12	280
15:37–41	63n
15:38–39	195
21:8–9	267
24:17	172
28:9 10	182

Deuteronomy

2:14	269
5:8–10	149

6:4	149
6:4ff.	63
6:8	195
11:13–21	63n
11:18	195
18:15	162, 272
18:15, 18	271
19:15	139, 201
21:1–9	201
22:12	195
22:23–24	171
23:1	306n
23:25	135n
24:1	191
25:5–10	150

Judges
13:4	216

1 Samuel
1:11	216
2:1–10	217
21:1–6	135
30:1, 12–13	183

2 Samuel
5:8	194

1 Kings
16–22	468
17:1	473
19:11	140

2 Kings
1:9–12	473
9:30–37	468

2 Chronicles
10:5, 12	183
24:20–22	196

Ezra
3–6	62n

Esther
4:16–5:1	183

Job
1:10	146
9:8	140
38:16	140

Psalm
8:2	194
22:1	156
22:15	287
22:18	287
22:21	417
69:21	203, 287
69:22	203
69:9	265
77:19	140
78:2	185
80:8–18	282
82:6	277
91:11–12	174
95:7–11	426
110:1	151
110:4	429
113–18	153
118:26–27	194
139:21–22	176

Proverbs
10:22	146

Isaiah
5:1–7	149
5:1–7	282
5:24–25	161n
6:10	280
7:14	171
11:1	172
13–14	475
35:5–6	182
40	207
40:3	307
42:1–4	183
44:3	302
45:21	318
46–48	475
52:13–53:12	120
53:4	179
53:7–8	307
53:12	240
56:3ff.	306n
56:7	194
61:1	182
61:1–2	219
62:11	194
66:1–2	306

Jeremiah
2:21	282
7:11	194
19:1, 11	201
23:5	172
31:15	172
31:31–34	428

33:15 — 172
50–51 — 475

Ezekiel
19:10–14 — 282
26–28 — 475
36:24–27 — 302
36:25–27 — 267
37:7, 12–13 — 203
39:29 — 302

Daniel
1:12, 14 — 466
2:44 — 113
4:1–37 — 172
4:12, 21 — 185n
7:13 — 134
7:9–14 — 120
9:27 — 151n, 357, 473, 474
11:31 — 151n, 357
12:11 — 151n, 357
12:2 — 203
12:2–3 — 150

Hosea
6:6 — 180, 182
10:1 — 282
11:1 — 172

Joel
2:28–29 — 302
2:28–32 — 303

Amos
9:11–12 — 318

Micah
5:2 — 172, 274

Haggai — 62n

Zechariah
1–8 — 62n
9:9 — 194
11:12–13 — 201
13:7 — 152
14:1–11 — 194

Malachi
4:5 — 144, 216

Passages Relating to Textual Criticism

Matthew
8:14 — 98n
10:23 — 103n, 107
16:13–20 — 107
21:22 — 89

Mark
1:19 — 98n
2:7 — 98n
2:15 — 97n
8:27–30 — 107
9:1 — 103n
11:24 — 89
13:32 — 103n

Luke
1:1–4 — 97, 102
4:38 — 98n
5:21 — 98n
5:29 — 97n
9:18–20 — 107
11:9 — 103n

John
1:14 — 102
5:3 — 89
20:30–31 — 102

Romans
1:1–4 — 104
10:9 — 104

1 Corinthians
7:6–40 — 104
7:10–11 — 102
10:19 — 90
11:23ff. — 104
15:3ff. — 104
15:5–8 — 102

1 John
1:1–4 — 102

Revelation
8:13 — 89

New Testament Readings

Matthew
1:1–17 — 170
1:18–25 — 171
2:1–12 — 171
2:13–23 — 172
3:1–17 — 172
4:1–11 — 173
4:12–25 — 174
5:1–16 — 174

5:17–48	176	26:47–56	201
6:1–18	177	26:57–68	201
6:19–34	177	26:69–75	201
7:1–12	178	27:1–10	201
7:13–29	178	27:11–14	201
8:1–15	179	27:15–26	202
8:16–22	179	27:27–44	202
8:23–9:8	179	27:45–61	203
9:9–17	180	27:62–28:20	203
9:18–34	180	**Mark**	
9:35–10:42	181	1:1–8	131
11:1–12:50	181	1:9–11	133
13:1–52	184	1:12–13	133
13:53–58	186	1:14–20	133
14:1–12	186	1:21–28	133
14:13–21	186	1:29–34	134
14:22–33	186	1:35–45	134
14:34–15:20	186	2:1–3:6	134
15:21–28	187	3:7–19	135
15:29–39	187	3:20–35	136
16:1–12	187	4:1–34	136
16:13–20	187	4:35–5:43	137
16:21–28	188	6:1–6	139
17:1–13	188	6:6–29	140
17:14–20	189	6:30–44	140
17:22–23	189	6:45–56	140
17:24–27	189	7:1–23	141
18:1–35	189	7:24–30	141
19:1–12	191	7:31–37	141
19:13–26	191	8:1–9	142
19:27–20:16	191	8:10–21	142
20:17–21:17	193	8:22–26	143
21:18–22:14	194	8:27–9:1	143
22:15–22	195	9:2–13	143
22:23–33	195	9:14–29	144
22:34–40	195	9:30–32	144
22:41–46	195	9:33–50	145
23:1–12	195	10:1–12	145
23:13–39	196	10:13–45	146
24:1–14	196	10:46–52	147
24:15–31	197	11:1–10	147
24:32–51	197	11:11–25	147
25:1–13	197	11:26–12:12	149
25:14–30	198	12:13–27	149
25:31–46	199	12:28–44	151
26:1–5	200	13:1–37	151
26:6–16	200	14:1–11	152
26:17–25	200	14:12–31	152
26:26–29	200	14:32–72	153
26:30–46	200	15:1–20	154

15:20–47	156	15:1–32	233
16:1–7	156	16:1–13	235
16:8	158	16:14–18	236
		16:19–31	236
Luke		17:1–10	238
1:1–4	215	17:11–19	238
1:5–56	215	17:20–37	238
1:57–80	217	18:1–8	238
2:1–20	217	18:9–17	239
2:21–40	218	18:18–30	239
2:41–52	218	18:31–34	239
3:1–20	218	18:35–43	240
3:21–38	219	19:1–10	240
4:14–30	219	19:11–27	240
4:31–44	221	19:28–48	240
5:1–11	221	20:1–26	241
5:12–16	221	20:27–44	241
5:17–26	221	20:45–21:4	241
5:27–39	221	21:5–38	242
6:1–11	223	22:1–6	242
6:12–49	223	22:7–13	242
7:1–10	223	22:14–23	242
7:11–17	223	22:24–30	243
7:18–35	224	22:31–34	243
7:36–50	224	22:35–38	244
8:1–21	224	22:39–46	244
8:22–25	225	22:47–53	244
8:26–39	225	22:54–71	245
8:40–56	226	23:1–5	245
9:1–6	226	23:6–12	245
9:7–9	226	23:13–25	246
9:10–17	226	23:26–31	247
9:18–27	226	23:32–43	247
9:28–36	227	23:44–49	248
9:37–43	227	23:50–24:12	248
9:43–50	227	24:13–35	250
9:51–62	227	24:36–53	250
10:1–16	228		
10:17–24	228	**John**	
10:25–37	228	1:1–18	262
10:38–42	229	1:19–34	264
11:1–13	229	1:35–42	264
11:14–36	230	1:43–51	264
11:37–52	230	2:1–12	264
11:53–12:59	230	2:13–22	266
13:1–9	231	2:23–3:21	266
13:10–21	231	3:22–4:42	267
13:22–30	231	4:43–54	268
13:31–35	231	5:1–47	268
14:1–24	232	6:1–71	271
14:25–35	233	7:1–9	272

7:10–52	273		**Romans**	
8:11–59	274		1:1–3:20	383
9:1–41	275		3:21–31	384
10:1–21	276		4:1–5:21	384
10:22–42	277		6:1–8:39	385
11:1–44	277		9:1–11:36	386
11:45–54	278		12:1–15:13	387
11:55–12:11	279		15:14–16:27	387
12:12–50	279		**1 Corinthians**	
13:1–20	280		1:1–4:21	362
13:21–30	280		5:1–7:40	363
13:31–38	281		8:1–11:1	365
14:1–31	281		11:2–16	365
15:1–27	283		11:17–34	365
16:1–33	283		12:1–14:40	366
17:1–26	283		15:1–58	367
18:1–11	284		16:1–24	368
18:12–27	284		**2 Corinthians**	
18:28–40	285		1:1–3:3	373
19:1–16	285		3:4–7:16	374
19:17–22	286		8:1–9:15	374
19:23–27	287		10:1–13:13	374
19:28–37	287		**Galatians**	
19:38–42	288		1:1–10	348
20:1–31	288		1:11–2:21	348
21:1–25	290		3:1–5:12	350
Acts			5:13–6:10	350
1:1–26	302		6:11–18	351
2:1–47	303		**Ephesians**	
3:1–4:31	303		1:1–23	400
4:32–5:11	305		2:1–3:21	400
5:12–42	305		4:1–16	400
6:1–8:1	305		4:17–5:14	401
8:1–40	306		5:15–6:24	402
9:1–31	307		**Philippians**	
9:32–11:18	308		1:1–30	406
11:19–30	310		2:1–30	406
12:1–25	310		3:1–4:23	407
13:1–14:28	314		**Colossians**	
15:1–35	318		1:1–2:23	395
15:36–18:22	319		3:1–4:18	396
18:23–19:41	325		**1 Thessalonians**	
20:1–21:16	327		1:1–3:13	354
21:17–23:35	329		4:1–5:28	355
24:1–27	332		**2 Thessalonians**	
25:1–12	334		1:1–3:18	357
25:13–27	334			
26:1–32	334			
27:1–28:31	335			

1 Timothy

1:1–20	414
2:1–3:16	415
4:1–6:21	415

2 Timothy

1:1–4:22	416

Titus

1:1–3:15	416

Philemon

1–25	392

Hebrews

1:1–2:18	426
3:1–4:16	427
5:1–6:20	427
7:1–10:18	429
10:19–13:25	430

James

1:1–2:26	435
3:1–5:20	436

1 Peter

1:1–12	441
1:13–3:22	441
4:1–5:14	442

2 Peter

1:1–21	445
2:1–3:18	446

1 John

1:1–5:21	450

2 John

1–13	451

3 John

1–15	452

Jude

1–25	447

Revelation

1:1–3:22	465
4:1–5:14	470
6:1–8:5	472
8:6–11:19	473
12:1–17	474
13:1–14:20	474
15:1–16:21	475
17:1–18:24	475
19:1–20:15	475
21:1–22:21	476

General Index

This index excludes items in the charts except for the Jewish Religious Calendar.

Abba, 120, 153, 418
Acts, Book of, 295–337
Adam, 384
Aeneas, 308
Agrapha, 95
Agriculture, 53
Albinus, 37
Alexander the Great, 21–22
Alexandria, 22, 43, 44, 46, 79, 80, 422
Amanuensis, 88, 343
Ambivius, 37
Ananias and Sapphira, 329
Anna, 216
Annas, 284
Annius Rufus, 37
Anointing of Jesus, 152, 200, 279
Antichrist, 357–58, 450, 474
Antinomianism, 350
Antioch in Syria, 46, 309–10, 314, 348, 477
Antioch of Pisidia, 315–17
Antiochus III, 23
Antiochus IV, Epiphanes, 23–25, 276
Antipas. *See* Herod Antipas
Antipater, 11
Antitheses, 175–77
Antony, 29, 32, 320

Apocalypse, 457, 478
Apocalyptic literature, 70–71, 457–76
Apocrypha, 68–69, 87, 90
Apollo, 56
Apollonius, 25
Apollos, 325, 360, 362, 422, 424
Apology, 127, 374–75
Apostasy, 427, 428, 436
Apostles. *See further* Disciples, 87, 135, 139–40, 181, 226, 302
Aqueduct, 316, 333
Aramaic language, 43, 68, 159
Arcadian Way, 328
Arch of Titus, 29, 342
Arch of Galerius, 352
Archelaus, 33–34
Areopagus, 321
Armor of God, 401–402
Artemis, 326, 327
Ascension, 250, 302–303
Asia Minor, map, 345
Asiarchs, 326
Athens, 79, 321, 324
Attis, 59
Augustus, 29–34, 149, 217
Autograph, 88
Babylon, 438–39, 475

Banking. *See* Business
Baptism, 113, 131, 146–47, 173, 219, 267, 302, 267–68, 385, 442, 449
Bar Cochba, or Khokba, 35
Bar-Jesus. *See* Elymas
Barabbas, 477
Barnabas, 305, 309–10, 314–19, 422, 477
Beast and false prophet, vision of, 474
Beatitudes, 174, 208
Beelzebul, 136
Benedictus, 217
Berea, 321
Bethesda. *See* Bethzatha
Bethzatha, 270–71, 273
Biblical anthropology, 322
Bishops, 414–15
Blessings, 384, 400
Body of Christ, 367, 397, 401
Bowls, 474
Bultmann, R., 101, 108
Business, 53
Caesarea, 33, 331–33, 393
Caiaphas, 201, 284, 278
Caligula, 30, 58, 357
Cana, 264–65
Canon, 85–88, 433, 443, 450–51, 458
Capernaum, 220–21
Catholic, 431–32
Centurion, 223
Cephas. *See* Peter
Cerinthus, 449
Charismata, 366
Chenoboskion. *See* Nag Hammadi
Children, 146
Chrestus, 323, 376
Christian community, 189–91, 237–38
Cilician Gates, 294
Claudius, 30, 335, 376, 378, 387
Claudius Lysias, 329, 331
Cleopatra, 22, 29, 32, 320
Clement, 126, 128, 376, 423
Clothing, 47, 50
Codex, 88–89
Coin, 154
Colossae, 391–95
Colosseum, 336
Colossian heresy, 394–95
Colossians, 392–96
Commerce, 43–44

Communal living, 305
Communication, 43–44
Consistent eschatology, 114
Conzelmann, H., 105
Coponius, 37
Corinth, 323, 360
Corinthians, First, 359–68
Corinthians, Second, 369–75
Cornelius, 188, 308
Coverdale Bible, 91
Crispus, 323, 359
Cronus, 56
Crucifixion, 112, 127, 143, 152, 155–56, 188, 202–203, 242, 247–48, 285–87
Cuspius Fadus, 37
Cybele, 58, 59
Cynicism, 61
Cyprus, 314–15
Day of Atonement, 69
Deacons, 305, 412, 414–15
Dead Sea, 71
Dead Sea Scrolls, 27, 71–72, 73, 75, 169, 259, 412, 447
Dedication, Feast of, 69, 276
Demetrius, 326, 452
Demetrius II, 26
Demythologization, 101–102
Descent into hell, 441–42
Diana. *See* Artemis
Diaspora, Dispersion, 79, 273, 303, 328
Dionysus, 25, 58, 458
Diotrephes, 452
Disciples, 78, 133, 179, 228, 239, 242, 264, 275
Divorce, 145–46, 175–76, 190–91, 364
Docetism, 449
Dodd, C. H., 104, 115, 169, 308
Domitian, 31, 58, 437, 459
Dorcas. *See* Tabitha
Dress. *See* Clothing
Education, 46
Egypt, map, 90
Elders, 412, 415, 435
Election, 151–52, 256–57, 386, 419, 428
Elijah, 144, 227, 473
Elizabeth, 209, 215, 217
Elymas, 314

Emmaus disciples, 248–50

Emperor worship, 57–58

Enoch, 473

Entertainment, 51

Epaphras, 394

Epaphroditus, 402, 404

Ephesians, 397–402

Ephesus, 325–27, 360, 390–91, 452, 466

Epicureanism, 61

Epiphanes. *See* Antiochus IV, Epiphanes

Epistles, 341–453

Erastus, 377–78, 403

Eratosthenes, 53

Eschatology, 354–57, 419–20

Essenes, 27, 75–76, 79, 111

Ethiopian eunuch, 306

Evangelists, 125–26, 206, 309

Exorcism, 60, 133–34, 137–38, 144, 225, 230

Expiation, 384

Ezra, 77

Faith, 114, 225, 355, 375, 383, 384, 435

Family, 49

Farmer, W. R., 97

Fasting, 222

Feasts, festivals (Jewish), 25, 68, 69, 272–74

Feeding of the five thousand, 140, 186, 271–72, 291

Feeding of the four thousand, 142

Felix, 34, 37, 331–32, 329

Festus, 34, 37, 333–34

Fig tree, 147, 148, 194

Fish, miracle of, 221, 290

Fish, parable of, 185

Florus, 34, 37

Food, 47

Food dedicated to idols, 364–65

Foot washing, 256, 280

Forgiveness, 189–90, 435–36

Form criticism, 99–104

Fragmentary theory, 410

Futurist, 461

Gaius, 452

Galatians, 344–51

Gallio, 324, 359

Gamaliel, 79, 305, 307

Gate of St. Paul, 391

Gemarah, 72

Genealogies of Jesus, 162, 170–71, 207, 219

Gerasene demoniacs,

Gethsemane, 153, 200, 244, 282, 284, 287

Gladiatorial shows, 51

Gloria in Excelsis Deo, 218

Glossolalia, 366

Gnosticism, 60–61, 257, 395, 411–12, 448

God–fearers, 73, 279, 315, 317, 321, 344

Golden Rule, 178

Good Samaritan, parable of, 228–29

Good Shepherd Discourse, 275–77

Goodspeed, E. J., 398

Gospel of Thomas, 95–96

Grace, 400, 419

Great Commission, 163, 204, 207, 302

Great Tribulation, 151, 450, 457, 461–62, 472–73, 474–75

Greek language, 43, 68, 79, 88, 330

Griesbach, J., 97

Guilt, 383

Hades, 188, 56

Hadrian, 35

Hagaddah, 72

Halakah, 72

Hanukkah, Feast of, 68, 69, 276

Harvests, 474

Hasideans, Hasidim, 24, 26, 74, 75

Hasmonean Kingdom, 27

Hasmoneans. *See* Maccabees

Hazzan, 64

Hebraists, 79, 305, 307, 477

Hebrew language, 43, 68, 159

Hebrews, 421–30

Hellenistic empires, 22–23

Hellenists, 25, 79, 259, 305, 477

Hellenization, 21–22, 74, 79

Hermes, 315, 217

Herod Agrippa I, 34, 310

Herod Agrippa II, 34, 334–35

Herod Antipas, 33, 77, 139–40, 219, 226, 231–32

Herodians, 77, 135, 150

Herodias, 33

Herod Philip, 33

Herod the Great, 31–33, 65, 172, 310, 334

Heterodoxy, 445–46

Higher criticism, 105–106

Hillel, 72

Historicist, 460–61

Historicity, 170

Holy conduct, 401, 435, 437

Homes, houses, 46–47, 48

Householder, parable of, 186

House of Onias, 23

House of Tobias, 23

Hymenaeus and Alexander, 414

Idealist, 460

Immortality. *See* Resurrection

Incarnation, 262–63

Industry. *See* Business

Irenaeus, 126, 128, 252, 459

Jairus, 226

James, Epistle of, 432–36

James the Apostle and son of Zebedee, 34

James the Brother of Jesus, 87, 310, 318, 348, 446

Jamnia, 35

Jannes and Jambres, 417

Jason, 23–25–321

Jerane, 90, 126

Jerusalem, 25, 34, 35, 193, 310, 328, 331, 345

Jerusalem Council, 296, 318–19

Jesus' life and ministry, 106–08, 111–17

Jewish wars, 35

John, First, 448–50

John, Second, 450–51

John, Third, 450–52

John, Gospel of, 252–91

John the Baptist, 33, 111–14, 128, 131–33, 140, 172–73, 209, 217, 218–19, 223–24, 263–64, 267, 271, 325

Jonah, 183–84

Jonathan Maccabeus, 26

Jordan River, 132

Joseph of Arimathea, 203, 248, 288

Judaism, 25, 62–80, 86, 111–13, 259, 303, 305, 317, 344, 394, 418, 421

Judaizing controversy, 318, 344, 406–07

Judas Iscariot, 152–53, 200–201, 280–81, 284, 305

Judas Maccabeus, 25–26, 65, 276

Jude, 87, 444, 446–48

Julius Caesar, 29, 320

Justification, 315–17, 349–50, 375–76, 379–80, 384, 419, 435

Kenosis, 406

Kerygma, 104–05

King James (Authorized) Version, 90, 298

Kingdom of God, or Heaven, 113–14, 163, 172, 227

Labor, 53

Laborers in the vineyard, parable of, 192–93, 376

Languages, 43, 366 (tongues)

Laodicea, 398, 468–69

Last Supper, 116–17, 152–53

Latin, 43, 88

Latin Vulgate, 90

Law of love, 365

Lawyer, 77, 228–29, 230–31

Lazarus, 116, 277–78

Lectionaries, 89

Leper(s), 134, 207, 221, 238

Letters, 341, 43

Levi, 221–22

Libertinism, 61, 350

Light, 175, 256

Lingua franca, 22

Logia, 159–60

Logos, 256, 262–63

Lord's Prayer, 114, 177, 229–30

Lord's Supper, 117, 200, 265–66, 419

Lost coin, parable of, 233–34

Lost sheep, parable of, 233

Lot's wife, 238

Luke, 53, 86–87, 206, 295–96, 393, 422

Luke, Gospel of, 205–50

Lystra, 317–18

Maccabean Revolt, 25

Maccabean Independence, 26

Maccabees, 25–26, 74

Magi, 171

Magnificat, 217

Mammon, 177–78

Man of Macedonia, 319

Manuscripts, 88–89

Maranatha, 368

Marcellus, 37

Marcion, 411

Mark (John Mark), 87, 126, 315, 319, 439

Mark, Gospel of, 125–58

Mark-Q, 97–99, 160

Marriage, 145–46, 175–76, 364, 385, 401

Marriage feast, parable of, 194, 376

Marriage supper, vision of, 475

Mars' Hill, 321–22

Mary, 170–71, 209, 216–18, 279, 432

Mary and Martha, 208, 229, 277

Mary Magdalene, 288–89

Maryllus, 37

Masada, 34, 35

Mattathias, 25–26

Matthew, Gospel of, 159–204

Matthew the Apostle, 87, 180

Matthias, 302–03

Medicine, 53–54

Melchizedek, 429

Menelaus, 24–25

Menorah, 276

Messiah, messiahship, messianism, messianic prophecy, messianic secret, 73–74, 77, 120, 126–27, 131, 162, 170, 186, 302, 315, 470, 477

Millennium, 461, 472, 475, 476

Miracles, 37, 115–16, 134, 137–39, 140–43, 179–80, 275

Mishnah, 72

Missions, 180–81

Montefiore, H., 424

Morals, 50–51

Moses, 144, 227, 262, 267, 271, 374, 426, 473

Mount Gerizim, 269

Mount of Olives, 286

Mustard seed, parable of, 183

Mystery religions, 58–59, 395

Mythology, 56–57, 102

Nag Hammadi, 61, 95

Nativity of Jesus, 171, 208, 217–18

Nazarene, 172

Nazareth, 172, 219–20

Nero, 30, 298, 357, 458–59

New Jerusalem, 475–76

New Testament book chart, 480–81

New Testament history chart, 39

Nicolaitans, 466

Nicodemus, 266–67, 280

North Galatia, 345–46

Octavian. *See* Augustus

Old Testament, 25, 39, 63, 68–69, 71–75, 78–79, 87, 168–70, 175, 388, 418

Olivet Discourse, 151–52, 353

One hundred and forty–four thousand, 472, 474

Onesimus, 391–93

Onias III, 23

Oral tradition, 96–97, 99, 115

Original sin, 384

Ostraca, 44

Osiris, 59

Oxyrhynchus, 95–96

Paganism, 25, 50–51, 56–62

Palestine, map, 84

Palm Sunday, 116

Papias, 126, 159, 253

Papyrus, 44, 88–89, 95, 255, 341–43

Parables, 115, 136–37, 149, 174–87, 194, 224–25

Paraclete, 257, 282–83

Paralytic(s), 221

Parenetic, 343–44

Parousia, 196, 355, 357–58, 475

Passover, Feast of, 68, 69, 116–17, 152, 242–44, 279, 285

Patmos, 456

Paul, 34, 78, 87, 95, 305–06, 307, 310–15, 317–37, 390–91, 407, 421–22, 477

Pauline theology, 307, 349, 417–20

Pax Romana, 29

Pentecost, Feast of, 68, 69, 117, 302–03

Pentateuch, 22

Perga, 315, 318

Pergamum, 458, 466–68

Persecution, 181–82, 241–42, 429, 437, 441–42, 458–59

Peter, 34, 86–87, 126, 143, 153, 187–88, 264, 281, 284, 290–91, 303–04, 308, 310, 348, 362

Peter, First, 86, 437–42

Peter, Second, 86, 443–46

Pharisee and the publican, parable of,

239–40, 376

Pharisees, 26, 27, 74, 75, 78–79, 135, 141–42, 150, 187, 195–96, 230–33, 273, 275, 331

Philadelphia, 468

Philemon, 391–92

Philip, 264, 279, 306, 423

Philippi, 319–20

Philippian jailer, 320–21

Philippians, 402–08

Philo, 79, 263

Philosophy, 61–62, 79

Phoebe, 378

Pilate. *See* Pontius Pilate

Plato, 60–61

Potemic, 258–59, 396, 403, 443, 446, 448

Polycarp, 459

Pompey, 27, 29

Pontifex Maximus, 57

Pontius Pilate, 34, 37, 154–55, 201–02, 245–47, 284–85

Pool of Bethzatha, 270–71, 273

Population, 43

Poseidon, 56

Pounds, parable of, 240

Praetorian Guard, 403–04

Prayer, 208, 229, 414

Preterist, 460

Priscilla and Aquila, 323–24, 325, 359, 387, 422–24

Prodigal son, parable of, 207, 234–35, 376

Propitiation, 383–84

Proselytes, 73, 111, 279, 303, 315, 317

Pseudepigrapha, 69–71, 447–48

Pseudonymity, 409–10

Ptolemies, 22–23

Ptolemy Philadelphus, 22

Publicans, 48

Purim, Feast of, 68, 69

Q, 97–99

Qumran. *See* Dead Sea Scrolls

Rabbis, 65, 72, 74, 77–78, 195

Rapture, 355, 461–62, 470

Realized Eschatology, 144, 258

Reconcile, 384

Redaction criticism, 105

Religious calendar of the Jews, 68, 69

Repentant thief, 248

Resurrection, 117–19, 150, 152, 156–57, 203–04, 250, 281, 288–89, 302, 321–22, 367

Revelation, Book of, 151, 283, 353, 457–76

Rich young ruler, 191, 236–37

Roads, 42, 44, 45

Roman citizenship, 331, 334

Roman empire, governors, and emperors, 28–37

Roman state religion, 57

Romans, 375–87

Roman worship, 45

Rome, 335–37, 376, 439, 475

Rylands Fragment, 252

Sabbath, 25, 74, 119, 134–35, 223, 231, 268–71

Sadducees, 75, 149–50, 187, 241, 331

Salt, 174, 233, 396

Samaritan woman, 268

Sanctification, 283, 380

Sanhedrin, 78, 116, 147–50, 152–55, 200, 241–42, 245–46, 278–79, 305, 331–33

Sardis, 467, 468

Saul. *See* Paul

Scepticism, 62

Sceva, 326

Schools. *See* Education

Schweitzer, Albert, 107, 114

Science, 53–54

Scribes, 77–78, 141, 150, 195–96, 331

Scroll, 470

Seals, 460, 470–72

Seed, parable of, 224

Seleucids, 22, 23–24

Septuagint, 22, 68, 70, 169, 296, 411, 422

Sergius Paulus, 314

Sermon on the Mount, 174–79, 434

Sermon on the Plain, 223

Seven Last Words, 117, 287

Shammai, 72

Sheep and goats, judgment of, 199

Shema, 63

Shemone Esreh, 63

Sicarii, 77

Silas, Silvanus, 319–25, 359, 423, 438, 444

Siloam, 275

Simeon, 209
Simon Magus (the sorcerer), 306
Simon of Cyrene, 156, 247, 286
Simon Peter. *See* Peter
Simon the Hasmonean, or Maccabean, 26
Sitz im Leben, 101
Slaves, 49, 79, 349, 385
Smyrna, 466
Social classes, 48–49
Sosthenes, 324
Source criticism, 96–99
Sources of Jesus' life, 94–96
South Galatia, 346–47
Sower, parable of, 224
Stadium, 52
Stephen, 305–06
Stoicism, 61, 401
Straight Street, 309
Superstition, 59–60, 62
Synagogue, 62–68, 219–21, 315, 317, 377
Syncretism, 59–60
Synoptic gospels, 96–100, 254, 292
Syro-Phoenician woman, 141
Syzygos, 408
Tabernacles, Feast of, 68, 69, 253, 272–74
Tabitha, 308
Talents, parable of, 198
Talmud, 72, 79
Tares and wheat, parable of, 185
Targums, 68, 263
Tax, 149–50, 189, 195, 387
Teacher, 77, 119–20, 264
Temple, 32, 34, 66–69, 147–49, 153, 194, 218, 240–42, 265–66
Temple of Apollo, 323
Temptation of Jesus, 133, 173–74, 219
Ten virgins, parable of, 197–98
Tertullus, 332
Textual criticism, 88–92
Theater, 52, 316, 330, 458
Theophilus, 205, 206, 299
Thessalonians, First, 353–56
Thessalonians, Second, 356–58
Thessalonica, 321–353
Thomas, 289
Thyatira, 468
Tiberius, 30, 31, 37, 111, 190

Timothy, 319, 353–54, 359, 360, 403
Timothy, First, 413–15
Timothy, Second, 416–17
Titus, 370
Titus, Epistle of, 415–16
Tomb, 157
Torah, 35, 62, 75, 79
Trade guilds, 53
Transfiguration, 116, 143–44, 188–89, 226–27, 302, 445
Translation, 355, 366
Transportation, 43–44
Treasure, parable of, 185
Trial, 112, 245
Tribulation. *See* Great Tribulation
Triumphal entry, 116, 147, 193–94, 240, 279
Trumpets, 472–73
Two sons, parable of, 194
Tychicus, 397
Tyndale, Williams, 90
Typology, 168–69
Unjust steward, parable of, 235–36
Upper Room Discourse, 281–82
Uranus, 56
Valerius Gratus, 37
Valley of Hinnom, 202
Ventidius Cumanus, 37
Vespasian, 31
Via Dolorosa, 247
Vine, 282–83
Vineyard, parable of, 149, 241
Vineyards, 192
Virgin birth, 171, 432
Walking on water, 140, 186
Wealth, 146
Wheat and tares, parable of, 185
Widow and the judge, parable of, 238–39
Widows, 305, 412, 415
Widow's mite(s), 151
Witnesses, vision of, 473
Woman and child, vision of, 473
Woman taken in adultery, 224
Zacchaeus, 207, 240, 376
Zacharias, 209, 215–16
Zealots, 77
Zerubbabel, 62
Zeus, 25, 56–57, 317, 466–67

❖

The text of *A Survey of the New Testament*,
Third Edition, was set in 11-point Berling typeface.
Display features were set in Berling and Syntax. The interior
design was created by Gary Gnidovic. The compositor was Sherri L.
Korhorn of the Composition Department of Zondervan Publishing
House, using QuarkXPress on a Macintosh computer. The editors
were Gary Knussman and James E. Ruark. The photographs
and maps were supplied by Carta, Jerusalem, Israel.